"If you are looking for a job ... before you go to the newspapers and the help-wanted ads, listen to Bob Adams, publisher of *The Metropolitan New York JobBank*."

-Tom Brokaw, *NBC*

"Help on the job hunt ... Anyone who is job hunting in the New York area can find a lot of useful ideas in a new paperback called *The Metropolitan New York JobBank* ..."

-Angela Taylor, *New York Times*

"One of the better publishers of employment almanacs is Adams Media Corporation ... publisher of *The Metropolitan New York JobBank* and similarly named directories of employers in Texas, Boston, Chicago, Northern and Southern California, and Washington DC. A good buy ..."

-Wall Street Journal's
National Business Employment Weekly

"Because our listing is seen by people across the nation, it generates lots of resumes for us. We encourage unsolicited resumes. We'll always be listed [in *The Chicago JobBank*] as long as I'm in this career."

-Tom Fitzpatrick, Director of Human Resources
Merchandise Mart Properties, Inc.

"Job hunting is never fun, but this book can ease the ordeal ... [*The Los Angeles JobBank*] will help allay fears, build confidence, and avoid wheel-spinning."

-Robert W. Ross, *Los Angeles Times*

"Job hunters can't afford to waste time. *The Minneapolis-St. Paul JobBank* contains information that used to require hours of research in the library."

-Carmella Zagone
Minneapolis-based Human Resources Administrator

"*The Florida JobBank* is an invaluable job-search reference tool. It provides the most up-to-date information and contact names available for companies in Florida. I should know--it worked for me!"

-Rhonda Cody, Human Resources Consultant
Aetna Life and Casualty

"*The Boston JobBank* provides a handy map of employment possibilities in Greater Boston. This book can help in the initial steps of a job search by locating major employers, describing their business activities, and for most firms, by naming the contact person and listing typical professional positions. For recent college graduates, as well as experienced professionals, *The Boston JobBank* is an excellent place to begin a job search."
-Juliet F. Brudney, Career Columnist
Boston Globe

"No longer can jobseekers feel secure about finding employment just through want ads. With the tough competition in the job market, particularly in the Boston area, they need much more help. For this reason, *The Boston JobBank* will have a wide and appreciative audience of new graduates, job changers, and people relocating to Boston. It provides a good place to start a search for entry-level professional positions."
-*Journal of College Placement*

"*The Phoenix JobBank* is a first-class publication. The information provided is useful and current."
-Lyndon Denton
Director of Human Resources and Materials Management
Apache Nitrogen Products, Inc.

"[*The Ohio JobBank* is] a good resource for the job hunter."
-Virginia Tyler, Human Resources Manager
Battelle Columbus Operations/Ohio

"*The Ohio JobBank* is a very helpful tool for locating and researching potential employers. It's easy to use and even gives advice on winning the job."
-Judith G. Bishop, Manager of Employment
Barberton Citizens Hospital

"*The Seattle JobBank* is an essential resource for job hunters."
-Gil Lopez, Staffing Team Manager
Battelle Pacific Northwest Laboratories

"I read through the "Basics of Job Winning" and "Resumes" sections [in *The Dallas-Ft. Worth JobBank*] and found them to be very informative, with some positive tips for the job searcher. I believe the strategies outlined will bring success to any determined candidate."
-Camilla Norder, Professional Recruiter
Presbyterian Hospital of Dallas

"Through *The Dallas-Ft. Worth JobBank,* we've been able to attract high-quality candidates for several positions."
-Rob Bertino, Southern States Sales Manager
CompuServe

What makes the JobBank series the nation's premier line of employment guides?

With vital employment information on thousands of employers across the nation, the JobBank series is the most comprehensive and authoritative set of career directories available today.

Each book in the series provides information on **dozens of different industries** in a given city or area, with the primary employer listings providing contact information, telephone numbers, addresses, a summary of the firm's business, and in many cases descriptions of the firm's typical professional job categories, the principal educational backgrounds sought, and the fringe benefits offered.

In addition to the **detailed primary employer listings,** the 1996 JobBank books give telephone numbers and addresses for **thousands of additional employers.**

All of the reference information in the JobBank series is as up-to-date and accurate as possible. Every year, the entire database is thoroughly researched and verified by mail and by telephone. Adams Media Corporation publishes **more local employment guides more often** than any other publisher of career directories.

In addition, the JobBank series features important information about the local job scene -- **forecasts on which industries are the hottest, overviews of local economic trends,** and **lists of regional professional associations,** so you can get your job hunt started off right.

Hundreds of discussions with job hunters show that they prefer information organized geographically, because most people look for jobs in specific areas. The JobBank series offers **20 regional titles,** from Minneapolis to Houston, and from Boston to San Francisco. Jobseekers moving to a particular area can review the local employment data not only for information on the type of industry most common to that region, but also for names of specific companies.

A condensed, but thorough, review of the entire job search process is presented in the chapter **The Basics of Job Winning**, a feature which has received many compliments from career counselors. In addition, each JobBank directory includes a section on **resumes and cover letters** the *New York Times* has acclaimed as "excellent."

The JobBank series gives job hunters the most comprehensive, timely, and accurate career information, organized and indexed to facilitate the job search. An entire career reference library, JobBank books are the consummate employment guides.

Published by Adams Media Corporation
260 Center Street, Holbrook, MA 02343

Manufactured in the United States of America.

Because addresses and telephone numbers of smaller companies change rapidly, we recommend you call each company and verify the information before mailing to the employers listed in this book. Mass mailings are not recommended.

While the publisher has made every reasonable effort to obtain and verify accurate information, occasional errors are inevitable due to the magnitude of the database. Should you discover an error, or if a company is missing, please write the editors at the above address so that we may update future editions.

"This publication is designed to provide accurate and authoritative information with regard to the subject matter covered. It is sold with the understanding that the publisher is not engaged in rendering legal, accounting, or other professional advice. If legal advice or other expert assistance is required, the services of a competent professional person should be sought."
  --From a *Declaration of Principles* jointly adopted by a Committee of the American Bar Association and a Committee of Publishers and Associations

The appearance of a listing in the book does not constitute an endorsement from the publisher.

Cover photo courtesy of Tennessee Tourist Development.

This book is available at quantity discounts for bulk purchases.
For information, call 800/872-5627.

Visit our home page at http://www.adamsjobbank.com

The
Tennessee
JobBank
3rd Edition

Reference Editor
Steven Graber

Series Editor
Jennifer J. Pfalzgraf

Associate Editor
Marcie DiPietro

Editorial Assistants
Tami M. Forman
Lissa Harnish
Andy Richardson

ADAMS MEDIA CORPORATION
Holbrook, Massachusetts

Top career publications from Adams Media Corporation

The JobBank Series:

each JobBank book is $15.95

The Atlanta JobBank, 1996
The Boston JobBank, 1996
The Carolina JobBank, 4th Ed.
The Chicago JobBank, 1996
The Dallas-Ft. Worth JobBank, 1996
The Denver JobBank, 8th Ed.
The Detroit JobBank, 6th Ed.
The Florida JobBank, 1996
The Houston JobBank, 1996
The Los Angeles JobBank, 1996
The Minneapolis-St. Paul JobBank, 1996
The Missouri JobBank, 1st Ed.
The Metropolitan New York JobBank, 1996
The Ohio JobBank, 1996
The Greater Philadelphia JobBank, 1996
The Phoenix JobBank, 6th Ed.
The San Francisco Bay Area JobBank, 1996
The Seattle JobBank, 1996
The Tennessee JobBank, 3rd Ed.
The Metropolitan Washington JobBank, 1996

The National JobBank, 1996
(Covers the entire U.S.: $270.00 hc)

The JobBank Guide to Employment Services, 1996-1997
(Covers the entire U.S.: $160.00 hc)

Other Career Titles:

The Adams Cover Letter Almanac ($10.95)
The Adams Jobs Almanac, 1996 ($15.95)
The Adams Resume Almanac ($10.95)

America's Fastest Growing Employers, 2nd Ed. ($16.00pb, $30.00 hc)
Career Shifting ($9.95)
Careers and the College Grad ($12.95)
Careers and the Engineer ($12.95)
Careers and the MBA ($12.95)
Cold Calling Techniques (That Really Work!), 3rd Ed. ($7.95)
The Complete Resume & Job Search Book for College Students ($9.95)
Cover Letters That Knock 'em Dead, 2nd Ed. ($10.95)
Every Woman's Essential Job Hunting & Resume Book ($10.95)
The Harvard Guide to Careers in the Mass Media ($7.95)
High Impact Telephone Networking for Job Hunters ($6.95)
How to Become Successfully Self-Employed, 2nd Ed. ($9.95)
The Job Hunter's Checklist ($5.95)
The Job Search Handbook ($6.95)
Knock 'em Dead, The Ultimate Jobseeker's Handbook, 1996 ($12.95)
The Lifetime Career Manager ($20.00 hc)
The MBA Advantage ($12.95)
The Minority Career Book ($9.95)
The National Jobline Directory ($7.95)
The New Rules of the Job Search Game ($10.95)
Outplace Yourself ($15.95 pb)
Over 40 and Looking for Work? ($7.95)
Reengineering Yourself ($12.95)
The Resume Handbook, 2nd Ed. ($7.95)
Resumes That Knock 'em Dead, 2nd Ed. ($10.95)
300 New Ways to Get a Better Job ($7.95)

To order these books or additional copies of this book,
send check or money order (including $4.50 for postage) to:
Adams Media Corporation, 260 Center Street, Holbrook MA 02343
(Foreign orders please call for shipping rates.)

Ordering by credit card? Just call 800/USA-JOBS (In Massachusetts, call 617/767-8100).
Please check your favorite retail outlet first.

TABLE OF CONTENTS

SECTION ONE: INTRODUCTION

How to Use This Book/10
An introduction to the most effective way to use The Tennessee JobBank.

The Tennessee Job Market/14
An informative economic overview designed to help you understand all of the forces shaping the Tennessee job market.

SECTION TWO: THE JOB SEARCH

The Basics of Job Winning/22
A condensed review of the basic elements of a successful job search campaign. Includes advice on developing an effective strategy, time planning, preparing for interviews, interview techniques, etc. Special sections address unique situations faced by those jobseekers who are currently employed, those who have lost a job, and college students conducting their first job search.

Resumes and Cover Letters/37
Advice on creating a strong resume. Includes sample resumes and cover letters.

SECTION THREE: PRIMARY EMPLOYERS

The Employers/54
The Tennessee JobBank *is organized according to industry. Many listings include the address and phone number of each major firm listed, along with a description of the company's basic product lines and services, and, in many cases, a contact name and other relevant hiring information. Also included are hundreds of secondary listings providing addresses and phone numbers for small- and medium-sized employers.*

SECTION FOUR: EMPLOYMENT SERVICES

Temporary Employment Agencies/318
Includes addresses, phone numbers, and descriptions of companies specializing in temporary placement of clients. Also includes contact names, specializations, and a list of positions commonly filled.

Permanent Employment Agencies/319
Includes addresses, phone numbers, and descriptions of companies specializing in permanent placement of clients. Also includes contact names, specializations, and a list of positions commonly filled.

Executive Search Firms/322
Includes addresses, phone numbers, and descriptions of companies specializing in permanent placement of executive-level clients. Also includes contact names, specializations, and a list of positions commonly filled.

Career Services/325
Includes addresses, phone numbers, and descriptions of companies specializing in career services.

SECTION FIVE: INDEX

Alphabetical Index of Primary Employers/328
Includes larger employer listings only. Does not include employers that fall under the headings "Additional Employers."

HOW TO USE THIS BOOK

Right now, you hold in your hands one of the most effective job hunting tools available anywhere. In *The Tennessee JobBank*, you will find a wide array of valuable information to help you launch or continue a rewarding career. But before you open to the book's employer listings and start calling about current job openings, take a few minutes to learn how best to put the resources presented in *The Tennessee JobBank* to work for you.

The Tennessee JobBank will help you to stand out from other jobseekers. While many people looking for a new job rely solely on newspaper help-wanted ads, this book offers you a much more effective job-search method -- direct contact. The direct contact method has been proven twice as effective as scanning the help-wanted ads. Instead of waiting for employers to come looking for you, you'll be far more effective going to them. While many of your competitors will use trial and error methods in trying to set up interviews, you'll learn not only how to get interviews, but what to expect once you've got them.

In the next few pages, we'll take you through each section of the book so you'll be prepared to get a jump-start on your competition:

The Tennessee Job Market: An Overview

To get a feel for the state of the local job scene, read the introductory section called *The Tennessee Job Market*. In it, we'll recap the economy's recent performance and the steps that local governments and business leaders are taking to bring new jobs to the area.

Even more importantly, you'll learn where the local economy is headed. What are the prospects for the industries that form the core of the region's economy? Which industries are growing fastest and which ones are laying off? Are there any companies or industries that are especially hot?

To answer these questions for you, we've pored over local business journals and newspapers and interviewed local business leaders and labor analysts. Whether you are new to the area and need a source of regional information, or are a life-long resident just looking for a fresh start in a new job, you'll find this section to be a concise thumbnail sketch of where the jobs are.

This type of information is potent ammunition to bring into an interview. Showing that you're well versed in current industry trends helps give you an edge over job applicants who haven't done their homework.

Basics of Job Winning

Preparation. Strategy. Time-Management. These are three of the most important elements of a successful job search. *Basics of Job Winning* helps you address these and all the other elements needed to find the right job.

One of your first priorities should be to define your personal career objectives. What qualities make a job desirable to you? Creativity? High pay?

Prestige? Use *Basics of Job Winning* to weigh these questions. Then use the rest of the chapter to design a strategy to find a job that matches your criteria.

In *Basics of Job Winning,* you'll learn which job-hunting techniques work, and which don't. We've reviewed the pros and cons of mass mailings, help-wanted ads and direct contact. We'll show you how to develop and approach contacts in your field; how to research a prospective employer; and how to use that information to get an interview and the job.

Also included in *Basics of Job Winning*: interview dress code and etiquette, the "do's and don'ts" of interviewing, sample interview questions, and the often forgotten art of what to do after the interview. We also deal with some of the unique problems faced by those jobseekers who are currently employed, those who have lost a job, and college students conducting their first job search.

Resumes and Cover Letters

The approach you take to writing your resume and cover letter can often mean the difference between getting an interview and never being noticed. In this section, we discuss different formats, as well as what to put on (and what to leave off) your resume. We review the benefits and drawbacks of professional resume writers, and the importance of a follow-up letter. Also included in this section are sample resumes and cover letters which you can use as models.

The Employer Listings

Employers are listed alphabetically by industry, and within each industry, by company names. When a company does business under a person's name, like "John Smith & Co.", the company is usually listed by the surname's spelling (in this case "S"). Exceptions occur when a company's name is widely recognized, like "JCPenney" or "Howard Johnson Motor Lodge." In those cases, the company's first name is the key ("J" and "H" respectively).

The Tennessee JobBank covers a very wide range of industries. Each company profile is assigned to one of the industry chapters listed below.

Accounting and Management Consulting
Advertising/Marketing and Public
Relations
Aerospace
Apparel and Textiles
Architecture, Construction, and
Engineering
Arts and Entertainment/Recreation
Automotive
Banking/Savings and Loans
Biotechnology, Pharmaceuticals and
Scientific R&D
Business Services and Non-Scientific
Research
Charities and Social Services

Chemicals/Rubber and Plastics
Communications: Telecommunications
and Broadcasting
Computer Hardware, Software and
Services
Educational Services
Electronic/Industrial Electrical
Equipment
Environmental and Waste Management
Services
Fabricated/Primary Metals and Products
Financial Services
Food and Beverage/Agriculture
Government

*Health Care: Services, Equipment and
    Products
Hotels and Restaurants
Insurance
Legal Services
Manufacturing and Wholesaling: Misc.
    Consumer
Manufacturing and Wholesaling: Misc.
    Industrial*

*Mining/Gas/Petroleum/Energy Related
Paper and Wood Products
Printing and Publishing
Real Estate
Retail
Stone, Clay, Glass and Concrete Products
Transportation
Utilities: Electric/Gas/Water*

Many of the company listings offer detailed company profiles. In addition to company names, addresses, and phone numbers, these listings also include contact names or hiring departments, and descriptions of each company's products and/or services. Many of these listings also include a variety of additional information including:

Common positions - A list of job titles that the company commonly fills when it is hiring, organized in alphabetical order from Accountant to X-ray Technician. Note: Keep in mind that *The Tennessee JobBank* is a directory of major employers in the area, not a directory of openings currently available. Many of the companies listed will be hiring, others will not. However, since most professional job openings are filled without the placement of help-wanted ads, contacting the employers in this book directly is still a more effective method than browsing the Sunday papers.

Educational backgrounds sought - A list of educational backgrounds that companies seek when hiring.

Benefits - What kind of benefits packages are available from these employers? Here you'll find a broad range of benefits, from the relatively common (medical insurance) to those that are much more rare (health club membership; child daycare assistance).

Special programs - Does the company offer training programs, internships or apprenticeships? These programs can be important to first time jobseekers and college students looking for practical work experience. Many employer profiles will include information on these programs.

Parent company - If an employer is a subsidiary of a larger company, the name of that parent company will often be listed here. Use this information to supplement your company research before contacting the employer.

Number of employees - The number of workers a company employs.

Companies may also include information on other U.S. locations and any stock exchange the firm may be listed on.

Because so many job openings are with small and mid-sized employers, we've also included the addresses and phone numbers of such employers. While none of these listings include any additional hiring information, many of them do offer rewarding career opportunities. These companies are found under each industry heading. Within each industry, they are organized by the type of product or service offered.

A note on all employer listings that appear in *The Tennessee JobBank*. This book is intended as a starting point. It is not intended to replace any effort that you, the jobseeker, should devote to your job hunt. Keep in mind that while a great deal of effort has been put into collecting and verifying the company profiles provided in this book, addresses and contact names change regularly. Inevitably, some contact names listed herein have changed even before you read this. We recommend you contact a company before mailing your resume to ensure nothing has changed.

At the end of each industry section, we have included a directory of other industry-specific resources to help you in your job search. These include: professional and industrial associations, many of which can provide employment advice and job search help; magazines that cover the industry; and additional directories that may supplement the employer listings in this book.

Employment Services

Immediately following the employer listings section of this book are listings of local employment services firms. Many jobseekers supplement their own efforts by contracting "temp" services, head hunters, and other employment search firms to generate potential job opportunities.

This section is a comprehensive listing of such firms, arranged alphabetically under the headings Employment Agencies, Temporary Agencies, and Executive Search Firms. Each listing includes the firm's name, address, telephone number and contact person. Most listings also include the industries the firm specializes in, the type of positions commonly filled, and the number of jobs filled annually.

Index

The Tennessee JobBank index is a straight alphabetical listing.

THE TENNESSEE JOB MARKET: AN OVERVIEW

After a boom year following a long struggle to come out of the national recession of the early '90s, Tennessee's economy slowed down somewhat during 1995. The state's unemployment rate hovered at 5 percent in October 1995, up from 4.3 percent a year earlier. At the same time, however, the state unemployment rate remained below the November 1995 national average of 5.6 percent. All told, between November 1994 and November 1995, Tennessee employers added 42,400 new non-farm workers to their payrolls.

The Service Sector

By far, the fastest-growing sector of the Tennessee economy is the service sector, following the national shift from a manufacturing-based economy to one that is service-based. About 190,000 workers are employed in the Tennessee health services industry alone. During the November 1994 to November 1995 period, the number of health services jobs grew by about 6,900. This growth should continue as the number of senior citizens increases, and new life-saving medical technology is developed.

In fact, the health care service sector has surpassed all other categories in job growth in Tennessee and is not expected to slow down any time soon. From 1990 to 2000, the majority of high-growth jobs will be health care occupations, such as home health aides, physical therapists, nursing aides, and medical technicians, with registered nurses in the lead. The health care industry in Tennessee is led by **Columbia/HCA Corporation**, operator of over 300 hospitals and 125 surgical centers. This cutting-edge health care giant recently raised its net profits by 15 percent through improved purchasing management, according to a *Fortune* magazine article. The firm recently moved its corporate headquarters back to Nashville after a brief relocation to Louisville, Kentucky. The new Columbia/HCA headquarters will employ 1,600 people at an average salary of $60,862, numbers that are sure to generate a positive impact on the entire Nashville economy.

Other up-and-coming health care companies with excellent employment opportunities include **PhyCor**, **American HomePatient**, and **Quorum Health Group**. PhyCor, also of Nashville, operates primary care health clinics and is unique in its reliance on physicians' input in making corporate decisions. The company has been expanding rapidly in recent years.

American HomePatient, headquartered in Franklin, provides home health care services and leases and sells home medical equipment and supplies. The company's revenues grew from about $5.7 million in 1991 to about $90.2 million in 1994. Equally impressive, the company's profitability has increased even faster.

Brentwood-based Quorum provides management and consulting services for over 250 acute care hospitals and owns 11 hospitals. Since 1990, profits climbed from a loss of $7.8 million in 1990, to $36.2 million in 1994. Meanwhile, the company's staff has more than doubled.

Business Services

Business services are another major source of job growth. One of Tennessee's largest business services companies is **Federal Express**, which chose Memphis as its corporate headquarters location in 1993. The overnight delivery giant employs more than 8,000 and the Memphis hub is the company's largest package and document sorting facility in the nation. And with FedEx headquarters right in Tennessee, local businesses receive FedEx deliveries eight hours earlier than competitors in other states.

In addition to FedEx, many other Tennessee business services companies are also faring well. **TomKats, Inc.** in Nashville, made *Inc.* magazine's 1994 list of fastest-growing private companies. This food service firm began as a caterer to country music video productions and special events and has now served directors, stars, and crews on more than 70 movie sets. Another good bet for service jobseekers in Nashville -- **Corporate Child Care Management Services**. Also an *Inc.* 500 company, CCCMS develops and manages employer-sponsored child development centers.

Financial Services

Tennessee's financial services, insurance, and real estate sector is also a major generator of employment in the state. Between November 1994 and November 1995, this group of industries created 2,700 new jobs.

While financial and real estate services each added over 1,000 new workers during 1995, job growth in the insurance industry has been somewhat mixed -- with only 300 new jobs. **Provident Life and Accident Insurance** of Chattanooga, which employs over 4,000 workers nationwide, has been laying off in recent years. Meanwhile, **Midland Financial Group**, a Memphis-based underwriter and marketer of auto insurance, employs just 280 people, and has seen sales and profitability skyrocket.

In financial services, jobseekers might consider several of the state's larger banking institutions. Both **First Tennessee National Corporation** and **Union Planters Corporation** have been adding staff in recent years. Among investment houses, one of the most successful has been **Morgan Keenan**. Between 1990 and 1994, the company's revenues grew by more than 166 percent, while profits grew by an astounding 497 percent over that same time period.

Entertainment and Hospitality

The entertainment and hospitality industries have always fared well in Tennessee. The Music State's rich heritage draws tourists from all over the world to Nashville, the birthplace of the now-revitalized country music scene, as well as to Memphis, the site of Elvis Presley's Graceland estate. No single company has dominated the country music scene more than **Gaylord Entertainment Company**, the *Fortune* 500 broadcasting and entertainment giant. Gaylord, Nashville's largest private employer, operates Opryland, the huge theme park, entertainment center, and hotel complex. Gaylord also owns two country music cable television stations -- **The Nashville Network (TNN)** and **Country Music Television (CMT)**, and is planning further expansion in Europe.

The Promus Companies are also one of Tennessee's biggest players in the entertainment and tourism industries. This multi-tiered hotel and entertainment corporation is comprised of **Harrah's Casinos** and the hotel chains **Embassy Suites, Hampton Inn**, and **Homewood Suites**. Headquartered in Memphis, the corporation is continually expanding and its help-wanted ads frequent the Memphis papers. Another promising company for jobseekers: Knoxville's **Regal Theaters**, a chain of movie houses featuring over 10 theaters at each location. Regal was also classified by *Fortune* as one of the nation's fastest-growing firms.

Manufacturing and Distribution

Tennessee, particularly the Memphis area, has long been cast as a manufacturing and distribution center. Although Tennessee's economy has now diversified, manufacturers still account for a significant part of the state's economy. However, in the 12 months following October 1994 the total number of manufacturing jobs fell by 12,400. Hardest hit were apparel workers, who lost 4,600 jobs during the year, well over half of the 7,900 jobs lost by all nondurable goods workers. Among those making durable goods, the toughest losses were felt by industrial machinery and equipment manufacturers, who shed 1,700 jobs over the year. Furniture and fixtures companies followed closely behind, laying off 1,600 workers.

With such a high percentage of job loss concentrated in just a few industries, jobseekers should note that there are some manufacturing industries in Tennessee that did some actual hiring. For instance, the number of lumber and wood products workers rose by 400; stone, clay, and glass products companies' hires rose by 200; the printing and publishing industries hired another 400; and rubber and plastics jobs were up by 200. One example of a manufacturer that is hiring in these industries is **J.M. Huber** in Spring City, which produces oriented strand board. The company recently announced a $95 million expansion that will create 125 jobs.

Automobiles and Auto Parts

Jobseekers in manufacturing industries should also look closely at Tennessee's important auto and auto parts industry. Up until the mid-1980s, manufacturing in the Southeast as a region was largely based upon the apparel, textile, and food processing industries. While these sectors still employ thousands of workers throughout the region, the transportation industry -- and the auto and auto parts industries, in particular, have changed the manufacturing sector's landscape in the South over the past decade. And few states have benefited from this trend as much as Tennessee.

The Volunteer State's economy is graced by a high number of auto supply companies that are direct beneficiaries when car and truck sales are strong, and 1994 was a banner year for Detroit. One company that has reaped the rewards is **Ezon, Inc.**, the nation's third largest independent wholesale distributor of auto parts and chemicals. Another is **Daikin Manufacturing**, a provider of parts to nearly every auto manufacturer in North America. Daikin recently opened a new plant in Eastbridge Business Park in Knox County. Then there's **Bridgestone Metalpha USA Inc.**, a producer of high-grade steel cord used in Bridgestone tires. The company recently opened a plant in Clarksville that will eventually employ 280. There's also **Specialty Tires of America**, which recently chose a 50-acre site in Unicoi County for an operation that is expected to have 225 employees when production begins in the fall of 1996. And **Form Rite Corporation**, another auto equipment company, recently expanded its Surgoinsville operation including the addition of 400 new jobs.

Tennessee is also known for its own automotive manufacturing plants, specifically **Saturn** in Spring Hill, and **Nissan Motor Manufacturing** in Smyrna. During 1995, Nissan announced that it will build an engine manufacturing facility in Dechard. The facility will be Nissan's first expansion site outside of Smyrna. The four-valve, dual-overhead-cam engines will be supplied for the 1998 model Altima, which will be built in Smyrna. Annual production capacity at the plant will be 200,000 engines, with production scheduled to start in the spring of 1997. The plant is expected to employ about 200, and hiring was expected to begin during the spring of 1996. Until now, Altima engines had been built in Mexico.

In another development, **Nippondenso Tennessee** announced in 1995 that it plans to build a facility in the McMinn County Interstate Industrial Park in Athens. When the site becomes operational in 1997 it will employ about 160 people. Nippondenso Tennessee makes advanced technology components and systems for automakers.

The auto industry does have its pitfalls, however. From one year to the next, auto sales can vary widely, depending on larger trends in the national economy. And when sales of new cars to consumers are down, sales of new auto parts to the Big Three Detroit automakers also drop.

Strong Demand for Technical Workers

The most successful jobseekers are those who can find potential employers that are having problems meeting their goals and offer themselves as the solution. For example, because most manufacturing jobs of the past required little technical knowledge, many Tennessee companies are having difficulty finding workers that are skilled enough to operate advanced electronics. And this isn't just a problem for high-tech employers. As Dan Bradley, the human resource manager for the Memphis distribution center of **Williams-Sonoma** told *The Memphis Business Journal*, "There are a lot of types of businesses around, but we all found out that we have the same problems in finding people with some knowledge of the skills required for the types of jobs we offer." According to Bradley, while Williams-Sonoma has no trouble filling traditional warehouse-type jobs, opportunities are best for computer programmers and other positions where advanced skills and a knowledge of electronics are required.

High-Technology

While there may still be shortages of skilled technical workers in the state, Tennessee does support a vibrant high-tech community. In fact, eastern Tennessee is one of the nation's major centers for high-technology, with hundreds of small and large companies lining the **Oak Ridge/Knoxville Technology Corridor**. The Technology Corridor is a network of office parks, supported by the presence of the **Tennessee Valley Authority** headquarters and the **University of Tennessee** at Knoxville. Three **U.S. Department of Energy** facilities are based in the corridor, including the **Oak Ridge National Laboratory**, which is one of the largest federal research and development centers. These institutions provide extensive education and training opportunities for area businesses. They have also played a role in creating new businesses by taking part in technology transfer. Two good bets for jobseekers include **National Psychopharmaceutical Laboratory**, which analyzes the effects of psychopharmacological drugs on the bloodstream, and **Science Application International Corporation**, which provides engineering, environmental, and informational services.

Other Manufacturing Industries

Another group of manufacturers that has avoided large layoffs is instrument manufacturers. This group includes many medical equipment manufacturers that have reaped the benefits of the rising demand for health care services. One such employer is **Sofamor/Danek Group**. *Fortune* magazine classified this manufacturer of spinal surgery implants and instruments as one of the fastest-growing companies in the nation.

Even in the pockets of the manufacturing job market where layoffs have been higher, there are companies that are hiring. That's even true in the beleaguered food processing sector, which shed 400 Tennessee jobs between November 1994 and November 1995. For example, the well-known agricultural giant **Tyson Foods** recently opened a processing plant, hatchery, and feed mill in northwest Tennessee. The plant is expected to employ up to 1,500 and provide contract opportunities for neighboring family farms.

And while the electronic equipment sector laid off about 800 workers between November 1994 and November 1995, **Alexander Batteries** has begun turning out rechargeable batteries in Norma, with employment expected to eventually grow to 1,000. Other manufacturers that have been expanding or launching new operations include: **N.N. Ball & Roller** of Mountain City; **AAA Coatings** of Smithville; **IRC Parts and Supply** of LaVergne; **Newell Home Hardware** of Memphis; **Clayton Homes** of Savannah; and **Birmingham Steel** of Memphis.

Memphis: America's Distribution Center

While Memphis used to be somewhat overshadowed by Nashville in the national spotlight, the city is increasingly being seen as more than just Elvis' hometown. Much of the credit for that goes to an advertising campaign launched back in 1981 and supported by the city's Chamber of Commerce, the advertising agency **Walker & Associates**, and the growing number of distribution companies that have moved to town. According to *Advertising Age* magazine, Memphis has been able to attract 55 new distribution operations since 1993 alone through a direct mail and magazine advertising campaign. The Chamber of Commerce estimates that 103,000 new jobs have been created since 1985, and that well over half of them are the result of the campaign.

One industry that benefits directly from Memphis' role as a distribution center is agribusiness. Tennessee trades almost half of the nation's cotton and is home to three of the world's largest cotton dealers, **Dunavant Enterprises**, **Hohenburg Brothers**, and the **Allenburgh Company**. Dunavant Enterprises is the largest cotton merchant in the world, as well as Memphis' largest private employer, specializing in cotton merchandising, warehousing, and ginning.

Hardwood and other wood and paper products are also important products in Memphis, as are soybeans, meat, and other foods. **Agricenter International** is located in Memphis as well. This huge exhibition center brings together the most technologically advanced methods of farming and farm equipment at various trade shows and conferences.

Retail

In the coming months there will be numerous retail opportunities in Tennessee, with retail sales associate positions second only to registered nurses in job growth. **Proffit's**, the specialty department store chain, has been adding thousands of employees to its payroll every year. And **Wal-Mart**, the nation's largest retailer, announced in 1995 that it had chosen Greene County as the site for a $30 million regional distribution center which will bring with it about 600 jobs. The initial hiring of about 400 locals was scheduled to begin during the summer of 1996 with the number of jobs expected to climb to 600 within two years. The bad news: most of these and other retail industry jobs are low-paid and low-skilled. The fact that retailers like **Dollar General** of Nashville and **Service Merchandise** of Brentwood are also doing extensive hiring reflects the shift in the consumer market toward convenience and economy. Dollar General is a rapidly expanding, cut-price merchandiser featuring items that range in price from $1 to $25. Service Merchandise, a department store chain, operates mostly through catalog sales, and its retail locations reflect the catalog's style. A sample of every item is on the floor, some encased in glass. Customers select an item number, then cash out and pick up the item on the way out, where it has materialized on a baggage carousel-like conveyor belt.

Even those with more expensive tastes can find bargains in Tennessee: **Warehouse Row** factory store outlet features 35 upscale shops in two renovated railroad warehouses situated in the center of Chattanooga. The complex is listed on the *National Register of Historic Places* and outlet stores include **J. Peterman**, **Cole Haan**, and **Polo/Ralph Lauren**, all of which report brisk sales.

For further information, jobseekers can contact:

Department of Economic and Community Development
320 6th Avenue North, 8th Floor
Nashville, TN 37243-0405
615/741-1094

Tennessee Department of Employment Security
Nashville, TN 37245-1000
615/741-2131

THE BASICS OF JOB WINNING:
A CONDENSED REVIEW

This chapter is divided into four sections. The first section explains the fundamentals that every jobseeker should know, especially first-time jobseekers. The following three sections deal with special situations faced by specific types of jobseekers: those who are currently employed, those who have lost a job, and college students.

THE BASICS:
Things Everyone Needs To Know

Career Planning   The first step to finding your ideal job is to clearly define your objectives. This is better known as career planning (or life planning if you wish to emphasize the importance of combining the two). Career planning has become a field of study in and of itself.

If you are thinking of choosing or switching careers, we particularly emphasize two things. First, choose a career where you will enjoy most of the day-to-day tasks. This sounds obvious, but most of us have at one point or another been attracted by a glamour industry or a prestigious job title without thinking of the most important consideration: Would we enjoy performing the everyday tasks the position entails?

The second key consideration is that you are not merely choosing a career, but also a lifestyle. Career counselors indicate that one of the most common problems people encounter in job-seeking is that they fail to consider how well-suited they are for a particular position or career. For example, some people, attracted to management consulting by good salaries, early responsibility, and high-level corporate exposure, do not adapt well to the long hours, heavy travel demands, and constant pressure to produce. Be sure to ask yourself how you might adapt to not only the day-to-day duties and working environment that a specific position entails, but also how you might adapt to the demands of that career or industry choice as a whole.

Choosing Your Strategy   Assuming that you've established your career objectives, the next step of the job search is to develop a strategy. If you don't take the time to develop a strategy and lay out a plan, you may find yourself going in circles after several weeks of randomly searching for opportunities that always seem just beyond your reach.

The most common job-seeking techniques are:

- following up on help-wanted advertisements
- using employment services
- relying on personal contacts
- contacting employers directly (the Direct Contact method)

Many professionals have been successful in finding better jobs using each one of these approaches. However, the Direct Contact method boasts twice the success rate of the others. So unless you have specific reasons to believe that other strategies would work best for you, Direct Contact should form the foundation of your job search.

If you prefer to use other methods as well, try to expend at least half your effort on Direct Contact, spending the rest on all of the other methods combined. Millions of other jobseekers have already proven that Direct Contact has been twice as effective in obtaining employment, so why not benefit from their experience?

With your strategy in mind, the next step is to work out the details of **Setting** your search. The most important detail is setting up a schedule. Of course, **Your** since job searches aren't something most people do regularly, it may be **Schedule** hard to estimate how long each step will take. Nonetheless, it is important to have a plan so that you can monitor your progress.

When outlining your job search schedule, have a realistic time frame in mind. If you will be job-searching full-time, your search could take at least two months or more. If you can only devote part-time effort, it will probably take at least four months.

You probably know a few currently employed people who seem to spend their whole lives searching for a better job in their spare time. Don't be one of them. If you are presently working and don't feel like devoting a lot of energy to job-seeking right now, then wait. Focus on enjoying your present position,

> **The first step in beginning your job search is to clearly define your objectives.**

performing your best on the job, and storing up energy for when you are really ready to begin your job search.

Those of you who are currently unemployed should remember that job-hunting is tough work physically and emotionally. It is also intellectually demanding work that requires you to be at your best. So don't tire yourself out by working on your job campaign around the clock. At the same time, be sure to discipline yourself. The most logical way to manage your time while looking for a job is to keep your regular working hours.

If you are searching full-time and have decided to choose several different contact methods, we recommend that you divide up each week, designating some time for each method. By trying several approaches at once, you can evaluate how promising each seems and alter your schedule accordingly. But be careful -- don't judge the success of a particular technique just by the sheer number of interviews you obtain. Positions advertised in the newspaper, for instance, are likely to generate many more interviews per opening than positions that are filled without being advertised.

If you are searching part-time and decide to try several different contact methods, we recommend that you try them sequentially. You simply won't have enough time to put a meaningful amount of effort into more than one method at once. Estimate the length of your job search, and then allocate so many weeks or months for each contact method, beginning with Direct Contact.

And remember that all schedules are meant to be broken. The purpose of setting a schedule is not to rush you to your goal but to help you periodically evaluate how you're progressing.

The Direct Contact Method

Once you have scheduled your time, you are ready to begin your search in earnest. If you decide to begin with the Direct Contact method, the first step is to develop a checklist for categorizing the types of firms for which you'd like to work. You might categorize firms by product line, size, customer-type (such as industrial or consumer), growth prospects, or geographical location. Your list of important criteria might be very short. If it is, good! The shorter it is, the easier it will be to locate a company that is right for you.

Now you will want to use this *JobBank* book to assemble your list of potential employers. Choose firms where *you* are most likely to be able to find a job. Try matching your skills with those that a specific job demands. Consider where your skills might be in demand, the degree of competition for employment, and the employment outlook at each company.

Separate your prospect list into three groups. The first 25 percent will be your primary target group, the next 25 percent will be your secondary group, and the remaining names you can keep in reserve.

After you form your prospect list, begin work on your resume. Refer to the Resumes and Cover Letters section following this chapter to get ideas.

Once your resume is complete, begin researching your first batch of prospective employers. You will want to determine whether you would be happy working at the firms you are researching and to get a better idea of what their employment needs might be. You also need to obtain enough information to sound highly informed about the company during phone conversations and in mail correspondence. But don't go all out on your research yet! You probably won't be able to arrange interviews with some of these firms, so save your big research effort until you start to arrange interviews. Nevertheless, you should plan to spend several hours researching each firm. Do your research in batches to save time and energy. Start with this book, and find out what you can about each of the firms in your primary target group. Contact any pertinent professional associations that may be able to help you learn more about an employer. Read industry

> The more you know about a company, the more likely you are to catch an interviewer's eye. (You'll also face fewer surprises once you get the job!)

publications looking for articles on the firm. (Addresses of associations and names of important publications are listed after each industrial section of employer listings in this book.) Then try additional resources at your local library. Keep organized, and maintain a folder on each firm.

If you discover something that really disturbs you about the firm (they are about to close their only local office), or if you discover that your chances of getting a job there are practically nil (they have just instituted a hiring freeze), then cross them off your prospect list. If possible,

---

DEVELOPING YOUR CONTACTS:
NETWORKING

Some career counselors feel that the best route to a better job is through somebody you already know or through somebody to whom you can be introduced. These counselors recommend that you build your contact base beyond your current acquaintances by asking each one to introduce you, or refer you, to additional people in your field of interest.

The theory goes like this: You might start with 15 personal contacts, each of whom introduces you to three additional people, for a total of 45 additional contacts. Then each of these people introduces you to three additional people, which adds 135 additional contacts. Theoretically, you will soon know every person in the industry.

Of course, developing your personal contacts does not work quite as smoothly as the theory suggests because some people will not be able to introduce you to anyone. The further you stray from your initial contact base, the weaker your references may be. So, if you do try developing your own contacts, try to begin with as many people that you know personally as you can. Dig into your personal phone book and your holiday greeting card list and locate old classmates from school. Be particularly sure to approach people who perform your personal business such as your lawyer, accountant, banker, doctor, stockbroker, and insurance agent. These people develop a very broad contact base due to the nature of their professions.

---

supplement your research efforts by contacting individuals who know the firm well. Ideally you should make an informal contact with someone at that particular firm, but often a direct competitor, or a major supplier or customer, will be able to supply you with just as much information. At the very least, try to obtain whatever printed information the company has available -- not just annual reports, but product brochures and any other printed materials that the firm may have to offer, either about its operations or about career opportunities.

Getting The Interview
Now it is time to arrange an interview, time to make the Direct Contact. If you have read many books on job-searching, you may have noticed that most of these books tell you to avoid the personnel office like the plague. It is said that the personnel office never hires people; they screen candidates. Unfortunately, this is often the case. If you can identify the appropriate manager with the authority to hire you, you should try to contact that person directly. However, this will take a lot of time in each case, and often you'll be bounced back to personnel despite your efforts. So we suggest that initially you begin your Direct Contact campaign through personnel offices. If it seems that the firms on your prospect list do little hiring through personnel, you might consider some alternative courses of action.

The three obvious means of initiating Direct Contact are:

- Showing up unannounced
- Mail
- Phone calls

Cross out the first one right away. You should never show up to seek a professional position without an appointment. Even if you are somehow lucky enough to obtain an interview, you will appear so unprofessional that you will not be seriously considered.

Mail contact seems to be a good choice if you have not been in the job market for a while. You can take your time to prepare a letter, say exactly what you want, and of course include your resume. Remember that employers receive many resumes every day. Don't be surprised if you do not get a response to your inquiry, and don't spend weeks waiting for responses that may never come. If you do send a letter, follow it up (or precede it) with a phone call. This will increase your impact, and because of the initial research you did, will underscore both your familiarity with and your interest in the firm.

Another alternative is to make a "Cover Call." Your Cover Call should be just like your cover letter: concise. Your first statement should interest the employer in you. Then try to subtly mention your familiarity with the firm. Don't be overbearing; keep your introduction to three sentences or less. Be pleasant, self-confident, and relaxed. This will greatly increase the chances of the person at the other end of the line developing the conversation. But don't press. If you are asked to follow up with "something in the mail," this signals the conversation's natural end. Don't try to prolong the conversation once it has ended, and don't ask what they want to receive in the mail. Always send your resume and a highly personalized follow-up letter, reminding the addressee of the phone conversation. *Always* include a cover letter if you are asked to send a resume.

> **Always include a cover letter if you are asked to send a resume.**

Unless you are in telephone sales, making smooth and relaxed cover calls will probably not come easily. Practice them on your own, and then with your friends or relatives.

If you obtain an interview as a result of a telephone conversation, be sure to send a thank-you note reiterating the points you made during the

DON'T BOTHER WITH MASS MAILINGS OR BARRAGES OF PHONE CALLS

Direct Contact does not mean burying every firm within a hundred miles with mail and phone calls. Mass mailings rarely work in the job hunt. This also applies to those letters that are personalized -- but dehumanized -- on an automatic typewriter or computer. Don't waste your time or money on such a project; you will fool no one but yourself.

The worst part of sending out mass mailings, or making unplanned phone calls to companies you have not researched, is that you are likely to be remembered as someone with little genuine interest in the firm, who lacks sincerity -- somebody that nobody wants to hire.

HELP WANTED ADVERTISEMENTS

Only a small fraction of professional job openings are advertised. Yet the majority of jobseekers -- and quite a few people not in the job market -- spend a lot of time studying the help wanted ads. As a result, the competition for advertised openings is often very severe.

A moderate-sized employer told us about their experience advertising in the help wanted section of a major Sunday newspaper:

It was a disaster. We had over 500 responses from this relatively small ad in just one week. We have only two phone lines in this office and one was totally knocked out. We'll never advertise for professional help again.

If you insist on following up on help wanted ads, then research a firm before you reply to an ad. Preliminary research might help to separate you from all of the other professionals responding to that ad, many of whom will have only a passing interest in the opportunity. It will also give you insight about a particular firm, to help you determine if it is potentially a good match. That said, your chances of obtaining a job through the want ads are still much smaller than they are with the Direct Contact method.

conversation. You will appear more professional and increase your impact. However, unless specifically requested, don't mail your resume once an interview has been arranged. Take it with you to the interview instead.

Preparing For The Interview

Once the interview has been arranged, begin your in-depth research. You should arrive at an interview knowing the company upside-down and inside-out. You need to know the company's products, types of customers, subsidiaries, parent company, principal locations, rank in the industry, sales and profit trends, type of ownership, size, current plans, and much more. By this time you have probably narrowed your job search to one industry. Even if you haven't, you should still be familiar with the trends in the firm's industry, the firm's principal competitors and their relative performance, and the direction in which the industry leaders are headed.

Dig into every resource you can! Read the company literature, the

> **You should arrive at an interview knowing the company upside-down and inside-out.**

trade press, the business press, and if the company is public, call your stockbroker (if you have one) and ask for additional information. If possible, speak to someone at the firm before the interview, or if not, speak to someone at a competing firm. The more time you spend, the better. Even if you feel extremely pressed for time, you should set aside several hours for pre-interview research.

If you have been out of the job market for some time, don't be surprised if you find yourself tense during your first few interviews. It will probably happen every time you re-enter the market, not just when you seek your first job after getting out of school.

Tension is natural during an interview, but knowing you have done a thorough research job should put you more at ease. Make a list of questions that you think might be asked in each interview. Think out your answers carefully and practice them with a friend. Tape record your responses to the problem questions. If you feel particularly unsure of your interviewing skills, arrange your first interviews at firms you are not as interested in. (But remember it is common courtesy to seem enthusiastic about the possibility of working for any firm at which you interview.) Practice again on your own after these first few interviews. Go over the difficult questions that you were asked.

Interview Attire

How important is the proper dress for a job interview? Buying a complete wardrobe of Brooks Brothers pinstripes or Donna Karan suits, donning new wing tips or pumps, and having your hair styled every morning are not enough to guarantee you a career position as an investment banker. But on the other hand, if you can't find a clean, conservative suit or won't take the time to wash your hair, then you are just wasting your time by interviewing at all.

Top personal grooming is as important as finding appropriate clothes for a job interview. Careful grooming indicates both a sense of thoroughness and self-confidence. This is not the time to make a statement -- take out the extra earrings and avoid any garish hair colors not found in nature. Women should not wear excessive makeup, and both men and women should refrain from wearing any perfume or cologne (it only takes a small spritz to leave an allergic interviewer with a fit of sneezing and a bad impression of your meeting). Men should be freshly shaven, even if the interview is late in the day, and men with long hair should have it pulled back and neat.

Men applying for any professional position should wear a suit, preferably in a conservative color such as navy or charcoal gray. It is easy to get away with wearing the same dark suit to consecutive interviews at the same company; just be sure to wear a different shirt and tie for each interview.

Women should also wear a businesslike suit. Professionalism still dictates a suit with a skirt, rather than slacks, as proper interview garb for women. This is usually true even at companies where pants are acceptable attire for female employees. As much as you may disagree with this guideline, the more prudent time to fight this standard is after you land the job.

SKIRT VS. PANTS:
An Interview Dilemma

For those women who are still convinced that pants are acceptable interview attire, listen to the words of one career counselor from a prestigious New England college:

I had a student who told me that since she knew women in her industry often wore pants to work, she was going to wear pants to her interviews. Almost every recruiter commented that her pants were "too casual," and even referred to her as "the one with the pants." The funny thing was that one of the recruiters who commented on her pants had been wearing jeans!

The final selection of candidates for a job opening won't be determined by dress, of course. However, inappropriate dress can quickly eliminate a first-round candidate. So while you shouldn't spend a fortune on a new wardrobe, you should be sure that your clothes are adequate. The key is to dress at least as formally or slightly more formally and more conservatively than the position would suggest.

What To Bring   Be complete. Everyone needs a watch, a pen, and a notepad. Finally, a briefcase or a leather-bound folder (containing extra, *unfolded*, copies of your resume) will help complete the look of professionalism.

Sometimes the interviewer will be running behind schedule. Don't be upset, be sympathetic. There is often pressure to interview a lot of candidates and to quickly fill a demanding position. So be sure to come to your interview with good reading material to keep yourself occupied and relaxed.

The Interview   The very beginning of the interview is the most important part because it determines the tone for the rest of it. Those first few moments are especially crucial. Do you smile when you meet? Do you establish enough eye contact, but not too much? Do you walk into the office with a self-assured and confident stride? Do you shake hands firmly? Do you

---

BE PREPARED:
Some Common Interview Questions

Tell me about yourself...

Why did you leave your last job?

What excites you in your current job?

Where would you like to be in five years?

How much overtime are you willing to work?

What would your previous/present employer tell me about you?

Tell me about a difficult situation that you
faced at your previous/present job.

What are your greatest strengths?

What are your greatest weaknesses?

Describe a work situation where you took initiative
and went beyond your normal responsibilities.

Why do you wish to work for this firm?

Why should we hire you?

make small talk easily without being garrulous? It is human nature to judge people by that first impression, so make sure it is a good one. But most of all, try to be yourself.

Often the interviewer will begin, after the small talk, by telling you about the company, the division, the department, or perhaps, the position. Because of your detailed research, the information about the company should be repetitive for you, and the interviewer would probably like nothing better than to avoid this regurgitation of the company biography. So if you can do so tactfully, indicate to the interviewer that you are very familiar with the firm. If he or she seems intent on providing you with background information, despite your hints, then acquiesce.

But be sure to remain attentive. If you can manage to generate a brief discussion of the company or the industry at this point, without being forceful, great. It will help to further build rapport, underscore your interest, and increase your impact.

Soon (if it didn't begin that way) the interviewer will begin the questions, many of which you will have already practiced. This period of the interview usually falls into one of two categories (or somewhere in between): either a structured interview, where the interviewer has a prescribed set of questions to ask; or an unstructured interview, where the interviewer will ask only leading questions to get you to talk about

> **The interviewer's job is to find a reason to turn you down; your job is to not provide that reason.**
>
> -John L. LaFevre, author, *How You Really Get Hired*
>
> Reprinted from the 1989/90 *CPC Annual,* with permission of the National Association of Colleges and Employers (formerly College Placement Council, Inc.), copyright holder.

yourself, your experiences, and your goals. Try to sense as quickly as possible in which direction the interviewer wishes to proceed. This will make the interviewer feel more relaxed and in control of the situation.

Remember to keep attuned to the interviewer and make the length of your answers appropriate to the situation. If you are really unsure as to how detailed a response the interviewer is seeking, then ask.

As the interview progresses, the interviewer will probably mention some of the most important responsibilities of the position. If applicable, draw parallels between your experience and the demands of the position as detailed by the interviewer. Describe your past experience in the same manner that you do on your resume: emphasizing results and achievements and not merely describing activities. But don't exaggerate. Be on the level about your abilities.

The first interview is often the toughest, where many candidates are screened out. If you are interviewing for a very competitive position, you will have to make an impression that will last. Focus on a few of your greatest strengths that are relevant to the position. Develop these points carefully, state them again in different words, and then try to summarize them briefly at the end of the interview.

Often the interviewer will pause toward the end and ask if you have any questions. Particularly in a structured interview, this might be the one chance to really show your knowledge of and interest in the firm. Have a list prepared of specific questions that are of real interest to you. Let your questions subtly show your research and your knowledge of the firm's activities. It is wise to have an extensive list of questions, as several of them may be answered during the interview.

> **Getting a job offer is a lot like getting a marriage proposal. Someone is not going to offer it unless they're pretty sure you're going to accept it.**
>
> -Marilyn Hill,
> Associate Director,
> Career Center,
> Carleton College

Do not turn your opportunity to ask questions into an interrogation. Avoid reading directly from your list of questions, and ask questions that you are fairly certain the interviewer can answer (remember how you feel when you cannot answer a question during an interview).

Even if you are unable to determine the salary range beforehand, do not ask about it during the first interview. You can always ask about it later. Above all, don't ask about fringe benefits until you have been offered a position. (Then be sure to get all the details.)

Try not to be negative about anything during the interview (particularly any past employer or any previous job). Be cheerful. Everyone likes to work with someone who seems to be happy.

Don't let a tough question throw you off base. If you don't know the answer to a question, simply say so -- do not apologize. Just smile. Nobody can answer every question -- particularly some of the questions that are asked in job interviews.

Before your first interview, you may be able to determine how many rounds of interviews there usually are for positions at your level. (Of course it may differ quite a bit even within the different levels of one firm.) Usually you can count on attending at least two or three interviews, although some firms are known to give a minimum of six interviews for all professional positions. While you should be more relaxed as you return for subsequent interviews, the pressure will be on. The more prepared you are, the better.

Depending on what information you are able to obtain, you might want to vary your strategy quite a bit from interview to interview. For instance, if the first interview is a screening interview, then be sure a few of your strengths really stand out. On the other hand, if later interviews are primarily with people who are in a position to veto your hiring, but not to push it forward, then you should primarily focus on building rapport as opposed to reiterating and developing your key strengths.

If it looks as though your skills and background do not match the position the interviewer was hoping to fill, ask him or her if there is another division or subsidiary that perhaps could profit from your talents.

Write a follow-up letter immediately after the interview, while it is still fresh in the interviewer's mind (see the sample follow-up letter format found in the Resumes and Cover Letters chapter). Then, if you haven't heard from the interviewer within a week, call to stress your continued interest in the firm, and the position, and request a second interview. **After The Interview**

THE BALANCING ACT:
Looking For A New Job While Currently Employed

For those of you who are still employed, job-searching will be particularly tiring because it must be done in addition to your normal work responsibilities. So don't overwork yourself to the point where you show up to interviews looking exhausted and start to slip behind at your current job. On the other hand, don't be tempted to quit your present job! The long hours are worth it. Searching for a job while you have one puts you in a position of strength.

If you're expected to be in your office during the business day, then you have additional problems to deal with. How can you work interviews into the business day? And if you work in an open office, how can you even call to set up interviews? As much as possible you should keep up the effort and the appearances on your present job. So maximize your use of the lunch hour, early mornings, and late afternoons for calling. If you keep trying, you'll be surprised how often you will be able to reach the executive you are trying to contact during your out-of-office hours. You can catch people as early as 8 a.m. and as late as 6 p.m. on frequent occasions. **Making Contact**

Your inability to interview at any time other than lunch just might work to your advantage. If you can, try to set up as many interviews as possible for your lunch hour. This will go a long way to creating a relaxed atmosphere. (Who isn't happy when eating?) But be sure the interviews don't stray too far from the agenda on hand. **Scheduling Interviews**

Lunchtime interviews are much easier to obtain if you have substantial career experience. People with less experience will often find no alternative to taking time off for interviews. If you have to take time off, you have to take time off. But try to do this as little as possible. Try to take the whole day off in order to avoid being blatantly obvious about your job search, and try to schedule two to three interviews for the same day. (It is

> **Try calling as early as 8 a.m. and as late as 6 p.m. You'll be surprised how often you will be able to reach the executive you want during these times of the day**

very difficult to maintain an optimum level of energy at more than three interviews in one day.) Explain to the interviewer why you might have to juggle your interview schedule -- he/she should honor the respect you're showing your current employer by minimizing your days off and will probably appreciate the fact that another prospective employer is interested in you.

References   What do you tell an interviewer who asks for references? Just say that while you are happy to have your former employers contacted, you are trying to keep your job search confidential and would rather that your current employer not be contacted until you have been given a firm offer.

IF YOU'RE FIRED OR LAID OFF:
Picking Yourself Up and Dusting Yourself Off

If you've been fired or laid off, you are not the first and will not be the last to go through this traumatic experience. In today's changing economy, thousands of professionals lose their jobs every year. Even if you were terminated with just cause, do not lose heart. Remember, being fired is not a reflection on you as a person. It is usually a reflection of your company's staffing needs and its perception of your recent job performance and attitude. And if you were not performing up to par or enjoying your work, then you will probably be better off at another company anyway.

> **Be prepared for the question "Why were you fired?" during job interviews.**

A thorough job search could take months, so be sure to negotiate a reasonable severance package, if possible, and determine what benefits, such as health insurance, you are still legally entitled to. Also, register for unemployment compensation immediately. Don't be surprised to find other professionals collecting unemployment compensation -- it is for everyone who has lost their job.

Don't start your job search with a flurry of unplanned activity. Start by choosing a strategy and working out a plan. Now is not the time for major changes in your life. If possible, remain in the same career and in the same geographical location, at least until you have been working again for a while. On the other hand, if the only industry for which you are trained is leaving, or is severely depressed in your area, then you should give prompt consideration to moving or switching careers.

Avoid mentioning you were fired when arranging interviews, but be prepared for the question "Why were you fired?" during an interview. If you were laid off as a result of downsizing, briefly explain, being sure to reinforce that your job loss was not due to performance. If you were in fact fired, be honest, but try to detail the reason as favorably as possible and portray what you have learned from your mistakes. If you are confident one of your past managers will give you a good reference, tell the interviewer to contact that person. Do not to speak negatively of your past employer and try not to sound particularly worried about your status of being temporarily unemployed.

Finally, don't spend too much time reflecting on why you were let go or how you might have avoided it. Think positively, look to the future, and be sure to follow a careful plan during your job search.

THE COLLEGE STUDENT:
How To Conduct Your First Job Search

While you will be able to apply many of the basics covered earlier in this chapter to your job search, there are some situations unique to the college student's job search.

Perhaps the biggest problem college students face is lack of **Gaining** experience. Many schools have internship programs designed to give **Experience** students exposure to the field of their choice, as well as the opportunity to make valuable contacts. Check out your school's career services department to see what internships are available. If your school does not have a formal internship program, or if there are no available internships that appeal to you, try contacting local businesses and offering your services -- often, businesses will be more than willing to have any extra pair of hands (especially if those hands are unpaid!) for a day or two each week. Or try contacting school alumni to see if you can "shadow" them for a few days, and see what their day-to-day duties are like. Either way, try to begin building experience as early as possible in your college career.

THE GPA QUESTION

You are interviewing for the job of your dreams. Everything is going well: you've established a good rapport, the interviewer seems impressed with your qualifications, and you're almost positive the job is yours. Then you're asked about your GPA, which is pitifully low. Do you tell the truth and watch your dream job fly out the window?

Never lie about your GPA (they may request your transcript, and no company will hire a liar). You can, however, explain if there is a reason you don't feel your grades reflect your abilities, and mention any other impressive statistics. For example, if you have a high GPA in your major, or in the last few semesters (as opposed to your cumulative college career), you can use that fact to your advantage.

What do you do if, for whatever reason, you weren't able to get experience directly related to your desired career? First, look at your previous jobs and see if there's anything you can highlight. Did you supervise or train other employees? Did you reorganize the accounting system, or boost productivity in some way? Accomplishments like these demonstrate leadership, responsibility, and innovation -- qualities that most companies look for in employees. And don't forget volunteer activities and school clubs, which can also showcase these traits.

On-Campus Recruiting

Companies will often send recruiters to interview on-site at various colleges. This gives students a chance to get interviews at companies that may not have interviewed them otherwise, particularly if the company schedules "open" interviews, in which the only screening process is who is first in line at the sign-ups. Of course, since many more applicants gain interviews in this format, this also means that many more people are rejected. The on-campus interview is generally a screening interview, to see if it is worth the company's time to invite you in for a second interview. So do everything possible to make yourself stand out from the crowd.

The first step, of course, is to check out any and all information your school's career center has on the company. If the information seems out of date, call the company's headquarters and ask to be sent the latest annual report, or any other printed information.

Many companies will host an informational meeting for interviewees, often the evening before interviews are scheduled to take place. DO NOT MISS THIS MEETING. The recruiter will almost certainly ask if you attended. Make an effort to stay after the meeting and talk with the company's representatives. Not only does this give you an opportunity to find out more information about both the company and the position, it also makes you stand out in the recruiter's mind. If there's a particular company that you had your heart set on, but you weren't able to get an interview with them, attend the information session anyway. You may be able to convince the recruiter to squeeze you into the schedule. (Or you may discover that the company really isn't suited for you after all.)

Try to check out the interview site beforehand. Some colleges may conduct "mock" interviews that take place in one of the standard interview rooms. Or you may be able to convince a career counselor (or even a custodian) to let you sneak a peek during off-hours. Either way, having an idea of the room's setup will help you to mentally prepare.

Be sure to be at least 15 minutes early to the interview. The recruiter may be running ahead of schedule, and might like to take you early. But don't be surprised if previous interviews have run over, resulting in your 30-minute slot being reduced to 20 minutes (or less). Don't complain; just use whatever time you do have as efficiently as possible to showcase the reasons *you* are the ideal candidate.

LAST WORDS

A parting word of advice. Again and again during your job search you will be rejected. You will be rejected when you apply for interviews. You will be rejected after interviews. For every job offer you finally receive, you probably will have been rejected a multitude of times. Don't let rejections slow you down. Keep reminding yourself that the sooner you go out and get started on your job search, and get those rejections flowing in, the closer you will be to obtaining the job you want.

RESUMES AND COVER LETTERS

When filling a position, a recruiter will often have 100-plus applicants, but time to interview only a handful of the most promising ones. As a result, he or she will reject most applicants after only briefly skimming their resumes.

Unless you have phoned and talked to the recruiter -- which you should do whenever you can -- you will be chosen or rejected for an interview entirely on the basis of your resume and cover letter. Your cover letter must catch the recruiter's attention, and your resume must hold it. (But remember -- a resume is no substitute for a job search campaign. *You* must seek a job. Your resume is only one tool.)

RESUME FORMAT:
Mechanics of a First Impression

The Basics

Recruiters dislike long resumes, so unless you have an unusually strong background with many years of experience and a diversity of outstanding achievements, keep your resume length to one page. If you must squeeze in more information than would otherwise fit, try using a smaller typeface or changing the margins.

Keep your resume on standard 8-1/2" x 11" paper. Since recruiters often get resumes in batches of hundreds, a smaller-sized resume may get lost in the pile. Oversized resumes are likely to get crumpled at the edges, and won't fit easily in their files.

First impressions matter, so make sure the recruiter's first impression of your resume is a good one. Print your resume on quality paper that has weight and texture, in a conservative color such as white, ivory, or pale gray. Use matching paper and envelopes for both your resume and cover letter.

Getting It On Paper

Modern photocomposition typesetting gives you the clearest, sharpest image, a wide variety of type styles, and effects such as italics, bold-facing, and book-like justified margins. It is also much too expensive for many jobseekers. And improvements in laser printers mean that a computer-generated resume can look just as impressive as one that has been professionally typeset.

A computer or word processor is the most flexible way to type your resume. This will allow you to make changes almost instantly and to store different drafts on disk. Word processing and desktop publishing systems also offer many different fonts to choose from, each taking up different amounts of space. (It is generally best to stay between 9-point and 12-point font size.) Many other options are also available, such as bold-facing for emphasis, justified margins, and the ability to change and manipulate spacing.

The end result, however, will be largely determined by the quality of the printer you use. You need at least "letter quality" type for your resume. Do not use a "near letter quality" or dot matrix printer. Laser printers will generally provide the best quality.

Household typewriters and office typewriters with nylon or other cloth ribbons are *not* good enough for typing your resume. If you don't have access to a quality word processor, hire a professional who can prepare your resume with a word processor or typesetting machine.

Don't make your copies on an office photocopier. Only the personnel office may see the resume you mail. Everyone else may see only a copy of it, and copies of copies quickly become unreadable. Either print out each copy individually, or take your resume to a professional copy shop, which generally use professionally-maintained, extra-high-quality photocopiers and charge fairly reasonable prices.

Proof With Care Whether you typed it yourself or paid to have it produced professionally, mistakes on resumes are not only embarrassing, but will usually remove you from further consideration (particularly if something obvious such as your name is misspelled). No matter how much you paid someone else to type, write, or typeset your resume, *you* lose if there is a mistake. So proofread it as carefully as possible. Get a friend to help you. Read your draft aloud as your friend checks the proof copy. Then have your friend read aloud while you check. Next, read it letter by letter to check spelling and punctuation.

If you are having it typed or typeset by a resume service or a printer, and you can't bring a friend or take the time during the day to proof it, pay for it and take it home. Proof it there and bring it back later to get it corrected and printed.

> The one piece of advice I give to everyone about their resume is: show it to people, show it to people, show it to people. Before you ever send out a resume, show it to at least a dozen people.
>
> -Cate Talbot Ashton, Associate Director, Career Services, Colby College

If you wrote your resume on a word processing program, also use that program's built-in spell checker to double-check for spelling errors. But keep in mind that a spell checker will not find errors such as "to" for "two" or "wok" for "work." It's important that you still proofread your resume, even after it has been spell-checked.

Types Of Resumes The two most common resume formats are the functional resume and the chronological resume (examples of both types can be found at the end of this chapter). A functional resume focuses on skills and de-emphasizes job titles, employers, etc. A functional resume is best if you have been out of the work force for a long time and/or if you want to highlight specific skills and strengths that your most recent jobs don't necessarily reflect.

Choose a chronological format if you are currently working or were working recently, and if your most recent experiences relate to your desired field. Use reverse chronological order. To a recruiter your last job and your latest schooling are the most important, so put the last first and list the rest going back in time.

Your name, phone number, and a complete address should be at the **Organization** top of your resume. Try to make your name stand out by using a slightly larger font size or all capital letters. Be sure to spell out everything -- never abbreviate St. for Street or Rd. for Road. If you are a college student, you should also put your home address and phone number at the top.

Next, list your experience, then your education. If you are a recent graduate, list your education first, unless your experience is more important than your education. (For example, if you have just graduated from a teaching school, have some business experience, and are applying for a job in business, you would list your business experience first.)

Keep everything easy to find. Put the dates of your employment and education on the left of the page. Put the names of the companies you worked for and the schools you attended a few spaces to the right of the dates. Put the city and state, or the city and country, where you studied or worked to the right of the page.

This is just one suggestion that may work for you. The important thing is simply to break up the text in some way that makes your resume visually attractive and easy to scan, so experiment to see which layout works best for your resume. However you set it up, stay consistent. Inconsistencies in fonts, spacing, or tenses will make your resume look sloppy. Also, be sure to use tabs to keep your information vertically lined up, rather than the less precise space bar.

RESUME CONTENT:
Say It With Style

You are selling your skills and accomplishments in your resume, so it **Sell Yourself** is important to inventory yourself and know yourself. If you have achieved something, say so. Put it in the best possible light. But avoid subjective statements, such as "I am a hard worker" or "I get along well with my coworkers." Just stick to the facts.

While you shouldn't hold back or be modest, don't exaggerate your achievements to the point of misrepresentation. Be honest. Many companies will immediately drop an applicant from consideration (or fire a current employee) if inaccurate information is discovered on a resume or other application material.

Keep It Brief
Write down the important (and pertinent) things you have done, but do it in as few words as possible. Your resume will be scanned, not read, and short, concise phrases are much more effective than long-winded sentences. Avoid the use of "I" when emphasizing your accomplishments. Instead, use brief phrases beginning with action verbs.

While some technical terms will be unavoidable, you should try to avoid excessive "technicalese." Keep in mind that the first person to see your resume may be a human resources person who won't necessarily know all the jargon -- and how can they be impressed by something they don't understand?

Also, try to keep your paragraphs at six lines or shorter. If you have more than six lines of information about one job or school, put it in two or more paragraphs. The shorter your resume is, the more carefully it will be examined. Remember: your resume usually has between eight and 45 seconds to catch an employer's eye. So make every second count.

Job Objective
A functional resume may require a job objective to give it focus. One or two sentences describing the job you are seeking can clarify in what capacity your skills will be best put to use.

Examples: An entry-level position in the publishing industry.
A challenging position requiring analytical thought and excellent writing skills.

Don't include a job objective in a chronological resume. Even if you are certain of exactly what type of job you desire, the presence of a job objective might eliminate you from consideration for other positions that a recruiter feels are a better match for your qualifications. But even though you may not put an objective on paper, having a career goal in mind as you write can help give your resume a sense of direction.

Work Experience
Some jobseekers may choose to include both "Relevant Experience" and "Additional Experience" sections. This can be useful, as it allows the jobseeker to place more emphasis on certain experiences and to de-emphasize others.

Emphasize continued experience in a particular job area or continued interest in a particular industry. De-emphasize irrelevant positions. Delete positions that you held for less than four months (unless you are a very recent college grad or still in school).Stress your results, elaborating on how you contributed in your previous jobs. Did you increase sales, reduce costs, improve a product, implement a new program? Were you promoted? Use specific numbers (i.e., quantities, percentages, dollar amounts) whenever possible.

Mention all relevant responsibilities. Be specific, and slant your past accomplishments toward the position that you hope to obtain. For example, do you hope to supervise people? If so, then state how many people, performing what function, you have supervised.

Keep it brief if you have more than two years of career experience. **Education** Elaborate more if you have less experience. If you are a recent grad with two or more years of college, you may choose to include any high school activities that are directly relevant to your career. If you've been out of school for awhile, list post-secondary education only.

Mention degrees received and any honors or special awards. Note individual courses or research projects you participated in that might be relevant for employers. For example, if you are an English major applying for a position as a business writer, be sure to mention any business or economics courses.

USE ACTION VERBS

How you write your resume is just as important as *what* you write. The strongest resumes use short phrases beginning with action verbs. Below, we've listed a few of the action verbs you may want to use. (This list is not all-inclusive.)

achieved	developed	integrated	purchased
administered	devised	interpreted	reduced
advised	directed	interviewed	regulated
analyzed	discovered	invented	reorganized
arranged	distributed	launched	represented
assembled	eliminated	maintained	researched
assisted	established	managed	resolved
attained	evaluated	marketed	restored
budgeted	examined	mediated	restructured
built	executed	monitored	revised
calculated	expanded	negotiated	scheduled
collaborated	expedited	obtained	selected
collected	facilitated	operated	served
compiled	formulated	ordered	sold
completed	founded	organized	solved
computed	generated	participated	streamlined
conducted	headed	performed	studied
consolidated	identified	planned	supervised
constructed	implemented	prepared	supplied
consulted	improved	presented	supported
controlled	increased	processed	tested
coordinated	initiated	produced	trained
created	installed	proposed	updated
designed	instituted	provided	upgraded
determined	instructed	published	wrote

Highlight Impressive Skills   Be sure to mention any computer skills you may have. You may wish to include a section entitled "Additional Skills" or "Computer Skills," in which you list any software programs you know. An additional skills section is also an ideal place to mention fluency in a foreign language.

Personal Data   This section is optional, but if you choose to include it, keep it very brief (two lines maximum). A one-word mention of hobbies such as fishing, chess, baseball, cooking, etc., can give the person who will interview you a good way to open up the conversation. It doesn't hurt to include activities that are unusual (fencing, bungee jumping, snake-charming) or that somehow relate to the position or the company you're applying to (for instance, if you are a member of a professional organization in your industry). Never include information about your age, health, physical characteristics, marital status, or religious affiliation.

References   The most that is needed is the sentence, "References available upon request," at the bottom of your resume. If you choose to leave it out, that's fine.

HIRING A RESUME WRITER:
Is It The Right Choice for You?

If you write reasonably well, it is to your advantage to write your own resume. Writing your resume forces you to review your experience and figure out how to explain your accomplishments in clear, brief phrases. This will help you when you explain your work to interviewers.

If you write your resume, everything will be in your own words -- it will sound like you. It will say what you want it to say. If you are a good writer, know yourself well, and have a good idea of which parts of your background employers are looking for, you should be able to write your own resume better than

> Those things [marital status, church affiliations, etc.] have no place on a resume. Those are illegal questions, so why even put that information on your resume?
>
> -Becky Hayes, Career Counselor
> Career Services, Rice University

anyone else can. If you decide to write your resume yourself, have as many people review and proofread it as possible. Welcome objective opinions and other perspectives.

When To Get Help   If you have difficulty writing in "resume style" (which is quite unlike normal written language), if you are unsure of which parts of your background you should emphasize, or if you think your resume would make your case better if it did not follow one of the standard forms outlined either here or in a book on resumes, then you should consider having it professionally written.

There are two reasons even some professional resume writers we know have had their resumes written with the help of fellow professionals. First, they may need the help of someone who can be objective about their background, and second, they may want an experienced sounding board to help focus their thoughts.

The best way to choose a writer is by reputation -- the **If You Hire** recommendation of a friend, a personnel director, your school placement **A Pro** officer, or someone else knowledgeable in the field.

Important questions:
- "How long have you been writing resumes?"
- "If I'm not satisfied with what you write, will you go over it with me and change it?"
- "Do you charge by the hour or a flat rate?"

There is no sure relation between price and quality, except that you are unlikely to get a good writer for less than $50 for an uncomplicated resume and you shouldn't have to pay more than $300 unless your experience is very extensive or complicated. There will be additional charges for printing.

Few resume services will give you a firm price over the phone, simply because some resumes are too complicated and take too long to do for a predetermined price. Some services will quote you a price that applies to almost all of their customers. Once you decide to use a specific writer, you should insist on a firm price quote before engaging their services. Also, find out how expensive minor changes will be.

COVER LETTERS:
Quick, Clear, and Concise

Always mail a cover letter with your resume. In a cover letter you can show an interest in the company that you can't show in a resume. You can also point out one or two skills or accomplishments the company can put to good use.

The more personal you can get, the better. If someone known to the **Make It** person you are writing has recommended that you contact the company, **Personal** get permission to include his/her name in the letter. If you have the name of a person to send the letter to, address it directly to that person (after first calling the company to verify the spelling of the person's name, correct title, and mailing address). Be sure to put the person's name and title on both the letter and the envelope. This will ensure that your letter will get through to the proper person, even if a new person now occupies this position. But even if you don't have a contact name and are simply addressing it to the "Personnel Director" or the "Hiring Partner," definitely send a letter.

Type cover letters in full. Don't try the cheap and easy ways, like using a computer mail merge program, or photocopying the body of your letter and typing in the inside address and salutation. You will give the impression that you are mailing to a host of companies and have no particular interest in any one.

Cover letter dos and don'ts

- *Do* keep your cover letter brief and to the point.
- *Do* be sure it is error-free.
- *Don't* just repeat information verbatim from your resume.
- *Don't* overuse the personal pronoun "I."
- *Don't* send a generic cover letter -- show your personal knowledge of and interest in that particular company.
- *Do* accentuate what you can offer the company, not what you hope to gain from them.

FUNCTIONAL RESUME
(Prepared on a word processor and laser printed.)

PENELOPE FRANCES PANZ
430 Miller's Crossing
Essex Junction VT 05452
802/555-9354

Objective
A position as a graphic designer commensurate with my acquired skills and expertise.

Summary
Extensive experience in plate making, separations, color matching, background definition, printing, mechanicals, color corrections, and personnel supervision. A highly motivated manager and effective communicator. Proven ability to:

- **Create Commercial Graphics**
- **Produce Embossed Drawings**
- **Color Separate**
- **Control Quality**
- **Resolve Printing Problems**
- **Analyze Customer Satisfaction**

Qualifications

Printing:
Knowledgeable in black and white as well as color printing. Excellent judgment in determining acceptability of color reproduction through comparison with original. Proficient at producing four or five color corrections on all media, as well as restyling previously reproduced four-color artwork.

Customer Relations:
Routinely work closely with customers to ensure specifications are met. Capable of striking a balance between technical printing capabilities and need for customer satisfaction through entire production process.

Specialties:
Practiced at creating silk screen overlays for a multitude of processes including velo bind, GBC bind, and perfect bind. Creative design and timely preparation of posters, flyers, and personalized stationery.

Personnel Supervision:
Skillful at fostering atmosphere that encourages highly talented artists to balance high-level creativity with maximum production. Consistently meet or beat production deadlines. Instruct new employees, apprentices, and students in both artistry and technical operations.

Experience
Graphic Arts Professor, University of Vermont, Burlington VT (1987-1993).
Manager, Design Graphics, Barre VT (1993-present).

Education
Massachusetts Conservatory of Art, Ph.D. 1987
University of Massachusetts, B.A. 1984

CHRONOLOGICAL RESUME
(Prepared on a word processor
and laser printed.)

MAURICE DUPETREAUX
412 Maple Court
Seattle, WA 98404
(206) 555-6584

EXPERIENCE

THE CENTER COMPANY   Seattle, WA
Systems Programmer   1993-present
- Develop and maintain over 100 assembler modules.
- Create screen manager programs, using Assembler and Natural languages, to trace input and output to the VTAM buffer.
- Install and customize Omegamon 695 and 700 on IBM mainframes.
- Develop programs to monitor complete security control blocks, using Assembler and Natural.
- Produce stand-alone IPLs and create backrests on IBM 3380 DASD.

INFO TECH, INC.   Seattle, WA
Technical Manager   1991-1993
- Designed and managed the implementation of a network providing the legal community with a direct line to Supreme Court cases, using Clipper on IBM 386s.
- Developed a system which catalogued entire library inventory, using Turbo Pascal on IBM AT.
- Used C to create a registration system for university registrar on IBM AT.

EDUCATION

SALEM STATE UNIVERSITY   Salem, OR
    B.S. in Computer Science.   1989
    M.S. in Computer Science.   1991

COMPUTER SKILLS

- Programming Languages: C, C + +, Assembler, COBOL, Natural, Turbo Pascal, dBASE III+, and Clipper.
- Software: VTAM, Complete, TSO, JES 2, ACF 2, Omegamon 695 and 700, and Adabas.
- Operating Systems: MVS/XA, MVS/SP, MS-DOS, and VMS.

FUNCTIONAL RESUME
(Prepared on an office-
quality typewriter)

LORRAINE AVAKIAN
70 Monback Avenue
Oshkosh, WI 54901
(608) 586-1243

OBJECTIVE:
To contribute over eight years of experience in promotion, communications, and administration to an entry-level position in advertising.

SUMMARY OF QUALIFICATIONS:
- Performed advertising duties for small business.
- Experience in business writing and communications skills.
- General knowledge of office management.
- Demonstrated ability to work well with others, in both supervisory and support staff roles.
- Type 75 words per minute.

SELECTED ACHIEVEMENTS AND RESULTS:
Promotion:
Composing, editing, and proofreading correspondence and PR materials for own catering service. Large-scale mailings.

Communication:
Instruction; curriculum and lesson planning; student evaluation; parent-teacher conferences; development of educational materials. Training and supervising clerks.

Computer Skills:
Proficient in MS Word, Lotus 1-2-3, Excel, and Filemaker Pro.

Administration:
Record-keeping and file maintenance. Data processing and computer operations, accounts receivable, accounts payable, inventory control, and customer relations. Scheduling, office management, and telephone reception.

WORK HISTORY:
Teacher; Self-Employed (owner of catering service); Floor Manager; Administrative Assistant; Accounting Clerk.

EDUCATION:
Beloit College, Beloit, WI, BA in Education, 1987

CHRONOLOGICAL RESUME
(Prepared on a word processor and laser printed)

T. WILLIAM MAGUIRE
16 Charles Street
Marlborough CT 06447
203/555-9641

EDUCATION

Keene State College, Keene NH
Bachelor of Arts in Elementary Education, 1995
- Graduated *magna cum laude*
- English minor
- Kappa Delta Pi member, inducted 1993

EXPERIENCE
September 1995-
Present

Elmer T. Thienes Elementary School, Marlborough CT
Part-time Kindergarten Teacher
- Instruct kindergartners in reading, spelling, language arts, and music.
- Participate in the selection of textbooks and learning aids.
- Organize and supervise class field trips and coordinate in-class presentations.

Summers
1993-1995

Keene YMCA, Youth Division, Keene NH
Child-care Counselor
- Oversaw summer program for low-income youth.
- Budgeted and coordinated special events and field trips, working with Program Director to initiate variations in the program.
- Served as Youth Advocate in cooperation with social worker to address the social needs and problems of participants.

Spring 1995

Wheelock Elementary School, Keene NH
Student Teacher
- Taught third-grade class in all elementary subjects.
- Designed and implemented a two-week unit on Native Americans.
- Assisted in revision of third-grade curriculum.

Fall 1994

Child Development Center, Keene NH
Daycare Worker
- Supervised preschool children on the playground and during art activities.
- Created a "Peter Rabbit Corner," where children could quietly look at books or take a voluntary "time-out."

ADDITIONAL INTERESTS

Martial arts, skiing, politics, reading, writing.

GENERAL MODEL
FOR A COVER LETTER

Your mailing address
Date

Contact's name
Contact's title
Company
Company's mailing address

Dear Mr./Ms. _____:

Immediately explain why your background makes you the best candidate for the position that you are applying for. Describe what prompted you to write (want ad, article you read about the company, networking contact, etc.). Keep the first paragraph short and hard-hitting.

Detail what you could contribute to this company. Show how your qualifications will benefit this firm. Describe your interest in the corporation. Subtly emphasizing your knowledge about this firm and your familiarity with the industry will set you apart from other candidates. Remember to keep this letter short; few recruiters will read a cover letter longer than half a page.

If possible, your closing paragraph should request specific action on the part of the reader. Include your phone number and the hours when you can be reached. Mention that if you do not hear from the reader by a specific date, you will follow up with a phone call. Lastly, thank the reader for their time, consideration, etc.

Sincerely,

(signature)

Your full name (typed)

Enclosure (use this if there are other materials, such as your resume, that are included in the same envelope)

SAMPLE COVER LETTER

16 Charles Street
Marlborough CT 06447
March 16, 1996

Ms. Lia Marcusson
Assistant Principal
Jonathon Daniels Elementary School
43 Mayflower Drive
Keene NH 03431

Dear Ms. Marcusson:

Janet Newell recently informed me of a possible opening for a third grade teacher at Jonathon Daniels Elementary School. With my experience instructing third-graders, both in schools and in summer programs, I feel I would be an ideal candidate for the position. Please accept this letter and the enclosed resume as my application.

Jonathon Daniels' educational philosophy that every child can learn and succeed interests me, since it mirrors my own. My current position at Elmer T. Thienes Elementary has reinforced this philosophy, heightening my awareness of the different styles and paces of learning and increasing my sensitivity toward special needs children. Furthermore, as a direct result of my student teaching experience at Wheelock Elementary School, I am comfortable, confident, and knowledgeable working with third-graders.

I look forward to discussing the position and my qualifications for it in more detail. I can be reached at 203/555-9641 evenings or 203/555-0248 weekdays. If I do not hear from you before Tuesday of next week, I will call to see if we can schedule a time to meet. Thank you for your time and consideration.

Sincerely,

Bill Maguire

T. William Maguire

Enclosure

GENERAL MODEL FOR A
FOLLOW-UP LETTER

Your mailing address
Date

Contact's name
Contact's title
Company
Company's mailing address

Dear Mr./Ms._____:

Remind the interviewer of the reason (i.e., a specific opening, an informational interview, etc.) you were interviewed, as well as the date. Thank him/her for the interview, and try to personalize your thanks by mentioning some specific aspect of the interview.

Confirm your interest in the organization (and in the opening, if you were interviewing for a particular position). Use specifics to re-emphasize that you have researched the firm in detail and have considered how you would fit into the company and the position. This is a good time to say anything you wish you had said in the initial meeting. Be sure to keep this letter brief; a half-page is plenty.

If appropriate, close with a suggestion for further action, such as a desire to have an additional interview, if possible. Mention your phone number and the hours that you can be reached. Alternatively, you may prefer to mention that you will follow up with a phone call in several days. Once again, thank the person for meeting with you, and state that you would be happy to provide any additional information about your qualifications.

Sincerely,

(signature)

Your full name (typed)

ACCOUNTING AND MANAGEMENT CONSULTING

As the number of accounting graduates drops and the economy strengthens, all types of accounting professionals will benefit. According to the Bureau of Labor Statistics, the number of accounting jobs may grow by as much as 40 percent by the year 2005. A recent survey conducted by Robert Half International found that the best opportunities for accountants were in the financial, insurance, and real estate sector, followed by the retail and wholesale industries.

Even faster growth is projected for the management consulting industry, where the number of jobs is expected to grow almost three times faster than the rate for all industries. The increasing complexity of business will contribute to industry growth. Among other things, today's managers must worry about rapid technological innovations, changes in government regulations, growing environmental concerns, continuing reduction of trade barriers, and globalization of markets. Because it has become difficult to keep abreast of these changing conditions, corporations, institutions, and governments will increasingly need the aid of well-trained, well-informed management consulting professionals.

ARTHUR ANDERSEN & COMPANY
165 Madison Avenue, Memphis TN 38103. 901/525-4451. **Contact:** Mark Mosley, Manager. **Description:** One of the six largest certified public accounting firms in the world. Organized in 1913, Arthur Andersen & Company has offices in 40 countries. The company operates in the following divisions: Audit (offering assignments in all types of businesses and industries); Tax (offering assignments involving consultation and compliance in all areas of taxation, including income, real estate, trust, and gift taxation); and Management Information Consulting (offering opportunities for both entry-level and experienced personnel in providing professional systems and consulting services to clients in a wide-range of businesses and industries). Arthur Andersen is a segment of The Arthur Andersen Worldwide Organization, one of the leading providers of professional services in the world. With over 72,000 people in 74 countries, the global practice of its member firms is conducted in more than 350 locations, through two business units: Arthur Andersen for audit, tax, business advisory, and speciality consulting services; and Andersen Consulting for global management and technology consulting. Arthur Andersen & Company, SC is the coordinating entity of the Worldwide Organization.

DELOITTE & TOUCHE
424 Church Street, Suite 2400, Nashville TN 37219. 615/259-1800. **Contact:** Tom Walker, Partner. **Description:** An international firm of certified public accountants, providing professional accounting, auditing, tax, and management consulting services to widely diversified clients. Deloitte & Touche operates more than 500

offices throughout the world, and has a specialized program consisting of some 25 national industry groups and 50 functional (technical) groups that cross industry lines. Groups are involved in various disciplines, including accounting, auditing, taxation, management advisory services, small and growing businesses, mergers and acquisitions, and computer applications. **Corporate headquarters location:** Wilton CT.

DELOITTE & TOUCHE
4022 Sells Drive, Hermitage TN 37076. 615/391-7600. **Contact:** Bruce Webb, Director of Human Resources. **Description:** An international firm of certified public accountants, providing professional accounting, auditing, tax, and management consulting services to widely diversified clients. Deloitte & Touche operates more than 500 offices throughout the world, and has a specialized program consisting of some 25 national industry groups and 50 functional (technical) groups that cross industry lines. Groups are involved in various disciplines, including accounting, auditing, taxation, management advisory services, small and growing businesses, mergers and acquisitions, and computer applications. **Corporate headquarters location:** Wilton CT.

ERNST & YOUNG
Nationsbank Plaza, 414 Union Street, Suite 2100, Nashville TN 37219-1779. 615/252-2000. **Contact:** Mr. Horice Page, OMP. **Description:** A worldwide certified public accounting organization, with operations in three main areas: Auditing and Accounting; Tax Services; and Management Consulting. The company has approximately 5,000 professionals and 600 partners and directors in offices throughout the United States and abroad. **Corporate headquarters location:** New York NY.

PERFORMANCE DEVELOPMENT CORPORATION
109 Jefferson Avenue, Oak Ridge TN 37830. 423/482-9004. **Contact:** Dewitt Beeler, Human Resource Director. **Description:** Establishes entire management programs for other corporations.

TENERA L.P.
Advantage Place, 308 North Peters Road, Suite 280, Knoxville TN 37922. 423/531-0806. **Contact:** Ann Hutton, Office Manager. **Description:** A broad-based national consulting firm offering a wide range of products and services. Management Consulting includes strategic planning, organizational effectiveness reviews, management process evaluation, expert witness and litigation support, and integrated resource management. Information Systems and Software offers applications software for maintenance management, operations management, project management, materials management, and general management. Engineering Services include electrical engineering, instrumentation and control engineering, and emergency preparedness services. Government Environmental Services include pre-audit planning and preparation activities, on-site activities, compliance reporting, permitting, quality assurance, and design review for RCRA. Through Compliance Management, the company provides compliance support services to the Department of Energy. Self-Assessment services range from monitoring and improving self-assessment programs to evaluating specific segments of a program. Operations and Maintenance

Support focuses on systems, components, and processes. Strategic Process Management (SPM) includes establishing objectives for the process to be examined; modeling the existing process based on reviews of existing documentation; validating the existing process for efficiency, agreement with industry practice, and conformance with appropriate requirements; identifying opportunities for improvement and carefully assessing the impact on the organization; and revising process procedures to implement client-approved changes. Issue Management is centered around the TENERA Integrated Resource Management System. Safety Assessment and Risk Management includes the use of probabilistic risk and safety assessment techniques, and Materials Management Support includes custom support in engineering and technical services, management services, and comprehensive materials management.

Note: Because addresses and telephone numbers of smaller companies change rapidly, we recommend you call each company to verify the information below before inquiring about job opportunities. Mass mailings are not recommended.

Additional employers with under 250 employees:

ACCOUNTING, AUDITING, AND BOOKKEEPING SERVICES

Frazee Tate & Associates
5100 Poplar Ave, Suite 300, Memphis TN 38137-4002. 901/682-9611.

Medaphis Physician Service
3212 W End Ave, Nashville TN 37203-1338. 615/383-0547.

MANAGEMENT SERVICES

Healthcare Properties Inc.
102 Woodmont Blvd, Nashville TN 37205-2287. 615/297-1020.

BUSINESS CONSULTING SERVICES

Paige Inc.
1808 W End Ave, Nashville TN 37203-2507. 615/329-9760.

Management Resources Co.
761 Old Hickory Blvd, Suite 400, Brentwood TN 37027-4513. 615/377-3100.

Taliafaro Inc.
1 Vantage Way #290, Nashville TN 37228-1515. 615/259-4332.

OC Tanner Co.
2301 21st Ave S, Nashville TN 37212-4908. 615/297-1300.

Inforum Inc.
424 Church St, Nashville TN 37219-2301. 615/742-8844.

PMT Services
2 Maryland Farms, Suite 200, Brentwood TN 37027-5007. 615/221-9867.

PST Inc.
6060 Poplar Ave, Memphis TN 38119-3981. 901/681-0400.

Brady & Horne Company
25 College Park Cv, Jackson TN 38301-8706. 901/423-1438.

Gridiron Industries
6202 Chapman Hwy, Knoxville TN 37920-5940. 423/577-0890.

EBM
123 N Church St, Murfreesboro TN 37130-3639. 615/849-9534.

LB Smith Inc.
1231 Bridgestone Pkwy, La Vergne TN 37086-3510. 615/793-3888.

Williams' Co. of Orlando Inc.
1155 Bell Rd, Antioch TN 37013-3701. 615/731-2900.

North Park of Tennessee Inc.
2051 Hamill Rd, Hixson TN 37343-4082. 423/870-1300.

Profitts Inc.
101 Northgate Mall, Chattanooga TN 37415-6939. 423/875-2734.

Colorado Prime Corp.
404 Bna Dr, Suite 200, Nashville TN

37217-2520.
615/366-1173.

**Pyramid Diagnostic
Service**
661 N Mendenhall Rd,
Suite 105, Memphis
TN 38122-4704.
901/681-0020.

SimmCo.
1360 N Washington
St, Brownsville TN
38012-1607.
901/772-0221.

**The Wexner
Companies Inc.**
4391 Barfield Rd,
Memphis TN 38117-
2417. 901/523-0769.

Vencor Inc.
709 Walnut St,
Chattanooga TN
37402-1916.

**William and Company
Inc.**
516 6th Ave S,
Nashville TN 37203-
4235. 615/726-2640.

Comfort Control Inc.
659 Thompson Ln,
Nashville TN 37204-
3668. 615/256-8131.

Peer Consultants PC
575 Oak Ridge Tpke,
Oak Ridge TN 37830-
7173. 423/483-3191.

Onsite
9041 Executive Park
Dr, Knoxville TN
37923-4621.
423/694-7611.

**For more information on career opportunities in accounting and management
consulting:**

Associations

**AMERICAN ACCOUNTING
ASSOCIATION**
5717 Bessie Drive, Sarasota FL
34233. 813/921-7747. An
academically-oriented accounting
association that offers two
quarterly journals, a semi-annual
journal, a newsletter, and a wide
variety of continuing education
programs.

**AMERICAN INSTITUTE OF
CERTIFIED PUBLIC
ACCOUNTANTS**
1211 Avenue of the Americas,
New York NY 10036. 212/596-
6200. A national professional
organization for all CPAs. AICPA
offers a comprehensive career
package to students.

**AMERICAN MANAGEMENT
ASSOCIATION**
Management Information Service,
135 West 50th Street, New York
NY 10020. 212/586-8100.
Provides a variety of publications,
training videos, and courses, as
well as an Information Resource
Center, which provides
management information, and a
library service.

**ASSOCIATION OF GOVERNMENT
ACCOUNTANTS**
2200 Mount Vernon Avenue,
Alexandria VA 22301. 703/684-
6931.

**ASSOCIATION OF
MANAGEMENT CONSULTING**

FIRMS
521 Fifth Avenue, 35th Floor,
New York NY 10175. 212/697-
9693. Offers certification
programs.

**INSTITUTE OF INTERNAL
AUDITORS**
49 Maitland Avenue, Altamont
Springs FL 32701. 407/830-
7600. Publishes magazines and
newsletters. Provides information
on current issues, a network of
more than 50,000 members in
100 countries, and professional
development and research
services.

**INSTITUTE OF MANAGEMENT
ACCOUNTANTS**
10 Paragon Drive, Box 433,
Montvale NJ 07645-1760.
201/573-9000. Offers a Certified
Management Accountant
Program, periodicals, seminars,
educational programs, a research
program, a financial management
network, and networking
services.

**INSTITUTE OF MANAGEMENT
CONSULTANTS**
521 Fifth Avenue, 35th Floor,
New York NY 10175. 212/697-
8262. Offers certification and
professional development and a
directory of members.

**NATIONAL ASSOCIATION OF
TAX PRACTITIONERS**
720 Association Drive, Appleton
WI 54914. 414/749-1040. Offers
seminars, research, newsletters,

preparer worksheets, state chapters, insurance, and other tax-related services.

NATIONAL BUSINESSWOMEN'S LEADERSHIP ASSOCIATION
6901 West 63rd Street, P.O. Box 2949, Shawnee Mission KS 66201-1349. World Wide Web address: http://www.natsem.com. A professional organization dedicated to advancing the careers of women in management.

NATIONAL SOCIETY OF PUBLIC ACCOUNTANTS
1010 North Fairfax Street, Alexandria VA 22314. 703/549-6400. Offers professional development services, government representation, a variety of publications, practice aids, low-cost group insurance, and annual seminars.

Directories

AICPA DIRECTORY OF ACCOUNTING EDUCATION
American Institute of Certified Public Accountants, 1211 Avenue of the Americas, New York NY 10036. 212/596-6200. $150.00. Only available to AICPA members.

ACCOUNTING FIRMS AND PRACTITIONERS
American Institute of Certified Public Accountants, 1211 Avenue of the Americas, New York NY 10036. 212/596-6200. $150.00. Only available to AICPA members.

Magazines

CPA JOURNAL
530 Fifth Avenue, New York NY 10136. 212/719-8300. Published monthly by The New York State Society.

CPA LETTER
American Institute of Certified Public Accountants, 1211 Avenue of the Americas, New York NY 10036. 212/596-6200.

JOURNAL OF ACCOUNTANCY
American Institute of Certified Public Accountants, 1211 Avenue of the Americas, New York NY 10036. 212/596-6200.

MANAGEMENT ACCOUNTING
Institute of Management Accounting, 10 Paragon Drive, Montvale NJ 07645. 201/573-9000.

WENDELL'S REPORT FOR CONTROLLERS
Warren, Gorham, and Lamont, Inc., 210 South Street, Boston MA 02111. 617/423-2020.

ADVERTISING, MARKETING, AND PUBLIC RELATIONS

Due to several trends shaping the industry, finding a job in advertising is as tough today as it has ever been. To remain competitive, the industry's largest firms have been downsizing to save money for larger campaigns. On the other hand, smaller agencies are increasingly specializing in fields such as direct marketing and public relations in order to gain a stronger presence in the market. Meanwhile, the growing cable industry has opened the door to new business opportunities, as has the Internet. Increasingly, advertisers are using the information highway to conduct business, as well as to target specific "digital" audiences.

In the public relations field, there has been an explosion in the number and range of consultants in the marketplace. Partially as a result of the recession of the early '90s, many senior executives who were released from their contracts at major firms have launched companies of their own.

ADVO INC.
5541 Distroplex Cove, Memphis TN 38118-6345. 901/794-0804. **Contact:** Human Resources. **Discription:** A direct mail advertising company. **Corporate headquarters location:** Windsor, CT. **Listed on:** New York Stock Exchange. **Number of employees nationwide:** 5,500.

THE ADVERTISING CHECKING BUREAU INC.
80 Monroe Avenue, Third Floor, Memphis TN 38103. 901/526-3281. **Contact:** Jackie Redner, Human Resources. **Description:** An advertising agency.

BOZELL WORLDWIDE, INC.
50 North Front Street, Suite 970, Memphis TN 38103. 901/525-4900. **Contact:** Human Resources. **Description:** One of 63 international full-service advertising offices. Bozell also offers public relations services such as corporate relations, marketing support, employee relations, financial relations, government affairs, and community relations. The staff includes specialists in marketing, media, account service, creative work, research, public relations, finance, agriculture, and broadcast affairs. **Corporate headquarters location:** New York NY.

BUNTIN GROUP
1001 Hawkins Street, Nashville TN 37203. **Contact:** Debbie Goodwin, Director of Human Resources. **Description:** An advertising agency.

DYE, VAN MOL, & LAWRENCE
209 Seventh Avenue North, Nashville TN 37219. 615/244-1818. **Contact:** Ronald Roberts, Account Executive. **Description:** A public relations agency.

SPRING PUBLISHING & ADVERTISING
1615 Bluff City Hwy, Bristol TN 37620. 423/968-1112. **Contact:** Human Resources. **Description:** Publishes ads for the Yellow Pages.

J. WALTER THOMPSON COMPANY
White Station Tower, 5050 Poplar Avenue, Suite 1000, Memphis TN 38115. 901/682-9656. **Contact:** Human Resources. **Description:** Memphis office of the worldwide advertising and public relations firm.

Note: Because addresses and telephone numbers of smaller companies change rapidly, we recommend you call each company to verify the information below before inquiring about job opportunities. Mass mailings are not recommended.

Additional employers with under 250 employees:

MISC. ADVERTISING SERVICES

R&E Enterprises
1414 Mana Ln, East Ridge TN 37412-2228. 423/867-2107.

3M National Advertising Co.
1431 Poplar Ln,

Nashville TN 37210-4519. 615/256-4400.

DIRECT MAIL ADVERTISING SERVICES

First Image Print & Mail
501 Great Circle Rd, Nashville TN 37228-1310. 615/255-3150.

Argus Mailing Services
3001 Lakeview Rd, Memphis TN 38116-1505. 901/396-9904.

Preferred Mail Processing
4481 Pleasant Hill Rd, Memphis TN 38118-7525. 901/541-1993.

For more information on career opportunities in advertising, marketing, and public relations:

Associations

ADVERTISING RESEARCH FOUNDATION
641 Lexington Avenue, New York NY 10022. 212/751-5656. Fax: 212/319-5265. World Wide Web address: http://www.arfsite.org/arf. A nonprofit organization comprised of advertising, marketing, and media research companies. For institutions only.

AMERICAN ASSOCIATION OF ADVERTISING AGENCIES
666 Third Avenue, New York NY 10017. 212/682-2500. Offers educational and enrichment benefits such as publications, videos, and conferences.

AMERICAN MARKETING ASSOCIATION
250 South Wacker Drive, Suite 200, Chicago IL 60606-5819. 312/831-2764. Fax: 312/648-5625. World Wide Web address: http://www.ama.org. An association with nearly 50,000 members worldwide. Offers 25 annual conferences, library and research services, and 25 annual issues of *Marketing News.*

DIRECT MARKETING ASSOCIATION
1120 Avenue of Americas, New York NY 10036-6700. 212/768-7277. Offers monthly newsletters, seminars, and conferences.

INTERNATIONAL ADVERTISING ASSOCIATION
521 Fifth Avenue, Suite 1807, New York NY 10175. 212/557-1133.

LEAGUE OF ADVERTISING AGENCIES
2 South End Avenue #4C, New York NY 10280. 212/945-4991. Seminars available.

MARKETING RESEARCH ASSOCIATION
2189 Silas Deane Highway, Suite #5, Rocky Hill CT 06067. 860/257-4008. Publishes several magazines and newsletters.

PUBLIC RELATIONS SOCIETY OF AMERICA
33 Irving Place, New York NY 10003. 212/995-2230. Publishes three magazines for public relations professionals.

Directories

AAAA ROSTER AND ORGANIZATION
American Association of Advertising Agencies, 666 Third Avenue, 13th Floor, New York NY 10017. 212/682-2500.

DIRECTORY OF MINORITY PUBLIC RELATIONS PROFESSIONALS
Public Relations Society of America, 33 Irving Place, New York NY 10003. 212/995-2230.

O'DWYER'S DIRECTORY OF PUBLIC RELATIONS FIRMS
J. R. O'Dwyer Company, 271 Madison Avenue, Room 600, New York NY 10016. 212/679-2471.

PUBLIC RELATIONS CONSULTANTS DIRECTORY
American Business Directories, Division of American Business Lists, 5711 South 86th Circle, Omaha NE 68127. 402/593-4500.

PUBLIC RELATIONS JOURNAL / REGISTER ISSUE
Public Relations Society of America, 33 Irving Place, New York NY 10003. 212/995-2230.

STANDARD DIRECTORY OF ADVERTISING AGENCIES
Reed Reference Publishing Company, P.O. Box 31, New Providence NJ 07974. 800/521-8110.

Magazines

ADVERTISING AGE
Crain Communications, 740 North Rush Street, Chicago IL 60611. 312/649-5316.

ADWEEK
BPI, 1515 Broadway, 12th Floor, New York NY 10036-8986. 212/536-5336.

BUSINESS MARKETING
Crain Communications, 740 North Rush Street, Chicago IL 60611. 312/649-5260.

JOURNAL OF MARKETING
American Marketing Association, 250 South Wacker Drive, Suite 200, Chicago IL 60606. 312/648-0536.

THE MARKETING NEWS
American Marketing Association, 250 South Wacker Drive, Suite 200, Chicago IL 60606. 312/648-0536.

PR REPORTER
PR Publishing Company, P.O. Box 600, Exeter NH 03833. 603/778-0514.

PUBLIC RELATIONS JOURNAL
Public Relations Society of America, 33 Irving Place, New York NY 10003. 212/995-2230.

PUBLIC RELATIONS NEWS
Phillips Publishing Inc., 1202 Seven Locks Road, Suite 300, Potomac MD 20854. 301/340-1520.

AEROSPACE

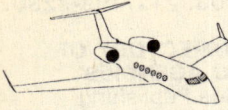

The aerospace industry, wracked by layoffs throughout the early '90s, has yet to pull out of its tailspin. As ever, the slump is being fueled by declining commercial aircraft orders and further defense cuts. As a result, research and development dollars have been trimmed, and many of the biggest firms in the industry have now merged. As of early 1996, the industry was continuing to shrink -- and is now dominated by fewer, larger companies.

While this consolidation has led to a surge in profits, it also means that rapid downsizing will continue. Some analysts believe that even though the defense industry has cut well over 1 million jobs since the late '80s, the industry still needs to cut its workforce by another 30 percent.

Many companies are trying to shift to commercial production, reducing their dependence on dwindling defense contracts. Even so, defense purchases still support a significant number of aerospace workers. Over the long haul, the industry's focus on advanced technology will mean more professional and technical positions -- with engineers leading the way.

BOEING DEFENSE & SPACE GROUP - OAK RIDGE, INC.
767 Boeing Oak Ridge, P.O. Box 851, Oak Ridge TN 37831. 423/481-7111. **Contact:** Frank Elkins, Director of Human Resources. **Description:** Boeing Defense & Space Group operates a manufacturing plant which primarily works on subassemblies for commercial jetliners built by the Boeing Commercial Airplane Group. The balance of the work involves defense projects, including building components and supplying the turret for the U.S. Army's Pedestal Mounted Stinger/Avenger air defense system built by Boeing Defense & Space Group. Boeing owns 1,400 acres, all within Oak Ridge city limits, and employs about 780 people, with approximately 90 percent hired locally. Overall, the Boeing Company is one of the largest aerospace firms in the United States, one of the nation's top exporters, and one of the world's leading manufacturers of commercial jet transports. The company is a major U.S. government contractor, with capabilities in missile and space, electronic systems, military aircraft, helicopters, and information systems management. Boeing is divided into three business segments: Commercial Aircraft, Defense and Space, and Computer Services. The Boeing Commercial Airplane Group, with approximately 70,000 employees, is the company's largest operating unit. The primary role of Boeing Computer Services is to support the company's computing needs, including systems development, data processing, and telecommunications. Boeing Information Services, Inc., a wholly owned subsidiary based in Vienna, VA, also develops and manages large-scale information systems for selected agencies of the federal government. **NOTE:** The Boeing Defense & Space Group has been substantially consolidated and streamlined in response to the downward trend in U.S. military spending. Over the past five years, company employment has been reduced from approximately 55,000 to less than 30,000. **Corporate headquarters location:** Seattle WA. **Parent company:** The Boeing Company.

CASTILLION INC.
P.O. Box 1108, Shelbyville TN 37160. 615/685-9057. **Contact:** T.J. Judge, Human Resources Manager. **Description:** A manufacturer of aircraft parts.

HOWMET CORPORATION
5650 Commerce Boulevard, Morristown TN 37814. 423/587-4910. **Contact:** Ruby Glasscock, Human Resources Director. **Description:** Manufactures ceramic cores for aircraft engines. Howmet is 67-percent owned by Pechiney, a diversified international corporation that has operations in packaging, aluminum, turbine components, and related industrial sectors.

SVERDRUP TECHNOLOGY INC.
600 William Northern Boulevard, Tullahoma TN 37388. 615/455-6400. **Contact:** Gary Spendlow, Manager of Professional Placement. **Description:** A professional and engineering services firm supporting NASA, Department of Defense entities, and private companies. Projects typically involve advanced aeronautical, technological, and testing programs. **Common positions include:** Aerospace Engineer; Civil Engineer; Electrical/Electronics Engineer; Mechanical Engineer. **Educational backgrounds include:** Engineering. **Benefits:** Dental Insurance; Disability Coverage; Life Insurance; Medical Insurance; Pension Plan; Profit Sharing; Savings Plan; Tuition Assistance. **Corporate headquarters location:** This Location. **Parent company:** Sverdrup Corporation (St. Louis, MO).

TEXTRON AEROSTRUCTURES
P.O. Box 210, Nashville TN 37202. 615/361-2000. **Contact:** Wanda Willliams, Human Resources. **Description:** Manufactures C1-30 cargo planes.

For more information on career opportunities in aerospace:

Associations

AIR TRANSPORT ASSOCIATION OF AMERICA
1301 Pennsylvania Avenue NW, Suite 1100, Washington DC 20004. 202/626-4000. A trade association for the major U.S. airlines.

AMERICAN INSTITUTE OF AERONAUTICS AND ASTRONAUTICS
85 John Street, 4th Floor, New York NY 10038. 212/349-1120. Membership required. Publishes six journals and books.

FUTURE AVIATION PROFESSIONALS OF AMERICA
4959 Massachusetts Boulevard, Atlanta GA 30337. 770/997-8097. Publishes a monthly newsletter which monitors the job market for flying jobs; a pilot employment guide, outlining what is required to become a pilot; and a directory of aviation employers.

NATIONAL AERONAUTIC ASSOCIATION OF USA
1815 North Fort Meyer Drive, Suite 700, Arlington VA 22209. 703/527-0226. Publishes a magazine. Membership required.

PROFESSIONAL AVIATION MAINTENANCE ASSOCIATION
500 NW Plaza, Suite 1016, St. Ann MO 63074. 314/739-2580. Members' resumes are distributed to companies who advise the organization of employment opportunities. Many local chapters also provide job referrals. Members have access to the Worldwide Membership Directory.

APPAREL AND TEXTILES

The apparel industry is facing an uncertain future. Women's apparel prices dropped 4.4 percent in 1994, and many experts expect continued deflation through 1996. Consumers have remained disinterested in new fashions and refuse to pay higher prices. Textile and apparel mills are under pressure from the other end of the supply chain as well -- the cost of cotton and other raw materials has remained at close to record highs, with raw cotton prices jumping 35 percent in 1994. As a result, many textile producers have recently reported significant drops in earnings. However, improved consumer confidence, more attractive fashions, and lower prices may prod consumers to buy. This will eventually increase business for mills. Especially hot: sales of men's suits. This trend is expected to continue as men look for upscale casual wear to accommodate more relaxed dress codes. The highest consumer demand in apparel will probably be for lower-priced clothing produced for discount stores.

ACME BOOT COMPANY, INC.
P.O. Box 749, Clarksville TN 37041-0749. 615/552-2000. **Contact:** Deborah Melson, Manager of Human Resources. **Description:** Acme Boot Company, Inc. manufactures, markets, and retails footwear. **Common positions include:** Accountant/Auditor; Computer Programmer; Computer Systems Analyst; Credit Manager; Customer Service Representative; Electrical/Electronics Engineer; Manufacturer's/Wholesaler's Sales Rep.; Operations/Production Manager; Quality Control Supervisor; Store Manager; Wholesale and Retail Buyer. **Educational backgrounds include:** Accounting; Business Administration; Computer Science; Finance. **Benefits:** 401K; Disability Coverage; Employee Discounts; Life Insurance; Medical Insurance; Pension Plan. **Corporate headquarters location:** This Location. **Other U.S. locations:** El Paso TX. **Parent company:** Farley Industries. **Operations at this facility include:** Administration; Divisional Headquarters; Sales; Service. **Listed on:** Privately held. **Number of employees at this location:** 200. **Number of employees nationwide:** 1,600.

ALLENBURG COMPANY
P.O. Box 3254, Cordova TN 38088-3254. 901/383-5000. **Contact:** Patsy Schoonever, Human Resources. **Description:** A cotton dealer.

AMERICAN UNIFORM COMPANY
P.O. Box 2130, Cleveland TN 37320. 423/476-6561. **Contact:** Mike Christian, Personnel Manager. **Description:** A manufacturer of uniforms for waitresses and nurses, as well as men's work clothes.

ANGELICA UNIFORM GROUP
P.O. Box 188, Collinwood TN 38450. 615/724-9194. **Contact:** Darryl Metheny, Human Resources. **Description:** Manufacturers of a variety of commercial uniforms.

AQUATECH INC.
P.O. Box 2249, Cookeville TN 38502. 615/528-5184. **Contact:** Mr. Connie Donaldson, Human Resources. **Description:** Aquatech Inc. washes, treats, and presses clothing for apparel manufacturers. The company's primary business is the pre-wash and stone-wash of Levi's brand jeans. **Corporate headquarters location:** This Location. **Other U.S. locations:** McMinnville TN.

BUSTER BROWN APPAREL, INC.
P.O. Box 5008, Chattanooga TN 37406. 615/493-2308. **Fax:** 615/493-2463. **Contact:** Carol Martin, Human Resources Director. **Description:** Manufactures children's apparel and socks. **Common positions include:** Accountant/Auditor; Computer Programmer; Computer Systems Analyst; Designer; Industrial Engineer. **Educational backgrounds include:** Accounting; Art/Design; Computer Science; Engineering. **Corporate headquarters location:** This Location. **Other U.S. locations:** Alabama; Georgia; North Carolina; Virginia. **Operations at this facility include:** Administration; Manufacturing; Research and Development; Sales; Service. **Listed on:** Privately held. **Number of employees at this location:** 850. **Number of employees nationwide:** 3,500.

CAMEL MANUFACTURING COMPANY
125 First Street, La Follette TN 37766. 423/562-0527. **Contact:** Janis Wilson, Human Resources. **Description:** A company contracted by the government for the manufacture of tents and other products.

CARHARDT
P.O. Box 280, Dover TN 37058. 615/232-5341. **Contact:** Rita Collins, Human Resources. **Description:** A clothing manufacturer. **Corporate headquarters location:** Oshkosh WI. **Listed on:** NASDAQ.

CHARLESTON HOSIERY
P.O. Box 2190, Cleveland TN 37320. 423/472-5095. **Contact:** Ms. Chris Leonard, Human Resources. **Description:** A manufacturer of men's, women's, and children's socks.

CRESCENT HOSIERY MILLS
P.O. Box 669, Niota TN 37826. 423/568-2101. **Contact:** Steve Burce, Human Resources Director. **Description:** A manufacturer of men's, women's, and children's socks.

DELTA APPAREL
P.O. Box 248, Decatur TN 37322-0248. 423/334-5726. **Contact:** Human Resources. **Description:** A manufacturer of sweatshirts for adults and children.

DELTA APPAREL
Highway 68, Tellico Plains TN 37385. 423/253-2171. **Contact:** Human Resources. **Description:** A manufacturer of sweatshirts for adults and children.

DIXIE YARNS, INC.
P.O. Box 751, Chattanooga TN 37401. 423/698-2501. **Contact:** Derek Davis, Vice President. **Description:** A yarn producing mill.

DUNAVANT ENTERPRISES
3797 New Getwell Road, Memphis TN 38118. 901/369-1500.
Contact: Sherly Cooley, Human Resources Director. **Description:** One of the world's largest cotton dealers. Activities of Dunavant Enterprises include the merchandising, warehousing, and ginning of cotton. **Number of employees at this location:** 300.

DYERSBURG FABRICS INC.
1315 Phillips Street, P.O. Box 767, Dyersburg TN 38024. 901/285-2323. **Contact:** Allen Tillman, Human Resources Director. **Description:** A fabric mill. **Common positions include:** Accountant/Auditor; Biological Scientist/Biochemist; Blue-Collar Worker Supervisor; Chemical Engineer; Civil Engineer; Computer Programmer; Computer Systems Analyst; Customer Service Representative; Electrician; Human Resources Specialist; Management Trainee; Purchasing Agent and Manager. **Benefits:** 401K; Dental Insurance; Life Insurance; Medical Insurance; Pension Plan; Profit Sharing. **Operations at this facility include:** Administration; Divisional Headquarters; Manufacturing; Regional Headquarters; Research and Development. **Listed on:** New York Stock Exchange. **Number of employees at this location:** 1,200.

EAST TENNESSEE UNDERGARMENT
P.O. Box 100, Elizabethton TN 37644. 423/542-4146. **Contact:** Florance Presson, Human Resources. **Description:** Manufactures women's undergarments.

EDEN INDUSTRIES
P.O. Box 419, Manchester TN 37355. 615/728-5130. **Contact:** Maxine Rogers, Human Resources. **Description:** A manufacturer of men's and boys' robes and pajamas. Brand names include Oscar de la Renta and Disney.

ELK BRAND MANUFACTURING COMPANY
1601 County Hospital Road, Nashville TN 37218. 615/254-4300. **Contact:** David Manning, Human Resources. **Description:** A manufacturer of women's jeans.

GALAXY CARPET MILLS INC.
P.O. Box 348, South Pittsburg TN 37380-0348. 423/837-7192. **Contact:** Human Resources. **Description:** Manufactures yarn to be used in carpet production.

GENESCO, INC.
Genesco Park, Suite 436, P.O. Box 731, Nashville TN 37202-0731. 615/367-7000. **Contact:** Human Resources. **Description:** Founded in 1924 in Nashville, Genesco markets, distributes, and manufactures branded men's, women's, and children's shoes and boots and men's tailored clothing. The company's owned and licensed footwear brands, sold through both wholesale and retail channels, include Johnston & Murphy, J. Murphy, Domani, Dockers, Nautica, and Jarman men's shoes; Laredo and Code West boots; Toddler University, Kids University, and Street Hot children's shoes; and Mitre athletic shoes. Genesco's tailored clothing labels, all of which the company manufactures and sells at wholesale through The Greif Companies, include Perry Ellis, Perry Ellis Portfolio, Mondo di Marco, Kilgour, French & Stanbury, and Grays by Gary Wasserman. A

Genesco subsidiary, GCO Apparel Company, also manufactures more moderately-priced, quality men's tailored clothing, primarily for the private label market. Genesco products are sold at wholesale to more than 7,000 retailers, including a number of leading department, specialty, and discount stores. Products are also sold at retail through the company's own network of 518 retail shoe stores, including Johnston & Murphy, Jarman, Journeys, and Boot Factory, and leased shoe departments. Genesco's footwear products are supplied through the company's own manufacturing facilities as well as a through variety of overseas and other domestic sources.

GEORGIA BOOT/DURANGO
P.O. Box 10, Franklin TN 37068-0010. 615/794-1556. **Contact:** Patsy Walker, Human Resources. **Description:** A footwear manufacturer.

GLENOIT MILLS
P.O. Box 400, Jacksboro TN 37757. 423/753-2196. **Contact:** Human Resources. **Description:** Manufactures imitation furs.

HARTMANN LUGGAGE COMPANY
P.O. Box 550, Lebanon TN 37087. 615/444-5000. **Contact:** Katherine Stillwell, Human Resources. **Description:** A luggage manufacturer.

HOHENBERG BROTHERS COMPANY
P.O. Box 193, Memphis TN 38101. 901/529-4200. **Contact:** Craig Clemmenson, Human Resources. **Description:** A cotton merchandising and warehousing company. **Number of employees at this location:** 175. **Number of employees nationwide:** 300.

KAYSER-ROTH HOSIERY INC.
425 North Gateway Avenue, Rockwood TN 37854. 423/354-0410. **Contact:** Human Resources. **Description:** A hosiery manufacturer. **Corporate headquarters location:** Greensboro NC.

LEGGETT & PLATT, INC.
400 Davidson Street, Nashville TN 37213. 615/734-1600. **Fax:** 615/256-1331. **Contact:** Judy Martin, Human Resources Manager. **Description:** Specializes in the manufacturing and marketing of a broad line of components for the furniture and bedding industries. Leggett & Platt products also include select lines of commodity fibers and carpet cushioning materials. A variety of diversified products are produced and sold in different markets. The Textile Products Division is an operating division of Leggett & Platt, involved in the manufacture of products made from recycled materials. This includes bedding and furniture fiber components, textile commodities, industrial wiping cloths, and synthetic fiber carpet cushion. This division participates in trading and marketing products with a national and international customer base. **Corporate headquarters location:** Carthage MO. **Other U.S. locations:** Villa Rica GA; Pineville NC; Cincinnati OH; Nashville TN; Mexica TX. **Operations at this facility include:** Divisional Headquarters.

LEON-FERENBACH INC.
P.O. Box 450, Johnson City TN 37605. 423/926-7161. **Contact:** Dee Harrison, Human Resources. **Description:** A manufacturer of thread yarn.

LEVI STRAUSS & COMPANY
2292 Skyview Drive, Centerville TN 37033. 615/729-4291. **Contact:** Bill Burkert, Human Resources. **Description:** Designs, manufactures, and markets worldwide a diversified line of apparel, primarily jeans and jeans-related products under the brand names Levi's and Brittania. The company also makes the Dockers line of clothing for U.S. markets. Operates 44 manufacturing and warehouse facilities and eight distribution centers in the U.S., and 22 and 19, respectively, overseas. **Corporate headquarters location:** San Francisco CA.

LEVI STRAUSS & COMPANY
2307 West Beaver Creek Drive, Powell TN 37849. 423/938-5384. **Contact:** Sherry Rosenbaum, Human Resources. **Description:** Designs, manufactures, and markets worldwide a diversified line of apparel, primarily jeans and jeans-related products under the brand names Levi's and Brittania. The company also makes the Dockers line of clothing for U.S. markets. Levi Strauss & Company has 44 manufacturing and warehousing facilities and eight distribution centers in the U.S. Overseas, the company operates 22 manufacturing and warehousing facilities as well as 19 distribution centers. **Corporate headquarters location:** San Francisco CA.

LEVI STRAUSS & COMPANY
1808 Cherry Street, Knoxville TN 37917. 423/546-2770. **Contact:** Nate Garlington, Human Resources. **Description:** Designs, manufactures, and markets worldwide a diversified line of apparel, primarily jeans and jeans-related products under the brand names Levi's and Brittania. The company also makes the Dockers line of clothing for U.S. markets. Levi Strauss & Company has 44 manufacturing and warehousing facilities and eight distribution centers in the U.S. Overseas, the company operates 22 manufacturing and warehousing facilities as well as 19 distribution centers. **Corporate headquarters location:** San Francisco CA.

LEVI STRAUSS & COMPANY
P.O. Box 915, Mountain City TN 37683. 423/727-8011. **Contact:** Gail Gambill, Human Resources. **Description:** Designs, manufactures, and markets worldwide a diversified line of apparel, primarily jeans and jeans-related products under the brand names Levi's and Brittania. The company also makes the Dockers line of clothing for U.S. markets. Levi Strauss & Company has 44 manufacturing and warehousing facilities and eight distribution centers in the U.S. Overseas, the company operates 22 manufacturing and warehousing facilities as well as 19 distribution centers. **Corporate headquarters location:** San Francisco CA.

LEVI STRAUSS & COMPANY
P.O. Box 1236, Johnson City TN 37605. 423/929-0146. **Contact:** Diana Davis, Human Resources. **Description:** Designs, manufactures, and markets worldwide a diversified line of apparel, primarily jeans and jeans-related products under the brand names Levi's and

Brittania. The company also makes the Dockers line of clothing for U.S. markets. Levi Strauss & Company has 44 manufacturing and warehousing facilities and eight distribution centers in the U.S. Overseas, the company operates 22 manufacturing and warehousing facilities as well as 19 distribution centers. **Corporate headquarters location:** San Francisco CA.

MAJOR LEAGUE INC.
P.O. Box 518, Tellico Plains TN 37385. 423/253-2113. **Contact:** Debbie Miller. **Description:** Manufactures T-shirts, sweatshirts, shorts, and sweatpants.

MOUNTAIN CITY GLOVE MANUFACTURING COMPANY
RR 4, Box 353, Mountain City TN 37683. 423/727-6191. **Contact:** Human Resources. **Description:** Manufactures gloves.

THE NEW CHEROKEE CORPORATION
730 Middle Creek Road, Sevierville TN 37862. 423/453-2825. **Contact:** Johnny Smith, Human Resources. **Description:** A textile mill specializing in cloth weaving.

NIOTA HOSIERY TEXTILE MILLS COMPANY
1145 Congress Parkway, Athens TN 37303. 423/745-8636. **Contact:** Mr. Ferris Chestnut, Human Resources. **Description:** A manufacturer of socks.

OSHKOSH B'GOSH INC.
P.O. Box 388, Celina TN 38551-0388. 615/243-4181. **Contact:** Kendra Smith, Human Resources. **Description:** This location manufactures children's clothing, excluding overalls, as well as casual apparel and related products for adults. Founded in 1895, OshKosh B'Gosh, then known as Grove Manufacturing Company, manufactured overalls for railroad workers and farmers. The company took its present name in 1937 and is now best known for its children's overalls and other apparel. The company now sells OshKosh B'Gosh products in 58 countries, and is aggressively pursuing growth opportunities around the world. In 1993, OshKosh segmented the children's wear division into Baby B'Gosh and OshKosh B'Gosh, a distinction designed to appeal to the parents of a broader age range of infants and children. Products are sold through catalogs and in department and specialty stores. OshKosh B'Gosh also operates 40 outlet stores in 26 geographically dispersed states. Other business includes Essex Outfitters, a wholly-owned subsidiary of OshKosh B'Gosh, which manufactures children's clothing under the Genuine Kids name (formerly Trader Kids, in association with Boston Traders). **Corporate headquarters location:** Oshkosh WI. **Other U.S. locations:** Dover TN; Gainesboro TN; McEwen TN. **Listed on:** NASDAQ.

OSHKOSH B'GOSH INC.
P.O. Box 280, McEwen TN 37101. 615/582-6816. **Contact:** Karen Jones, Human Resources Manager. **Description:** This location manufactures children's overalls, as well as casual apparel and related products for adults. Founded in 1895, OshKosh B'Gosh, then known as Grove Manufacturing Company, manufactured overalls for railroad workers and farmers. The company took its present name in 1937 and is now best known for its children's overalls and other

apparel. The company now sells OshKosh B'Gosh products in 58 countries, and is aggressively pursuing growth opportunities around the world. In 1993, OshKosh segmented the children's wear division into Baby B'Gosh and OshKosh B'Gosh, a distinction designed to appeal to the parents of a broader age range of infants and children. Products are sold through catalogs and in department and specialty stores. OshKosh B'Gosh also operates 40 outlet stores in 26 geographically dispersed states. Other business includes Essex Outfitters, a wholly-owned subsidiary of OshKosh B'Gosh, which manufactures children's clothing under the Genuine Kids name (formerly Trader Kids, in association with Boston Traders). **Corporate headquarters location:** Oshkosh WI. **Other U.S. locations:** Celina TN; Dover TN; Gainesboro TN. **Listed on:** NASDAQ.

OSHKOSH B'GOSH INC.
P.O. Box 6, 330 Birch Street, Gainesboro TN 38562. 615/268-0224. **Contact:** Tommy Donahue, Human Resources. **Description:** This location manufactures children's wear in sizes 3-6 months and 6-9 months, as well as casual apparel and related products for adults. Founded in 1895, OshKosh B'Gosh, then known as Grove Manufacturing Company, manufactured overalls for railroad workers and farmers. The company took its present name in 1937 and is now best known for its children's overalls and other apparel. The company now sells OshKosh B'Gosh products in 58 countries, and is aggressively pursuing growth opportunities around the world. In 1993, OshKosh segmented the children's wear division into Baby B'Gosh and OshKosh B'Gosh, a distinction designed to appeal to the parents of a broader age range of infants and children. Products are sold through catalogs and in department and specialty stores. OshKosh B'Gosh also operates 40 outlet stores in 26 geographically dispersed states. Other business includes Essex Outfitters, a wholly-owned subsidiary of OshKosh B'Gosh, which manufactures children's clothing under the Genuine Kids name (formerly Trader Kids, in association with Boston Traders). **Corporate headquarters location:** Oshkosh WI. **Other U.S. locations:** Celina TN; Dover TN; McEwen TN. **Listed on:** NASDAQ.

PCA APPAREL INDUSTRIES INC.
P.O. Box 271, Manchester TN 37355. 615/728-3281. **Contact:** Marvin Bunde, Manager of Administrative Services. **Description:** Manufactures pajamas.

PERMNA COLOR INC.
P.O. Box 1439, Cleveland TN 37364. 423/479-4102. **Contact:** Kenny Higgins, Personnel Manager. **Description:** Provides garment-dyeing services to the apparel industry.

RED KAP INDUSTRIES
1688 Harriman Highway, Harriman TN 37748. 423/882-0755. **Contact:** Kay Seaton, Office Manager. **Description:** This location manufactures men's work shirts. Red Kap Industries manufactures occupational apparel as a division of VF Corporation, an international apparel company. The company specializes in apparel that captures the specific corporate image and style of different businesses. In 1993, a new line of durable press, easy-care, 100 percent cotton products was introduced. Other specialties include safety and flame resistant products, including high-visibility and reflective trim

garments, as well as fluid resistant and other protective apparel. Brand names of work utility wear include Big Ben and WorkWear. **Corporate headquarters location:** Nashville TN. **Other U.S. locations:** Dickson TN; Sparta TN; Wartburg TN. **Parent company:** VF Corporation.

RED KAP INDUSTRIES
240 Red Kap Road, Wartburg TN 37887. 423/346-6234. **Contact:** Elizabeth Barker, Human Resources. **Description:** This location is a sewing factory for various apparel items. Red Kap Industries manufactures occupational apparel as a division of VF Corporation, an international apparel company. The company specializes in apparel that captures the specific corporate image and style of different businesses. In 1993, a new line of durable press, easy-care, 100 percent cotton products was introduced. Other specialties include safety and flame resistant products, including high-visibility and reflective trim garments, as well as fluid resistant and other protective apparel. Brand names of work utility wear include Big Ben and WorkWear. **Corporate headquarters location:** Nashville TN. **Other U.S. locations:** Dickson TN; Harriman TN; Sparta TN. **Parent company:** VF Corporation.

RED KAP INDUSTRIES
212 Highway 46, Dickson TN 37055. 615/446-9071. **Contact:** Ann Irwin, Office Manager. **Description:** This location manufactures work shirts. Red Kap Industries manufactures occupational apparel as a division of VF Corporation, an international apparel company. The company specializes in apparel that captures the specific corporate image and style of different businesses. In 1993, a new line of durable press, easy-care, 100 percent cotton products was introduced. Other specialties include safety and flame resistant products, including high-visibility and reflective trim garments, as well as fluid resistant and other protective apparel. Brand names of work utility wear include Big Ben and WorkWear. **Corporate headquarters location:** Nashville TN. **Other U.S. locations:** Harriman TN; Sparta TN; Wartburg TN. **Parent company:** VF Corporation.

RED KAP INDUSTRIES
545 Marriott Drive, Nashville TN 37214. 615/391-1200. **Contact:** Gary Williams, Human Resources. **Description:** Red Kap Industries manufactures occupational apparel as a division of VF Corporation, an international apparel company. Specializes in apparel that captures the specific corporate image and style of different businesses. In 1993, a new line of durable press, easy-care 100 percent cotton products was introduced. Other specialties include safety and flame resistant products, including high-visibility and reflective trim garments, as well as fluid resistant and other protective apparel. Brand names of work utility wear include Big Ben and WorkWear. **Corporate headquarters location:** This Location. **Other U.S. locations:** Dickson TN; Harriman TN; Sparta TN; Wartburg TN. **Parent company:** VF Corporation.

REEMAY, INC.
70 Old Hickory, P.O. Box 511, Old Hickory TN 37138-3651. 615/847-7000. **Contact:** Ron Wade, Human Resources Director. **Description:** A yarn producing mill.

ROANE HOSIERY INC.
P.O. Box 431, Harriman TN 37748. 423/882-0121. **Contact:** George Wilson III, President. **Description:** Manufacturers of a variety of women's sheer hosiery.

ROCKFORD MANUFACTURING COMPANY
3901 Little River Road, Rockford TN 37853-3305. 423/970-3131. **Contact:** Van Myers, Treasurer. **Description:** A textile manufacturer specializing in rough yarns.

SCT YARNS
P.O. Box 791, Chattanooga TN 37401. 423/622-3131. **Contact:** Floyd Craig, Director of Human Resources. **Description:** A yarn spinning mill.

SAN ANTONIO SHOE COMPANY
P.O. Box 1136, Tullahoma TN 37388. 615/455-2222. **Contact:** Human Resources. **Description:** A shoe manufacturer. This plant manufactures ladies' shoes, which are then marketed nationwide under the S.A.S. brand name. **Corporate headquarters location:** San Antonio TX.

SCOTTS HILL LEISUREWEAR
P.O. Box 98, Scotts Hill TN 38374. 901/549-3161. **Contact:** Human Resources. **Description:** Manufactures women's leisurewear.

SHAW INDUSTRIES INC.
P.O. Box 703, South Pittsburg TN 37380. 423/837-8651. **Contact:** Tom Boulere, Human Resources. **Description:** A carpeting manufacturer specializing in tufted floor coverings and related products. The company manufactures and sells tufted carpet for both residential and commercial use. In 1994, Shaw Industries purchased 11 state-of-the-art Michel Van De Wiele looms to accommodate its growing woven rug manufacturing operations. All products are marketed through retailers, distributors, and other end-users and are exported to over 150 countries. Brand names include Philadelphia Carpet Company, Fashion Statements, Expressive Designs, Sutton, Shaw Commercial Carpets, ShawRugs, Stratton Commercial Carpets, and Salemcarpets. This location prepares and twists yarn for carpets that are manufactured at other locations. **Corporate headquarters location:** Dalton GA. **Listed on:** New York Stock Exchange; Pacific Exchange. **Number of employees nationwide:** 24,000.

SIGNAL APPAREL COMPANY
P.O. Box 4296, Chattanooga TN 37405. 423/752-2032. **Contact:** Donna Langsom, Human Resources. **Description:** Signal Apparel Company manufactures fabric from which it produces T-shirts, fleece garments, and other sportswear. The products of the division are sold primarily to wholesalers, distributors, screenprinters, and to certain retail accounts. In addition to sales to its own customers, Signal Sportwear is a source of products for the Riddell Athletic division, Signal Artwear, and HeritageSportwear. Riddell Athletic currently has a license agreement with National Football Properties, Inc. to produce activewear bearing NFL logos and trademarks for sale in upscale specialty stores, department stores, and specialty catalog houses. Signal Artwear purchases unprinted shirts and tops

from Signal Apparel and produces its finished products through the addition of a variety of silkscreened and embroidered graphics derived under license from popular cartoons, movies, and television shows, as well as original concepts produced by an internal art staff. Heritage Sportwear produces a designer line of tailored knits designed primarily by Joan Vass. **Corporate headquarters location:** This Location. **Other U.S. locations:** Bean Station TN; New Tazewell TN.

HORACE SMALL APPAREL COMPANY

P.O. Box 1269, Nashville TN 37202. 615/320-1000. **Contact:** Glen Rogers, Assistant Vice President of Human Resources. **Description:** A manufacturer of industrial uniforms for such professions as police officers and postal workers.

SMITHVILLE MANUFACTURING INC.

215 West Market Street, Smithville TN 37166-1731. 615/597-4045. **Contact:** Linda Bates, Personnel Director. **Description:** An apparel manufacturer specializing in contract work for companies such as L.L. Bean and Land's End.

STAR HOSIERY INC.

P.O. Box 5206, Chattanooga TN 37406. 423/698-0660. **Fax:** 423/622-9838. **Contact:** Marvin Graves, Personnel Manager. **Description:** Manufactures greige hosiery, primarily socks. **Common positions include:** Accountant/Auditor; Human Resources Specialist; Quality Control Supervisor. **Benefits:** Dental Insurance; Disability Coverage; Employee Discounts; Life Insurance; Medical Insurance. **Corporate headquarters location:** This Location. **Operations at this facility include:** Administration; Manufacturing; Research and Development; Sales. **Number of employees at this location:** 450.

TENNESSEE WOOLEN MILLS
PILLOWTEX CORPORATION

218 North Maple Street, Lebanon TN 37087. 615/444-6060. **Fax:** 615/449-6706. **Contact:** Tammie Russell, Human Resources Manager. **Description:** A textile manufacturer specializing in the production of blankets. **Common positions include:** Accountant/Auditor; Buyer; Clerical Supervisor; Customer Service Representative; Electrical/Electronics Engineer; Electrician; General Manager; Industrial Engineer; Industrial Production Manager; Management Trainee; Mechanical Engineer; Purchasing Agent and Manager; Quality Control Supervisor. **Educational backgrounds include:** Accounting; Business Administration; Engineering; Marketing. **Benefits:** 401K; Disability Coverage; Employee Discounts; Life Insurance; Medical Insurance; Tuition Assistance. **Corporate headquarters location:** Dallas TX. **Other U.S. locations:** Nationwide. **Operations at this facility include:** Manufacturing. **Listed on:** New York Stock Exchange. **Number of employees at this location:** 400. **Number of employees nationwide:** 5,000.

TEXAS BOOT COMPANY

127 East Forrest Avenue, Lebanon TN 37087. 615/444-5440. **Contact:** Bob Reed, Executive Vice President of Manufacturing. **Description:** This location is the main administrative office for a manufacturer of western boots. The company has four plants in

Tennessee and sells its products across the United States and Canada, with limited exports.

TEXAS BOOT COMPANY
231 Western Avenue, Hartsville TN 37074. 615/374-2211. **Contact:** Human Resources. **Description:** Manufactures western boots. The company has four Tennessee plants, and sells its products across the United States and Canada, with limited exports.

TRI-CON INDUSTRIES LIMITED
315 Airport Road, Livingston TN 38570. 615/823-7301. **Contact:** Human Resources. **Description:** Manufactures canvas car seat covers.

UNITED KNITTING APPAREL INC.
310 Industrial Drive, P.O. Box 3748, Cleveland TN 37311. 423/476-9163. **Contact:** Kay Hightower, Human Resources Manager. **Description:** A manufacturer of knit fabrics. **Number of employees at this location:** 300.

VOLUNTEER KNIT APPAREL INC.
403 Old Knoxville Highway, New Tazewell TN 37825. 423/626-8000. **Contact:** Larry Evans, Plant Manager. **Description:** Manufactures T-shirts, sweatshirts, tank tops, and shorts.

WSW MANUFACTURING
320 Alexander Street, Bradford TN 38316-8657. 901/742-3901. **Contact:** Human Resources. **Description:** Manufactures children's garments, primarily sleepwear.

WASHTEX INDUSTRIES INC.
P.O. Box 1809, Dyersburg TN 38025. 901/286-1374. **Contact:** Robert Elrod, Human Resources. **Description:** Provides wet-processing for the apparel industry.

WILSON SPORTING GOODS
UNIFORM MANUFACTURING FACILITY
P.O. Box 938, Cookeville TN 38501. 615/528-2576. **Contact:** Human Resources. **Description:** Manufactures basketball, football, and baseball uniforms.

Note: Because addresses and telephone numbers of smaller companies change rapidly, we recommend you call each company to verify the information below before inquiring about job opportunities. Mass mailings are not recommended.

Additional employers with under 250 employees:

BROADWOVEN FABRIC MILLS

ADH Manufacturing Inc.
1417 Tennessee Ave, Etowah TN 37331-1229. 423/263-5451.

M. Fine & Sons Manufacturing Co. Inc.
110 E Commerce St, Loretto TN 38469-2300. 615/853-4355.

Val D'Or Inc.
539 W Colonial St,

Woodbury TN 37190-1448. 615/563-5954.

Action Knitwear Inc.
P.O. Box 189, Bean Station TN 37708-0189. 423/993-3352.

Clay Sportswear
RR 1, Moss TN
38575-9801.
615/258-3490.

Damy Industries Inc.
P.O. Box 969, Athens
TN 37371-0969.
423/745-7620.

**Lincoln County
Manufacturing Inc.**
600 6th Ave,
Fayetteville TN
37334-2042.
615/433-3507.

**Little King
Manufacturing Co.**
238 E Walnut St,
Alamo TN 38001-
1120. 901/696-5517.

Master Slack Corp.
P.O. Box 226, Bolivar
TN 38008-0226.
901/658-5247.

Omega Apparel Inc.
P.O. Box 556,
Smithville TN 37166-
0556. 615/597-8889.

**Southwest Apparel
Corp.**
P.O. Box 829,
Waynesboro TN
38485-0829.
615/722-3684.

Winning Moves Inc.
6201 Cayce Ln,
Columbia TN 38401-
5421. 615/380-9229.

**NARROW FABRIC
AND OTHER
SMALLWARES MILLS**

**Datrek Professional
Bags**
2413 Industrial Dr,
Springfield TN 37172-
5014. 615/384-1230.

Volunteer Apparel Inc.
3311 Highway 61 E,
Luttrell TN 37779-
2045. 423/992-4360.

KNITTING MILLS

**Pittsburg Knitting Mills
Inc.**
212 E 1st St, S
Pittsburg TN 37380-
1560. 423/837-6794.

**Sweetwater Hosiery
Mills**
818 N Main St,
Sweetwater TN
37874-2600.
423/337-6161.

Mirror Images
2021 Richard Jones
Rd, Nashville TN
37215-2860.
615/292-3381.

Master Apparel Corp.
95 Ball Park St,
Somerville TN 38068-
1711. 901/465-3530.

Rivoli Mills
2301 E 28th St,
Chattanooga TN
37407-3629.
423/622-3126.

**Somerville Mills
Manufacturing Co.**
P.O. Box 279,
Somerville TN 38068-
0279. 901/465-5353.

Tex-Tenn Corp.
P.O. Box 8219, Gray
TN 37615-0219.
423/477-2611.

United Knitting Inc.
P.O. Box 3748,
Cleveland TN 37320-
3748. 423/476-9163.

TEXTILE FINISHING

**Appalachian Finishing
Works**
P.O. Box 3601,
Knoxville TN 37927-
3601. 423/523-6217.

Pershield Inc.
P.O. Box 152,
Sweetwater TN
37874-0152.
423/337-7811.

**Watauga Industries
Inc.**
P.O. Box 1180,
Elizabethton TN
37644-1180.
423/543-5063.

Volunteer Automat
3756 Ringgold Rd,
East Ridge TN 37412-
1652. 423/698-6016.

CARPETS AND RUGS

Tennessee Mat Co.
1414 4th Ave S,
Nashville TN 37210-
4123. 615/254-8381.

**YARN AND THREAD
MILLS**

Trenton Mills
400 Factory St,
Trenton TN 38382-
2012. 901/855-1323.

**Hartsville Garment
Corp.**
226 Broadway,
Hartsville TN 37074-
1345. 615/374-3083.

**La Grange Molded
Products**
369 Chemwood Dr,
Newport TN 37821-
8150. 423/623-9869.

Master Casual Wear
P.O. Box 28, Ripley
TN 38063-0028.
901/635-9415.

COATED FABRICS

SSM Industries Inc.
211 Ellis St, Spring
City TN 37381-5223.
423/365-4048.

NONWOVEN FABRICS

**Kasbar National
Industries**
801 N James
Campbell Blvd,
Columbia TN 38401-
2680. 615/388-4551.

MEN'S AND BOYS' CLOTHING

Benton Manufacturing Co.
P.O. Box B, Benton TN 37307-1002. 423/338-5893.

Duck Head Apparel Co.
Indl Park Rd, Jellico TN 37762. 423/784-9431.

Freedom Industries Inc.
180 Freedom Ave, Murfreesboro TN 37129-6926. 615/896-3800.

Jetricks Co. Inc.
P.O. Box 428, Selmer TN 38375-0428. 901/645-3455.

KMA Manufacturing Inc.
214 E Henson St, Livingston TN 38570-1950. 615/823-5601.

Measure-Up Inc.
300 College St, Lafayette TN 37083-1704. 615/666-6664.

Mt. Pleasant Manufacturing
7025 Industrial Park Rd, Mount Pleasant TN 38474-1074. 615/379-5885.

River Heights Inc.
P.O. Box 365, Selmer TN 38375-0365. 901/645-3264.

Tennessee River Inc.
102 Industrial Dr, Waynesboro TN 38485-2433. 615/722-9021.

Appalachian Corp.
P.O. Box 369, Monterey TN 38574-0369. 615/839-2295.

Green Apparel Inc.
320 E Main St, Greenfield TN 38230-1620. 901/235-2247.

Robinson Manufacturing Co.
P.O. Box 56, Clarkrange TN 38553-0056. 615/863-3218.

Action Apparel Inc.
P.O. Box 157, Ramer TN 38367-0157. 901/645-9676.

Henry I. Siegel Co. Inc.
Siegel Dr, Tiptonville TN 38079. 901/253-6616.

HPH Apparel Manufacturing
136 Industrial Park Rd, Piney Flats TN 37686-4413. 423/538-7159.

Lexington Apparel
223 Pine St, Lexington TN 38351-2154. 901/968-0144.

Seiver Industries
1131 Dolly Parton Pkwy, Sevierville TN 37862-3710. 423/453-5519.

Sew Fine Inc.
1643 Robert C Jackson Dr, Maryville TN 37801-3776. 423/977-1243.

Doyle Shirt Manufacturing
P.O. Box 128, Doyle TN 38559-0128. 615/657-2281.

LC King Manufacturing Co.
P.O. Box 367, Bristol TN 37621-0367. 423/764-5188.

Blue Collar Tees
5286 Longmeadow Dr, Memphis TN 38134-4378. 901/377-3109.

Chalk Line Inc.
Blue Ribbon Pkwy, Shelbyville TN 37160. 615/684-4114.

DCB Corp.
233 Industrial Park Rd, Madisonville TN 37354-6134. 423/442-2271.

Delong Sportswear Inc.
985 N Broadway St, Dayton TN 37321-1125. 423/775-6818.

Hartsville Sportswear Inc.
P.O. Box 21, Hartsville TN 37074-0021. 615/374-4725.

River Valley Mills Inc.
119 Dyer St, Columbia TN 38401-4551. 615/381-9731.

Robinson Manufacturing Co.
Hwy 20 W, Parsons TN 38363. 901/847-3251.

Rockwood Sportswear Inc.
P.O. Box 417, Rockwood TN 37854-0417. 423/354-4066.

Sports Belle Inc.
P.O. Box 50243, Knoxville TN 37950-0243. 423/938-2063.

WE Stephens Manufacturing
1255 W Madison St, Pulaski TN 38478-2641. 615/363-1771.

WOMEN'S AND MISSES' CLOTHING

DNT Inc.
P.O. Box 477, Byrdstown TN 38549-0477. 615/864-3101.

Overton Shirt Makers
Indl Pk, Livingston TN 38570. 615/823-5627.

I. Appel Corp.
122 S Franklin Ave,
Henderson TN 38340-
2620. 901/989-7181.

Santini Corp.
2397 Highway 43 S,
Leoma TN 38468-
5209. 615/852-2752.

Todd Uniform Inc.
P.O. Box 246, Maury
City TN 38050-0246.
901/656-2178.

Daun-Ray Casuals
1811 Old Estill
Springs Rd, Tullahoma
TN 37388-5510.
615/455-8033.

**Decaturville
Manufacturing**
P.O. Box 397,
Decaturville TN
38329-0397.
901/852-4610.

**La-Del Manufacturing
Co.**
1608 N Mahr Ave,
Lawrenceburg TN
38464-2202.
615/762-7412.

**Normak International
Inc.**
1507 9th Ave,
Knoxville TN 37917-
6145. 423/525-6284.

Sportswear Associates
1107 Scottsville Rd,
Lafayette TN 37083-
2213. 615/666-4685.

Todd Uniform Inc.
P.O. Box 440, Ripley
TN 38063-0440.
901/635-3073.

Formfit Rogers Inc.
700 Freeman St,
Lafayette TN 37083-
1122. 615/666-2222.

HEAD WEAR

Park Industries Inc.
1 Park Pl, Manchester
TN 37355. 615/728-
6700.

**CHILDREN'S AND
INFANTS' CLOTHING**

Garan Inc.
115 Dorsky St,
Adamsville TN 38310-
2412. 901/632-3321.

Hickory Hills Industries
1 Ash St, Clifton TN
38425. 615/676-
3331.

Bill Sills Sportswear
484 E Main St,
Huntingdon TN
38344-4203.
901/986-2217.

Cozy Dozy Inc.
1127 5th St, Bristol
TN 37620-4413.
423/968-5151.

**Kellwood Co.
Outerwear Division**
102 Factory St,
Greenfield TN 38230-
1529. 901/235-2231.

Keneric Corp.
305 Dillard St, Ridgely
TN 38080-1523.
901/264-5524.

Liggett Corp.
P.O. Box 5140, South
Fulton TN 38257-
0140. 901/479-1631.

**FABRICATED TEXTILE
PRODUCTS**

Big Horn Inc.
1222 E 38th St,
Chattanooga TN
37407-2438.
423/867-9901.

LeSportsac Inc.
313 E Meeting St,
Dandridge TN 37725-
4910. 423/397-3448.

**LEATHER TANNING
AND FINISHING**

Valmore Leather
940 E Trinity Ln,
Nashville TN 37207-
4732. 615/227-9755.

**BOOT AND SHOE
CUT STOCK AND
FINDINGS**

Laredo Code West
200 Dabbs Ave,
Hohenwald TN 38462-
1954. 615/796-7388.

FOOTWEAR

**Lea-Wayne Knitting
Mills Inc.**
5231 Commerce Blvd,
Morristown TN
37814-1044.
423/586-7513.

**Stetson Boot & Shoe
Co.**
P.O. Box 140,
Dresden TN 38225-
0140. 901/364-2202.

**MISC. LEATHER
GOODS**

Simco Leather Co. Inc.
1800 Daisy St,
Chattanooga TN
37406-2403.
423/624-3331.

**APPAREL
WHOLESALE**

**Robinson
Manufacturing Co.**
245 Lands Rd,
Madisonville TN
37354-6132.
423/442-1084.

Designs by Norvell
High Street,
Watertown TN 37184.
615/237-9724.

Signal Knitting Mills
Hwy 11 W North,
Rutledge TN 37861.
423/767-2141.

Lisa Deb Casuals Inc.
537 5th Ave S,
Nashville TN 37203-
4211. 615/254-5001.

For more information on career opportunities in the apparel and textiles industries:

Associations

**AMERICAN APPAREL
MANUFACTURERS
ASSOCIATION**
2500 Wilson Boulevard, Suite
301, Arlington VA 22201.
703/524-1864. Publishes
numerous magazines,
newsletters, and bulletins for the
benefit of employees in the
apparel manufacturing industry.

**AMERICAN TEXTILE
MANUFACTURERS INSTITUTE**
Office of the Chief Economist,
1801 K Street NW, Suite 900,
Washington DC 20006-1301.
202/862-0500. Fax: 202/862-
0570. The national trade
association for the domestic
textile industry. Members are
corporations only.

THE FASHION GROUP
597 5th Avenue, 8th Floor, New
York NY 10017. 212/593-1715.
A nonprofit organization for
professional women in the fashion
industries (apparel, accessories,
beauty, and home). Offers career
counseling workshops 18 times
per year.

**INTERNATIONAL ASSOCIATION
OF CLOTHING DESIGNERS**
475 Park Avenue South, 17th
Floor, New York NY 10016.
212/685-6602. Fax: 212/545-
1709.

Directories

AAMA DIRECTORY
American Apparel Manufacturers
Association, 2500 Wilson
Boulevard, Suite 301, Arlington
VA 22201. 703/524-1864. A
directory of publications
distributed by the American

Apparel Manufacturers
Association.

APPAREL TRADES BOOK
Dun & Bradstreet Inc., 430
Mountain Avenue, New
Providence NJ 07974. 908/665-
5000.

**FAIRCHILD'S MARKET
DIRECTORY OF WOMEN'S AND
CHILDREN'S APPAREL**
Fairchild Publications, 7 West
34th Street, New York NY
10001. 212/630-4000.

Magazines

ACCESSORIES
Business Journals, 50 Day Street,
P.O. Box 5550, Norwalk CT
06856. 203/853-6015.

AMERICA'S TEXTILES
Billiam Publishing, 37 Villa Road,
Suite 111, P.O. Box 103,
Greenville SC 29615. 864/242-
5300.

APPAREL INDUSTRY MAGAZINE
Shore Communications Inc., 6255
Barfield Road, Suite 200, Atlanta
GA 30328-4893. 404/252-8831.

BOBBIN
Bobbin Publications, P.O. Box
1986, 1110 Shop Road, Columbia
SC 29202. 803/771-7500.

TEXTILE HILIGHTS
American Textile Manufacturers
Institute, Office of the Chief
Economist, 1801 K Street NW,
Suite 900, Washington DC
20006.

WOMEN'S WEAR DAILY (WWD)
Fairchild Publications, 7 West
34th Street, New York NY
10001. 212/630-4000.

ARCHITECTURE, CONSTRUCTION, AND ENGINEERING

The U.S. Department of Labor has estimated 1.2 million new construction jobs from 1992 through 2005, due to the need to replace aging experienced workers. Residential construction will grow slowly, as a result of the expected decline in population growth. Industrial construction, however, will be stronger because of an increase in exports by manufacturers. Heavy construction is growing faster than the industry average, with much activity in highway, bridge, and street construction.

Job prospects for engineers have been good for a number of years, and will continue to improve into the next century. Employers will need more engineers as they increase investment in equipment in order to expand output. In addition, engineers will find work improving the nation's deteriorating infrastructure.

ADAMS, CRAFT, HERZ, WALKER
P.O. Box 5838, Oak Ridge TN 37831. 423/482-4451. **Contact:** Human Resources. **Description:** Adams, Craft, Herz, Walker offers architectural, engineering, planning, and surveying services.

AMERICAN TECHNICAL ASSOCIATES, INC.
P.O. Box 10844, Knoxville TN 37939. 423/588-5751. **Contact:** Ken Allisen, Manager of Human Resources. **Description:** Provides technical and consulting services. Serving industries with technically-qualified, highly-skilled engineers, designers, draftsmen, technicians, and computer specialists.

APAC
HARRISON DIVISION
P.O. Box 359, Alcoa TN 37701. 423/983-3100. **Contact:** Charlie Espiritu, Personnel Manager. **Description:** A construction company.

BARGE, WAGGONER, SUMNER & CANNON
162 Third Avenue North, Nashville TN 37201. 615/254-1500. **Contact:** Vicki Phillips, Director of Human Resources. **Description:** An employee-owned design firm offering services in engineering, architecture, planning, landscape architecture, and surveying. Civil engineering services include site engineering and utilities design, grading, drainage, traffic impact studies, traffic signal system design, and transportation facility planning and design. Planning services are used by city, county, and regional authorities. Barge, Waggoner, Sumner & Cannon is supported by in-house engineers, architects, planners, and landscape architects providing services to private developers on projects ranging from small residential developments to mixed-use projects of more than 6,000 acres. Services include zoning and land use controls, airport master planning, housing and community development, environmental assessments, feasibility analyses, grant program administration, recreation facilities, and park

design. Architectural services are used in office buildings, multi-level parking garages, historic restoration, and commercial, institutional, and recreational facilities. The engineering and architectural staff offer services in industrial buildings and facilities design as well. The firm also provides environmental engineering services for water treatment and distribution systems, wastewater collection and treatment systems, and for solid and hazardous waste projects. **Corporate headquarters location:** This Location. **Other U.S. locations:** Dothan AL; Huntsville AL; Montgomery AL; Indianapolis IN; Lexington KY; Jackson MS; Miamisburg OH; Blountville TN; Knoxville TN; Memphis TN; Oak Ridge TN.

BARGE, WAGGONER, SUMNER & CANNON
800 South Gay Street, Plaza Tower, Suite 2400, Knoxville TN 37929. 423/637-2810. **Contact:** Human Resources. **Description:** An employee-owned design firm offering services in engineering, architecture, planning, landscape architecture, and surveying. Civil engineering services include site engineering and utilities design, grading, drainage, traffic impact studies, traffic signal system design, and transportation facility planning and design. Planning services are used by city, county, and regional authorities. Barge, Waggoner, Sumner & Cannon is supported by in-house engineers, architects, planners, and landscape architects providing services to private developers on projects ranging from small residential developments to mixed-use projects of more than 6,000 acres. Services include zoning and land use controls, airport master planning, housing and community development, environmental assessments, feasibility analyses, grant program administration, recreation facilities, and park design. Architectural services are used in office buildings, multi-level parking garages, historic restoration, and commercial, institutional, and recreational facilities. The engineering and architectural staff offer services in industrial buildings and facilities design as well. The firm also provides environmental engineering services for water treatment and distribution systems, wastewater collection and treatment systems, and for solid and hazardous waste projects. **Corporate headquarters location:** Nashville TN. **Other U.S. locations:** Dothan AL; Huntsville AL; Montgomery AL; Indianapolis IN; Lexington KY; Jackson MS; Miamisburg OH; Blountville TN; Memphis TN; Morristown TN; Oak Ridge TN.

BARGE, WAGGONER, SUMNER & CANNON
1093 Commerce Park Drive, Suite 500, Oak Ridge TN 37830. 423/481-0496. **Contact:** Ray Evans, Executive Vice President. **Description:** An employee-owned design firm offering services in engineering, architecture, planning, landscape architecture, and surveying. Civil engineering services include site engineering and utilities design, grading, drainage, traffic impact studies, traffic signal system design, and transportation facility planning and design. Planning services are used by city, county, and regional authorities. Barge, Waggoner, Sumner & Cannon is supported by in-house engineers, architects, planners, and landscape architects providing services to private developers on projects ranging from small residential developments to mixed-use projects of more than 6,000 acres. Services include zoning and land use controls, airport master planning, housing and community development, environmental assessments, feasibility analyses, grant program administration, recreation facilities, and park design. Architectural services are used

in office buildings, multi-level parking garages, historic restoration, and commercial, institutional, and recreational facilities. The engineering and architectural staff offer services in industrial buildings and facilities design as well. The firm also provides environmental engineering services for water treatment and distribution systems, wastewater collection and treatment systems, and for solid and hazardous waste projects. **Corporate headquarters location:** Nashville TN. **Other U.S. locations:** Dothan AL; Huntsville AL; Montgomery AL; Indianapolis IN; Lexington KY; Jackson MS; Miamisburg OH; Blountville TN; Knoxville TN; Memphis TN; Morristown TN.

BARGE, WAGGONER, SUMNER & CANNON
6750 Poplar Avenue, Suite 720, Memphis TN 38138. 901/755-7166. **Contact:** Human Resources. **Description:** An employee-owned design firm offering services in engineering, architecture, planning, landscape architecture, and surveying. Civil engineering services include site engineering and utilities design, grading, drainage, traffic impact studies, traffic signal system design, and transportation facility planning and design. Planning services are used by city, county, and regional authorities. Barge, Waggoner, Sumner & Cannon is supported by in-house engineers, architects, planners, and landscape architects providing services to private developers on projects ranging from small residential developments to mixed-use projects of more than 6,000 acres. Services include zoning and land use controls, airport master planning, housing and community development, environmental assessments, feasibility analyses, grant program administration, recreation facilities, and park design. Architectural services are used in office buildings, multi-level parking garages, historic restoration, and commercial, institutional, and recreational facilities. The engineering and architectural staff offer services in industrial buildings and facilities design as well. The firm also provides environmental engineering services for water treatment and distribution systems, wastewater collection and treatment systems, and for solid and hazardous waste projects. **Corporate headquarters location:** Nashville TN. **Other U.S. locations:** Dothan AL; Huntsville AL; Montgomery AL; Indianapolis IN; Lexington KY; Jackson MS; Miamisburg OH; Blountville TN; Knoxville TN; Morristown TN; Oak Ridge TN.

BARGE, WAGGONER, SUMNER & CANNON
1135 West Third North Street, Georgian Court, Suite 100, Morristown TN 37814. 423/586-6134. **Contact:** Human Resources. **Description:** An employee-owned design firm offering services in engineering, architecture, planning, landscape architecture, and surveying. Civil engineering services include site engineering and utilities design, grading, drainage, traffic impact studies, traffic signal system design, and transportation facility planning and design. Planning services are used by city, county, and regional authorities. Barge, Waggoner, Sumner & Cannon is supported by in-house engineers, architects, planners, and landscape architects providing services to private developers on projects ranging from small residential developments to mixed-use projects of more than 6,000 acres. Services include zoning and land use controls, airport master planning, housing and community development, environmental assessments, feasibility analyses, grant program administration, recreation facilities, and park design. Architectural services are used

in office buildings, multi-level parking garages, historic restoration, and commercial, institutional, and recreational facilities. The engineering and architectural staff offer services in industrial buildings and facilities design as well. The firm also provides environmental engineering services for water treatment and distribution systems, wastewater collection and treatment systems, and for solid and hazardous waste projects. **Corporate headquarters location:** Nashville TN. **Other U.S. locations:** Dothan AL; Huntsville AL; Montgomery AL; Indianapolis IN; Lexington KY; Jackson MS; Miamisburg OH; Blountville TN; Knoxville TN; Memphis TN; Oak Ridge TN.

BARGE, WAGGONER, SUMNER & CANNON
P.O. Box 1057, Blountville TN 37617. 423/323-6226. **Contact:** Dennis Ward, Office Manager. **Description:** An employee-owned design firm offering services in engineering, architecture, planning, landscape architecture, and surveying. Civil engineering services include site engineering and utilities design, grading, drainage, traffic impact studies, traffic signal system design, and transportation facility planning and design. Planning services are used by city, county, and regional authorities. Barge, Waggoner, Sumner & Cannon is supported by in-house engineers, architects, planners, and landscape architects providing services to private developers on projects ranging from small residential developments to mixed-use projects of more than 6,000 acres. Services include zoning and land use controls, airport master planning, housing and community development, environmental assessments, feasibility analyses, grant program administration, recreation facilities, and park design. Architectural services are used in office buildings, multi-level parking garages, historic restoration, and commercial, institutional, and recreational facilities. The engineering and architectural staff offer services in industrial buildings and facilities design as well. The firm also provides environmental engineering services for water treatment and distribution systems, wastewater collection and treatment systems, and for solid and hazardous waste projects. **Corporate headquarters location:** Nashville TN. **Other U.S. locations:** Dothan AL; Huntsville AL; Montgomery AL; Indianapolis IN; Lexington KY; Jackson MS; Miamisburg OH; Knoxville TN; Memphis TN; Morristown TN; Oak Ridge TN.

BELL CONSTRUCTION COMPANY, INC.
P.O. Box 363, Brentwood TN 37024. 615/373-4343. **Contact:** Randy Brent, Senior Vice President. **Description:** A construction company. **Number of employees at this location:** 200.

BLAINE CONSTRUCTION CORPORATION
120 Market Place Boulevard, Knoxville TN 37922. 423/693-8900. **Contact:** Sherri Housely, Human Resources. **Description:** A construction company.

CH2M HILL
599 Oak Ridge Turnpike, Oak Ridge TN 37830. 423/483-9032. **Contact:** Human Resources. **Description:** Established in 1946 in Corvallis, Oregon, CH2M Hill is a group of employee-owned companies operating under the names CH2M Hill, Inc., Industrial Design Corporation, Operations Management International, CH2M Hill International, and CH2M Hill Engineering. The company objective

is to provide planning, engineering design, and operation and construction management services to help clients apply technology, safeguard the environment, and develop infrastructure. The professional staff includes specialists in environmental engineering and waste management, water management, transportation, industrial facilities, and a broad spectrum of infrastructure systems. This location works under contract with the Martin Marietta-managed Hazardous Waste and Remedial Action Program (HAZWRAP). It also subcontracts to Bechtel National, Inc., at the Oak Ridge National Library. **Corporate headquarters location:** Denver CO. **Number of employees nationwide:** 5,000.

CENTEX FORCUM LANNOM INC.
350 Gerald Ford Memorial Highway, Dyersburg TN 38024. 901/285-6503. **Contact:** Jerome Campbell, Human Resources. **Description:** A commercial construction company.

CLAYTON HOMES, INC.
4726 Airport Highway, Louisville TN 37777. 423/970-7200. **Contact:** Greg Stanley, Human Resources Manager. **Description:** A vertically integrated builder and seller of low- to medium-priced manufactured homes. Provides complete financing and insurance services to its retail customers, and develops communities for manufactured housing. **Common positions include:** Accountant/Auditor; Adjuster; Collector; Computer Programmer; Computer Systems Analyst; Credit Manager; Customer Service Representative; Financial Analyst; Investigator. **Educational backgrounds include:** Accounting; Business Administration; Computer Science; Finance; Mathematics. **Benefits:** 401K; Dental Insurance; Disability Coverage; Employee Discounts; Life Insurance; Medical Insurance; Savings Plan. **Corporate headquarters location:** This Location. **Operations at this facility include:** Administration; Regional Headquarters. **Listed on:** New York Stock Exchange. **Number of employees nationwide:** 4,000.

DEMENT CONSTRUCTION COMPANY
178 Airways Boulevard, Jackson TN 38301. 901/424-6306. **Contact:** Bill Dement, President. **Description:** A company specializing in bridge and road construction.

FLINTCO INC.
3447 Cazassa Road, Memphis TN 38116. 901/396-1746. Contact: Human Resources. Description: General contractors of industrial buildings.

FLUOR CORPORATION
565 Marriott Drive, Suite 750, Nashville TN 37214. 615/391-1880. **Contact:** Human Resources. **Description:** A construction company.

W.L. HAILEY AND COMPANY
P.O. Box 40646, Nashville TN 37204. 615/255-3161. **Fax:** 615/256-1316. **Contact:** Joy James, Administrative Secretary. **Description:** A construction company engaged in the construction of pipeline, bridges, tunnels, marine structures, and treatment plants. The pipelines range from 1/8-inch control lines in water and in sewerage treatment plants to massive 11-foot by 16-foot 6-inch cast-in-place concrete combination storm and sanitary sewers. The

pipelines are constructed from a variety of materials and sizes, from 1/2-inch copper water service lines to 108-inch pre-cast, pre-stressed concrete water mains and from 6-inch vitrified clay collector sewers to 11-foot diameter pre-cast concrete pipe. Pipelines are also constructed of brick, iron, steel, stainless steel, wood, cement, asbestos, and plastic. Coupled with a wide variety of jointing methods, the pipelines are laid in a range of conditions, including earth and rock trenches, in tunnels, beneath rivers and lakes, supported by bridges, hung from ceilings, and supported on the floors and walls of buildings. Bridge construction utilizes specialized processes including cofferdams using steel sheet piling to depths of 70-feet, underwater excavation, single pours of up to 2,200 yards of concrete, and demolition of old bridges. The construction of docks and other river-front structures includes underwater rock and dirt excavation, steel and wood pile driving, construction of steel sheet pile cells, large diameter drilling into deep underwater rock, and erection of structural steel docks. W.L. Hailey also constructs water treatment and wastewater treatment plants, as well as raw water intakes and treated wastewater outfalls for municipalities and industries.

HARDAWAY GROUP, INC.
P.O. Box 60464, Nashville TN 37206. 615/254-5461. **Fax:** 615/255-5107. **Contact:** Randy Swainehart, Human Resource Director. **Description:** A general contractor also engaged in residential and commercial property management and real estate sales. **Common positions include:** Accountant/Auditor; Blue-Collar Worker Supervisor; Civil Engineer; Claim Representative; Clerical Supervisor; Computer Programmer; Computer Systems Analyst; Construction and Building Inspector; Construction Contractor and Manager; Cost Estimator; Draftsperson; Electrical/Electronics Engineer; Human Resources Specialist; Mechanical Engineer; Property and Real Estate Manager; Real Estate Agent. **Educational backgrounds include:** Accounting; Business Administration; Computer Science; Construction; Engineering; Finance; Marketing. **Benefits:** 401K; Dental Insurance; Life Insurance; Medical Insurance; Savings Plan. **Corporate headquarters location:** This Location. **Subsidiaries include:** Hardaway Construction Corporation of Tennessee; Hardaway Management Company, Inc.; and Hardaway Realty, Inc. **Operations at this facility include:** Administration. **Listed on:** Privately held. **Number of employees nationwide:** 900.

HOMES BY OAKWOOD
1887 Mines Road, Pulaski TN 38478-9419. 615/424-0733. **Contact:** Human Resources. **Description:** A plant that manufactures mobile homes.

JBF ASSOCIATES
Technology Drive, 1000 Technology Park Center, Knoxville TN 37932. 423/966-5232. **Fax:** 423/966-5287. **Contact:** Mary Mix, Personnel Director. **Description:** JBF Associates offers engineering consulting for system safety and reliability, and provides probabilistic risk assessment to the energy, defense, petrochemical, and manufacturing industries. **Common positions include:** Chemical Engineer; Mechanical Engineer; Nuclear Engineer; Petroleum Engineer. **Educational backgrounds include:** Engineering. **Benefits:** 401K; Disability Coverage; Life Insurance; Medical Insurance.

Corporate headquarters location: This Location. **Listed on:** Privately held. **Number of employees at this location:** 70.

THE JORDAN COMPANIES
4661 Burbank Road, Memphis TN 38118. 901/363-2121. **Contact:** Doris Monroe, Personnel Manager. **Description:** Manufactures aluminum windows and doors.

KIRBY BUILDING SYSTEMS INC.
P.O. Box 390, Portland TN 37148. 615/889-0020. **Contact:** Charles Wilcox, Director of Personnel. **Description:** Manufactures prefabricated metal buildings and components.

MARVIN WINDOWS & DOORS
101 Marvin Road, Ripley TN 38063. 901/635-5190. **Contact:** Kent Carter, Director of Human Resources. **Description:** Manufactures windows and doors and related building materials.

OGDEN ENVIRONMENTAL AND ENERGY SERVICES COMPANY, INC.
1009 Commerce Park Drive, #100, Oak Ridge TN 37830. 423/481-8002. **Contact:** Kathy Carko, Human Resources Director. **Description:** Offers broad-based engineering services, including geotechnical, mining, civil, and environmental engineering.

PARSONS AND TOWER
1055 Commerce Park Drive, Suite 200, Oak Ridge TN 37830. 423/482-1434. **Contact:** Mike Tulay, Manager of Operations and Administration. **Description:** Offers engineering, consulting, and construction services.

PHILLIPS & JORDAN INC.
6621 Wilbanks Road, Knoxville TN 37912. 423/688-8342. **Contact:** Mona Napier, Human Resources Manager. **Description:** A land clearing and excavation contractor.

PROFESSIONAL LOSS CONTROL, INC.
P.O. Box 585, Kingston TN 37763. 423/376-1131. **Contact:** Judy Smith, Vice President of Finance. **Description:** Professional Loss Control, Inc., located in the Tennessee Technology Corridor, provides engineering services in the areas of fire protection, safety, and environmental protection.

RAYTHEON ENGINEERS, INC.
9111 Cross Park Drive, #480, Knoxville TN 37923. 423/690-8610. **Contact:** Human Resources. **Description:** Raytheon Engineers provides full-service engineering and design for the chemical process, steel and metals, and nuclear and fossil power generation industries. The parent company, Raytheon Company, is a diversified, technology-based company ranked among the 100 largest U.S. industrial corporations. Raytheon has 110 facilities in 28 states, plus the District of Columbia. Overseas facilities and representative offices are located in 26 countries, principally in Europe, the Middle East, and the Pacific Rim. The company has four business segments: Electronics, Major Appliances, Aircraft Products, and Energy and Environmental. **Corporate headquarters location:** Lexington MA. **Parent company:** Raytheon Company.

REPUBLIC BUILDERS PRODUCTS
Highway 22 & Como Road, P.O. Box 580, McKenzie TN 38201. 901/352-3383. **Contact:** Human Resources. **Description:** Republic Builders Products produces doors and door frames for industrial use.

STEIN CONSTRUCTION COMPANY
P.O. Box 5246, Chattanooga TN 37406. 423/698-0271. **Contact:** John Miller, Personnel Manager. **Description:** A construction company.

THETA TECHNOLOGIES
101 East Tennessee Avenue, Oak Ridge TN 37830. 423/482-0056. **Contact:** Kathy Buchanan, Human Resource Director. **Description:** Offers engineering subcontracting and project management support.

VARCO-PRUDEN BUILDINGS
6000 Poplar Avenue, Suite 400, Memphis TN 38119. 901/767-5910. **Contact:** Human Resources Manager. **Description:** Varco-Pruden Buildings designs and manufactures pre-engineered metal building systems for the low-rise, non-residential market. **Common positions include:** Civil Engineer; Draftsperson. **Educational backgrounds include:** Engineering. **Benefits:** Dental Insurance; Disability Coverage; Life Insurance; Medical Insurance; Pension Plan; Savings Plan; Tuition Assistance. **Corporate headquarters location:** This Location. **Other U.S. locations:** Pine Bluff AR; Turlock CA; St. Joseph MO; Kernersville NC; Evansville WI. **Parent company:** United Dominion Industries. **Operations at this facility include:** Administration; Research and Development; Sales. **Listed on:** New York Stock Exchange. **Number of employees nationwide:** 10,300.

Note: Because addresses and telephone numbers of smaller companies change rapidly, we recommend you call each company to verify the information below before inquiring about job opportunities. Mass mailings are not recommended.

Additional employers with under 250 employees:

ENGINEERING SERVICES

GRW Engineers Inc.
179 Belle Forest Cir, Nashville TN 37221-2111. 615/662-1977.

Compliance Engineering LP
109 McMurry Blvd, Hartsville TN 37074-1107. 615/374-4715.

Greiner Inc.
Highway 51 N, Halls TN 38040. 901/836-5083.

MTI Engineering Services
727 N Eastman Rd, Kingsport TN 37664-3152. 423/378-3633.

Parsons De Leuw Inc.
5885 Ridgeway Center Pkwy #100, Memphis TN 38120-4011. 901/767-0044.

ARCHITECTURAL SERVICES

Hart Freeland Roberts Inc.
72 Stonebridge Blvd, Jackson TN 38305-2038. 901/668-8063.

Allen & Hoshall Inc.
9041 Executive Park Dr, Knoxville TN 37923-4621. 423/693-7881.

GENERAL CONTRACTORS

APAC-Tennessee Inc.
1311 N Mud Island Rd, Memphis TN 38103-1001. 901/523-2464.

Merico Abatement Contractors Inc.
1750 Lincoln St, Kingsport TN 37664-5156. 423/247-9399.

Centex-Rodgers Construction
2620 Elm Hill Pike,
Nashville TN 37214-3108. 615/889-4400.

Choctaw Transportation Co.
1307 E Court St,
Dyersburg TN 38024-4810. 901/286-0012.

Constructions Concepts
7200 US Highway 64,
Oakland TN 38060-3402. 901/465-4040.

Crowder Construction Co.
705 Bluff City Hwy,
Bristol TN 37620-4609. 423/652-9065.

Dale Inc.
P.O. Box 50875,
Knoxville TN 37950-0875. 423/970-2600.

Fischer Construction Co.
1321 Murfreesboro Pike, Suite 520,
Nashville TN 37217-2648. 615/367-1977.

Foote Brothers Construction
7428 Igou Gap Rd,
Chattanooga TN 37421-3133.
423/892-6600.

Interstate Contractors
2064 Fishing Ford Rd,
Belfast TN 37019-2056. 615/276-2400.

J&S Construction Company
71 C C Camp Rd,
Cookeville TN 38501-4471. 615/528-7478.

Memphis Construction Co.
117 Demase St,
Portland TN 37148-1423. 615/325-7710.

Robert K. Chaney Construction
418 Dover Rd,
Clarksville TN 37042-4160. 615/647-3483.

The Strauss Company Inc.
147A N Market St,
Chattanooga TN 37405-3904.
423/265-3201.

Lawhead & Associates
7512 Kerri Way,
Knoxville TN 37909-2329. 423/531-4754.

R. Lafferty & Son
500 Attaway Rd,
Cunningham TN 37052. 615/387-3482.

Ray Bell Construction Co.
255 Wilson Pike Cir,
Brentwood TN 37027-5207. 615/373-4343.

Valley Land Construction
2191 Oakview Ave,
Dyersburg TN 38024-1617. 901/286-5899.

Richards Remodeling & Contracting
622 Silver St,
Lewisburg TN 37091-2644. 615/359-0469.

Jim Walter Homes
2600 Music Valley Dr,
Nashville TN 37214-1208. 615/883-7601.

Jim Walter Homes
3400 Ringgold Rd,
East Ridge TN 37412-1206. 423/622-5191.

Cambridge Constructors Inc.
701 S Church St,
Murfreesboro TN 37130-4925.
615/896-5842.

Lad Homes Inc.
780 Tissington Dr,
Collierville TN 38017-1529. 901/854-5230.

GENERAL INDUSTRIAL CONTRACTORS

Covington Metal Building & Contracting
202 Providence Blvd,
Clarksville TN 37042-4324. 615/645-2375.

Morton Buildings Inc.
1263 Anderson Ave,
Brownsville TN 38012-3543.
901/772-3950.

United Structures of America
214 Fountain Head Rd, Portland TN 37148-1662.
615/325-7351.

Johnson & Galyon Inc.
1130 Atlantic Ave,
Knoxville TN 37917-3705. 423/688-1111.

MCDR Inc.
5100 Wheelis Dr,
Suite 200, Memphis TN 38117-4531.
901/761-0911.

ROAD CONSTRUCTION

Dillard Paving
431 Haynie Ave,
Nashville TN 37207-3905. 615/228-7176.

Harrison Construction
Vonore Rd,
Sweetwater TN 37874. 423/337-3679.

Simpson Construction Shop
178 Durkee Rd NE,
Cleveland TN 37323-6400. 423/476-5286.

BRIDGE, TUNNEL, AND HIGHWAY CONSTRUCTION

Bridge Builders Inc.
RR 1, McMinnville TN 37110-9801.
615/668-4166.

McKinnon Bridge Co. Inc.
205 Eddy Ln, Franklin TN 37064-2935. 615/794-2552.

HEAVY CONSTRUCTION

Smith Mechanical Contractors Inc.
1509 Riverport Rd, Kingsport TN 37660-3545. 423/246-3611.

Contech Construction Products
301 S Perimeter Park Dr, Nashville TN 37211-4143. 615/781-4217.

PLUMBING, HEATING, AND A/C

Rock City Mechanical
2715 Grandview Ave, Nashville TN 37211-2224. 615/251-3045.

KLM Mechanical Contractors
210 Omohundro Pl, Nashville TN 37210-2204. 615/254-5494.

Noland Company
2016 American Way Rd, Kingsport TN 37660-4700. 423/246-8171.

Noland Company
7526 A E Beaty Dr, Memphis TN 38134. 901/373-5300.

Apex Supply Co. Inc.
780 Berry Rd, Nashville TN 37204-2827. 615/383-5936.

ELECTRICAL WORK

Travis Electric Company
4400 Michigan Ave, Nashville TN 37209-2216. 615/385-0250.

Electric Motor Service Inc.
1420 Highway 51, By-Pass E, Dyersburg TN 38024. 901/285-6241.

Cornerly Electrical Concepts
515 Airport Rd, Chattanooga TN 37421-3536. 423/490-0006.

Roadrunner Electric
8219 Neal Rd, Arrington TN 37014-9112. 615/395-4828.

TAM Electric Company Inc.
3832 Watman Ave, Memphis TN 38118-6043. 901/363-0513.

Townsend Electric Company
503 Airways Blvd, Jackson TN 38301-5739. 901/423-2800.

Mid States Electric Co. Inc.
117 N Conalco Dr, Jackson TN 38301-3619. 901/423-9482.

ROOFING, SIDING, AND SHEET METAL WORK

Centimark
1710 N Shelby Oaks Dr, Suite 15, Memphis TN 38134-7403. 901/377-2314.

Design-Systems Builders Inc.
627 Norris Ave, Nashville TN 37204-3707. 615/256-0993.

WATER WELL DRILLING

Boyles Bros. Drilling Co.
803 Samsonite Blvd, Murfreesboro TN 37129-5525. 615/896-5132.

Foremost Drills
325 Tammy Dr, Powell TN 37849-3448. 423/947-5355.

Long Foundation Drilling Co.
3014 Brandau Rd, Hermitage TN 37076-3501. 615/885-5664.

MISC. SPECIAL TRADE CONTRACTORS

Scott Contractors
1619 Panama St, Memphis TN 38108-1995. 901/386-1981.

Wright Bros. Construction Co.
1500 Lauderdale Memorial Hwy N, Charleston TN 37310-6641. 423/336-2261.

Nashville Machine Co. Inc.
520 Interstate Blvd S, Nashville TN 37210-4610. 615/256-5251.

CONSTRUCTION MATERIALS WHOLESALE

APAC Tennessee Inc.
1850 Elm Hill Pike, Nashville TN 37210-3710. 615/885-1234.

Jones Brothers Inc.
820 Old Ezell Rd, Nashville TN 37217-2931. 615/360-9181.

Lafarge Corporation
1740 61st Ave N, Nashville TN 37209-1313. 615/350-7384.

Reynolds Aluminum Building Products
3352 Democrat Rd, Memphis TN 38118-1524. 901/366-6622.

Lowe's Contractor Sales Division
6006 Lee Hwy, Chattanooga TN

37421-2937.
423/892-2440.

**PLUMBING, HEATING,
AND A/C EQUIPMENT
WHOLESALE**

**Young Radiator
Company**
1000 Young Dr,
Lexington TN 38351-
9200. 901/968-3617.

Kohler Co.
8245 Tournament Dr,
Memphis TN 38125-
8898. 901/748-2270.

For more information on career opportunities in architecture, construction, and engineering:

Associations

**AACE INTERNATIONAL: THE
ASSOCIATION FOR TOTAL COST
MANAGEMENT**
209 Prairie Avenue, Suite 100,
P.O. Box 1557, Morgantown WV
26507-1557. 304/296-8444.
800/858-2678. Toll-free number
provides information on
scholarships for undergraduates.
Fax: 304/291-5728. A
membership organization which
offers *Cost Engineering,* a
monthly magazine; employment
referral services; technical
reference information and
assistance; insurance; and a
certification program accredited
by the Council of Engineering
Specialty Boards.

**AMERICAN ASSOCIATION OF
ENGINEERING SOCIETIES**
1111 19th Street NW, Suite 608,
Washington DC 20036-3690.
202/296-2237. A multi-
disciplinary organization of
professional engineering societies.
Publishes reference works,
including *Who's Who in
Engineering Directory of
Engineering Societies and Related
Organizations,* and the *Thesaurus
of Engineering and Scientific
Terms,* as well as statistical
reports from studies conducted by
the Engineering Workforce
Commission.

**AMERICAN CONSULTING
ENGINEERS COUNCIL**
1015 15th Street NW, Suite 802,
Washington DC 20005. 202/347-
7474. Fax: 202/898-0068. A
national organization of more than
5,000 member firms. Offers *Last
Word,* a weekly newsletter;
American Consulting Engineer
magazine; life and health
insurance programs; books,
manuals, video and audiotapes,
and contract documents;

conferences and seminars; and
voluntary peer reviews.

**AMERICAN INSTITUTE OF
ARCHITECTS**
1735 New York Avenue NW,
Washington DC 20006. 202/626-
7300. 800/365-2724. Contact
toll-free number for brochures.

**AMERICAN SOCIETY FOR
ENGINEERING EDUCATION**
1818 N Street NW, Suite 600,
Washington DC 20036. 202/331-
3500. Promotes engineering
education. Publishes monthly
magazines.

**AMERICAN SOCIETY OF CIVIL
ENGINEERS**
345 East 47th Street, New York
NY 10017. 212/705-7496. Toll-
free number: 800/548-2723. A
membership organization which
offers subscriptions to *Civil
Engineering* magazine and *ASCE
News,* discounts on various other
publications, seminars, audio and
videotapes, specialty conferences,
an annual convention, group
insurance programs, and pension
plans.

**AMERICAN SOCIETY OF
HEATING, REFRIGERATING AND
AIR CONDITIONING ENGINEERS**
1791 Tullie Circle NE, Atlanta GA
30329. 404/636-8400. Fax:
404/321-5478. A society of
50,000 members which offers
handbooks, a monthly journal, a
monthly newspaper, discounts on
other publications, group
insurance, continuing education,
and registration discounts for
meetings, conferences, seminars,
and expositions.

**AMERICAN SOCIETY OF
LANDSCAPE ARCHITECTS**
4401 Connecticut Avenue NW,
Washington DC 20008. 202/686-
2752. World Wide Web address:

http://www.asla.org. Look for Joblink for employment listings.

AMERICAN SOCIETY OF MECHANICAL ENGINEERS
345 East 47th Street, New York NY 10017. 212/705-7722. Handles educational materials for certified engineers, as well as scholarships.

AMERICAN SOCIETY OF NAVAL ENGINEERS
1452 Duke Street, Alexandria VA 22314. 703/836-6727. Holds symposiums based on technical papers. Publishes a journal and newsletter bimonthly.

AMERICAN SOCIETY OF PLUMBING ENGINEERS
3617 Thousand Oaks Boulevard, Suite 210, Westlake CA 91362-3694. 805/495-7120. Provides technical and educational information.

AMERICAN SOCIETY OF SAFETY ENGINEERS
1800 East Oakton Street, Des Plaines IL 60018-2187. 847/692-4121. Jobline service available at ext. 243. Fax: 847/296-3769. A membership organization offering *Professional Safety*, a monthly journal; educational seminars; an annual professional development conference and exposition; technical publications; certification preparation programs; career placement services; and group and liability insurance programs.

ASSOCIATED BUILDERS AND CONTRACTORS
1300 North 17th Street, Rosslyn VA 22209. 703/812-2000. Sponsors annual career fair. Currently in the process of creating a service to find workers for construction companies.

ASSOCIATED GENERAL CONTRACTORS OF AMERICA, INC.
1957 E Street NW, Washington DC 20006. 202/393-2040. A full-service construction association of subcontractors, specialty contractors, suppliers, equipment manufacturers, and professional firms. Services include government relations, education and training, jobsite services, legal services, and information services.

ILLUMINATING ENGINEERING SOCIETY OF NORTH AMERICA
120 Wall Street, 17th Floor, New York NY 10005-4001. 212/248-5000. An organization for industry professionals involved in the manufacturing, design, specification, and maintenance of lighting systems. Conference held annually. Offers a Technical Knowledge Examination.

JUNIOR ENGINEERING TECHNICAL SOCIETY
1420 King Street, Suite 405, Alexandria VA 22314-2794. 703/548-JETS. Fax: 703/548-0769. E-mail address: jets@nas.edu. A nonprofit, educational society promoting interest in engineering, technology, mathematics, and science. Provides information to high school students and teachers regarding careers in engineering and technology.

NATIONAL ACTION COUNCIL FOR MINORITIES IN ENGINEERING
3 West 35th Street, New York NY 10001. 212/279-2626. Offers scholarship programs for students.

NATIONAL ASSOCIATION OF HOME BUILDERS
1201 15th Street NW, Washington DC 20005. 202/822-0200. A trade association promoting safe and affordable housing. Provides management services and education for members.

NATIONAL ASSOCIATION OF MINORITY ENGINEERING
1133 West Morse Boulevard, Suite 201, Winter Park FL 32789. 407/647-8839.

NATIONAL SOCIETY OF BLACK ENGINEERS
1454 Duke Street, Alexandria VA 22314. 703/549-2207. A nonprofit organization run by college students. Offers

scholarships, editorials, and magazines.

NATIONAL SOCIETY OF PROFESSIONAL ENGINEERS
1420 King Street, Alexandria VA 22314-2794. 703/684-2800. Call 703/684-2830 for scholarship information for students. Fax: 703/836-4875. A society of over 73,000 engineers. Membership includes the monthly magazine *Engineering Times;* continuing education; scholarships and fellowships; discounts on publications; health and life insurance programs; and employment service programs.

SOCIETY OF FIRE PROTECTION ENGINEERS
One Liberty Square, Boston MA 02109-4825. 617/482-0686. Fax: 617/482-8184. A professional society which offers members reports, newsletters, *Journal of Fire Protecting Engineering,* insurance programs, short courses, symposiums, tutorials, an annual meeting, and engineering seminars.

Directories

DIRECTORY OF ENGINEERING SOCIETIES
American Association of Engineering Societies, 1111 19th Street NW, Suite 608, Washington DC 20036. 202/296-2237. $185.00. Lists other engineering association members, publications, and convention exhibits.

DIRECTORY OF ENGINEERS IN PRIVATE PRACTICE
National Society of Professional Engineers, 1420 King Street, Alexandria VA 22314. 703/684-2800. $50.00. Lists members and companies.

Magazines

THE CAREER ENGINEER
National Society of Black Engineers, 1454 Duke Street, Alexandria VA 22314. 703/549-2207.

CAREERS AND THE ENGINEER
Adams Media Corporation, 260 Center Street, Holbrook MA 02343. 617/767-8100.

CHEMICAL & ENGINEERING NEWS
American Chemical Society 1155 16th Street NW, Washington DC 20036. 202/872-4600.

COMPUTER-AIDED ENGINEERING
Penton Publishing, 1100 Superior Avenue, Cleveland OH 44114. 216/696-7000.

EDN CAREER NEWS
Cahners Publishing Company, 275 Washington Street, Newton MA 02158. 617/964-3030.

ENGINEERING TIMES
National Society of Professional Engineers, 1420 King Street, Alexandria VA 22314. 703/684-2800.

NAVAL ENGINEERS JOURNAL
American Society of Naval Engineers, 1452 Duke Street, Alexandria VA 22314. 703/836-6727. Subscription: $48.00.

ARTS AND ENTERTAINMENT/RECREATION

Job opportunities in the entertainment and recreation industries are projected to increase 39 percent through the year 2005, faster than the average for all industries. Higher incomes, growth of leisure time due to a growing population of retirees, and increasing awareness of the health benefits of physical fitness will affect employment growth.

The market for leisure activities is changing. In the past, amusement and recreation services catered to those in their '20s and '30s who had steadily growing incomes. Now that those baby boomers have grown up, companies are targeting adults between 50 and 75 years old. -

In Hollywood, the past several years have been marked by mergers: Disney and ABC/Capital Cities, Westinghouse and CBS, Turner Broadcasting and Time Warner, and Seagram and MCA, to name a few of the biggest headline-stealers. And then there's the growing alliance between Hollywood and Silicon Valley. Microsoft, for example, has joined forces with NBC to create an online news station.

ALLIED DIGITAL TECHNOLOGIES CORPORATION
370 J.D. Yarnell Industrial Parkway, Clinton TN 37716-0460. 615/457-7772. **Fax:** 615/457-7799. **Contact:** Catherine Jones, Human Resources Manager. **Description:** Allied Digital Technologies Corporation is one of the nation's leading independent multimedia manufacturing companies, offering CD audio and CD-ROM mastering and replication, videocassette and audiocassette duplication, laser video disc recording, off-line and on-line video editing, motion picture film processing, film-to-tape and tape-to-film transfers, and complete finishing, packaging, warehousing and fulfilment services. The company is the result of the January 1995 merger of HMG Digital Technologies Corporation and Allied Fil Laboratory, Inc. Privately held Allied Film, with nine operating divisions in major cities nationwide, was one of the top four video duplicators in the U.S. in terms of sales. According to statistics from the Recording Industry Association of America, HMG Digital Technologies Corporation, a publicly held company, was the largest independent replicator of music audiocassettes in the U.S., one of the largest duplicators of music videos, and a leading independent replicator of CD audio and CD-ROM optical disc products. Allied Digital Technologies is one of only two independent manufacturers in North America providing audio, video, and CD replication.

BMG MUSIC (RCA RECORDS)
One Music Circle North, Nashville TN 37203. 615/664-1200. **Contact:** Ms. Janell Sanders, Human Resources Director. **Description:** Local offices of the national record company.

CAPITOL NASHVILLE
3322 West End Avenue, 11th Floor, Nashville TN 37203. 615/269-2000. **Contact:** Ms. Corey Terrano, Director of Office Services. **Description:** Local offices of the record company.

GAYLORD ENTERTAINMENT COMPANY
One Gaylord Drive, Nashville TN 37214. 615/316-6000. **Contact:** Human Resources. **Description:** A diversified entertainment and communications company operating principally in three industry divisions: entertainment, cable networks, and broadcasting. Gaylord owns and operates Opryland, the theme park, entertainment center, and hotel complex. The company also owns the Grand Old Opry, the General Jackson Showboat, Fiesta Texas, and Opryland Music Group. New operations include the Wildhorse Saloon, Nashville on Stage, the BellSouth Senior Classic at Opryland Golf Tournament, and the Ryman Auditorium Renovation. Three cable network television stations make up the fastest growing division of Gaylord Entertainment: the Nashville Network, Country Music Television, and CMT Europe. The broadcasting division owns two television stations in Texas and one in Seattle, and two radio stations in Tennessee and one in Oklahoma City.

OPRYLAND USA
2800 Opryland Drive, Nashville TN 37214. 615/889-6600. **Contact:** Rick Haynes, Manager of Personnel. **Description:** Opryland USA dates back to first broadcast of the radio program Grand Ole Opry on the radio station WSM in November 1925. The Grand Ole Opry has now been broadcasting for 70 years, and has become a springboard for what has become Opryland USA. The Opryland USA theme park features live entertainment, amusement park rides, shops, restaurants, museums, riverboat cruises and more. Facilities include Ryman Auditorium, The Wildhorse Saloon, Opryland River Taxis, The Nashville Network (TNN) studios, the 1,891-room Opryland Hotel, the Springhouse Golf Club, Grand Ole Opry Sightseeing Tours, Cumberland River Cottage, and even the Opryland USA KOA Kampground. Opryland USA is owned and operated by Gaylord Entertainment, a diversified entertainment and communications company operating principally in three industry divisions: entertainment, cable networks, and broadcasting. The broadcasting division owns two television stations in Texas and one in Seattle, and two radio stations in Tennessee and one in Oklahoma City. **Parent company:** Gaylord Entertainment Company.

REGAL CINEMAS, INC.
7132 Commercial Park Drive, Knoxville TN 37918. 423/922-1123. **Contact:** Debbie Robertson, Director of Human Resources. **Description:** Founded in November, 1989, Regal Cinemas, Inc. is a leading motion picture exhibitor in the eastern United States. The company, which is headquartered in Knoxville, Tennessee, primarily shows first-run movies and, at December 30, 1993, operated 45 multi-screen theaters with an aggregate of 359 screens in 10 states. According to Regal management, the company's prominent concession stands are designed for rapid service and efficiency. Through optimizing the product mix, special promotions, and cross selling, Regal seeks to maximize concession revenues. In a growing number of Regal theaters, patrons can enjoy specialty cafes serving non-traditional theater fare such as cappuccino, fruit juices, cookies

and muffins, soft pretzels, and yogurt. With a wide range of seating capacities within the same theater complex, Regal's auditoriums feature plush seating, wide aisles, cupholder arm rests, and elegant wall treatments.

SONY MUSIC
34 Music Square West, Nashville TN 37203. 615/742-4321. **Contact:** Human Resources. **Description:** Local offices of a national record company.

SUN ENTERTAINMENT
3106 Belmont Boulevard, Nashville TN 37212. 615/385-1960. **Contact:** John Singleton, Vice President. **Description:** Offices of a music company.

THE TRACK
575 Parkway, Pigeon Forge TN 37863-3226. 423/453-4777. **Contact:** Human Resources. **Description:** A track and general recreation center.

WARNER REPRISE/NASHVILLE
20 Music Square East, Nashville TN 37203. 615/748-8000. **Contact:** Human Resources. **Description:** Local offices of a national record company.

Note: Because addresses and telephone numbers of smaller companies change rapidly, we recommend you call each company to verify the information below before inquiring about job opportunities. Mass mailings are not recommended.

Additional employers with under 250 employees:

MOTION PICTURE THEATERS

Carmike Cinemas Inc.
2298 Metrocenter Blvd, Nashville TN 37228-1315. 615/254-3144.

Downtown West Cinema 4
1640 Downtown West Blvd, Knoxville TN 37919-5408. 423/693-0505.

THEATRICAL PRODUCERS AND SERVICES

Kari Estrin Management
1415 Sumner Ave, Nashville TN 37206-2533. 615/262-0883.

Uhuru Dance Co. Inc.
1107 Chapel Ave, Nashville TN 37206-2446. 615/227-0400.

Variety Services Inc.
401 Chestnut St, Chattanooga TN 37402-4924. 423/267-4440.

PHYSICAL FITNESS FACILITIES

Body Shapers
2750 Executive Park NW, Cleveland TN 37312-2722. 423/478-1682.

Memorial Health & Wellness Center
1150 Gallatin Rd S, Madison TN 37115-4611. 615/860-0952.

AMUSEMENT AND RECREATION SERVICES

Fairfield Glade Riding Stables
Chestnut Hill Rd, Crossville TN 38555. 615/484-0110.

Wentworth Gallery Inc.
4465 Poplar Ave, Memphis TN 38117-3739. 901/682-8099.

Memphis Sports Shooting Association
9428 Old Brownsville Rd, Arlington TN 38002-9339. 901/867-8277.

For more information on career opportunities in arts, entertainment and recreation:

Associations

AMERICAN ASSOCIATION OF MUSEUMS
1225 I Street NW, Suite 200, Washington DC 20005. 202/289-1818. Fax: 202/289-6578. Publishes *AVISO,* a monthly newsletter containing employment listings for the entire country.

AMERICAN COUNCIL FOR THE ARTS
1 East 53rd Street, New York NY 10022. 212/223-2787. Fax: 212/980-4857. Visual Artist Information Hotline: 800/232-2789. A nonprofit organization for the literary, visual, and performing arts. Supports K-12 education and promotes public policy through meetings, forums, and seminars.

AMERICAN CRAFTS COUNCIL
72 Spring Street, New York NY 10012. 212/274-0630. Operates a research library. Publishes *American Crafts* magazine.

AMERICAN DANCE GUILD
31 West 21st Street, New York NY 10010. 212/627-3790. Holds an annual conference with panels, performances, and workshops. Operates a job listings service (available at a discount to members.)

AMERICAN FEDERATION OF MUSICIANS
1501 Broadway, Suite 600, New York NY 10036. 212/869-1330. Membership required.

AMERICAN FEDERATION OF TELEVISION AND RADIO ARTISTS
260 Madison Avenue, New York NY 10016. 212/532-0800. Membership required.

AMERICAN FILM INSTITUTE
John F. Kennedy Center for the Performing Arts, Washington DC 20566. 202/828-4000.

AMERICAN GUILD OF MUSICAL ARTISTS
1727 Broadway, New York NY 10019. 212/265-3687.

AMERICAN MUSIC CENTER
30 West 26th Street, Suite 1001, New York NY 10010-2011. 212/366-5260. Fax: 212/366-5265. A nonprofit research and information center for contemporary music and jazz. Provides information services and grant programs. World Wide Web address: http://www.amc.net/amc/.

AMERICAN SOCIETY OF COMPOSERS, AUTHORS, AND PUBLISHERS (ASCAP)
One Lincoln Plaza, New York NY 10023. 212/621-6000. Fax: 212/724-9064. A membership association which licenses members' work and pays members royalties. Offers showcases and educational seminars and workshops.

AMERICAN SYMPHONY ORCHESTRA LEAGUE
1156 15th Street NW, Suite 4800, Washington DC 20005. 202/628-0099.

AMERICAN ZOO AND AQUARIUM ASSOCIATION
Oglebay Park, Wheeling WV 26003. 304/242-2160. Produces a monthly newspaper.

ASSOCIATION OF INDEPENDENT VIDEO AND FILMMAKERS
625 Broadway, 9th Floor, New York NY 10012. 212/473-3400.

NATIONAL ARTISTS' EQUITY ASSOCIATION
P.O. Box 28068, Central Station, Washington DC 20038-8068. 202/628-9633. A national, nonprofit organization dedicated to improving economic, health, and legal conditions for visual artists.

NATIONAL DANCE ASSOCIATION
1900 Association Drive, Reston VA 22091. 703/476-3436. Fax: 703/476-9527. Promotes the development and implementation of philosophies and policies in all forms of dance and in dance education at all levels.

NATIONAL ENDOWMENT FOR THE ARTS
1100 Pennsylvania Avenue NW, Washington DC 20506. 202/682-5400.

NATIONAL RECREATION AND PARK ASSOCIATION
2775 South Quincy Street, Suite 300, Arlington VA 22206. 703/820-4940. Fax: 703/671-6772. A national, nonprofit service organization. Offers professional development and training opportunities in recreation, parks, and leisure services. Publishes a newsletter and magazine.

PRODUCERS GUILD OF AMERICA
400 South Beverly Drive, Suite 211, Beverly Hills CA 90212. 310/557-0807.

SCREEN ACTORS GUILD
5757 Wilshire Boulevard, Los Angeles CA 90036-3600. 213/954-1600.

THEATRE COMMUNICATIONS GROUP
355 Lexington Avenue, New York NY 10017. 212/697-5230.

WOMEN'S CAUCUS FOR ART
Moore College of Art, 20th & The Parkway, Philadelphia PA 19103. 215/854-0922. Fax: 215/854-0915. A national organization of professionals in the visual arts. Over 3,700 members. Membership includes an annual conference; participation in juried shows; local chapter meetings and regional conferences; publications including an annual exhibition catalog of honors awards and a quarterly newsletter; and insurance programs.

Directories

ARTIST'S MARKET
Writer's Digest Books, 1507 Dana Avenue, Cincinnati OH 45207. 513/531-2222.

CREATIVE BLACK BOOK
866 3rd Avenue, 3rd Floor, New York NY 10022. 212/254-1330.

PLAYERS GUIDE
165 West 46th Street, New York NY 10036. 212/869-3570.

ROSS REPORTS TELEVISION
Television Index, Inc., 40-29 27th Street, Long Island City NY 11101. 718/937-3990.

Magazines

AMERICAN ARTIST
One Astor Place, 1515 Broadway, New York NY 10036. 212/764-7300. 800/346-0085, ext. 477.

AMERICAN CINEMATOGRAPHER
American Society of Cinematographers, P.O. Box 2230, Hollywood CA 90028. 213/969-4333.

ART BUSINESS NEWS
Myers Publishing Company, 19 Old Kings Highway South, Darien CT 06820. 203/656-3402.

ART DIRECTION
10 East 39th Street, 6th Floor, New York NY 10016. 212/889-6500.

ARTFORUM
65 Bleecker Street, New York NY 10012. 212/475-4000.

ARTWEEK
12 South First Street, Suite 520, San Jose CA 95113. 408/279-2293.

AVISO
American Association of Museums, 1225 I Street NW, Suite 200, Washington DC 20005. 202/289-1818.

BACK STAGE
1515 Broadway, New York NY 10036. 212/764-7300.

BILLBOARD
Billboard Publications, Inc., 1515 Broadway, New York NY 10036. 212/764-7300.

CASHBOX
157 West 57th Street, Suite 503, New York NY 10019. 212/245-4224.

CRAFTS REPORT
300 Water Street, Wilmington DE
19801. 302/656-2209.

DRAMA-LOGUE
P.O. Box 38771, Los Angeles CA
90038. 213/464-5079.

HOLLYWOOD REPORTER
5055 Wilshire Boulevard, 6th

Floor, Los Angeles CA 90036.
213/525-2000.

VARIETY
249 West 17th Street, New York
NY 10011. 212/779-1100.
800/323-4345.

WOMEN ARTIST NEWS
300 Riverside Drive, New York
NY 10025. 212/666-6990.

AUTOMOTIVE

The automotive industry saw a big turnaround in 1994, with sales of new cars and trucks reaching a six-year high. Unfortunately, the boom didn't last. Rising interest rates in early 1995 put the brakes on auto sales. Although the year can't be classified as truly weak, 1995 sales dropped 2.6 percent off 1994's pace. Rising steel prices have also put pressure on the Big Three automakers to cut costs and boost productivity, so don't look for job opportunities to grow very rapidly in '96. Even so, analysts are predicting a 2 percent sales gain in 1996, spurred in part by dropping interest rates.

Jobseekers should look to auto parts suppliers in addition to the Big Three. While Detroit is using fewer suppliers than in the past, the suppliers that are under contract are being asked to supply more of the finished product. Look for large employers with financial backing and superior skills.

ALCOA FUJIKURA, LTD.
105 Westpark Drive, Suite 200, Brentwood TN 37027-5010. 615/370-2100. **Contact:** Gus Agostinelli, Vice President of Human Resources. **Description:** ALCOA Fujikura manufactures motor vehicle parts and accessories. **Common positions include:** Accountant/Auditor; Design Engineer; Electrical/Electronics Engineer; Financial Analyst; Manufacturer's/Wholesaler's Sales Rep.; Marketing Specialist; Mechanical Engineer. **Parent company:** ALCOA (Aluminum Corporation of America).

ALLIEDSIGNAL CORPORATION
BRAKING SYSTEMS
3000 20th Street NE, Cleveland TN 37323. 423/478-0700. **Contact:** Noe Gaton, Personnel Department. **Description:** As a division of Braking Systems, this location manufactures brake linings, non-asbestos disc brakes, block brakes, and segments for both original and used cars. Overall, AlliedSignal Corporation serves a broad spectrum of industries through more than 40 strategic businesses, which are grouped into three sectors: Aerospace, Automotive, and Engineered Materials. AlliedSignal Aerospace business units include Engines, Air Transport Avionics, General Aviation Avionics, Aerospace Systems and Equipment, Controls and Accessories, Fluid Systems, Aircraft Landing Systems, Technical Services Corporation, and Government Electronics Systems. AlliedSignal Engineered Materials does business in fibers, chemicals, plastics, and advanced materials. AlliedSignal Automotive business units include Braking Systems, Safety Restraint Systems, AlliedSignal Truck Brake Systems Company (an alliance with Knorr-Bremse AG), Filters and Spark Plugs, Automotive Aftermarket, and Aftermarket Europe. **Corporate headquarters location:** Southfield MI. **Parent company:** AlliedSignal Corporation. **Number of employees at this location:** 600.

ALLIEDSIGNAL CORPORATION
SAFETY RESTRAINT SYSTEMS
1601 MidPark Road, Knoxville TN 37921. 423/584-9141. **Fax:** 423/558-4704. **Contact:** Andrew Shelton, Senior Human Resources

Representative. **Description:** As part of Safety Restraint Systems, this location manufactures automotive seat belts. Overall, AlliedSignal Corporation serves a broad spectrum of industries through more than 40 strategic businesses, which are grouped into three sectors: Aerospace, Automotive, and Engineered Materials. AlliedSignal Aerospace business units include Engines, Air Transport Avionics and General Aviation Avionics, Aerospace Systems and Equipment, Controls and Accessories, Fluid Systems, Aircraft Landing Systems, Technical Services Corporation, and Government Electronics Systems. AlliedSignal Engineered Materials does business in fibers, chemicals, plastics, and advanced materials. AlliedSignal Automotive business units include Braking Systems, Safety Restraint Systems, Turbocharging Systems, AlliedSignal Truck Brake Company (alliance with Knorr-Bremse AG), Filters and Spark Plugs, Automotive Aftermarket, and Aftermarket Europe. **Corporate headquarters location:** Southfield MI. **Number of employees at this location:** 700. **Number of employees nationwide:** 86,000.

ALLIEDSIGNAL CORPORATION
SAFETY RESTRAINTS DIVISION
1644 Mustang Drive, Maryville TN 37801. 423/984-5007. **Contact:** Human Resources. **Description:** As a division of Safety Restraint Systems, this location produces passenger-side auto air bag assemblies. Overall, AlliedSignal Corporation serves a broad spectrum of industries through more than 40 strategic businesses, which are grouped into three sectors: Aerospace, Automotive, and Engineered Materials. AlliedSignal Aerospace business units include Engines, Air Transport Avionics and General Aviation Avionics, Aerospace Systems and Equipment, Controls and Accessories, Fluid Systems, Aircraft Landing Systems, Technical Services, and Government Electronic Systems. AlliedSignal Engineered Materials does business in fibers, chemicals, plastics, and advanced materials. AlliedSignal Automotive business units include Braking Systems, Safety Restraint Systems, Turbocharging Systems, AlliedSignal Truck Brake Systems Company (alliance with Knorr-Bremse AG), Filters and Spark Plugs, Automotive Aftermarket, and Aftermarket Europe. **Corporate headquarters location:** Southfield MI. **Number of employees at this location:** 350. **Number of employees nationwide:** 86,000.

BTR SEALING SYSTEMS
1713 Henry G. Lane Street, Maryville TN 37801. 423/984-7600. **Contact:** Jim Nelson, Human Resources. **Description:** Manufacturers of seals and weather-stripping for automobiles.

BOSCH AUTOMOTIVE MOTORS INC.
250 East Main Street, Hendersonville TN 37075. 615/822-2850. **Contact:** Bill McShain, Human Resources. **Description:** Manufactures motors for automobiles. **Parent company:** Robert Bosch, Inc.

C.K.R. INDUSTRIES INC.
590 Baxter Lane, Winchester TN 37398. 615/967-5189. **Contact:** Human Resources. **Description:** Produces moldings and automotive parts, which the company then supplies to Nissan, as well as a number of other car companies.

CALSONIC YORUZU CORPORATION

395 Mount Industrial Drive, Morrison TN 37357. 615/668-7700. **Contact:** Bill Goodman, Employee Relations Supervisor. **Description:** A manufacturer of stamped auto parts. **Common positions include:** Automotive Engineer; Computer Engineer; Computer Programmer; Design Engineer; Manufacturing Engineer; Mechanical Engineer.

CAMDEN CASTING CENTER

501 Overhead Bridge Road, Camden TN 38320. 901/584-4691. **Contact:** Jack Adkins, Industrial Relations Manager. **Description:** Manufactures ductile iron castings for the automotive industry. **Common positions include:** Accountant/Auditor; Administrator; Blue-Collar Worker Supervisor; Buyer; Department Manager; General Manager; Human Resources Specialist; Industrial Engineer; Purchasing Agent and Manager; Quality Control Supervisor. **Educational backgrounds include:** Accounting; Business Administration; Chemistry; Engineering. **Benefits:** Dental Insurance; Disability Coverage; Life Insurance; Medical Insurance; Pension Plan; Tuition Assistance. **Corporate headquarters location:** Dayton OH. **Operations at this facility include:** Administration; Divisional Headquarters; Manufacturing; Sales.

COOPER AUTOMOTIVE
WAGNER LIGHTING DIVISION

P.O. Box 87, Sparta TN 38583. 615/738-2261. **Contact:** Tim Caldwell, Human Resources. **Description:** Manufactures automotive lighting.

DANA CORPORATION
SPICER TRANSMISSION DIVISION

5428 North National Drive, Knoxville TN 37914. 423/637-7294. **Fax:** 423/523-1042. **Contact:** Human Resources. **Description:** Dana Corporation, founded in 1905, is a global leader in engineering, manufacturing, and marketing of products and systems for the worldwide vehicular, industrial, and mobile off-highway original equipment markets and is a major supplier to the related aftermarkets. Dana is also a leading provider of lease financing services in selected markets. The company's products include: drivetrain components, such as axles, driveshafts, clutches, and transmissions; engine parts, such as gaskets, piston rings, seals, pistons, and filters; chassis products, such as vehicular frames and cradles and heavy duty side rails; fluid power components, such as pumps, motors, and control valves; and industrial products, such as electrical and mechanical brakes and clutches, drives, and motion control devices. Dana's vehicular components and parts are used on automobiles, pickup trucks, vans, minivans, sport utility vehicles, medium and heavy trucks, and off-highway vehicles. The company's industrial products include mobile off-highway and stationary equipment applications. Dana Corporation has over 55,000 employees worldwide at almost 700 facilities in 27 countries. **Corporate headquarters location:** Toledo OH.

DOUGLAS & LOMASON COMPANY

3000 Kefauver Drive, Milan TN 38358. 901/686-0805. **Contact:** Brad Shelby, Human Resources Manager. **Description:** Manufactures and distributes bumpers, trim, and complete automobile seats. **Corporate headquarters location:** Farmington Hills MI.

EZON CORPORATION
1900 Exeter Road, Germantown TN 38138. 901/755-5555. **Contact:** Sarah Blankenship, Human Resources Manager. **Description:** One of the largest independent wholesale distributors of automotive parts and chemicals in the country. **Listed on:** Privately held.

FINDLAY INDUSTRIES
1095 Mount View Industrial Boulevard, Morrison TN 37357. 615/668-2858. **Contact:** Human Resources. **Description:** Manufactures seat covers and door panels for automobiles.

GKN/PARTS INDUSTRIES CORPORATION
601 South Dudley Street, Memphis TN 38104. 901/523-7711. **Contact:** Human Resources. **Description:** A wholesaler of motor vehicle supplies and parts.

HARMAN AUTOMOTIVE INDUSTRIES INC.
P.O. Box 4628, Seiverville TN 37864-4628. **Contact:** Human Resources. **Description:** Manufactures outside mirrors for Chrysler and General Motors.

HASTINGS MANUFACTURING
5112 North National Drive, Knoxville TN 37914. 423/523-5916. **Contact:** Human Resources. **Description:** Manufactures and sells automotive piston rings, filters, fuel pumps, oil additives, and mechanics' hand tools.

HENNESSY INDUSTRIES INC.
1601 J.P. Hennessy Drive, La Vergne TN 37086. 615/641-7533. **Contact:** Lou Morroer, Director of Human Resources. **Description:** Manufactures automotive equipment including engines and related parts.

JOHNSON CONTROLS, INC.
659 Natchez Trace Drive, Lexington TN 38351-4125. 901/968-3601. **Contact:** Danny Azvill, Human Resources. **Description:** This location of Johnson Controls manufactures automotive hardware, specifically seat adjusters and recliners. Founded in 1885, Johnson Controls is now a global market leader in automotive seating, facility services and control systems, plastic packaging, and automotive batteries. These industries make up the four business units of the company: Automotive, Controls, Plastics, and Battery. The automotive business produces complete seat systems, seating components, and interior trim systems for cars, light trucks, and vans. The controls segment is involved in the installation and service of facility management and control systems, retrofit and service of mechanical equipment and lighting systems in non-residential buildings, and on-site management of facility operations and maintenance. The plastics unit manufactures plastic containers for beverages, food, personal care, and household items, as well as manufacturing, installing, and servicing plastics blowmolding machinery systems. The battery segment manufactures automotive batteries for the replacement and original equipment markets and specialty batteries for telecommunications and uninterruptible power

supply (UPS) applications. **Corporate headquarters location:** Milwaukee WI.

JOHNSON CONTROLS, INC.
1890 Mines Road, Pulaski TN 38478-9504. 615/363-5666. **Contact:** Mr. Terry Birdsong. **Description:** This facility of Johnson Controls produces foam used in the manufacture of automotive seating. Founded in 1885, Johnson Controls is now a global market leader in automotive seating, facility services and control systems, plastic packaging, and automotive batteries. These industries make up the four business units of the company: Automotive, Controls, Plastics, and Battery. The automotive business produces complete seat systems, seating components, and interior trim systems for cars, light trucks, and vans. The controls segment is involved in the installation and service of facility management and control systems, retrofit and service of mechanical equipment and lighting systems in non-residential buildings, and on-site management of facility operations and maintenance. The plastics unit manufactures plastic containers for beverages, food, personal care, and household items, as well as manufacturing, installing, and servicing plastics blowmolding machinery systems. The battery segment manufactures automotive batteries for the replacement and original equipment markets and specialty batteries for telecommunications and uninterruptible power supply (UPS) applications. **Corporate headquarters location:** Milwaukee WI.

JOHNSON CONTROLS, INC.
P.O. Box 989, 1210 East Madison, Athens TN 37371-0989. 423/745-5807. **Contact:** Charlotta Pickens, Human Resources Manager. **Description:** Founded in 1885, Johnson Controls is now a global market leader in automotive seating, facility services and control systems, plastic packaging, and automotive batteries. These industries make up the four business units of the company: Automotive, Controls, Plastics, and Battery. The automotive business produces complete seat systems, seating components, and interior trim systems for cars, light trucks, and vans. The controls segment is involved in the installation and service of facility management and control systems, retrofit and service of mechanical equipment and lighting systems in non-residential buildings, and on-site management of facility operations and maintenance. The plastics unit manufactures plastic containers for beverages, food, personal care, and household items, as well as manufacturing, installing, and servicing plastics blowmolding machinery systems. The battery segment manufactures automotive batteries for the replacement and original equipment markets and specialty batteries for telecommunications and uninterruptible power supply (UPS) applications. This location manufactures plastic cases for the batteries. **Corporate headquarters location:** Milwaukee WI.

MAHLE INC.
P.O. Box 748, Morristown TN 37815. 615/581-6603. **Contact:** Dennis Wheeler, Human Resources Manager. **Description:** Manufactures automotive engine parts.

MIDLAND BRAKE INC.
P.O. Box 490, Paris TN 38242. 901/642-4215. **Contact:** Art McKew, Human Resources Manager. **Description:** Manufactures

heavy-duty truck brake parts. The company also has a clutch line for heavy-duty trucks.

NASHVILLE PLASTIC PRODUCTS
660 Massman Drive, Nashville TN 37210. 615/883-0058. **Contact:** Human Resources. **Description:** Nashville Plastic Products performs injection-molding of parts for the automotive industry.

NISSAN MOTOR MANUFACTURING CORPORATION
983 Nissan Drive, Smyrna TN 37167. 615/459-1400. **Contact:** Employment Department. **Description:** U.S. corporate headquarters for the auto manufacturing division of Nissan. **NOTE:** The Employment Department only accepts applications for professional positions.

NORTH AMERICAN ROYALTIES
WHELAND FOUNDRY DIVISION
200 East Eighth Street, Chattanooga TN 37402. 423/265-3181. **Fax:** 423/266-5669. **Contact:** Rick Roberts, Labor Relations Manager. **Description:** Wheland Foundry, established in 1866, is the largest independent producer of cast iron automotive brake components in the United States. There are six automated tight flask molding lines and a centrifugal casting plant at Broad Street. The Middle Street ductile plant features three large, high-speed, flaskless Disamatic molding lines. Two gray iron foundries produce castings in the weight range of five to 180 pounds. The Middle Street operation produces ductile iron automotive and general purpose castings in the three to 70 pound range. Iron is melted in three of five cupolas daily and duplexed through seven of 10 induction furnaces at a rate of over 100 tons per hour. Approximately four million pounds of material are melted and poured during a normal work day. This metal can be cast into an average of 100,000 parts with a total weight of 1000 tons. Approximately 150 different gray and ductile iron castings are made at Wheland. In an average work week, 15 rail cars and 130 tractor trailer loads of castings are shipped to Wheland's customers, the major car manufacturers, and several large machining operations. Since Wheland Foundry began production of automotive castings over 40 years ago, more than 500 million castings have been made. Approximately 50 percent of U.S. built cars have one or more castings made at Wheland. **Common positions include:** Accountant/Auditor; Civil Engineer; Computer Programmer; Computer Systems Analyst; Electrical/Electronics Engineer; Electrician; Financial Analyst; General Manager; Human Resources Specialist; Industrial Engineer; Management Trainee; Mechanical Engineer; Metallurgical Engineer; Purchasing Agent and Manager; Registered Nurse. **Educational backgrounds include:** Business Administration; Engineering. **Benefits:** 401K; Dental Insurance; Disability Coverage; Life Insurance; Medical Insurance; Pension Plan; Tuition Assistance. **Corporate headquarters location:** This Location. **Other U.S. locations:** Warrenton GA. **Operations at this facility include:** Administration; Divisional Headquarters; Manufacturing; Sales. **Listed on:** Privately held. **Number of employees at this location:** 250. **Number of employees nationwide:** 1,450.

P.T. COMPONENTS, INC.
LINK BELT BEARING DIVISION
Eagle Bend Industrial Park, P.O. Box 330, Clinton TN 37716. 423/546-1175. **Contact:** Tom Plachinski, Human Resources. **Description:** A manufacturer of auto bearings.

PETERBILT MOTORS/PACCAR INC.
430 Myatt Drive, Madison TN 37115. 615/865-8910. **Contact:** Human Resources. **Description:** A truck manufacturer.

REPUBLIC AUTOMOTIVE PARTS, INC.
500 Wilson Pike Circle, Suite 115, P.O. Box 2088, Brentwood TN 37024. 615/373-2050. **Contact:** Michael Bouldin, Director of Human Resources. **Description:** Republic Automotive Parts, Inc. distributes a complete line of replacement parts for substantially all mass produced makes and models of automobiles manufactured within the last 15 years and most replacement parts for mass produced trucks and vans. The company also distributes a number of replacement parts for heavy-duty trucks, snowmobiles, motorcycles, farm and marine equipment and other similar types of machinery through its automotive distribution centers and stores. These are in excess of 100,000 separate parts of nationally and privately branded items distributed by the company. The company purchases replacement parts from over 100 principal suppliers and distributes them through automotive parts distribution centers. These centers sell to the company's jobber stores as well as to approximately 3,000 independent jobber stores. These stores in turn sell to service stations, repair shops, individuals and others, including automobile and truck dealers, fleet operators, leasing companies and mass merchandisers. The company also distributes new replacement parts used to repair vehicles damaged in collisions. Distribution centers located in Nashville and Atlanta sell to automotive collision repair shops and smaller parts distributors. **Corporate headquarters location:** This Location.

SW MANUFACTURING, INC.
1111 West Broad Street, Smithville TN 37166. 615/597-8870. **Fax:** 615/597-8876. **Contact:** Patty Burke, Personnel Manager. **Description:** An automotive manufacturing supplier and manufacturer of window regulators and seat adjusters. **Common positions include:** Accountant/Auditor; Computer Systems Analyst; Electrical/Electronics Engineer; Electrician; Human Resources Specialist; Industrial Engineer; Mechanical Engineer; Purchasing Agent and Manager; Quality Control Supervisor. **Educational backgrounds include:** Accounting; Computer Science; Engineering; Finance; Marketing. **Benefits:** 401K; Dental Insurance; Disability Coverage; Life Insurance; Medical Insurance; Tuition Assistance. **Corporate headquarters location:** This Location. **Parent company:** Shiroki Corporation (Japan). **Operations at this facility include:** Administration; Manufacturing; Research and Development; Sales. **Listed on:** Privately held. **Number of employees at this location:** 450.

SATURN CORPORATION
100 Saturn Parkway, P.O. Box 1500, Spring Hill TN 37174-1500. 615/486-5000. **Recorded Jobline:** 615/486-5731. **Contact:** Human Resources. **Description:** Manufactures motor vehicles. **Corporate**

headquarters location: Troy MI. **Parent company:** General Motors Corporation.

A.O. SMITH AUTOMOTIVE PRODUCTS COMPANY
P.O. Box 529, Milan TN 38358. 901/686-0891. **Contact:** Jerry Taylor, Human Resources. **Description:** Manufactures fabricated metal automotive products.

TBC CORPORATION
4770 Hickory Hill Road, P.O. Box 18181, Memphis TN 38141-0342. 901/363-8030. **Contact:** John Carter, Human Resources. **Description:** TBC is a marketer and distributor of automotive replacement products. The company's customers make up a distribution network of more than 185 regional distribution centers and 20,000 independent tire dealers throughout the North America. TBC's product line covers tires, tubes, batteries, custom wheels, ride-control products, filters, brakes, chassis parts, and automotive service equipment. The products are sold under the company's proprietary, well-established brand names. Developments at the company within recent years include the successful broadening of its product line and adding several services for distributors.

TEKSID ALUMINUM FOUNDRY INC.
DIVISION OF FIAT USA
1635 Old Columbia Road, Dickson TN 37055. 615/446-8110. **Fax:** 615/446-2460. **Contact:** Mitch Camp, Human Resources Manager. **Description:** Manufactures aluminum cylinder heads for Ford, Chrysler, G.M., and Daewoo. **Common positions include:** Accountant/Auditor; Administrative Services Manager; Blue-Collar Worker Supervisor; Computer Systems Analyst; Electrical/Electronics Engineer; Electrician; Human Resources Specialist; Materials Engineer; Mechanical Engineer; Metallurgical Engineer. **Educational backgrounds include:** Accounting; Business Administration; Chemistry; Engineering; Physics. **Benefits:** 401K; Dental Insurance; Disability Coverage; Life Insurance; Medical Insurance; Savings Plan; Tuition Assistance. **Corporate headquarters location:** This Location. **Parent company:** Fiat USA. **Operations at this facility include:** Administration; Divisional Headquarters; Manufacturing; Research and Development. **Listed on:** New York Stock Exchange. **Number of employees at this location:** 650.

TEXTRON AUTOMOTIVE COMPANY
100 Textron Way, Athens TN 37303. 423/745-8488. **Contact:** Human Resources. **Description:** Manufactures interior car parts. Nationally, Textron Inc. is a diversified conglomerate with over 30 separate companies in three primary areas: Aerospace and Defense Technology; Financial Services; and Communications. The company also manufactures outdoor equipment and specialty fasteners. **Parent company:** Textron Inc.

YAMAKAWA MANUFACTURING CORPORATION
201 Kirby Drive, P.O. Box 799, Portland TN 37148. 615/325-7311. **Contact:** David Milam, General Manager of Administration. **Description:** Manufactures automotive stampings.

Note: Because addresses and telephone numbers of smaller companies change rapidly, we recommend you call each company to verify the information below before inquiring about job opportunities. Mass mailings are not recommended.

Additional employers with under 250 employees:

AUTOMOTIVE STAMPINGS

Del-Met Corp.
113 Hazel Path,
Hendersonvlle TN
37075-3865.
615/822-2722.

EWI/Dover Products Co.
1 Dover Prdts Dr,
Dover TN 37058.
615/232-8090.

MOTOR VEHICLES AND EQUIPMENT

Flour County Architectual Metal Division
P.O. Box 629,
Johnson City TN
37605-0629.
423/928-2724.

Miller Industries
8503 Hilltop Dr,
Ooltewah TN 37363-
8831. 423/238-4171.

AE Clevite Engine Parts
2237 Byron Ave,
Murfreesboro TN
37129-1384.
615/896-6774.

Allison & Farber
201 Ball Park St,
Somerville TN 38068-
1704. 901/465-3678.

Alphatech Inc.
408 Municipal Dr,
Jefferson Cty TN
37760-5033.
423/475-9085.

Burner Systems International
1400 Higgs Rd,
Lewisburg TN 37091-
4402. 615/359-7241.

Crotty-Tennessee Inc.
P.O. Box 95,
Gainesboro TN 38562-
0095. 615/268-2035.

D&A Technology Inc.
201 Canaan Rd,
Mount Pleasant TN
38474-1059.
615/379-4994.

EWI Greenfield Products Co.
P.O. Box 85,
Greenfield TN 38230-
0085. 901/235-2244.

Flex Technologies Inc.
108 Brattontown Cir,
Lafayette TN 37083-
2623. 615/666-6677.

Form Rite
5961 Commerce Blvd,
Morristown TN
37814-1051.
423/587-1810.

Gabriel Ride Control Products
100 Westwood Pl,
Suite 300, Brentwood
TN 37027-5044.
7084628500.

Hastings Manufacturing Co.
P.O. Box 14825,
Knoxville TN 37914.
423/523-5916.

Moeller of TN Inc.
801 N Spring St,
Sparta TN 38583.
615/738-8090.

Morton Bendix
119 Air Bag Way,
Maryville TN 37801-
3793. 423/981-4600.

Plumley Companies
RR 2 Box 116B, South
Fulton TN 38257-
9802. 901/352-7941.

The Heil Co.
P.O. Box 160, Athens
TN 37371-0160.
423/745-5830.

MOTOR VEHICLE EQUIPMENT WHOLESALE

Auto Part Locators
1150 Linden Ave,
Memphis TN 38104-
6622. 901/272-0810.

Speedometer Repair Service
16 S Cleveland St,
Memphis TN 38104-
3502. 901/272-1196.

Fel-Pro Southeast
600 Bryan St, Old
Hickory TN 37138-
3152. 615/847-0140.

City Truck & Trailer Parts
3259 Millbranch Rd,
Memphis TN 38116-
3652. 901/332-2489.

Tranquility Motors
653 County Road
220, Athens TN
37303-7009.
423/745-2264.

AUTOMOTIVE REPAIR SHOPS

Earl Scheib Auto Painters
3605 E Magnolia Ave,
Knoxville TN 37914-
3908. 423/544-0020.

Nationwide Auto Parts
4804 Clinton Hwy,
Knoxville TN 37912-
3936. 423/688-0020.

Coleman Taylor Automatic Transmission
7981 Fischer Steel Rd,

Cordova TN 38018-6200. 901/754-2832.

Coleman Taylor Automatic Transmission
3674 S Mendenhall Rd, Memphis TN 38115-4801. 901/363-1288.

Express Lube
5012 Nolensville Rd, Nashville TN 37211-5414. 615/333-9820.

Dobbs Bros. Paint & Body Shop
2625 S Mendenhall Rd, Memphis TN 38115-1503. 901/363-6200.

Prevost Car Inc.
2520 Ewell Elliott Rd, Springfield TN 37172-5619. 615/382-7300.

Cummings Cumberland Inc.
706 Spence Ln,

Nashville TN 37217-1144. 615/366-4341.

American Bearing-Transmission
403 Bernard Ave, Knoxville TN 37917-7135. 423/546-7611.

Primus Automotive Etc.
1 Burton Hills Blvd, Suite 350, Nashville TN 37215-6104. 615/665-7900.

For more information on career opportunities in the automotive industry:

Associations

AMERICAN AUTOMOBILE MANUFACTURERS ASSOCIATION
1401 H Street NW, Suite 900, Washington DC 20005. 202/326-5500. Fax: 202/326-5567. A trade association consisting of the Big Three U.S. automakers: Chrysler, Ford, and General Motors. Sponsors research projects, distributes publications, and reviews social and public policies pertaining to the motor vehicle industry and its customers.

ASSOCIATION OF INTERNATIONAL AUTOMOBILE MANUFACTURERS
1001 19th Street North, Suite 1200, Arlington VA 22209. 703/525-7788.

AUTOMOTIVE SERVICE INDUSTRY ASSOCIATION
25 Northwest Point Boulevard, Suite 425, Elk Grove Village IL 60007-1035. 708/228-1310. Members are manufacturers and distributors of automobile replacement parts. Sponsors a trade show. Publishes educational guidebooks and training manuals.

AUTOMOTIVE SERVICE ASSOCIATION
1901 Airport Freeway, Suite 100, P.O. Box 929, Bedford TX 76095. 817/283-6205. Works with shops to find workers.

Publishes a monthly magazine with classified advertisements.

Directories

AUTOMOTIVE NEWS MARKET DATA BOOK
Crain Communications, Automotive News, 1400 Woodbridge Avenue, Detroit MI 48207-3187. 313/446-6000.

WARD'S AUTOMOTIVE YEARBOOK
Ward's Communications, 3000 Town Center, Suite 2750, Southville MI 48075. 810/357-0800.

Magazines

AUTOMOTIVE INDUSTRIES
Chilton Book Company, 201 King of Prussia Road, Radnor PA 19089. 800/695-1214.

AUTOMOTIVE NEWS
1400 Woodbridge Avenue, Detroit MI 48207. 313/446-6000.

WARD'S AUTO WORLD
Ward's Communications, Inc., 3000 Town Center, Suite 2750, Southville MI 48075. 810/357-0800.

WARD'S AUTOMOTIVE REPORTS
Ward's Communications, Inc., 3000 Town Center, Suite 2750, Southville MI 48075. 810/357-0800.

BANKING/SAVINGS AND LOANS

The banking industry has fared well over the past few years. Banks reported record earnings from 1992 to 1995. Low interest rates have decreased the number of bad loans and have increased investment profits. The early '90s were also a good time for banking professionals, who, despite numerous mergers and consolidations throughout the industry, avoided the large layoffs that hit workers in other industries. As a result of rising interest rates in early 1995, times have begun to change. Analysts argue that there are simply too many banks clogging the market. This glut of banks (over 10,000 in the United States as compared to 60 in Canada), the emphasis on multi-branch banking, and the decline in traditional transactions, has forced banks to consolidate and close branches. This has led to shrinking employment with dramatic layoffs of tellers, bank office workers, and managers. This trend will continue to take place into the next century.

FIRST AMERICAN CORPORATION

First American Center, Nashville TN 37237. 615/748-2000. **Contact:** Marlene Akin, Vice President of Human Resources. **Description:** First American Corporation is a bank holding company which was incorporated in 1968. First American's largest subsidiary is First American National Bank, which was established in 1883. First American is also the parent company of First American Trust Company, N.A., and First National Bank of Kentucky. The corporation currently operates 138 banking offices and the same number of automated banking machines. It operates in the following communities in Tennessee: Brentwood, Bristol, Chattanooga, Clarksville, Cleveland, Clinton, Cookeville, Crossville, Dayton, Dover, Franklin, Gallatin, Harriman, Jackson, Jefferson City, Johnson City, Kingsport, Kingston, Knoxville, Lebanon, Maryville, McMinnville, Memphis, Milan, Murfreesboro, Nashville, Oak Ridge, Paris, Rockwood, Smyrna, Spring City, Shelbyville, Waverly, and Woodbury; and it operates in Bowling Green and Franklin, Kentucky. Through is subsidiaries, First American Corporation engages in general commercial and retail banking and provides personal and corporate trust, agency, and investment services. First American National Bank is a member of the FDIC. **Corporate headquarters location:** This Location. **Listed on:** NASDAQ.

FIRST TENNESSEE BANK

300 Court Street, Memphis TN 38103. 901/543-4778. **Contact:** Bob Vezina, Director of Personnel. **Description:** A full-service commercial banking institution. Parent company, First Tennessee National Corporation, is one of the nation's 65 largest banking companies with assets of $9.6 billion. FTNC, whose principal subsidiary is First Tennessee National Bank Association (FTNBA), is the largest Tennessee-based bank holding company. Emphasizing convenient, quality service, FTBNA offers general banking products through 211 locations which serve 18 regions, including the five major metropolitan areas across the state. Mortgage banking provides

services through 96 offices in 20 states. In addition, consumer lending has 10 offices in five states. Through its membership in MOST, Gulfnet and PLUS, FTBNA allows regional and international automated teller machine (ATM) access at more than 100,000 locations. FTBNA offers related financial services including bond broker/agency services, mortgage banking, merchant credit card processing, nationwide check clearing, integrated check processing solutions, trust services, brokerage, venture capital, and credit life insurance. **Other subsidiaries include:** Planters Bank of Tunica, Mississippi (acquired in 1994); Cleveland Bank & Trust Company of Cleveland, Tennessee (acquired in 1994); and SNMC Management Corporation of Dallas, Texas (acquired in 1994). **Parent company:** First Tennessee National Corporation.

FIRST TENNESSEE NATIONAL CORPORATION
165 Madison Avenue, Memphis TN 38103. 901/523-4444. **Contact:** Human Resources. **Description:** First Tennessee National Corporation is one of the nation's 65 largest banking companies with assets of $9.6 billion. FTNC, whose principal subsidiary is First Tennessee National Bank Association (FTNBA), is the largest Tennessee-based bank holding company. Emphasizing convenient, quality service, FTBNA offers general banking products through 211 locations which serve 18 regions, including the five major metropolitan areas across the state. Mortgage banking provides services through 96 offices in 20 states. In addition, consumer lending has 10 offices in five states. Through its membership in MOST, Gulfnet and PLUS, FTBNA allows regional and international automated teller machine (ATM) access at more than 100,000 locations. FTBNA offers related financial services including bond broker/agency services, mortgage banking, merchant credit card processing, nationwide check clearing, integrated check processing solutions, trust services, brokerage, venture capital, and credit life insurance. **NOTE:** The Human Resources office is located at 300 Court Street, Memphis TN 38103, 901/543-4778. **Corporate headquarters location:** This Location. **Listed on:** NASDAQ.

FIRST UNION NATIONAL BANK OF TENNESSEE
150 Fourth Avenue North, Nashville TN 37219. 615/251-9200. **Contact:** Ms. Gari Cowan, Human Resources. **E-mail address:** comments@firstunion.com. **World Wide Web address:** http://www.firstunion.com. **Description:** A full-service commercial bank providing corporate and consumer services. First Union National Bank of Tennessee operates 54 offices. The parent company, First Union Corporation, is one of the nation's largest bank holding companies with subsidiaries which operate over 1,330 full-service bank branches in the South Atlantic states. These subsidiaries provide retail banking, retail investment, and commercial banking services. The corporation provides other financial services including mortgage banking, home equity lending, leasing, insurance and securities brokerage services from 222 branch locations. The corporation also operates one of the nation's largest ATM networks. **Corporate headquarters location:** This Location. **Parent company:** First Union Corporation (Charlotte, NC). **Listed on:** New York Stock Exchange. **Number of employees nationwide:** 31,858.

NATIONAL COMMERCE BANCORPORATION

One Commerce Square, Memphis TN 38150. 901/523-3434. **Contact:** Susan Arrison, Human Resources. **Description:** National Commerce Bancorporation is the parent company of National Bank of Commerce, NBC Knoxville Bank, and NBC Bank FSB. In addition to traditional banking services, the company offers the following: investment advice through Commerce Capital Management, Inc. and Brooks, Montague & Associates, Inc.; investment services through Commerce Investment Corporation; data processing capabilities through Commerce General Corporation; supermarket banking to licensed banks through National Commerce Bank Services, Inc.; and consumer financing through Commerce Finance Company. The corporation attributes it growth and profitability to conservative banking and "forward-thinking innovation." The company recently celebrated its 120th anniversary of being in business.

NATIONSBANK

800 Main Street, Nashville TN 37206. 615/749-3333. **Contact:** Personnel Department. **Description:** In addition to a complete selection of financial accounts, NationsBank offers a variety of services that are designed to make banking as easy and convenient as possible. NationsBank also offers an automatic savings transfer program, allowing regular transfer of money from checking to savings, and direct deposit. **Common positions include:** Bank Officer/Manager; Branch Manager; Customer Service Representative; Department Manager; Financial Analyst; Management Trainee; Services Sales Representative. **Educational backgrounds include:** Accounting; Business Administration; Economics; Finance; Liberal Arts; Marketing. **Benefits:** Daycare Assistance; Dental Insurance; Disability Coverage; Employee Discounts; Life Insurance; Medical Insurance; Pension Plan; Profit Sharing; Savings Plan; Tuition Assistance. **Special Programs:** Training Programs. **Corporate headquarters location:** This Location.

SUNTRUST BANK, EAST TENNESSEE, N.A.

700 East Hill Avenue, Knoxville TN 37997. 423/637-2411. **Contact:** Human Resources. **Description:** A full-service commercial bank. The parent company, SunTrust Banks, Inc., is a financial services company with three principal subsidiaries: SunTrust Banks of Florida, Inc. (formerly SunBanks, Inc.); SunTrust Banks of Georgia, Inc. (formerly Trust Company of Georgia); and SunTrust Banks of Tennessee, Inc. (Third National Corporation). Together, these subsidiaries operate 658 full-service banking offices in Florida, Georgia, Tennessee, and Alabama. The company's primary businesses include traditional deposit and credit services as well as trust and investment services. Additionally, SunTrust Banks, Inc. provides corporate finance, mortgage banking, factoring, credit cards, discount brokerage, credit-related insurance, and data processing and information services. **Parent company:** SunTrust Banks, Inc. (Atlanta GA).

SUNTRUST BANKS OF TENNESSEE, INC.

P.O. Box 305110, Nashville TN 37230-5110. 615/748-4000. **Contact:** Tom Vanetta, Human Resources Department. **Description:** A full-service commercial bank. The parent company, SunTrust Banks, Inc., is a financial services company with three principal subsidiaries: SunTrust Banks of Florida, Inc. (formerly SunBanks,

Inc.); SunTrust Banks of Georgia, Inc. (formerly Trust Company of Georgia); and SunTrust Banks of Tennessee, Inc. (Third National Corporation). Together, these subsidiaries operate 658 full-service banking offices in Florida, Georgia, Tennessee, and Alabama. The company's primary businesses include traditional deposit and credit services as well as trust and investment services. Additionally, SunTrust Banks, Inc. provides corporate finance, mortgage banking, factoring, credit cards, discount brokerage, credit-related insurance, and data processing and information services. **Parent company:** SunTrust Banks, Inc. (Atlanta GA).

TRANE SOUTHERN FEDERAL CREDIT UNION
2701 Wilma Rudolph Boulevard, Clarksville TN 37040. 615/645-3802. **Contact:** Ms. Parolea York, Branch Manager. **Description:** A credit union.

UNION PLANTERS NATIONAL BANK
7130 Goodlett Farms Parkway, Cordova TN 38018. 901/383-6000. **Contact:** Faye Weakley. **Description:** A bank with 234 offices in Tennessee, Arkansas, Mississippi, Kentucky, and Alabama. Union Planters National Bank also offers real estate mortgage, construction, consumer, and lease financing services. **Common positions include:** Accountant/Auditor; Administrator; Attorney; Bank Officer/Manager; Branch Manager; Computer Programmer; Credit Manager; Customer Service Representative; Department Manager; Economist/Market Research Analyst; Financial Analyst; General Manager; Human Resources Specialist; Management Trainee; Marketing Specialist; Operations/Production Manager; Systems Analyst; Technical Writer/Editor. **Educational backgrounds include:** Accounting; Business Administration; Communications; Computer Science; Economics; Finance; Marketing; Mathematics. **Benefits:** Dental Insurance; Disability Coverage; Employee Discounts; Flexible Benefits; Life Insurance; Medical Insurance; Savings Plan; Stock Option. **Corporate headquarters location:** This Location. **Parent company:** Union Planters Corporation. **Listed on:** New York Stock Exchange.

VOLUNTEER BANK
P.O. Box 549, Jackson TN 38302. 901/422-9200. **Contact:** Fran Turner, Personnel Officer. **Description:** Volunteer Bank, a subsidiary of BancorpSouth, provides commercial and retail banking, leasing, mortgage origination and servicing, and trust services. These services are provided to a variety of clients throughout western Tennessee, including Madison, Gibson, and McNairy counties. The client base ranges from corporate customers and local governments to individuals and other financial institutions. Volunteer Bank continues to expand its mortgage, credit card, and loan operations. BancorpSouth acquired Volunteer when it merged with Volunteer Bancshares, Inc. BancorpSouth also has a banking subsidiary in Tupelo MS, Bank of Mississippi, which offers similar services. **Corporate headquarters location:** Tupelo MS. **Parent company:** BancorpSouth, Inc. **Listed on:** NASDAQ.

Note: Because addresses and telephone numbers of smaller companies change rapidly, we recommend you call each company to verify the information below before inquiring about job opportunities. Mass mailings are not recommended.

Additional employers with under 250 employees:

COMMERCIAL BANKS

Amsouth Bank
P.O. Box 3325,
Cleveland TN 37320-
3325. 423/479-9661.

Bank of East Tennessee
P.O. Box 15993,
Knoxville TN 37901-
5993. 423/549-2200.

Cavalry Banking
1745 Memorial Blvd,
Murfreesboro TN
37129-1520.
615/890-2919.

First Citizens Bancshares Inc.
P.O. Box 370,
Dyersburg TN 38025-
0370. 901/285-4410.

First Farmers & Merchants
P.O. Box 1148,
Columbia TN 38402-
1148. 615/388-3145.

Hamilton Bank
P.O. Box 1677,
Johnson City TN
37605-1677.
423/461-1000

Security Trust Federal Savings & Loan
435 W 1st North St,
Morristown TN
37814-4640.
423/581-6210.

Tri-City Bank & Trust Co.
P.O. Box 277,
Blountville TN 37617-
0277. 423/323-3161.

Bank of Commerce
P.O. Box 187, Trenton
TN 38382-0187.
901/855-0772.

Barretville Bank & Trust Co.
P.O. Box 306,
Millington TN 38083-
0306. 901/829-4211.

Brownsville Bank
111 S Washington St,
Brownsville TN
38012-3033.
901/772-1201.

Charter Federal Savings Bank
330 N Cedar Bluff Rd,
Knoxville TN 37923-
4539. 423/690-0115.

Cleveland Bank & Trust Co.
P.O. Box 4170,
Cleveland TN 37320-
4170. 423/559-7600.

First Fidelity Savings Bank
P.O. Box 888,
Crossville TN 38557-
0888. 615/484-7565.

First State Bank Fayette County
16880 US Highway
64, Somerville TN
38068-6156.
901/465-3635.

Leader Federal Bank for Savings
3325 W End Ave,
Nashville TN 37203-
1035. 615/383-1560.

Peoples Bank & Trust
2 W Jackson St,
Cookeville TN 38501-
3926. 615/528-1768.

Tennessee Commercial Bank
P.O. Box 667,
Covington TN 38019-
0667. 901/476-2686.

Third National Bank
201 E Main St,

Murfreesboro TN
37130-3753.
615/849-7000.

Trans Financial Bank of TN
340 S Jefferson Ave,
Cookeville TN 38501-
3409. 615/528-5421.

Trans Financial Bank of TN
113 E Bockman Way,
Sparta TN 38583-
2010. 615/836-3197.

Wilson Bank & Trust
P.O. Box 768,
Lebanon TN 37088-
0768. 615/444-2265.

SAVINGS INSTITUTIONS

Heritage Federal Bancshares
110 E Center St,
Kingsport TN 37660-
4230. 423/378-8000.

Trans Financial Savings Bank
101 W Lincoln St
#1090, Tullahoma TN
37388-3570.
615/455-5411.

CREDIT UNIONS

TI Federal Credit Union
2700 S Roan St,
Johnson City TN
37601-7587.
423/434-2211.

AUB Employees' Credit Union
P.O. Box 689, Athens
TN 37371-0689.
423/745-4501.

Caney Fork Cooperative Credit Union
P.O. Box 272,
McMinnville TN

37110-0272.
615/473-3116.

**Chattanooga Quaker
Credit Union**
P.O. Box 1677,
Chattanooga TN
37401-1677.
423/698-1591.

**Jefferson County
Education Credit Union**
115 W Dumplin Valley
Rd, Dandridge TN
37725-4501.
423/397-2075.

**Johnson City Federal
Credit Union**
P.O. Box 833,
Johnson City TN
37605-0833.
423/928-8682.

**McNairy Co.
Educational Credit
Union**
170 W Court Ave,
Selmer TN 38375-
2134. 901/645-3267.

**Memphis Buckeye
Credit Union**

2899 Jackson Ave,
Memphis TN 38112-
2029. 901/320-8621.

**Rand McNally Credit
Union**
2901 Sidco Dr,
Nashville TN 37204-
3709. 615/254-9471.

**Tennessee Paper Mills
Credit Union**
P.O. Box 4058,
Chattanooga TN
37405-0058.
423/266-7381.

**Townsend Press
Credit Union**
330 Charlotte Ave,
Nashville TN 37201-
1108. 615/256-2480.

**Transit Employees
Credit Union**
213 Kentucky St,
Knoxville TN 37915-
1240. 423/523-1208.

**USTC Employees
Credit Union**
800 Harrison St,

Nashville TN 37203-
3336. 615/244-5270.

**WCQ Employees
Credit Union**
P.O. Box 284, Martin
TN 38237-0284.
901/587-9521.

Weavexx Credit Union
P.O. Box 1030,
Greeneville TN 37744-
1030. 423/639-1187.

**OFFICES OF BANK
HOLDING
COMPANIES**

CB&T Inc.
101 W Main St,
McMinnville TN
37110-2515.
615/473-5561.

**Community
Bancshares Inc.**
2175 S Germantown
Rd #104,
Germantown TN
38138-3857.
901/755-6067.

For more information on career opportunities in the banking/savings and loans industry:

Associations

**AMERICA'S COMMUNITY
BANKERS**
900 19th Street NW, Suite 400,
Washington DC 20006. 202/857-
3100. A trade association
representing the expanded thrift
industry. Members are institutions
(not individuals).

**AMERICAN BANKERS
ASSOCIATION**
1120 Connecticut Avenue NW,
Washington DC 20036. 202/663-
5221. Provides banking education
and training services, sponsors
industry programs and
conventions, and publishes
articles, newsletters, and the ABA
Service Member Directory.

Directories

AMERICAN BANK DIRECTORY
Thomson Financial Publications,
6195 Crooked Creek Road,
Norcross GA 30092. 770/448-
1011.

**AMERICAN SAVINGS
DIRECTORY**
McFadden Business Publications,
6195 Crooked Creek Road,
Norcross GA 30092. 770/448-
1011.

**BUSINESS WEEK/TOP 200
BANKING INSTITUTIONS ISSUE**
McGraw-Hill, Inc., 1221 Avenue
of the Americas, 39th Floor, New
York NY 10020. 212/512-4776.

**MOODY'S BANK AND FINANCE
MANUAL**
Moody's Investors Service, Inc.,
99 Church Street, First Floor,

New York NY 10007. 212/553-0300.

POLK'S BANK DIRECTORY
R.L. Polk & Co., P.O. Box 305100, Nashville TN 37320-5100. 615/889-3350.

RANKING THE BANKS/THE TOP NUMBERS
American Banker, Inc., 1 State Street Plaza, New York NY 10004. 212/943-6700.

Magazines

ABA BANKING JOURNAL
American Bankers Association, 1120 Connecticut Avenue NW, Washington DC 20036. 202/663-5221.

BANK ADMINISTRATION
1 North Franklin, Chicago IL 60606. 800/323-8552.

BANKERS MAGAZINE
Warren, Gorham & Lamont, Park Square Building, 31 St. James Avenue, Boston MA 02116-4112. 617/423-2020.

JOURNAL OF COMMERCIAL BANK LENDING
Robert Morris Associates, P.O. Box 8500 S-1140, Philadelphia PA 19178. 215/851-9100.

BIOTECHNOLOGY, PHARMACEUTICALS, AND SCIENTIFIC R&D

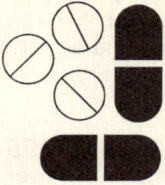

During the early '90s, the pharmaceutical industry was characterized by a mass of mergers and acquisitions, with drug companies concentrating on cutting costs to boost profit margins.

While more mergers may be on the way, most of the big staff cuts are history, and profitability is up. Even so, industry watchers don't expect the arrival of many big-selling new products in the near future, and many companies have slashed research and development budgets. According to the Pharmaceutical Research and Manufacturers of America, the 8 percent growth in R&D spending was the lowest in 20 years.

As more drug patents continue to expire, the impact will be felt by large pharmaceutical companies. There will be a negative impact on their sales growth. Conversely, the expired patents mean more opportunities for generic drug manufacturers, who should continue to gain market share through 1996.

GALBRAITH LABORATORIES, INC.
2323 Sycamore Drive, Knoxville TN 37921. 423/546-1335. **Fax:** 423/546-7209. **Contact:** Sherry McCreary, Manager of Human Resources. **Description:** Galbraith Laboratories, Inc. is the world's largest microanalytical laboratory. Since 1950, the lab has run over six million sample analyses on over a million and a half samples. Galbraith's operations include 300,000 tests and 60,000 quality control checks annually; 70 chemists, technicians and support personnel; 17,000 square feet of laboratory space; and 500 available procedures. For over 40 years, Galbraith has been providing expert laboratory services to all segments of industry, government, and the academic world. The company serves over 3,500 industrial firms, research foundations, government agencies, and universities, including 60 of the 100 largest U.S. corporations. Galbraith provides a full range of services to help meet as many client testing needs as possible in one lab -- from fast turnaround/high volume to highly specialized analysis. These services include analysis for all elements, trace analyses, physical property testing, environmental testing, compendium methods, and assays. Industry specific expertise includes pharmaceuticals, pulp and paper, plastics, environmental testing, agriculture, chemicals, petroleum, textiles, and mining, among others.

NATIONAL PSYCHOPHARMACOLOGY LABORATORY
9320 Park West Boulevard, Knoxville TN 37923. 423/690-8101. **Contact:** Associate Director. **Description:** National Psychopharmacology Laboratory (NPL) was established in 1978 as the first specialty laboratory to combine psychopharmacology and drug detection with the highest level of experience and a complete database. NPL is the nation's oldest on-site manager of psychiatric and addictionology laboratory services. The company offers assistance in program development, documentation for accreditation,

quality control support and data utilization. The company also provides on-site coordination, including phlebotomy service. NPL believes that it has set the benchmarks for every psychoactive compound since 1978. NPL is supported by a staff of scientists and clinicians in the specialties of psychiatry, psychopharmocology, toxicology, clinical pharmacy, addictionology and clinical chemistry. The company was the first to develop clinical assays for Prozac, Zoloft, Haldol, Mellaril, Navane, MHPG, Serentil, Clozaril, Paxil, and Stelazine.

NATIONAL REFERENCE LABORATORY
1400 Donelson Pike, Suite B10, Nashville TN 37217. 615/399-0713. **Contact:** Deborah Martin, Human Resources Manager. **Description:** A blood reference laboratory.

OAK RIDGE RESEARCH INSTITUTE (ORRI)
113 Union Valley Road, Oak Ridge TN 37830. 423/481-5000. **Contact:** Director. **Description:** ORRI does biomonitoring for the City of Oak Ridge, including radiological isotope analysis, environmental bioremediation, and asbestos analysis.

SCHERING-PLOUGH
3030 Jackson Avenue, P.O. Box 377, Memphis TN 38151. 901/320-2011. **Contact:** Beverly Daniels, Personnel, Administration & EEOC Manager. **Description:** Offices of the manufacturer of sun care products and laxatives. **Number of employees nationwide:** 2,000.

WEST END DIAGNOSTIC IMAGING
2611 West End Avenue, Suite 101, Nashville TN 37203. 615/320-7374. **Contact:** Human Resources. **Description:** A subdivision of St. Thomas Hospital specializing in diagnostic tests and imaging.

Note: Because addresses and telephone numbers of smaller companies change rapidly, we recommend you call each company to verify the information below before inquiring about job opportunities. Mass mailings are not recommended.

Additional employers with under 250 employees:

MEDICAL AND DENTAL LABORATORIES

Roche Biomedical Labs Inc.
9220 Park West Blvd, Knoxville TN 37923-4405. 423/531-6464.

Smithkline Beecham Clinic Labs
311 Princeton Rd,
Johnson City TN 37601-2046. 423/283-4342.

Mynatt Dental Laboratories
1303 Carter St, Chattanooga TN 37402-4412. 423/266-2713.

DRUGS, DRUG PROPRIETARIES, AND

DRUGGISTS' SUNDRIES

Chapman Drug Company Inc.
P.O. Box 50105, Knoxville TN 37950-0105. 423/522-3161.

NSS Inc.
556 Metroplex Dr, Nashville TN 37211-3133. 615/833-7530.

For more information on career opportunities in biotechnology, pharmaceuticals, and scientific R&D:

Associations

AMERICAN ASSOCIATION FOR CLINICAL CHEMISTRY
2101 L Street NW, Suite 202, Washington DC 20037-1526. 202/857-0717 or 800/892-1400. International scientific/medical society of individuals involved with clinical chemistry and other clinical labscience-related disciplines.

AMERICAN ASSOCIATION OF COLLEGES OF PHARMACY
1426 Prince Street, Alexandria VA 22314-2841. 703/739-2330. An organization composed of all U.S. pharmacy colleges and over 2,000 school administrators and faculty members. Career publications include: *Shall I Study Pharmacy?*, *Pharmacy: A Caring Profession*, and *A Graduate Degree in the Pharmaceutical Sciences: An Option For You?*

AMERICAN COLLEGE OF CLINICAL PHARMACY (ACCP)
3101 Broadway, Suite 380, Kansas City MO 64111. 816/531-2177. Operates ClinNet jobline at 412/648-7893 for both members and nonmembers, for a fee.

AMERICAN PHARMACEUTICAL ASSOCIATION
2215 Constitution Avenue NW, Washington DC 20037. 202/628-4410. Operates a resume referral service for all members.

AMERICAN SOCIETY FOR BIOCHEMISTRY AND MOLECULAR BIOLOGY
9650 Rockville Pike, Bethesda MD 20814-3996. 301/530-7145. A nonprofit scientific and educational organization whose primary scientific activities are in the publication of the *Journal of Biological Chemistry* and holding an annual scientific meeting. Also publishes a career brochure entitled *Unlocking Life's Secrets: Biochemistry and Molecular Biology*.

AMERICAN SOCIETY OF HEALTH SYSTEM PHARMACISTS
7272 Wisconsin Avenue, Bethesda MD 20814. 301/657-3000. Provides pharmaceutical education. Updates pharmacies on current medical developments. Offers a service for jobseekers for a fee.

BIOMEDICAL RESEARCH INSTITUTE
355 K Street, Chula Vista CA 91911-1209. 619/427-9940. Fax: 619/427-2634. A nonprofit organization which promotes scientific research and education and provides annual scholarships to students. Maintains a national Institutional Review Board.

BIOTECHNOLOGY INDUSTRY ORGANIZATION
1625 K Street NW, Suite 1100, Washington DC 20006-1604. 202/857-0244. Fax: 202/857-0237. Represents agriculture, biomedical, diagnostic, food, energy, and environmental companies.

NATIONAL PHARMACEUTICAL COUNCIL
1894 Preston White Drive, Reston VA 22091. 703/620-6390. Fax: 703/476-0904. An organization of research-based pharmaceutical companies. Fax requests to the attention of Pat Adams, Vice President of Finance and Administration.

Magazines

DRUG TOPICS
Medical Economics Company, 5 Paragon Drive, Montvale NJ 07645. 201/358-7200.

PHARMACEUTICAL ENGINEERING
International Society of Pharmaceutical Engineers, 3816 West Linebaugh Avenue, Suite 412, Tampa FL 33624. 813/960-2105.

BUSINESS SERVICES AND NON-SCIENTIFIC RESEARCH

The business services sector, which includes 16 of the 20 fastest growing industries, covers a broad spectrum of careers, including everything from adjustment and collection services to data processing companies. While the job outlook varies upon which service is being discussed, in general, the business services sector is among the fastest-growing in the nation. Increasingly, American companies are "outsourcing" functions like data processing to outside firms. Often large organizations will go so far as to hand over the management of their entire data center to an outside service provider. This trend is expected to boost opportunities for those who work for data processing services.

Other types of services that benefit from this trend include security firms and personnel services firms. Many businesses are using temporary workers instead of hiring new permanent staffers, thus avoiding the much higher overhead costs such as health insurance. Companies that supply these temporary workers, as well as those that place permanent workers, are among the fastest-growing in the nation. While one third of the jobs available are administrative support occupations, there is a growing trend toward specialization which will open up more positions for highly-skilled workers, such as engineers or managers.

ADVANCED COMPUTER ENTERPRISES
P.O. Box 4759, Maryville TN 37802. 615/982-0116. **Contact:** Human Resources. **Description:** Performs computer processing functions for financial institutions.

ANALYSAS CORPORATION
151 Lafayette Drive, Suite 310, Oak Ridge TN 37830. 423/576-1650. **Contact:** Susie Jimerson, Human Resources. **Description:** Provides technical and administrative support in areas such as program management, environmental regulatory analysis, waste management technology development, technical writing and editing, graphic arts, and word processing.

COMDATA HOLDINGS CORPORATION
5301 Maryland Way, Brentwood TN 37027. 615/370-7000. **Contact:** Amanda Kraus, Director of Human Resources. **Description:** Provides transaction processing and information services to the transportation, gaming, and retail industries. Comdata links more than 20,000 telecommunication ports of entry, processing over 100 million transactions per year. Services for the transportation industry increase productivity and control for trucking companies and truck stops. Products encompass fuel purchase, cash advance, driver settlement, money transfer, load matching, route planning, legalization permitting, fuel tax reporting, and management reporting. Comdata's consumer services include money transfer for emergencies or leisure activities. The company helps gaming

organizations adapt to new technologies such as smart cards, linked progressive slot machines, and player tracking systems. Retail services include a check acceptance network to shorten customer checkout time and reduce losses from returned checks. An integrated payment system combines check acceptance and credit and debit card approval into a single, in-lane system. **Common positions include:** Accountant/Auditor; Administrator; Advertising Clerk; Attorney; Buyer; Claim Representative; Commercial Artist; Computer Programmer; Credit Manager; Customer Service Representative; Department Manager; Financial Analyst; General Manager; Human Resources Specialist; Management Trainee; Marketing Specialist; Operations/Production Manager; Purchasing Agent and Manager; Services Sales Representative; Systems Analyst. **Educational backgrounds include:** Accounting; Business Administration; Communications; Computer Science; Finance; Liberal Arts; Marketing. **Corporate headquarters location:** This Location. **Other locations:** Toronto, Canada; Los Angeles CA; Denver CO; Atlanta GA; Cincinnati OH; Dallas TX. **Operations at this facility include:** Administration; Sales; Service. **Listed on:** NASDAQ. **Number of employees nationwide:** 1,800.

CORRECTIONS CORPORATION OF AMERICA

102 Woodmont Boulevard, Nashville TN 37205. 615/292-3100. **Fax:** 615/269-8635. **Contact:** Shirley Harbison, Human Resources. **Description:** Corrections Corporation of America is one of the leading private-sector providers of detention and corrections services to federal, state, and local governments. The company's subsidiary, Corrections Corporation International, furnishes similar services abroad. The company designs, finances, constructs, renovates, and manages new or existing facilities, as well as provides escort and court services and long-distance transportation of inmates. Its expertise covers adult and juvenile offenders at all levels of security classification.

DUN & BRADSTREET INFORMATION SERVICES

565 Marriott Drive, Suite 225, Nashville TN 37214. 615/883-2168. **Contact:** Human Resources. **Description:** Dun & Bradstreet is a seller of business information and related services. Major divisions include: Marketing Information Services, which offers research, information, and evaluation services; Risk Management and Business Marketing Information Services, which provides risk assessment information in 34 countries, publishes financial documents and debt ratings, and offers credit insurance, collection, and debt management; Software Services; and Directory Information Services, publishing 35 telephone company business directories. **Corporate headquarters location:** New York, NY. **Listed on:** New York Stock Exchange.

DUN & BRADSTREET INFORMATION SERVICES

6075 Poplar Avenue, Suite 401, Memphis TN 38119. 901/767-2300. **Contact:** Human Resources. **Description:** Dun & Bradstreet is a seller of business information and related services. Major divisions include: Marketing Information Services, which offers research, information, and evaluation services; Risk Management and Business Marketing Information Services, which provides risk assessment information in 34 countries, publishes financial documents and debt ratings, and offers credit insurance, collection, and debt management; Software Services; and Directory Information Services, publishing 35 telephone company business directories. **Corporate headquarters location:** New York, NY. **Listed on:** New York Stock Exchange.

GUARDSMARK, INC.

P.O. Box 45, Memphis TN 38101. 901/522-6000. **Contact:** Robert Oberman, Vice President of Human Resources. **Description:** Provides the following services: security, life safety, fire, protective, background screening, investigative, and consulting. **Listed on:** Privately held. **Number of employees at this location:** 700. **Number of employees nationwide:** 8,500.

INGRAM INDUSTRIES, INC.

4400 Harding Road, Nashville TN 37205. 615/298-8200. **Contact:** Michael Head, Vice President of Human Resources. **Description:** Offers transportation services, insurance, consumer products distribution services, and related services.

JEFFERSON-PILOT DATA SERVICES, INC.

785 Crossover Lane, Suite 141, P.O. Box 17469, Memphis TN 38187. 901/767-5230. **Contact:** Mr. Arch Martin, Regional Manager. **Description:** This location operates as part of the electronic data services sector of Jefferson-Pilot. Jefferson-Pilot is a holding company whose principal subsidiaries are Jefferson-Pilot Life Insurance Company, Jefferson-Pilot Fire and Casualty Company, and Jefferson-Pilot Title Insurance Company. The company also operates radio and television stations and produces televised sports programs.

MURRAY GUARD, INC.

58 Murray Guard Drive, Jackson TN 38305. 901/668-3400. **Contact:** Danny Underwood, Director of Personnel. **Description:** Provides security services for other corporations.

QUALITY COMPANIES, INC.

1991 Corporate Avenue, Memphis TN 38101. 901/395-8000. **Contact:** Human Resources. **Description:** Quality Companies, Inc. is engaged in the marketing of incentive programs for other companies, as well as individual and group travel programs.

Note: Because addresses and telephone numbers of smaller companies change rapidly, we recommend you call each company to verify the information below before inquiring about job opportunities. Mass mailings are not recommended.

Additional employers with under 250 employees:

LINEN SUPPLY

National Linen Service
1312 Louisiana St,
Memphis TN 38106-3924. 901/946-1691.

National Linen Service
2612 Western Ave,
Knoxville TN 37921-4530. 423/523-8118.

Initial USA Uniform & Linen Service
2302 Charlotte Ave,
Nashville TN 37203-1820. 615/320-7333.

Aratex Services Inc.
Tullahoma Highway,
Shelbyville TN 37160.
615/684-1123.

ADJUSTMENT AND COLLECTION SERVICES

ACB Business Services Inc.
136 Walton Ferry Rd,
Hendersonvlle TN 37075-3615.
615/822-5962.

Creditek Corp.
260 Cumberland Bnd,
Nashville TN 37228-
1804. 615/256-7001.

Medcol
28 White Bridge Rd,
Nashville TN 37205-
1428. 615/353-1060.

**CREDIT REPORTING
SERVICES**

**Credit Bureau of
Knoxville**
1014 Heiskell Ave,
Knoxville TN 37921-
1900. 423/544-1200.

**PHOTOCOPYING AND
DUPLICATING
SERVICES**

**Ameriscribe
Management Service
Inc.**
611 Commerce St,
Nashville TN 37203-
3742. 615/ 242-
0963.

**DISINFECTING AND
PEST CONTROL
SERVICES**

**Arrow-Mayfield Pest
Control**
3720 Amnicola Hwy,
Chattanooga TN
37406-1792.
423/629-7378.

**Cook's Pest Control
Inc.**
612 Ingleside Ave,
Athens TN 37303-
3770. 423/745-1011.

**Cook's Pest Control
Inc.**
4308 Middlebrook
Pike, Knoxville TN
37921-5539.
423/584-7700.

**Cook's Pest Control
Inc.**
47 Riverport Dr,
Jackson TN 38301-
5748. 901/424-3004.

**Cook's Pest Control
Inc.**
118 S 2nd St, Pulaski
TN 38478-3219.
615/363-1554.

**Orkin Exterminating
Co. Inc.**
2000 Highway 75,
Blountville TN 37617-
5831. 423/323-9801.

**Orkin Exterminating
Co. Inc.**
2104 Emory Rd W,
Powell TN 37849-
3790. 423/947-2233.

Spray's Pest Control
1001 Huntsville Hwy,
Fayetteville TN
37334-3441.
615/433-3353.

CH Heist Corp.
3700 Dickerson Rd,
Nashville TN 37207-
1316. 615/865-8381.

**Southeast Service
Corp.**
3126 Long Hollow
Pike, Hendersonvlle
TN 37075-8781.
615/824-8558.

**Southeast Service
Corp.**
301 E Jackson Ave,
Knoxville TN 37915-
1008. 423/546-8080.

**Wedgewood Towers
Maintenance**
1195 Wedgewood
Ave, Nashville TN
37203-5440.
615/383-6728.

**COMPUTER
PROCESSING AND
DATA PREPARATION
SERVICES**

Envoy Corp.
15 Century Blvd, Suite
600, Nashville TN
37214-3692.
615/885-3700.

Cad Lab
569 Stewarts Ferry
Pike, Nashville TN

37214-3414.
615/871-7294.

Decision Data
1410 Donelson Pike,
Nashville TN 37217-
2933. 615/399-2084.

Datamark America
236 Stewarts Ferry
Pike Ofc, Nashville TN
37214-3382.
615/889-5711.

**Innovative Computing
Corp.**
2851 Stage Village
Cv, Memphis TN
38134-4683.
901/385-0927.

SMS
3 Maryland Farms,
Suite 118, Brentwood
TN 37027-5005.
615/377-1244.

**DETECTIVE, GUARD,
AND ARMORED CAR
SERVICES**

**Vinson Guard Service
Inc.**
2008 E Magnolia Ave,
Knoxville TN 37917-
8026. 423/525-5047.

Wackenhut Security
4295 Cromwell Rd,
Chattanooga TN
37421-2166.
423/899-0605.

GuardCo.
2670 Union Avenue
Ext, Memphis TN
38112-4416.
901/458-1294.

**Tri-State Security
Agency**
4510 Hixson Pike,
Hixson TN 37343-
5039. 423/877-6600.

**Pinkerton Security
Services**
5800 Bldg,
Chattanooga TN
37411. 423/894-
5248.

Pinkerton Security & Investigation Service
295 Plus Park Blvd, Suite 102, Nashville TN 37217-1027. 615/367-1306.

Wells Fargo Guard Services
1838 Elm Hill Pike, Nashville TN 37210-3726. 615/885-9536.

A Able Detective Service
2555 Poplar Ave, Memphis TN 38112-3850. 901/454-0668.

Investigations Unlimited
9158 Westminister Cir, Chattanooga TN 37416-1525. 423/344-6765.

APB Investigations Inc.
9114 Hundley Rd, Chattanooga TN 37416-1517. 423/344-7177.

One Stop Investigations
4713 Robinwood Dr, Chattanooga TN 37416-3111. 423/499-9293.

MISC. BUSINESS SERVICES

STS Inc.
6047 Executive Centre Dr, Suite 3, Memphis TN 38134-7633. 901/382-5781.

Lynn Feathers Interiors
103 N Center St,

Collierville TN 38017-2615. 901/854-6079.

King & Ballow
220 4th Ave N, Nashville TN 37219-2102. 615/259-3456.

Mail Boxes Etc.
622 W Poplar Ave, Suite 5, Collierville TN 38017-2578. 901/853-1530.

Commercial Carriers Inc.
3585 Knight Arnold Rd, Memphis TN 38118-2736. 901/362-0870.

Calgon Corp.
322 Nancy Lynn Ln, Knoxville TN 37919-6054. 423/558-3043.

For more information on career opportunities in miscellaneous business services and non-scientific research:

Associations

AMERICAN SOCIETY OF APPRAISERS
P.O. Box 17265, Washington DC 20041. 703/478-2228. Toll-free number: 800/ASA-VALU. Fax: 703/742-8471. An international, nonprofit, independent appraisal organization. ASA teaches, tests, and awards designations.

EQUIPMENT LEASING ASSOCIATION OF AMERICA
1300 17th Street, Suite 1010,

North Arlington VA 22209. 703/527-8655.

NATIONAL ASSOCIATION OF PERSONNEL SERVICES
3133 Mt. Vernon Avenue, Alexandria VA 22305. 703/684-0180. Fax: 703/684-0071. Provides federal legislative protection, education, certification, and business products and services to its member employment service agencies.

CHARITIES AND SOCIAL SERVICES

The outlook for social service workers is better than average. In fact, opportunities for qualified applicants are expected to be excellent, partly due to the rapid turnover in the industry as a result of lower wages offered.

Note: Because of the high turnover rate and the continuous need for social services, the outlook for this industry has remained constant over the past few years.

AMERICAN RED CROSS
410 West Lytle Street, Murfreesboro TN 37130-3667. 615/893-4272. **Contact:** Human Resources. **Description:** American Red Cross' services include diaster relief, CPR training, and blood donations.

CHILDREN'S COMPREHENSIVE SERVICES, INC. (CCS)
805 South Church Street, P.O. Box 8, Murfreesboro TN 37133-0008. 615/896-3100. **Fax:** 615/986-5068. **Contact:** Lorri Wilson, Office Manager. **Description:** Children's Comprehensive Services, Inc. (CCS) provides a comprehensive array of education and treatment services for at-risk youth. CCS offers these services through the operation and management of special education schools, and both open and secured treatment centers for local, state, and federal government agencies in Alabama, California, Louisiana, and Tennessee. The company also provides management and marketing services to Helicon, Inc., a not-for-profit corporation which provides related services in California and Tennessee. CCS is one of the largest for-profit providers of these services in the United States.

MULTIPLE SCLEROSIS SOCIETY
6324 Papermill Road, Knoxville TN 37919. 423/558-8686. **Contact:** Human Resources. **Description:** A national nonprofit organization providing services such as health care equipment and financial aid.

MULTIPLE SCLEROSIS SOCIETY
6100 Building, Eastgate Center, Suite 4800, Chattanooga TN 37411. 423/954-9700. **Contact:** Sally Reeve, Human Resources. **Description:** A national nonprofit organization providing services such as health care equipment and financial aid.

OPPORTUNITY HOUSE
652 West Iris Drive, Nashville TN 37204-3121. 615/292-1657. **Contact:** Human Resources. **Description:** A half-way house for convicted felons.

THE SALVATION ARMY
140 North First Street, Nashville TN 37207-5929. 615/259-2348. **Contact:** Human Resources. **Description:** Nationwide, the Salvation Army offers services such as food, medical attention, and daycare for the homeless. **World Wide Web address:** http://www.winkcomm.com/saweb/home.htm.

Note: Because addresses and telephone numbers of smaller companies change rapidly, we recommend you call each company to verify the information below before inquiring about job opportunities. Mass mailings are not recommended.

Additional employers with under 250 employees:

JOB TRAINING AND VOCATIONAL REHABILITATION SERVICES

Northern Tennesee Private Industry Council
121 Waverly Plz, Waverly TN 37185-1531. 615/296-5872.

MISC. SOCIAL SERVICES

Hiwassee Mental Health Center
2600 Executive Park NW, Cleveland TN 37312-2720. 423/339-5920.

TN Opportunity Programs
115 Main Ave N, Fayetteville TN 37334-3055. 615/433-7487.

Youth Villages
148 Shipley St, Cookeville TN 38501-3458. 615/528-9771.

For more information on career opportunities in charities and social services:

Associations

AMERICAN COUNCIL OF THE BLIND
1155 15th Street NW, Suite 720, Washington DC 20005. 202/467-5081. Membership. Offers an annual conference, a monthly magazine, and scholarships.

CATHOLIC CHARITIES USA
1731 King Street, Suite 200, Alexandria VA 22314. 703/549-1390. Membership.

FAMILY SERVICE ASSOCIATION OF AMERICA
11700 West Lake Park Drive, Park Place, Milwaukee WI 53224. 414/359-1040. Membership.

NATIONAL COUNCIL ON FAMILY RELATIONS
3989 Central Avenue NE, Suite 550, Minneapolis MN 55421. 612/781-9331. Fax: 612/781-9348. Membership. Publishes two quarterly journals. Offers an annual conference and newsletters.

NATIONAL FEDERATION OF SOCIETIES FOR CLINICAL SOCIAL WORK, INC.
P.O. Box 3740, Arlington VA 22203. 703/522-3866. A lobbying organization. Offers newsletters and a conference every two years to membership organizations.

NATIONAL FEDERATION OF THE BLIND
1800 Johnson Street, Baltimore MD 21230. 410/659-9314. Membership of 50,000 in 600 local chapters. Publishes a monthly magazine.

NATIONAL MULTIPLE SCLEROSIS SOCIETY
733 Third Avenue, New York NY 10017. 212/986-3240. Toll-free: 800/344-4867. Publishes a quarterly magazine.

NATIONAL ORGANIZATION FOR HUMAN SERVICE EDUCATION
Brookdale Community College, Newman Springs Road, Lyncroft NJ 07738. 908/842-1900, ext. 546.

CHEMICALS/RUBBER AND PLASTICS

First the good news: Overall growth in the chemical industry is on the upswing. Chemical products and services are currently in high demand, thus creating a need for more workers, and recent price increases are holding steady.

Now the bad news: Costs for pollution reduction are rising. Factories are running at 85 percent capacity, and if companies increase spending on plant and equipment, an oversupply could result if economic growth slows too quickly.

Growth prospects for the domestic synthetic rubber industry remain mixed, reflecting the industry's dependence on tire manufacturing. The tire industry shows signs of stabilizing after undergoing a period characterized by massive restructuring, the effects of recession in the domestic market, and consistently high levels of imports.

In the plastics industry, greater reliance on computer-aided design and manufacturing is expected in the last half of the 1990s, as production is streamlined. These measures will be aimed at strengthening the industry's competitiveness in the areas of quality control and improved client relations.

ACE PRODUCTS INC.
850 Industrial Road, Newport TN 37821. 423/623-6025. **Contact:** Christine Williams, Personnel Manager. **Description:** Ace Products Inc. manufactures tires. **Common positions include:** Blue-Collar Worker Supervisor; Buyer; Chemist; Computer Programmer; Customer Service Representative; Department Manager; Draftsperson; General Manager; Human Resources Specialist; Industrial Agent/Broker; Manufacturer's/Wholesaler's Sales Rep.; Mechanical Engineer; Operations/Production Manager; Quality Control Supervisor. **Educational backgrounds include:** Business Administration; Chemistry; Engineering; Marketing. **Special Programs:** Training Programs. **Corporate headquarters location:** Los Angeles CA. **Operations at this facility include:** Manufacturing; Research and Development; Sales.

ARCADIAN PARTNERS
6750 Poplar Avenue, #600, Memphis TN 38138. 901/758-5200. **Contact:** Wanda Weeks, Manager of Human Resources. **Description:** Arcadian Partners, a master limited partnership, is an international producer and marketer of nitrogen fertilizers and chemicals used in agricultural and industrial applications. The partnership's principal products are ammonia, urea, ammonium nitrate, nitric acid, and nitrogen solutions. Ammonia, urea, and ammonium nitrate are sold to agricultural customers as fertilizers and to industrial customers as intermediate chemical feedstocks. Nitric acid is sold to industrial customers. Nitrogen solutions are the partnership's most versatile fertilizer products. Arcadian Partners' sales mix is favorably balanced with approximately 60 percent of sales to agricultural customers and 40 percent to industrial customers. With eight plants strategically located throughout the Midwest, the South, along the East Coast,

and in Trinidad, the partnership has easy access and low distribution costs to most U.S. agricultural and industrial markets east of the Rocky Mountains. In addition, the Trinidad plant is well-situated to serve Latin American and other world markets. **Corporate headquarters location:** This Location. **Listed on:** New York Stock Exchange.

BOSTON INDUSTRIAL PRODUCTS
P.O. Box 500, Hohenwald TN 38462. 615/796-3272. **Contact:** Human Resources. **Description:** Produces rubber hose for a variety of industrial purposes. **Parent company:** Dana Corporation.

BOSTON INDUSTRIAL PRODUCTS
P.O. Box 1708, Brentwood TN 37024. 615/377-6700. **Contact:** Norma Bowman, Manager of Human Resources. **Description:** Produces rubber hose, sheets, and conveyor belts for a variety of industrial purposes. **Parent company:** Dana Corporation.

BRIDGESTONE/FIRESTONE, INC.
One Bridgestone Park, P.O. Box 140991, Nashville TN 37214-0991. 615/391-0088. **Fax:** 615/872-2628. **Contact:** Human Resources. **Description:** Primarily engaged in the development, manufacture, and sale of a broad line of tires for the original equipment and replacement markets of the world. Manages its business through three primary operating groups: the World Tire Group is responsible for the design, development, testing, and manufacturing of tires throughout the world; the Sales and Marketing Group is a nationwide sales network which includes dealer outlets and automotive service centers; and the Corporate Development Group is responsible for corporate strategic planning activities. This location is a corporate marketing and sales headquarters for Bridgestone and Firestone tires. **Common positions include:** Accountant/Auditor; Clerical Supervisor; Computer Programmer; Computer Systems Analyst; Credit Manager; Customer Service Representative; Economist/Market Research Analyst; Education Administrator; Electrical/Electronics Engineer; Financial Analyst; Human Resources Specialist; Industrial Engineer; Manufacturer's/Wholesaler's Sales Rep.; Mechanical Engineer. **Educational backgrounds include:** Accounting; Business Administration; Communications; Computer Science; Engineering; Finance; Marketing. **Benefits:** 401K; Dental Insurance; Disability Coverage; Employee Discounts; Life Insurance; Medical Insurance; Pension Plan; Savings Plan; Tuition Assistance. **Special Programs:** Internships. **Operations at this facility include:** Divisional Headquarters; Marketing; Sales. **Number of employees at this location:** 360. **Number of employees nationwide:** 2,000.

BRYCE CORPORATION
4650 Shelby Air, Suite 1, Memphis TN 38118. 901/369-4400. **Contact:** Len Swett, Human Resources Manager. **Description:** A manufacturer of flexible packaging for snack foods and other products. Packaging is converted from plastic films.

C.C.L. CUSTOM MANUFACTURING INC.
1725 Third Street, Memphis TN 38109-7711. 901/947-5400. **Contact:** Human Resources. **Description:** Manufactures aerosols, fragrances, cosmetics, and toiletries.

CHATTEM, INC.

1715 West 38th Street, Chattanooga TN 37409. 423/821-7571. **Contact:** Matthew Brown, Personnel Director. **Description:** Chattem, Inc. and its wholly owned subsidiaries are primarily engaged in manufacturing and marketing branded consumer products and specialty chemicals. The consumer products are sold nationwide and in many international markets, primarily through independent and chain drug stores, drug wholesalers, mass merchandisers and food stores. Specialty chemicals are sold primarily to other manufacturing companies. Chattem, Inc. operates through the following divisions: Chattem Consumer Products, which include over the counter pharmaceuticals, cosmetics and toiletries; Chattem Chemicals, which include aluminum hydroxides, aluminum derivitives, glycine, and new product development operations; and Chattem International, which directs the international sales of Chattem Consumer Products. **Corporate headquarters location:** This Location.

COLONIAL RUBBER WORKS INC.

P.O. Box 807, Dyersburg TN 38025. 901/285-4353. **Contact:** Donny Brown, Manager of Human Resources. **Description:** Manufactures rubber compounds and sponge rubber moldings for gaskets and seals, as well as some plastic products.

CROSSVILLE RUBBER, INC.

P.O. Box 729, Crossville TN 38557. 615/484-5187. **Contact:** Department of Interest. **Description:** A manufacturer of rubber floor coverings for automotive original equipment, automotive aftermarket, and automotive replacements; and industrial rubber mats (i.e. welcome, kitchen, anti-fatigue, etc.) for over 35 years. This location is a union facility. **Common positions include:** Accountant/Auditor; Administrator; Blue-Collar Worker Supervisor; Buyer; Chemical Engineer; Chemist; Computer Programmer; Customer Service Representative; Department Manager; Electrical/Electronics Engineer; General Manager; Human Resources Specialist; Industrial Engineer; Management Trainee; Manufacturer's/Wholesaler's Sales Rep.; Mechanical Engineer; Operations/Production Manager; Purchasing Agent and Manager; Quality Control Supervisor. **Educational backgrounds include:** Business Administration; Chemistry; Computer Science; Engineering. **Benefits:** Dental Insurance; Disability Coverage; Life Insurance; Medical Insurance; Pension Plan; Profit Sharing; Tuition Assistance. **Special Programs:** Internships; Training Programs. **Corporate headquarters location:** This Location. **Operations at this facility include:** Administration; Manufacturing; Sales. **Listed on:** Privately held. **Number of employees nationwide:** 310.

DH COMPOUNDING COMPANY

1260 Carden Farm Road, P.O. Box 70, Clinton TN 37716. 423/457-1200. **Contact:** Marshall Lenne, Human Resources Director. **Description:** Producers of customized thermoplastic resins.

DAYCO PRODUCTS

1921 North Broad Street, Lexington TN 38351. 901/968-4281. **Contact:** Human Resources. **Description:** Manufactures rubber hoses for automotive, industrial, garden, hydraulic, and metal products.

DICO TIRE INC.
A SUBSIDIARY OF DYNEER CORPORATION
520 J.D. Yarnell Industrial Parkway, Clinton TN 37716. **Contact:** Mark Bright, Director of Human Resources. **Description:** Dico Tire is a developer, manufacturer, and marketer of selected types of industrial tires. Industrial tires and related services are provided for use by outdoor power, recreational, industrial, material handling, and light construction vehicle producers and end users.

EASTMAN CHEMICAL COMPANY
P.O. Box 1975, Kingsport TN 37662-9901. 423/229-4180. **Fax:** 423/224-0995. **Contact:** Ellen Payton, Personnel Representative. **Description:** Eastman Chemical Company is an international chemical company offering a broad line of plastic, chemical, and fiber products. Eastman is among the leading chemical companies in the United States and is a world leader in polyester plastics for packaging applications. The company is also a leading supplier of cellulose acetate filter tow (used in the manufacture of cigarette filters), as well as a leader in the coatings and fine chemicals markets. Eastman has a commanding position in many smaller markets, and is a leader in developing new uses for recycled polyester plastics. **Common positions include:** Accountant/Auditor; Chemical Engineer; Chemist; Computer Systems Analyst; Electrical/Electronics Engineer; Industrial Engineer; Mechanical Engineer; Metallurgical Engineer. **Educational backgrounds include:** Accounting; Chemistry; Computer Science; Engineering. **Benefits:** 401K; Dental Insurance; Disability Coverage; Employee Discounts; ESOP; Life Insurance; Medical Insurance; Pension Plan; Profit Sharing; Savings Plan; Tuition Assistance. **Special Programs:** Internships. **Corporate headquarters location:** This Location. **Other U.S. locations:** Batesville AK; Charlotte NC; Columbia SC; Longview TX. **Operations at this facility include:** Administration; Divisional Headquarters; Manufacturing; Research and Development; Sales; Service. **Listed on:** New York Stock Exchange. **Number of employees at this location:** 12,000. **Number of employees nationwide:** 18,500.

FOAMEX INTERNATIONAL, INC.
328 Hamblen Avenue, Morristown TN 37813. 423/581-8350. **Contact:** Brenda Blankenship, Human Resources Manager. **Description:** A manufacturer of flexible polyurethane foam. Products are classified into five groups: cushioning foams, carpet cushion foams, automotive foams, technical foams, and home comfort foams. Cushion foams are used for mattresses, quilting and borders, home and office furniture, computer and electronics packaging, and padding for health care. Customers include mattress manufacturers Sealy, Serta, Simmons, and Spring Air; furniture manufacturers Action Furniture Industries, Berkline, Ethan Allen, and La-Z-Boy; specialized packaging users Apple Computer, CompUSA, Hewlett-Packard, and Seagate Technology; and health care companies Invacare, Medline, Span America, and Sunrise Medical. Foamex manufactures classes of carpet cushion including prime, bonded, sponge rubber, and felt carpet cushion, synthetic grass turf, and a variety of textured carpeting and wallcovering. Customers include Color Tile, Carpetland USA, New York Carpets, Sears, and other floor covering distributors and retailers. Automotive foams include foams for cushioning and seating, acoustical foams, headliner foams, trim foams, and foams for door panel parts. Customers include Ford,

Chrysler, General Motors, Honda, Nissan, and Toyota. Technical foams include those for filtration, reservoiring, sound absorption and transmission, carburetors, high-speed inkjet printers, speaker grilles, oxygenators, and EKG pads, as well as cosmetic applicators, mop heads, paint brushes, and diapers. Customers include the AC Division of GM, Briggs & Stratton, and Hewlett-Packard. Home Comfort products include mattress pads, pillows, decorative bedding products, and draperies. Customers include Kmart, Montgomery Ward, Sears, Target, Allied, Federated Stores, JCPenney, Macy's, The May Company, Spiegel, and Toys-R-Us. **Corporate headquarters location:** East Providence RI. **Other U.S. locations:** Phoenix AZ; City of Industry CA; Fresno CA; Hayward CA; La Mirada CA; Ontario CA; Orange CA; Pico Rivera CA; San Bernardino CA; Union City CA; West Sacramento CA; Denver CO; Hialeah FL; Hialeah Gardens FL; Opa Locka FL; Orlando FL; Tampa FL; Athens GA; Conyers GA; Dalton GA; Boise ID; Chicago IL; Auburn IN; Elkhart IN; Ft. Wayne IN; La Porte IN; Loogootee IN; Southfield MI; Cape Girardeau MO; Verona MS; Conover NC; Cornelius NC; High Point NC; Monroe NC; Richfield NC; Omaha NE; Saddle Brook NJ; Santa Teresa NM; Sparks NV; Arcade NY; New York NY; Columbus OH; Tigard OR; Corry PA; Eddystone PA; Fairless Hills PA; Philadelphia PA; Williamsport PA; Rock Hill SC; Cookeville TN; Milan TN; New Tazewell TN; Dallas TX; Mesquite TX; Salt Lake City UT; Kent WA; Manitowoc WI. **Number of employees nationwide:** 5,400.

GOODYEAR TIRE & RUBBER COMPANY
P.O. Box 570, Union City TN 38281. 901/885-2310. **Contact:** Gail Tatriac, Personnel. **Description:** Goodyear Tire & Rubber Company's principal business is the development, manufacturing, distribution, and sale of tires for most applications worldwide. Goodyear also manufactures and sells a broad spectrum of rubber products and rubber-related chemicals for various industrial and consumer markets and provides auto repair services. The company operates 32 plants in the United States, 42 plants in 29 other countries, and more than 1,800 retail tire and service centers and other distribution facilities around the globe. Strategic business units of Goodyear Tire & Rubber include: North American Tire; Kelly-Springfield, Goodyear Europe; Goodyear Latin America; Goodyear Asia; Engineered Products; Chemicals; Celeron; and Goodyear Racing. This location is a manufacturing plant.

W.R. GRACE & COMPANY
100 North Main Building, 17th Floor, Memphis TN 38103. 901/522-2000. **Contact:** Mr. L.E. Ingram, Division Manager. **Description:** This location produces anhydrous ammonia. Overall, W.R. Grace & Company is a diversified worldwide enterprise consisting of energy production and services, retailing, restaurants, and other businesses. The firm operates over 2,500 facilities in 47 states and 42 foreign countries and employs 80,000 people. **Corporate headquarters location:** New York NY.

KYZEN CORPORATION
430 Harding Industrial Drive, Nashville TN 37211. 615/831-0888. **Fax:** 615/831-0889. **Contact:** Human Resources. **Description:** Kyzen Corporation manufactures and markets chemical solutions and processes which do not contain ozone depleting products, for use in high-technology cleaning applications, including electronic

assemblies, precision metal, and plastic components. The company also manufactures and markets process water reuse machines used in these chemical cleaning applications, and offers integrated process support services. These products can be sold as a package, as a cleaning process or as separate items that can be integrated into the customer's cleaning process. The company's customers include Motorola, Delco Electronics, Intel, Lockheed Martin, Kyocera, Boeing, Ford, United Technologies, Rockwell, and Rayovac. Because industrial cleaning is one of the largest single applications of ozone depleting chemicals, Kyzen was organized to develop chemical solutions and processes to replace ozone depleting chemicals used in the cleaning of electronic assemblies and precision metal components.

PLASTIC INDUSTRIES INC.
P.O. Box 669, Athens TN 37371. 423/745-6213. **Contact:** Human Resources. **Description:** Plastic Industries Inc. is engaged in the injection molding of plastics. The company's primary products are furniture parts.

TEAM TECHNOLOGIES INC.
5949 Commerce Boulevard, Morristown TN 37814-1051. 423/587-2199. **Contact:** Nancy Henrikson, Director of Personnel. **Description:** Contract manufacturers for a variety of plastic products, including dental devices and business accessories.

TECHMER PM
One Quality Circle, Clinton TN 37716. 423/457-6700. **Contact:** Phil Parrot, Human Resources Director. **Description:** A manufacturer of custom colorants and additives for plastics and fibers.

TENNESSEE PLASTIC & ENGINEERING INC.
1414 Devens Drive, Brentwood TN 37027. 615/370-3279. **Contact:** Human Resources. **Description:** Provides plastics engineering for industrial customers.

VINYLEX CORPORATION
2636 Byington Solway Road, Knoxville TN 37931. 423/690-2211. **Contact:** Human Resources. **Description:** Engaged in custom plastic extrusion.

WESTERN RESERVE PRODUCTS INC.
435 Calvert Drive, Gallatin TN 37066. 615/451-9700. **Contact:** Cheri Reynolds, Manager of Human Resources. **Description:** Engaged in plastic injection-molding.

Note: Because addresses and telephone numbers of smaller companies change rapidly, we recommend you call each company to verify the information below before inquiring about job opportunities. Mass mailings are not recommended.

Additional employers with under 250 employees:

ALKALIES AND CHLORINE

Velsicol Chemical Corp.
1199 Warford St,
Memphis TN 38108-
3418. 901/324-4401.

INDUSTRIAL GASES

BOC Gases
4551 N Access Rd,
Chattanooga TN
37415-3816.
423/877-4387.

INDUSTRIAL INORGANIC CHEMICALS

ICI Acrylics Inc.
P.O. Box 13328,
Memphis TN 38113-
0328. 901/942-0787.

Primester
1801 Warrick Dr,
Kingsport TN 37660-
5555. 423/229-1514.

PLASTICS MATERIALS, SYNTHETICS, AND ELASTOMERS

ABC Technologies Inc.
400 Abc Blvd, Gallatin
TN 37066-3715.
615/451-1524.

Comalloy International Corp.
481 Allied Dr,
Nashville TN 37211-
3333. 615/333-3453.

Constar International
89 Eastley St,
Collierville TN 38017-
2735. 901/853-8586.

DH Compounding Co.
1260 Carden Farm Dr,
Clinton TN 37716-
4120. 423/457-1200.

Elm Packaging
5837 Distribution Dr,
Memphis TN 38141-
8204. 901/795-2711.

STS International
4721 Trousdale Dr,
Nashville TN 37220-
1322. 615/831-2326.

Tennessee Press Inc.
1501 Washington
Ave, Knoxville TN
37917-6804.
423/525-8349.

Variform Inc.
1274 Industrial Blvd,
Jasper TN 37347-
5200. 423/942-6033.

Burton Rubber Processing
P.O. Box 377,
Jonesborough TN
37659-0377.
423/753-2196.

CHEMICAL AGENTS, SULFONATED OILS, AND RELATED PRODUCTS

BASF Corp.
3805 Amnicola Hwy,
Chattanooga TN
37406-1004.
423/493-2700.

PAINTS, VARNISHES, AND RELATED PRODUCTS

Homecrest Corp.
P.O. Box 550, Clinton
TN 37717-0550.
423/457-9403.

Jeld-Wen of TN
P.O. Box 688, Sparta
TN 38583-0688.
615/738-3515.

The Gilman Company
801 Riverfront Pkwy,
Chattanooga TN
37402-1615.
423/756-5185.

United Paint Co.
404 E Mallory Ave,
Memphis TN 38109-
2597. 901/775-1315.

INDUSTRIAL ORGANIC CHEMICALS

Allied Color Industries Inc.
P.O. Box 278, Vonore
TN 37885-0278.
423/884-6625.

Alco Chemical
909 Mueller Ave,
Chattanooga TN
37406-1334.
423/629-1405.

Delta Foremost Chemical
3915 Air Park St,
Memphis TN 38118-
9018. 901/363-4340.

GLI
365 Chemwood Dr,
Newport TN 37821-
8150. 423/623-1584.

QO Chemicals Inc.
3324 Chelsea Ave,
Memphis TN 38108-
1909. 901/324-8851.

Rhone-Poulenc Basic Chemicals
4600 Centennial Blvd,
Nashville TN 37209-
1545. 615/269-3414.

Velsicol Chemical Corp.
4902 Central Ave,
Chattanooga TN
37410-2009.
423/825-8213.

WR Grace & Co.
4000 N Hawthorne St,
Chattanooga TN
37406-1300.
423/698-3461.

ADHESIVES AND SEALANTS

Ken-Koat of Tennessee
P.O. Box 2668,
Lewisburg TN 37091-
1668. 615/359-1616.

PRINTING INK

John H. Harland Co.
P.O. Box 428,
Nashville TN 37202-
0428. 615/641-2655.

Rock-Tenn Co.
302 Hartman Dr,
Lebanon TN 37087-
2520. 615/444-6250.

Textile Printing Co.
6107 Ringgold Rd,
East Ridge TN 37412-
3829. 423/894-1110

Union Camp Corp.
P.O. Box 645,
Morristown TN
37815-0645.
423/581-8650.

CHEMICALS AND CHEMICAL PREPARATIONS

HBD Industries Inc.
1 Industrial Ln, Oneida
TN 37841-9515.
423/569-6301.

Porelon Inc.
P.O. Box 2999,
Cookeville TN 38502-
2999. 615/432-4000.

TIRES AND INNER TUBES

Pulaski Rubber Co.
P.O. Box I, Pulaski TN
38478-0909.
615/363-5583.

Taylor Pittsburgh
7 Rocky Mountain Rd,
Athens TN 37303-
2903. 423/745-3110.

RUBBER PRODUCTS

Aero Pro Corp.
544 English Mountain
Rd, Newport TN
37821-6836.
423/623-8818.

Baxter Pharmaseal Laboratories
2301 Buffalo Rd,
Johnson City TN
37604-7439.
423/434-5400.

Faultless Caster Corp.
109 Kirby Dr, Portland
TN 37148-2004.
615/325-6706.

Vulcan Corp. Rubber Products Division
P.O. Box 709,
Clarksville TN 37041-
0709. 615/645-6431.

UNSUPPORTED PLASTICS PRODUCTS

Sequentia Inc.
450 Highway 368,
Grand Junction TN
38039-5500.
901/764-2153.

PLASTICS PRODUCTS

Volunteer Fabricators Inc.
221 E Main St,
Morristown TN
37814-4738.
423/581-2224.

Drexel Chemical Co.
P.O. Box 9306,
Memphis TN 38190-
0306. 901/774-4370.

Recticel Foam
P.O. Box 1955,
Morristown TN
37816-1955.
423/587-4470.

Bryan Custom Plastics
515 N Poplar St,
Kenton TN 38233-
1024. 901/749-5372.

Burcliff Industries Inc.
RR 2, Box 700, Erin
TN 37061-9802.
615/289-4111.

Crane Interiors Inc.
P.O. Box 40,
Woodbury TN 37190-
0040. 615/563-4800.

Del-Met Corp.
840 Industrial Dr,
Winchester TN
37398-1246.
615/967-8544.

Dura Mechanical Components
114 Spicer Dr,
Gordonsville TN
38563-2142.
615/683-6651.

Fortune Plastics of TN Inc.
310 Hartman Dr,
Lebanon TN 37087-
2520. 615/444-4004.

Kenton Custom Molding
320 N Main St,
Kenton TN 38233-
1130. 901/749-0366.

Lin Pac Flexible Packaging
5725 Commerce Blvd,
Morristown TN
37814-1049.
423/586-8917.

Mark I Molded Plastics
P.O. Box 160, Henry
TN 38231-0160.
901/243-2312.

Oak Technical Inc.
208 Industrial Blvd,
Tullahoma TN 37388-
4070. 615/455-7011.

Plexco Inc.
P.O. Box 23530,
Knoxville TN 37933-
1530. 423/966-5822.

Valk Industries Inc.
RR 10, Box 668,
Greeneville TN 37743-
9810. 423/638-1284.

Wilton Corp.
110 Wilton Cir,
Winchester TN
37398-2537.
615/967-1471.

PLASTICS MATERIALS WHOLESALE

Duracraft
300 Entrance St, Halls TN 38040-1217. 901/836-5573.

Piedmont Plastics Inc.
725 Airpark Center Dr, Nashville TN 37217-2925. 615/361-0087.

CHEMICALS AND ALLIED PRODUCTS WHOLESALE

Nalco Chemical Co.
1255 Lynnfield Rd, Suite 109, Memphis TN 38119-5142. 901/681-9186.

Dowelanco
8001 Centerview Pkwy, Cordova TN 38018-4228. 901/755-8800.

PB&S Chemical Co.
133 N Conalco Dr, Jackson TN 38301-3665. 901/424-0585.

Harcros Chemicals Inc.
1418 Poplar Ln,

Nashville TN 37210-4520. 615/256-8636.

Helena Chemical Company
6075 Poplar Ave, Suite 500, Memphis TN 38119-4702. 901/761-0050.

IDA Inc.
1311 Rayburn St, Memphis TN 38106-4249. 901/775-2861.

Ideal Chemical & Supply Co.
4025 Air Park St, Memphis TN 38118-9036. 901/363-7720.

Tennessee Valley Chemicals
1338 Lewis St, Nashville TN 37210-3412. 615/242-8866.

PB&S Chemical Co. Inc.
1705 Boone St, Knoxville TN 37917-4804. 423/523-7171.

Tri-State Delta Chemical Co.
6800 Poplar Ave, Suite 100, Memphis

TN 38138-7404. 901/755-7566.

Terra International Inc.
6555 Quince Rd, Memphis TN 38119-8259. 901/758-1341.

BOC Gases
1008 Whites Creek Pike, Nashville TN 37207-5431. 615/226-1725.

Stanley Urban
3613 Craig Rd, East Ridge TN 37412-1507. 423/867-2462.

Ecolab Inc.
4600 Cromwell Ave, Memphis TN 38118-6309. 901/368-0090.

PAINTS, VARNISHES, AND SUPPLIES WHOLESALE

Crutchfield Wallcoverings
223 Cumberland St, Memphis TN 38112-3302. 901/323-4133.

Porter Paint Co.
3135 Poplar Ave, Memphis TN 38111-3501. 901/323-1155.

For more information on career opportunities in the chemicals/rubber and plastics industries:

Associations

AMERICAN ASSOCIATION FOR CLINICAL CHEMISTRY
2101 L Street NW, Suite 202, Washington DC 20037-1526. 202/857-0717 or 800/892-1400. International scientific/medical society of individuals involved with clinical chemistry and other clinical labscience-related disciplines.

AMERICAN CHEMICAL SOCIETY
Career Services, 1155 16th Street NW, Washington DC 20036. 202/872-4600.

AMERICAN INSTITUTE OF CHEMICAL ENGINEERS
345 East 47th Street, New York

NY 10017. 212/705-7338 or 800/242-4363. Provides leadership in advancing the chemical engineering profession as it meets the needs of society.

AMERICAN INSTITUTE OF CHEMISTS, INC.
7315 Wisconsin Avenue, Suite 502 E, Bethesda MD 20814. 301/652-2447. A professional organization supporting the social, economic, and career objectives of the individual scientist.

CHEMICAL MANAGEMENT & RESOURCES ASSOCIATION
60 Bay Street, Suite 702, Staten Island NY 10301. 718/876-8800. Fax: 718/720-4666. Engaged in marketing, marketing research,

business development, and planning for the chemical and allied process industries. Provides technical meetings, educational programs, and publications to members.

CHEMICAL MANUFACTURERS ASSOCIATION
2501 M Street NW, Washington DC 20037. 202/887-1100. A trade association that develops and implements programs and services and advocates public policy that benefits the industry and society.

THE ELECTROCHEMICAL SOCIETY
10 South Main Street, Pennington NJ 08534-2896. An international educational society dealing with electrochemical issues. Also publishes monthly journals.

SOAP AND DETERGENT ASSOCIATION
475 Park Avenue South, 27th Floor, New York NY 10016. 212/725-1262. A trade association and research center.

SOCIETY OF PLASTICS ENGINEERS
14 Fairfield Drive, P.O. Box 403, Brookfield CT 06804-0403. 203/775-0471. Dedicated to helping members attain higher professional status through increased scientific, engineering, and technical knowledge.

THE SOCIETY OF THE PLASTICS INDUSTRY, INC.
1275 K Street NW, Suite 400, Washington DC 20005. 202/371-5200. Promotes the development of the plastics industry and enhances public understanding of its contributions while meeting the needs of society.

Directories

CHEMICAL INDUSTRY DIRECTORY
State Mutual Book and Periodical Service, Order Department, 17th Floor, 521 5th Avenue, New York NY 10175. 516/537-1104.

CHEMICALS DIRECTORY
Cahners Publishing, 275 Washington Street, Newton MA 02158. 617/964-3030.

DIRECTORY OF CHEMICAL ENGINEERING CONSULTANTS
American Institute of Chemical Engineering, 345 East 47th Street, New York NY 10017. 212/705-7338.

DIRECTORY OF CHEMICAL PRODUCERS
SRI International, 333 Ravenswood Avenue, Menlo Park CA 94025. 415/326-6200.

Magazines

CHEMICAL & ENGINEERING NEWS
American Chemical Society 1155 16th Street NW, Washington DC 20036. 202/872-4600.

CHEMICAL MARKETING REPORTER
Schnell Publishing Company, 80 Brot Street, 23rd Floor, New York NY 10004. 212/248-4177.

CHEMICAL PROCESSING
Putnam Publishing Company, 301 East Erie Street, Chicago IL 60611. 312/644-2020.

CHEMICAL WEEK
888 7th Avenue, 26th Floor, New York NY 10106. 212/621-4900.

COMMUNICATIONS: TELECOMMUNICATIONS & BROADCASTING

The telecommunications and broadcasting industries are poised on the edge of a revolution. At long last, Congress has finally deregulated the telecommunications industry, allowing long-distance carriers, local phone companies, and cable TV operators to get into each other's businesses. For the first time, consumers will be able to choose their local phone company, and that company will probably also provide them with their cable hookups.

Business in the telecommunications industry has been booming even without deregulation. The industry continues to break new ground and reach more customers, especially in wireless phone service. However, the industry has been shaken by recent layoffs at AT&T.

In broadcasting, competition is high, especially for high-profile positions such as newscasters and DJs. In television, the hottest industry is cable. Cable companies are rapidly expanding, and opportunities for technical workers are growing. In radio, syndicated radio shows are tearing up the airwaves. Larger stations with more money, more experience, and bigger names are producing shows which smaller stations are picking up to save money. This increase in syndication will lead to continued competition in the radio industry.

A+ COMMUNICATIONS INC.
2416 Hillsboro Road, Nashville TN 37212-5318. 615/385-4500. **Contact:** Dot Abell, Manager of Personnel. **Description:** A+ Communications Inc. is a regional provider of paging, mobile communications, and telemessaging services through 36 offices operating in nine states throughout the Southeast. Formed in 1985 through the merger of various predecessor paging and telemessaging companies, A+ has grown significantly to become one of the largest paging providers within its market area and one of the largest multi-market telemessaging providers in the Southeast. **Educational backgrounds include:** Accounting; Data Processing; Finance; Telecommunications. **Corporate headquarters location:** This Location. **Other U.S. locations:** Birmingham AL; Huntsville AL; Mobile AL; Montgomery AL; Lakeland FL; Melbourne FL; Winter Park FL; Louisville KY; Baton Rouge LA; Harvey LA; Lafayette LA; Monroe LA; Sheveport LA; Baltimore MD; Gulfport MS; Jackson MS; Asheville NC; Charlotte NC; Greensboro NC; Raleigh NC; Winston-Salem NC; Columbia SC; Greenville SC; Antioch TN; Knoxville TN; Memphis TN; Chattanooga TN; Jackson TN.

BAGWELL ENTERTAINMENT/ROSS TELEVISION PRODUCTIONS
813 Northshore Drive, Suite 102, Knoxville TN 37919. 423/588-1732. **Contact:** Carmita Wright, Vice President of Administration. **Description:** Involved in the development of television programs.

BELL ATLANTIC BUSINESS SYSTEMS SERVICES, INC.
2525 Perimeter Place Drive, #209, Nashville TN 37214-3674. 615/391-0516. **Contact:** Human Resources. **Description:** Bell Atlantic Business Systems Services, Inc. provides computer and telecommunications services to business customers. **Common positions include:** Computer Engineer; Computer Systems Analyst; Electrical/Electronics Engineer.

CHANNEL ONE COMMUNICATIONS
125 West Jackson Avenue, Knoxville TN 37902. 423/546-1151. **Contact:** Florence Frank, Director of Human Resources. **Description:** Creators of a television program that is distributed to high schools. **NOTE:** Florence Frank should be contacted at: 600 Madison Avenue, New York NY 10022.

COUNTRY MUSIC TELEVISION
2806 Opryland Drive, Nashville TN 37214. 615/871-5830. **Contact:** Vanessa Seveire, Personnel. **Description:** A 24-hour country music video channel featuring top country hits.

GAYLORD ENTERTAINMENT/COMMUNICATIONS GROUP
2806 Opryland Drive, Nashville TN 37214. 615/871-6959. **Contact:** Human Resources. **Description:** The Broadcast Division of Gaylord Entertainment. Overall, Gaylord Entertainment Company provides diversified entertainment and communications services including the operation of a convention and resort complex, musical show park, and television and radio stations.

THE NASHVILLE NETWORK
2806 Opryland Drive, Nashville TN 37214. 615/889-6840. **Contact:** Human Resources. **Description:** A cable network serving 95 percent of American cable viewers with country music and country lifestyle programming.

NORTHERN TELECOM, INC.
200 Athens Way, Nashville TN 37228. 615/734-4000. **Contact:** Human Resources. **Description:** Designs, develops, manufactures, markets, sells, installs, and services central office switching equipment, integrated business systems, terminals transmission equipment, cable and outside plant products, and other telecommunications products and services. **Corporate headquarters location:** Research Triangle Park NC. **Other U.S. locations:** San Ramon CA; Stone Mountain GA; Morton Grove IL. **Number of employees nationwide:** 30,000.

SHARED TECHNOLOGIES INC.
424 Church Street, Suite 210, Nashville TN 37219. 615/259-1330. **Contact:** Human Resources. **Description:** Shared Technologies Inc. provides communications equipment and services, cellular business services, facilities management, and consulting services to businesses in virtually every industry and profession across the United States. Shared Technologies has on-site personnel in more than 95 field locations that provide sales, service, analysis, maintenance, and customized billing to over 3,000 businesses nationwide. The company categorizes its services into three divisions: Shared Tenant Services, Cellular Business Services, and Long-Distance Services. Shared Tenant Services offers such

products as telephone equipment and services, long-distance and local telephone service, 800 service, voice mail, copiers, facsimile machines, cellular rentals, and LANs. Cellular Business Services provides cellular phone services, wireless facsimile machines and pagers, and mobile telephones. Discounted long-distance services, 800 service, international calling plans, and calling cards are part of the Long-Distance Services Division. **NOTE:** Human Resources can be contacted at corporate headquarters: 100 Green Meadow Road, Suite 104, Wethersfield CT 06109. **Corporate headquarters location:** Wethersfield CT.

TDS TELECOM
P.O. Box 22995, Knoxville TN 37933. 423/966-4700. **Contact:** Rita Vaughn, Director of Human Resources. **Description:** Provides telecommunications, telephone, cable television, radio paging, and cellular services.

TRESP ASSOCIATES
687 Emory Valley Road, Oak Ridge TN 37830. 423/483-9400. **Contact:** Roy Jones, Director of Human Resources and Administration. **Description:** An automated data-processing telecommunications company.

Note: Because addresses and telephone numbers of smaller companies change rapidly, we recommend you call each company to verify the information below before inquiring about job opportunities. Mass mailings are not recommended.

Additional employers with under 250 employees:

TELEPHONE COMMUNICATIONS

Cellular One
P.O. Box 23463, Chattanooga TN 37422-3463. 423/892-2355.

ATS Phone & Data Systems
3915 S Mendenhall Rd, Memphis TN 38115-5919. 901/797-3000.

ATS Phone & Date Systems
1111 Northshore Dr Suite S-100, Knoxville TN 37919-4005. 423/584-4281.

Memphis Payphone Co.
5308 Sunnyside Cv, Memphis TN 38135-2226. 901/386-4281.

Bell South Mobility
2133 Green Hills Village Dr, Nashville TN 37215-2601. 615/292-1402.

Ben Lomand Rural Phone Cooperative
Hillsboro 596, Pelham 467, Hillsboro TN 37342. 615/596-2247.

Twin Lakes Telephone Cooperative
156 Broad St, Cookeville TN 38501. 615/858-3192.

South Central Bell
9733 Truckers Ln, Knoxville TN 37922-2297. 423/694-3601.

South Central Bell
3841 Green Hills Village Dr, Nashville TN 37215-2610. 615/665-6475.

South Central Bell
22 N Front St, Suite 970, Memphis TN 38103-2109. 901/577-1400.

South Central Bell
200 Krystal Blvd, Chattanooga TN 37402. 423/266-9061.

South Eastern Communications
4730 Nolensville Rd, Nashville TN 37211-5408. 615/781-1011.

Peoples Telephone Co.
9888 Roberts Rd, Silver Point TN 38582-6124. 615/858-5068.

Twin Lakes Telephone Co-op Corp.
P.O. Box 67, Gainesboro TN 38562-0067. 615/268-2151.

Tennessee Telephone Co.
7407 Andersonville Pike, Knoxville TN 37938-4236.
423/922-3535.

Vanguard Communications
2011 Richard Jones Rd, Nashville TN 37215-2804.
615/386-3565.

Phonetech Communications
72 Madison Ave, Memphis TN 38103-2107. 901/522-1205.

Telego
618 Grassmere Park, Suite 15, Nashville TN 37211-3643.
615/831-7902.

Executone Information Systems Inc.
2620 Thousand Oaks Blvd #2200, Memphis TN 38118-2434.
901/366-1505.

Telefacts Corporation
2826 Pedigo Pl, Thompsons Stn TN 37179-9268.
615/591-7333.

Communications Systems
3276 Commercial Pkwy, Memphis TN 38116-3278.
901/396-0930.

RADIO BROADCASTING STATIONS

WIMZ FM
901 E Summit Hill Dr, Suite 200, Knoxville TN 37915-1237.
423/525-6000.

WMTN AM
510 W Economy Rd, Morristown TN 37814-3223.
423/586-7993.

WPLN FM
222 8th Ave N, Nashville TN 37203-3502. 615/862-5810.

WSM AM
2644 McGavock Pike, Nashville TN 37214-1202. 615/889-6595.

WSMC FM
P.O. Box 870, Collegedale TN 37315-0870.
423/238-2905.

WUSY FM
P.O. Box 8799, Chattanooga TN 37414-0799.
423/892-3333.

WYFN AM
1940 Neelys Bend Rd, Madison TN 37115-5800. 615/868-4458.

TELEVISION BROADCASTING STATIONS

WBIR TV
1513 Hutchison Ave, Knoxville TN 37917-3833. 423/637-1010.

WATE TV
1306 N Broadway St, Knoxville TN 37917-6599. 423/637-6666.

WJHL TV
P.O. Box 1130, Johnson City TN 37605-1130.
423/926-2151.

WKNO TV
900 Getwell Rd, Memphis TN 38111-7418. 901/458-2521.

WPTY TV
2225 Union Ave, Memphis TN 38104-4316. 901/278-2424.

WREG TV
803 Channel 3 Dr, Memphis TN 38103-4603. 901/577-0100.

WTVC
410 W 6th St, Chattanooga TN 37402-1619.
423/756-5500.

WTVF
474 James Robertson Pkwy, Nashville TN 37219-1298.
615/244-5000.

CABLE/PAY TELEVISION SERVICES

Crown Cable Television
1850 Business Park Dr, Suite 101, Clarksville TN 37040-6000. 615/552-2288.

Sammons Communications
2300 S Roan St, Johnson City TN 37601-7527.
423/929-2101.

MISCELLANEOUS COMMUNICATIONS SERVICES

Cylix Communications Corp.
800 Ridge Lake Blvd Fl 3, Memphis TN 38120-9427.
901/761-1177.

For more information on career opportunities in the communications industries:

Associations

ACADEMY OF TELEVISION ARTS & SCIENCES
5220 Lankershim Boulevard, North Hollywood CA 91601. 818/754-2800.

AMERICAN WOMEN IN RADIO AND TELEVISION, INC.
1650 Tysons Boulevard, Suite 200, McLean VA 22102. 703/506-3290. A national, nonprofit professional organization of women and men who work in electronic media and related fields. Services include *News and Views,* a fax newsletter transmitted biweekly to members; Careerline, a national listing of job openings available to members only; and the AWRT Foundation, which supports charitable and educational programs and annual awards.

BROADCAST PROMOTION AND MARKETING EXECUTIVES
2029 Century Park East, Suite 555, Los Angeles CA 90028. 310/788-7600. Fax: 310/788-7616.

INTERACTIVE SERVICES ASSOCIATION
Suite 865, 8403 Colesville Road, Silver Springs MD 20910. 301/495-4955.

INTERNATIONAL TELEVISION ASSOCIATION
6311 North O'Connor Road, Suite 230, Irving TX 75309. 214/869-1112. Membership required.

NATIONAL ASSOCIATION OF BROADCASTERS
1771 N Street NW, Washington DC 20036. 202/429-5300, ext. 5490. Fax: 202/429-5343. Provides employment information.

NATIONAL CABLE TELEVISION ASSOCIATION
1724 Massachusetts Avenue NW, Washington DC 20036-1969. 202/775-3651. Fax: 202/775-3695. A trade association. Publications include *Cable Television Developments, Secure Signals, Kids and Cable, Linking Up, Only on Cable,* and *Producers' Sourcebook: A Guide to Program Buyers.*

U.S. TELEPHONE ASSOCIATION
1401 H Street NW, Suite 600, Washington DC 20005-2136. 202/326-7300.

Magazines

BROADCASTING AND CABLE
Broadcasting Publications Inc., 1705 DeSales Street NW, Washington DC 20036. 202/659-2340.

COMPUTER HARDWARE, SOFTWARE, AND SERVICES

Hardware and software: Companies are starting to invest more in corporate technology after several years of lean spending. Network servers have been the hot business product recently, and that trend will continue through 1996. Expect the boom in big machines -- parallel computers, mainframes, and minicomputers -- to support a growing interest in online databases, accessing the Internet, and e-mail. PCs will remain the strongest part of the hardware market. The composition of the software industry is shrinking with many firms merging or acquiring others. Despite consolidation in the industry, and despite the crisis at Apple Computer, the overall number of software jobs is still rising.

What's hot on the market? Although it still accounts for a tiny percentage of software sales, Internet-related software -- and World Wide Web browsing software in particular -- is quickly transforming the industry. Analysts predict that sales of Internet software will double every year through at least 2000, and by then sales could hit $4 billion a year.

Services: Computer services professionals perform three activities: systems integration, custom programming, and consulting/training. Consulting and integration are the fastest-growing segments in computing due to the demand for networking. With more computer power available, more computer support will be needed.

BELL ATLANTIC BUSINESS SYSTEMS SERVICES, INC.
2525 Perimeter Place Drive, #209, Nashville TN 37214-3674. 615/391-0516. **Contact:** Human Resources. **Description:** Bell Atlantic Business Systems Services, Inc. provides computer and telecommunications services to business customers. **Common positions include:** Computer Engineer; Computer Systems Analyst; Electrical/Electronics Engineer.

CONTROL TECHNOLOGY, INC.
P.O. Box 59003, Knoxville TN 37950. 423/584-0440. **Contact:** Human Resources. **Description:** Manufactures back-up support units for programmable controllers.

ELO-TOUCH SYSTEMS
105 Randolph Road, Oak Ridge TN 37830. 423/482-4100. **Contact:** Human Resources. **Description:** Designs and manufactures computer touch screen systems and software.

PERCEPTICS CORPORATION
725 Pellissippi Parkway, Suite 200N, Knoxville TN 37932-3350. 423/966-9200. **Contact:** Jim Disney, Human Resources Director. **Description:** Provides consulting, design, development, and fabrication of systems for image processing, pattern recognition, and computer vision.

SHARP MANUFACTURING COMPANY
Sharp Plaza Boulevard, Memphis TN 38193. 901/795-6510. **Contact:** Human Resources. **Description:** Manufactures computers and related equipment.

SIEMENS NIXDORF INFORMATION SYSTEMS, INC.
4701 Trousdale Drive Nashville TN 37220-1320. 615/333-2610. **Contact:** Human Resources. **Description:** A supplier of computer systems, software, and peripherals. The company also offers consulting, planning, and implementation services. **Common positions include:** Computer Systems Analyst; Customer Service Representative; Software Engineer. Educational Backgrounds include: Business Administration; Communications; Computer Science; Marketing. Benefits: 401K; Dental Insurance; Disability Coverage; Life Insurance; Medical Insurance; Tuition Assistance. **Corporate headquarters location:** Burlington MA. **Operations at this facility include:** Service. **Listed on:** Privately held.

UNISYS CORPORATION
321 Maple Lane, Blountville TN 37617-4748. 423/323-1464. **Contact:** Human Resources. **Description:** Unisys Corporation is a provider of information services, technology, and software. The company employs 49,000 people in 100 countries. Unisys specializes in developing business-critical solutions based on open information networks. The company's enabling software team creates a variety of software projects which facilitate the building of user applications and the management of distributed systems. The company's platforms group is responsible for UNIX Operating Systems running across a wide range of multiple processor server platforms, including all peripheral and communication drivers. The Unisys commercial parallel processing group is engaged in the development of a microkernel-based operating system, I/O device driver development, ATM hardware development, diagnostics, and system architects. The system management group is chartered with the overall management of development programs for UNIX desktop and entry server products.

UNISYS CORPORATION
105 Westpark Drive, Nashville TN 37207. 615/371-7800. **Contact:** Human Resources. **Description:** Unisys Corporation is a provider of information services, technology, and software. The company employs 49,000 people in 100 countries. Unisys specializes in developing business-critical solutions based on open information networks. The company's enabling software team creates a variety of software projects which facilitate the building of user applications and the management of distributed systems. The company's platforms group is responsible for UNIX Operating Systems running across a wide range of multiple processor server platforms, including all peripheral and communication drivers. The Unisys commercial parallel processing group is engaged in the development of a microkernel-based operating system, I/O device driver development, ATM hardware development, diagnostics, and system architects. The system management group is chartered with the overall management of development programs for UNIX desktop and entry server products.

Note: Because addresses and telephone numbers of smaller companies change rapidly, we recommend you call each company to verify the information below before inquiring about job opportunities. Mass mailings are not recommended.

Additional employers with under 250 employees:

COMPUTERS AND COMPUTER EQUIPMENT WHOLESALE

CNU Business Systems
101 E Webster St, Madison TN 37115-4803. 615/860-0455.

COMPUTER SOFTWARE, PROGRAMMING, AND SYSTEMS DESIGN

O'Brien's Computer Services
517 Sugar Hollow Rd, Piney Flats TN 37686-3126. 423/323-2567.

Computer Prep
1395 Green Orchard Cv, Memphis TN 38138-1913. 901/755-0329.

COMPUTER MAINTENANCE AND REPAIR

Ameridata
624 Grassmere Park, Suite 9, Nashville TN 37211-3662. 615/315-5400.

Computer Consoles Inc.
4230 Faronia Rd, Memphis TN 38116-6505. 901/345-6566.

Computer Network Consulting
124 N 3rd St, Pulaski TN 38478-3203. 615/363-9763.

Digital Servicenter
15 Century Blvd, Nashville TN 37214-3692. 615/871-7342.

Innovative Technical Group
3679 Graceland Dr, Memphis TN 38116-4464. 901/332-0256.

For more information on career opportunities in the computer industry:

Associations

ASSOCIATION FOR COMPUTING MACHINERY
1515 Broadway, 17th Floor, New York NY 10036. 212/869-7440. Membership required.

INFORMATION TECHNOLOGY ASSOCIATION OF AMERICA
1616 North Fort Myer Drive, Suite 1300, Arlington VA 22209. 703/522-5055.

MULTIMEDIA DEVELOPMENT GROUP
2601 Mariposa Street, San Francisco CA 94110. 415/553-2300. Fax: 415/553-2403. Internet: info@mdg.org. A nonprofit trade association dedicated to the business and market development of multimedia companies.

Magazines

COMPUTER-AIDED ENGINEERING
Penton Publishing, 1100 Superior Avenue, Cleveland OH 44114. 216/696-7000.

COMPUTERWORLD
IDG, 375 Cochituate Road, P.O. Box 9171, Framingham MA 01701-9171. 508/879-0700.

DATA COMMUNICATIONS
McGraw-Hill, 1221 Avenue of the Americas, New York NY 10020. 212/512-2000.

DATAMATION
Cahners Publishing, 275 Washington Street, Newton MA 02158. 617/964-3030.

IDC REPORT
International Data Corporation, Five Speen Street, Framingham MA 01701. 508/872-8200.

EDUCATIONAL SERVICES

Job prospects for college and university faculty, elementary school teachers, counselors, and education administrators should show moderate improvement throughout the '90s, although most of the openings will result from retirements. Among kindergarten and elementary school teachers, the best opportunities await those with training in special education. The employment outlook is also good for teacher aides, as many assist special education teachers, as school reforms call for more individual attention to students, and as the number of students who speak English as a second language rises. Adult education and secondary school teachers, and sports and physical fitness instructors and coaches are other occupations expected to grow faster than average.

BELMONT UNIVERSITY
1900 Belmont Boulevard, Nashville TN 37212. 615/383-7001. **Contact:** Human Resources. **Description:** Belmont University is a leading university with a Fall 1994 enrollment of 2,961 students from 45 states and 40 countries. Belmont University's six schools offer undergraduate degrees in 53 major areas of study with 36 minors, and master's degrees in business administration, accounting, education, music education and nursing. Belmont's six schools are as follows: the School of Business, the School of Religion, the School of Music, the School of Nursing, the School of Sciences, and the School of Humanities/Education. Belmont also offers the Belmont University Research Symposium (BURS), which gives students a chance to contribute to the pursuit of knowledge through original research. Belmont University dates back to the 19th Century when the grounds were known as Adelicia Acklen's Belle Monte estate. The antebellum mansion remains and is flanked by university buildings separated in age by a century. The first educational institution located on the site was the original Belmont College (1890-1913), which eventually joined Ward School and became Ward Belmont College for Women (1913-1951) In 1951, the Tennessee Baptist Convention founded the second Belmont College (1951-1991) with an initial coeducational enrollment of 136 students. Belmont College became a university in 1991.

CHRISTIAN BROTHERS UNIVERSITY
650 East Parkway South, Memphis TN 38104. 901/722-0200. **Contact:** Mr. Vernon Tabor, Director of Human Resources and Purchasing. **Description:** A university offering Bachelor of Arts, Bachelor of Science, Master's, and M.B.A. degrees.

EAST TENNESSEE STATE UNIVERSITY
Box 70564, Johnson City TN 37614. 423/929-4233. **Contact:** Department of Human Resources. **Description:** A state university.

LEE COLLEGE
P.O. Box 3450, Cleveland TN 37320-3450. 423/472-2111. **Contact:** David Painter, Human Resources. **Description:** Founded in 1918, Lee is a private, four-year, coeducational, liberal arts college affiliated with the Church of God. The administration believes it is the fastest-

growing independent college in Tennessee. The college is located near the natural Ocoee Region in Cleveland, Tennessee, 28 miles northeast of Chattanooga. The student-faculty ratio is 18 to one. More than 50 percent of full-time faculty have doctoral degrees. Lee College offers the following majors, which lead to Bachelor of Arts, Bachelor of Science, or Bachelor of Music Education degrees: Accounting, Bible and Theology, Biblical Studies, Biological Science, Business Administration, Business Education, Chemistry, Christian Education, Communication, Computer Information Systems, English, English/Reading, General Business, History, Human Development, Intercultural Studies, Mathematics, Mathematics Education, Mathematics/Science, Medical Technology, Modern Foreign Languages, Music, Music Education, Pastoral Ministry, Physical Education, Psychology, and Sociology.

LIBSCOMB UNIVERSITY
3901 Granny White Pike, Nashville TN 37204. 615/269-1000. **Contact:** Director of University. **Description:** A university.

MIDDLE TENNESSEE STATE UNIVERSITY
1301 East Main Street, Murfreesboro TN 37132. 615/898-2928. **Contact:** Gloria Jordan, Employment Office. **Description:** A state university. **Number of employees at this location:** 1,400.

MONTGOMERY BELL ACADEMY
4001 Harding Road, Nashville TN 37205. 615/298-5514. **Contact:** Bradford Gioia, Headmaster. **Description:** An all-male, private high school established in 1867.

NASHVILLE STATE TECHNICAL INSTITUTE
120 White Bridge Road, Nashville TN 37209. 615/353-3333. **Contact:** Norma Sheucraft, Director of Personnel. **Description:** A two-year technical institute, offering a variety of certificate and associate degree programs.

OAK RIDGE ASSOCIATED UNIVERSITIES
P.O. Box 117, Oak Ridge TN 37831. 423/576-3000. **Contact:** Human Resources. **Description:** A non-profit association of more than 50 colleges and universities acting as prime contractor for research, training, education, and information activities.

RHODES COLLEGE
2000 North Parkway, Memphis TN 38112. 901/726-3000. **Contact:** Claire Shapiro, Director of Human Resources. **Description:** A four-year college, offering Bachelor of Arts and Bachelor of Science degrees.

FATHER RYAN HIGH SCHOOL
700 Norwood Drive, Nashville TN 37204. 615/383-4200. **Contact:** Edward Krenson, Principal. **Description:** A co-ed private high school founded in 1927.

SOUTHERN COLLEGE OF SEVENTH-DAY ADVENTISTS
P.O. Box 370, Collegedale TN 37315. **Toll free phone:** 800/768-8437. **Contact:** Human Resources. **Description:** Southern College of Seventh-day Adventists is a four-year coeducational institution established by the Seventh-day Adventist Church primarily to serve

its constituents in the southeastern part of the United States. The mission of Southern College of Seventh-day Adventists is to provide students, faculty, and staff with an environment for balanced development of the intellectual, spiritual, physical, and social dimensions of life in harmony with biblical principles. In a context of liberal arts and professional curricula, the campus community emphasizes academic scholarship, vocational preparation, cultural understanding, and a relationship with Jesus Christ leading to a life of service.

STATE TECHNICAL INSTITUTE
5983 Macon Cove, Memphis TN 38134. 901/383-4111. **Contact:** Paul Thomas, Director of Personnel. **Description:** A two-year technical institute, offering associate's degrees.

TENNESSEE STATE UNIVERSITY
3500 John Merritt Boulevard, Nashville TN 37209. 615/963-5000. **Contact:** Ms. Fonda Terry, Employment Specialist. **Description:** A state university.

TENNESSEE TECHNOLOGICAL UNIVERSITY
Cookeville TN 38505. 615/372-3101. **Contact:** Personnel Department. **Description:** A technical university.

TREVECCA NAZARENE UNIVERSITY
333 Murfreesboro Road, Nashville TN 37210. 615/248-1200. **Contact:** Dr. Richard Baxter. **Description:** Trevecca Nazarene College, founded in 1901, is a fully accredited four-year liberal arts college in Nashville, Tennessee that exists to meet the higher education needs of the Church of the Nazarene. Its academic programs are based on Christian values that promote scholarship, critical thinking, and meaningful worship for students in preparation for lives of leadership and service to the church, the community and the world at large. As the official college of the Church of the Nazarene in the southeastern United States, Trevecca is guided by the doctrines and principles for conduct of the denomination. The school emphasizes both the authority of the Bible and doctrine, experience, and ethic of Christian holiness as interpreted by the Wesleyan tradition.

UNION UNIVERSITY
Highway 45 Bypass, Jackson TN 38305. 901/668-1818. **Contact:** Gary Carter, Vice President for Business Affairs. **Description:** Union University is a private, four-year, co-educational liberal arts college, fully-accredited and affiliated with the Tennessee Baptist Convention. Union University traces its roots back to 1823, making it the oldest of all the Southern Baptist colleges and universities. The campus is situated on 230 acres of rolling terrain in the city of Jackson, 80 miles east of Memphis and 120 miles west of Nashville. Union University's approach to learning weaves strong commitments to the Christian faith and the development of the whole person with a thoroughly professional approach to higher education. Union University offers a full liberal arts curriculum in more than 40 fields of study in the arts, sciences, humanities, and social sciences. Union's mission and ministry programs are an integral part of students lives and offer outstanding opportunities for community involvement and service.

UNIVERSITY OF TENNESSEE/CHATTANOOGA
615 McCallie Avenue, Chattanooga TN 37403. 423/755-4221. **Contact:** Personnel Department Services. **Description:** A campus of the state university.

UNIVERSITY OF TENNESSEE/KNOXVILLE
600 Henley Street, Suite 224, Knoxville TN 37996-4125. 423/974-5151. **Fax:** 423/974-3856. **Contact:** Recruitment and Staffing. **Description:** A state university. **Common positions include:** Accountant/Auditor; Attorney; Automotive Mechanic/Body Repairer; Buyer; Chemist; Clerical Supervisor; Computer Programmer; Computer Systems Analyst; Counselor; Draftsperson; Editor; Electrician; Financial Analyst; Human Resources Specialist; Librarian; Library Technician; Mechanical Engineer; Physician; Psychologist; Public Relations Specialist; Radio/TV Announcer/Broadcaster; Restaurant/Food Service Manager; Speech-Language Pathologist; Statistician; Technical Writer/Editor. **Educational backgrounds include:** Accounting; Biology; Business Administration; Computer Science; Liberal Arts. **Benefits:** 401K; Dental Insurance; Disability Coverage; Employee Discounts; Life Insurance; Medical Insurance; Tuition Assistance. **Operations at this facility include:** Administration. **Number of employees at this location:** 4,500.

VANDERBILT UNIVERSITY
Box 7700, Station B, Nashville TN 37235. 615/322-8300. **Fax:** 615/343-6388. **Contact:** Recruitment and Staffing. **Description:** A university and medical center. **Common positions include:** Accountant/Auditor; Architect; Attorney; Biological Scientist/Biochemist; Blue-Collar Worker Supervisor; Budget Analyst; Clerical Supervisor; Clinical Lab Technician; Computer Programmer; Computer Systems Analyst; Counselor; Dental Assistant/Dental Hygienist; Dental Lab Technician; Dietician/Nutritionist; Draftsperson; Editor; Education Administrator; EEG Technologist; EKG Technician; Electrical/Electronics Engineer; Financial Analyst; Health Services Manager; Human Resources Specialist; Librarian; Library Technician; Medical Records Technician; Medical Technologist; Nuclear Medicine Technologist; Occupational Therapist; Pharmacist; Physical Therapist; Preschool Worker; Psychologist; Public Relations Specialist; Purchasing Agent and Manager; Radiologic Technologist; Registered Nurse; Reporter; Research Assistant; Respiratory Therapist; Science Technologist; Social Worker; Speech-Language Pathologist; Statistician; Structural Engineer; Surgical Technician; Teacher; Technical Writer/Editor. **Educational backgrounds include:** Accounting; Art/Design; Biology; Business Administration; Chemistry; Computer Science; Liberal Arts. **Benefits:** 401K; Daycare Assistance; Dental Insurance; Disability Coverage; Employee Discounts; Life Insurance; Medical Insurance; Pension Plan; Tuition Assistance; Wellness Program. **Corporate headquarters location:** This Location. **Operations at this facility include:** Administration; Research and Development. **Number of employees at this location:** 12,000.

Note: Because addresses and telephone numbers of smaller companies change rapidly, we recommend you call each company to verify the information below before inquiring about job opportunities. Mass mailings are not recommended.

Additional employers with under 250 employees:

ELEMENTARY AND SECONDARY SCHOOLS

University School of Nashville
2000 Edgehill Ave,
Nashville TN 37212-2198. 615/327-8158.

Evangelical Christian School
P.O. Box 1030,
Cordova TN 38088-1030. 901/754-7774.

Harding Academy-Macon
1000 Cherry Rd,
Memphis TN 38117.
901/452-7801.

Baylor School
P.O. Box 1337,
Chattanooga TN 37401-1337.
423/267-8505.

Farragut Middle School
200 W End Ave,
Knoxville TN 37922-2893. 423/966-9756.

Dobyns Bennett High School
1800 Legion Dr,
Kingsport TN 37664-2658. 423/378-8400.

Bradley High School
1000 S Lee Hwy,
Cleveland TN 37311-5899. 423/476-0650.

Farragut High School
11237 Kingston Pike,
Knoxville TN 37922-2891. 423/966-9775.

Bartlett High School
5688 Woodlawn St,
Bartlett TN 38134-3498. 901/373-2620.

Germantown High School
7653 Old Poplar Pike,
Germantown TN 38138-5940.
901/756-2350.

Glencliff Comp High School
160 Antioch Pike,
Nashville TN 37211-3018. 615/333-5070.

Central High School
5321 Jacksboro Pike,
Knoxville TN 37918-3355. 423/689-1400.

Hunters Lane High School
1150 Hunters Ln,
Nashville TN 37207-1113. 615/860-1401.

Jackson Central-Merry High School
179 Allen Ave,
Jackson TN 38301-4496. 901/424-2200.

Whites Creek High School
7277 Old Hickory Blvd, Whites Creek TN 37189-9148.
615/876-5132.

Karns High School
2710 Byington Solway Rd, Knoxville TN 37931-3200.
423/539-8670.

North Side High School
3070 Humboldt Hwy,
Jackson TN 38305.
901/668-7866.

McGavock Comp High School
3150 McGavock Pike,
Nashville TN 37214-1634. 615/885-8850.

Sevier County High School
1200 Dolly Parton Pkwy, Sevierville TN 37862-3798.
423/453-1076.

West High School
3326 Sutherland Ave,
Knoxville TN 37919-4587. 423/594-4477.

Jackson County School District
205 W Gibson Ave,
Gainesboro TN 38562-9399. 615/268-0119.

Marshall County Board of Education
700 Jones Cir,
Lewisburg TN 37091-2427. 615/359-1581.

Cleveland City School District
4300 Mouse Creek Rd NW, Cleveland TN 37312-3303.
423/472-9571.

COLLEGES, UNIVERSITIES, AND PROFESSIONAL SCHOOLS

Freed Hardeman University
158 E Main St,
Henderson TN 38340-2306. 901/989-6000.

Knoxville College
901 College St,
Knoxville TN 37921-4799. 423/524-6500.

Lambuth University
Lambuth Blvd,
Jackson TN 38301.
901/425-2500.

Lemoyne Owen College
807 Walker Ave,
Memphis TN 38126-6595. 901/774-9090.

Milligan College
P.O. Box 500, Milligan Coll TN 37682-0500.
423/461-8700.

Tennessee Temple University
1815 Union Ave,
Chattanooga TN 37404-3587.
423/493-4100.

Tennessee Wesleyan College
P.O. Box 40, Athens

TN 37371-0040.
423/745-7504.

**University of the
South**
735 University Ave,
Sewanee TN 37383-
0001. 615/598-1000.

**JUNIOR COLLEGES
AND TECHNICAL
INSTITUTES**

**Cleveland State
Community College**
P.O. Box 3570,
Cleveland TN 37320-
3570. 423/472-7141.

**Columbia State
Community College**
P.O. Box 1315,
Columbia TN 38402-
1315. 615/540-2722.

**Jackson State
Community College**
2046 N Parkway,
Jackson TN 38301-
3797. 901/424-3520.

**Motlow State
Community College**
P.O. Box 88100,
Tullahoma TN 37388-
8100. 615/455-8511.

**Northeast State
Technical Community
College**
P.O. Box 246,
Blountville TN 37617-
0246. 423/323-3191.

**CHILD DAYCARE
SERVICES**

**Alex Greene YMCA
Daycare**
3700 Ashland City

Hwy, Nashville TN
37218-2614.
615/876-0909.

Carrousel Day Care
745 Bluff City Hwy,
Bristol TN 37620-
4647. 423/968-2012.

**Cindy's Group Day
Care**
4242 Lindawood Dr,
Nashville TN 37215-
3241. 615/385-0766.

**Circle Time
Therapeutic Nursery**
1201 E Chilhowie
Ave, Johnson City TN
37601-3403.
423/928-4686.

**Lake Country Child
Learning Center**
223 S Court St,
Tiptonville TN 38079-
1305. 901/253-7780.

YMCA Daycare
8207 Concord Rd,
Brentwood TN 37027-
6725. 615/373-0215.

**David Lipscomb BA
School Program**
4517 Granny White
Pike, Nashville TN
37204-4119.

Enrichment Preschools
208 3rd Ave N,
Nashville TN 37201-
1617. 615/242-5226.

**The Children's
Learning Center**
2035 Saint John Ave,
Dyersburg TN 38024-
2209. 901/285-4120.

**Kinder Care Learning
Center**
771 Walnut Knoll Ln,
Cordova TN 38018-
6301. 901/756-0313.

**Kinder Care Learning
Center**
1025 Jackson Rd,
Goodlettsville TN
37072-3599.
615/851-1361.

**Ms. Vickeys Group
Day Care**
6818 Scenic Dr,
Murfreesboro TN
37129-8278.
615/459-5047.

**Therapeutic Learning
Center**
1218 Madison St,
Clarksville TN 37040-
3820. 615/552-5964.

**The Young Hopefuls
Center**
422 N Academy St,
Murfreesboro TN
37130-2932.
615/893-8232.

**John Coleman Head
Start**
P.O. Box 1048,
Smyrna TN 37167-
1048. 615/355-9296.

**NW Tennessee Head
Start**
526 W Walnut Ave,
McKenzie TN 38201-
2124. 901/352-7951.

**North Springs Head
Start**
RR 1, Whitleyville TN
38588-9801.
615/621-3325.

For more information on career opportunities in educational services:

<u>Associations</u>

**AMERICAN ASSOCIATION OF
SCHOOL ADMINISTRATORS**
1801 North Moore Street,
Arlington VA 22209-9988.
703/528-0700. Fax: 703/841-
1543. An organization of school
system leaders. Membership
includes a national conference on

education; programs and
seminars; *The School
Administrator,* a monthly
magazine; *Leadership News,* a bimonthly newspaper; *The AASA
Professor,* a quarterly publication;
and a catalog of other
publications and audiovisuals.

AMERICAN FEDERATION OF TEACHERS
555 New Jersey Avenue NW, Washington DC 20001. 202/879-4400.

COLLEGE AND UNIVERSITY PERSONNEL ASSOCIATION
1233 20th Street NW, Suite 301, Washington DC 20036. 202/429-0311. Membership required.

NATIONAL ASSOCIATION OF BIOLOGY TEACHERS
11250 Roger Bacon Drive #19, Reston VA 22090-5202. 703/471-1134. Toll-free number: 800/406-0775. Fax: 703/435-5582. A professional organization for biology and life science educators. E-mail address: nabter@aol.com.

NATIONAL ASSOCIATION OF COLLEGE ADMISSION COUNSELORS
1631 Prince Street, Alexandria VA 22314. 703/836-2222. An education association of secondary school counselors, college and university admission officers, and related individuals who work with students as they make the transition from high school to post-secondary education.

NATIONAL ASSOCIATION OF COLLEGE AND UNIVERSITY BUSINESS OFFICERS
1 DuPont Circle, Suite 500, Washington DC 20036. 202/861-2500. Association for those involved in the financial administration and management of higher education. Membership required.

NATIONAL SCIENCE TEACHERS ASSOCIATION
1840 Wilson Boulevard, Arlington VA 22201-3000. 703/243-7100. Organization committed to the improvement of science education at all levels, preschool through college. Publishes five journals, a newspaper, and a number of special publications. Also conducts national and regional conventions.

Books

ACADEMIC LABOR MARKETS
Falmer Press, Taylor & Francis, Inc., 1900 Frost Road, Suite 101, Bristol PA 19007. 800/821-8312.

HOW TO GET A JOB IN EDUCATION
Adams Media Corporation, 260 Center Street, Holbrook MA 02343. 617/767-8100.

Directories

WASHINGTON HIGHER EDUCATION ASSOCIATION DIRECTORY
Council for Advancement and Support of Education, 11 DuPont Circle NW, Suite 400, Washington DC 20036 202/328-5900.

ELECTRONIC/INDUSTRIAL ELECTRICAL EQUIPMENT

Heading into 1996, industry analysts expect productivity in the fast-paced electronics industry to continue to spiral downward, even as the number of production workers in the industry levels off. Intense competition from overseas has companies cutting costs by sending labor-intensive operations to low-wage regions like the Far East and Mexico. On the other hand, the increased computerization of the industry is fueling the demand for highly-trained, knowledgeable workers.

Semiconductor manufacturers, in particular, are growing steadily. Starting out the year, the Semiconductor Industry Association forecasted a growth rate of about 15 percent. The year actually came in at 26 percent. Factors spawning a high demand for semiconductors: a surging PC market, new information highway markets, and a stronger telecommunications and consumer electronics market.

ADVANCE TRANSFORMER COMPANY
Highway 62, P.O. Box 926, Wartburg TN 37887. 423/346-6621.
Contact: Human Resources. **Description:** A manufacturer of transformers.

THE ALPHA CORPORATION OF TENNESSEE
P.O. Box 670, Collierville TN 38027-0670. 901/853-2450. **Contact:** Hazel Somogyi, Director of Human Resources. **Description:** The Alpha Corporation of Tennessee operates in two divisions under the names Glasteel, Inc. and Glasteel Industrial Laminates. Glasteel, Inc. manufactures fiberglass panels and Glasteel Industrial Laminates manufactures electronic circuit boards.

COLUMBUS ELECTRIC MANUFACTURING COMPANY
485 Industrial Park Road, Piney Flats TN 37686. 423/538-8191.
Fax: 423/538-3218. **Contact:** Connie Benton, Human Resources.
Description: Columbus Electrical Manufacturing Company has been serving the HVAC and appliance industry for over 35 years. The company manufactures a variety of controls, including low voltage thermostats, line voltage thermostats, special application thermostats, remote sensing thermostats, air sensing controls, safety controls, snap disc thermostats, relays and accessories.

COMPUTATIONAL SYSTEMS, INC. (CSI)
835 Innovation Drive, Knoxville TN 37932. 423/675-2110. **Fax:** 423/675-3100. **Contact:** Human Resources. **Description:** CSI is the world's largest manufacturer of Reliability-Based Maintenance (RBM) products and allied services. The RBM strategy integrates maintenance technologies such as vibration analysis, oil analysis, infrared thermography, and quality alignment and balancing. CSI is the technical leader in vibration analysis, with products in three major categories -- the periodic survey systems category, the pocket-

sized FFT analyzer category, and the advanced machinery analyzer category. CSI's tribology products and services include its Tribology Mini-Lab; its Tribology Total Solution system; and its Fluid Analysis Lab. CSI's infrared thermography systems include its focal-plane array camera, which delivers the most accurate temperature measurement in the predictive maintenance field, its IntraPort pen-based analyzer and Infranalysis data/image management system provide a systematic route-based approach to IR that saves time and simplifies diagnoses. CSI's alignment and balancing services include both electromechanical and laser alignment systems. **Common positions include:** Electrical/Electronics Engineer; Manufacturer's/Wholesaler's Sales Rep.; Mechanical Engineer; Nuclear Engineer; Software Engineer; Technical Writer/Editor. **Benefits:** 401K; Dental Insurance; Life Insurance; Medical Insurance; Profit Sharing; Tuition Assistance. **Corporate headquarters location:** This Location. **Operations at this facility include:** Administration; Manufacturing; Research and Development; Sales; Service. **Listed on:** Privately held. **Number of employees nationwide:** 310.

COORS TECHNICAL CERAMICS COMPANY
TENNESSEE OPERATIONS
1100 Commerce Park Drive, Oak Ridge TN 37830. 423/481-8021. **Fax:** 423/481-8022. **Contact:** Randy Wallace, Human Resources. **Description:** Coors Technical Ceramics Company is located near the Oak Ridge National Laboratory's High Temperature Materials Lab, to provide high-tech ceramics to the semiconductor, laser tube, prototype/research and development, aerospace, medical, defense and electronics industries. This facility manufactures alumina from 85 percent pure to 99.9 percent pure as well as mullite, zirconias, titanites, cordierites, quartz, silicon carbides, silicon nitrides, aluminum nitrides and other exotic and advanced materials. Coors Technical Ceramics dates back to 1894, when Adolph Coors helped found Herold China and Pottery Company in a deserted bottle-making factory that once served his company's brewery. Coors Technical Ceramics evolved when World War I prompted American potteries to manufacture chemical porcelainware that previously was only produced in Europe.

ELECTRIC RESEARCH
P.O. Box 1228, Dyersburg TN 38025. 901/285-9121. **Contact:** Human Resources. **Description:** Manufactures industrial electronic products.

EMERSON ELECTRIC COMPANY
1600 Industrial Park Road, P.O. Box 610, Paris TN 38242. 901/642-1124. **Contact:** Jerry Brenda, Human Resources. **Description:** Manufactures industrial electrical products.

FRANCE
P.O. Box 300, Fairview TN 37062. 615/799-0551. **Contact:** Human Resources. **Description:** Manufactures transformers.

GENERAL ELECTRIC MOTORS
2150 Northwest Broad Street, Murfreesboro TN 37129. 615/893-2900. **Contact:** Tom Lavalle, Human Resources. **Description:** As part of the diversified manufacturing company, this location manufactures electric motors. GE operates in the following areas:

aircraft engines (jet engines, replacement parts, and repair services for commercial, military, executive, and commuter aircraft); appliances; capital services (consumer services, financing, specialty insurance, and Kidder, Peabody investment bank and securities broker); industrial (lighting products, electrical distribution and control equipment, transportation systems products, electric motors and related products, and a broad range of electrical and electronic industrial automation products); technical products and services (medical systems and equipment sold worldwide to hospitals and medical facilities, as well as a full range of computer-based information and data interchange services for both internal use and external commercial and industrial customers); broadcasting (NBC); materials (plastics, ABS resins, silicones, and superabrasives); and power systems (products for the generation, transmission, and distribution of electricity).

MAGNETEK
P.O. Box 569, Ripley TN 38063. 901/635-2421. **Contact:** Paul Avery, Human Resources Manager. **Description:** Manufactures fractional horsepower motors. Overall, MagneTek manufactures electrical power distribution equipment. **NOTE:** MagneTek supports equal opportunity for all Americans, regardless of race, Color, religion, age, gender, marital status, sexual preference, disability (where reasonable accommodations can be made), or Veteran's status.

MORRILL ELECTRIC INC.
P.O. Box 531, Erwin TN 37650. 423/743-7000. **Contact:** Human Resources. **Description:** Manufactures small electric motors.

PANASONIC
5105 South National Drive, Knoxville TN 37914-6518. 423/673-0700. **Contact:** Joy Johnson, Personnel Director. **Description:** A manufacturer of electrolytic capacitors, audio stereo speakers, formed aluminum foil, and components for cellular telephones.

ROBERTSHAW CONTROLS COMPANY
P.O. Box 400, Knoxville TN 37901-0400. 423/546-0550. **Contact:** Jim Fair, Manager of Human Resources. **Description:** A manufacturer of control instrumentation. Products include automatic controls used in homes, commercial buildings, and industry to conserve energy and enable machinery to work efficiently and automatically. Products include level controls, including RF/microprocessor-based level controls and precision level controls; vibration detectors, including monitor and control; recorders and controllers; accessories; control valves, including diaphragm actuated; self-actuated regulators, including temperature regulators; and control systems, including system components. Robertshaw also produces Sylphon formed bellows and assemblies at this location, as well as automobile thermostats, caps, water outlet housings, and heater control valves. **Other U.S. locations:** Cookeville TN.

SQUARE D COMPANY
330 Weakley Road, Smyrna TN 37167. 615/459-5026. **Contact:** Human Resources. **Description:** Founded 1903, Square D is a manufacturer of electrical distribution products for the construction industry. Square D's industrial control and electrical distribution

products, systems, and services are used worldwide in industrial facilities and equipment, commercial and residential construction, and original equipment manufacturers' products. In addition to meeting all major standards, including ANSI, UL, NEMA, CSA, and IEC, products and services can also be tailored to meet specific local requirements. Square D operates in three sectors: Electrical Distribution, Industrial Control, and International. The Electrical Distribution Sector manufactures distribution equipment, power equipment, connectors (Anderson), and consumer products. In the Industrial Control Sector, the company provides control products, automation products, power protection systems (Topaz), infrared measurement products (Ircon), engineered systems (ESI), and technical services. In the International Sector, the company has operations in Canada, Latin America, Europe, and Asia Pacific. This location manufactures electrical switchgear. **Corporate headquarters location:** Palatine IL. **Parent company:** Groupe Schneider.

TELEDYNE ELECTRONIC TECHNOLOGIES
LEWISBURG FACILITY
1425 Higgs Road, P.O. Box 326, Lewisburg TN 37091-1326. 615/359-4531. **Contact:** Ed Daeghrity, Manager of Human Resources. **Description:** An electronics manufacturer.

THOMAS & BETTS CORPORATION
1555 Lynnfield Road, Memphis TN 38119. 901/682-7766. **Contact:** Human Resources. **Description:** Thomas & Betts Corporation is engaged in the design, manufacture, and marketing of electrical and electronic components and systems for connecting, fastening, protecting, and identifying wires, components, and conduits. The company's products include fittings and accessories for electrical raceways, solderless terminals for small wires and heavy power cables, wire fastening devices and markers, insulation products, flat cable, connectors and IC sockets for electronic applications, ceramic chip capacitors for electronic circuitry, fiber optic connectors and accessories, wire management systems, and customer specific products for major original equipment manufactures. Most of the products are used in numerous markets, from power generating plants to telecommunications to transportation equipment. **Corporate headquarters location:** This Location. **Listed on:** New York Stock Exchange.

THOMAS & BETTS CORPORATION
200 Challenger Drive, Portland TN 37148. 615/325-6800. **Contact:** Dick DeGeorge, Human Resources Director. **Description:** Thomas & Betts Corporation is engaged in the design, manufacture, and marketing of electrical and electronic components and systems for connecting, fastening, protecting, and identifying wires, components, and conduits. The company's products include fittings and accessories for electrical raceways, solderless terminals for small wires and heavy power cables, wire fastening devices and markers, insulation products, flat cable, connectors and IC sockets for electronic applications, ceramic chip capacitors for electronic circuitry, fiber optic connectors and accessories, wire management systems, and customer specific products for major original equipment manufactures. Most of the products are used in numerous markets, from power generating plants to telecommunications to transportation equipment. This location manufactures non-metallic

electrical outlet boxes. **Corporate headquarters location:** Memphis TN. **Listed on:** New York Stock Exchange.

Note: Because addresses and telephone numbers of smaller companies change rapidly, we recommend you call each company to verify the information below before inquiring about job opportunities. Mass mailings are not recommended.

Additional employers with under 250 employees:

TRANSFORMERS

ABB Power T&D Co. Inc.
RR 1 Box 96, Alamo TN 38001-9709. 901/696-5561.

The Bodine Co. Inc.
P.O. Box 460, Collierville TN 38027-0460. 901/853-7211.

ELECTRICAL INDUSTRIAL APPARATUS

Acco Contol Group Division of FKI Automotive
5200 Industrial Dr, Milan TN 38358-3175. 901/686-1532.

ELECTRIC LIGHTING AND WIRING EQUIPMENT

Chardon Electrical Components
1613 Industrial Rd, Greeneville TN 37745-3505. 423/638-1381.

Exide Corp. Speed Clip Division
P.O. Box 3548, Bristol TN 37625-3548. 423/968-1010.

ELECTRONIC COMPONENTS AND ACCESSORIES

CEI
2405A Industrial Dr, Springfield TN 37172-5014. 615/384-8555.

Computational Systems Inc.
835 Innovation Dr,

Knoxville TN 37932-2578. 423/675-2110.

Numark Inc.
1124 W Irish St, Greeneville TN 37743-5200. 423/639-0216.

ELECTRICAL ENGINE EQUIPMENT

Flex Technologies Inc.
104 Flex Ave, Portland TN 37148-1503. 615/325-2025.

ELECTRICAL EQUIPMENT, MACHINERY, AND SUPPLIES

Dejay Corporation
1750 Hal Henard Rd, Greeneville TN 37743-3143. 423/638-1888.

Electric Supply & Repair
2152 Swannanoa Ave, Kingsport TN 37664-3223. 423/247-1691.

ELECTRICAL EQUIPMENT WHOLESALE

Braid Electric Co.
299 Cowan St, Nashville TN 37213-1109. 615/242-6511.

Schott Corporation
1838 Elm Hill Pike, Suite 107, Nashville TN 37210-3726. 615/889-8800.

Tennessee Valley Electrical Supply
296 Adams Ave,

Memphis TN 38103-1986. 901/525-4751.

Industrial Automation Controls
1901 I A C Dr, Memphis TN 38116-3600. 901/345-7000.

Mills & Lupton Supply Co.
1623 Bartlett Rd, Memphis TN 38134-7106. 901/382-6033.

Graybar Electric Co. Inc.
210 N Highland Park Ave, Chattanooga TN 37404-2438. 423/698-8021.

Wholesale Electric
420 Press St, Kingsport TN 37660-3614. 423/246-2900.

Vari-Lite
5215 Linbar Dr, Nashville TN 37211-1031. 615/834-3190.

Nashville Light Bulb Supply
930 5th Ave S, Nashville TN 37203-4612. 615/254-5171.

Stowers Machinery Corp.
9960 Airport Pkwy, Blountville TN 37617-6361. 423/323-0400.

ELECTRONIC PARTS AND EQUIPMENT WHOLESALE

Carlton-Bates Company
100 Executive Dr,

Jackson TN 38305-
2319. 901/664-2714.

**Mitel Telecom
Systems Inc.**
1385 W Brierbrook
Rd, Germantown TN
38138-2208.
901/753-2525.

Telco Manufacturing
123 Seaboard Ln,
Franklin TN 37067-
8215. 615/377-9910.

Telepage Inc.
895 N White Station
Rd, Memphis TN
38122-3021.
901/685-9900.

Dreamhire
914 19th Ave S,
Nashville TN 37212-
2108. 615/321-5544.

Tenmark Telecom Inc.
903 Industrial Dr,
Murfreesboro TN
37129-4928.
615/890-3505.

**For more information on career opportunities in the electronic/industrial electrical
equipment industry:**

Associations

AMERICAN CERAMIC SOCIETY
735 Ceramic Place, Westerville OH
43081. 614/890-4700. 800/837-
1804. Provides ceramics futures
information. Membership required.

ELECTROCHEMICAL SOCIETY
10 South Main Street, Pennington
NJ 08534-2896. 609/737-1902.
Fax: 609/737-2743. An
international society which holds bi-
annual meetings internationally and
periodic meetings through local
sections. Publications include the
monthly *Journal of the
Electrochemical Society* and the
quarterly *Interface.*

**ELECTRONIC INDUSTRIES
ASSOCIATION**
2500 Wilson Boulevard, Arlington
VA 22201-3834. 703/907-7500.

**ELECTRONICS TECHNICIANS
ASSOCIATION**
602 North Jackson Street,
Greencastle IN 46135. 317/653-
8262. Offers published job-hunting
advice from the organization's
officers and members. Also offers
educational material and
certification programs.

**INSTITUTE OF ELECTRICAL AND
ELECTRONICS ENGINEERS (IEEE)**
345 East 47th Street, New York NY

10017. 212/705-7900. Toll-free
customer service line: 800/678-
4333.

**INSTITUTE OF ELECTRICAL AND
ELECTRONICS ENGINEERS (IEEE)**
1828 Elm Street NW, Suite 1202,
Washington DC 20036-5104.
Professional activities line:
202/785-0017. National information
line: 202/785-2180.

**INTERNATIONAL BROTHERHOOD
OF ELECTRICAL WORKERS**
1125 15th Street NW, Washington
DC 20005. 202/833-7000. Has
over 1,000 apprenticeship
programs.

**INTERNATIONAL SOCIETY OF
CERTIFIED ELECTRONICS
TECHNICIANS**
2708 West Berry Street, Ft. Worth
TX 76109. 817/921-9101.

**NATIONAL ELECTRONICS SALES
AND SERVICES ASSOCIATION**
2708 West Berry, Ft. Worth TX
76109. 817/921-9061. Provides
newsletters and directories to
members.

**SOCIETY OF MANUFACTURING
ENGINEERS (SME)**
One SME Drive, P.O. Box 930,
Dearborn MI 48121. 313/271-
1500. Offers a resume database for
members.

ENVIRONMENTAL AND WASTE MANAGEMENT SERVICES

According to the Environmental Protection Agency, the increase in environmental awareness over recent decades is more than just a trend. State and national legislation, such as the 1990 amendments to the Clean Air Act, has generated a new range of opportunities in skilled administrative, professional, and technical areas. However, the most critical need in the industry is for scientists and engineers. These two groups develop new solutions to old problems, and therefore are instrumental in the research and development stages.

On the other hand, the current climate in the Congress is significantly cooler towards environmental regulation than in years past. Many members of Congress argue that American business is already overburdened by the Federal government, and some propose that the Environmental Protection Agency itself be disbanded.

ABB ENVIRONMENTAL SYSTEMS
1400 Centerpoint Boulevard, Knoxville TN 37932-1966. 423/693-7550. **Contact:** Julie Pearson, Human Resources. **Description:** ABB Environmental Systems manufactures and operates particulate and SO2 removal systems for coal fired boilers and other industrial processes. The parent company, Asea, Brown, Boveri, Inc., is a supplier of industrial equipment and services for industries such as electric power generation, oil and gas exploration, and production and chemical refinement processing.

ADVANCED SCIENCES, INC. (ASI)
800 Oak Ridge Turnpike, Suite C102, Oak Ridge TN 37830. 423/483-1274. **Contact:** Human Resources. **Description:** A technical services consulting firm that provides innovative, multi-disciplinary solutions to a wide range of environmental challenges. A staff of environmental professionals provides quality services in the areas of: waste management, environmental sciences, advanced technologies, and bio-remediation. **NOTE:** All hiring is handled by the corporate headquarters at 6739 Academy Road Northeast, Albuquerque NM 87109. **Corporate headquarters location:** Albuquerque NM.

AMERICAN ECOLOGY
109 Flint Road, Oak Ridge TN 37830. 423/482-5532. **Contact:** Marcie Meldahl, Public Relations Manager. **Description:** American Ecology recycles nuclear components and materials and provides decontamination services.

BFI SOLID WASTE SYSTEMS
2400 Chipman Street, Knoxville TN 37917-6115. 423/522-8161. **Contact:** Human Resources. **Description:** A corporation engaged primarily in the collection and disposal of solid wastes for commercial, industrial, and residential customers. Services provided

include landfills, waste-to-energy programs, hazardous waste removal, and liquid waste removal. Worldwide operations at more than 500 facilities. **Corporate headquarters location:** Houston TX.

BATTELLE MEMORIAL INSTITUTION
151 Lafayette Drive, Suite 110, Oak Ridge TN 37830. 423/482-7945. **Contact:** Human Resources. **Description:** Battelle Memorial Institution provides environmental, safety, health, and waste management services.

BROWN & ROOT ENVIRONMENTAL
800 Oak Ridge Turnpike, Suite A600, Oak Ridge TN 37830. 615/483-9900. **Contact:** Cathy Frazee. **Description:** Provides engineering and environmental waste services.

C.A.C.I. -- AUTOMATED SCIENCES GROUP
800 Oak Ridge Turnpike, Suite A-300, Oak Ridge TN 37830. 615/482-6601. **Contact:** Judy Craig, Human Resources. **Description:** An energy and environmental technology and systems integration consulting firm. The environmental consulting group at this location is organized according to the following functional disciplines: environmental technology and engineering, regulatory compliance and analysis, health and safety programs, quality assurance and control, environmental information management systems, privatization, and energy. Programs include economic, safety, and environmental assessments of waste management alternatives; hazardous, radioactive and mixed waste management strategy development; facility design; operations; decontamination and decommissioning optimization, environmental regulation and policy analysis, environmental compliance strategy development, quality assurance and quality control program development and implementation; environmental systems; and environmental site assessments. **Common positions include:** Biological Scientist/Biochemist; Civil Engineer; Environmental Engineer; Geologist/Geophysicist; Nuclear Engineer. **Educational backgrounds include:** Biology; Engineering; Geology. **Benefits:** Dental Insurance; Life Insurance; Medical Insurance; Tuition Assistance. **Corporate headquarters location:** Silver Spring MD. **Other U.S. locations:** Huntsville AL; Dalgren VA. **Listed on:** Privately held. **Number of employees at this location:** 100. **Number of employees nationwide:** 275.

ENVIRONMENTAL SYSTEMS CORPORATION
200 Tech Center Drive, Knoxville TN 37912. 423/688-7900. **Contact:** Human Resources. **Description:** Manufacturers of custom-designed environmental and engineering systems and services for air quality monitoring, hazardous waste management, and ground water management for the coal and nuclear energy industry.

INTERNATIONAL TECHNOLOGY CORPORATION (IT)
312 Directors Drive, Knoxville TN 37923. 423/690-3211. **Fax:** 423/690-3626. **Contact:** C. Randy Beck, Manager, Human Resources, Southern Region. **Description:** International Technology Corporation (IT) delivers a full range of environmental management services through an integrated approach for total turnkey solutions. The company applies engineering, analytical, remediation and pollution control expertise to meet the environmental needs of its

clients, from site assessment through remediation. With a multidisciplinary staff of approximately 4,000 associates in more than 50 locations, the company can respond promptly in all environmental areas to the needs of industrial and governmental clients, both nationally and internationally. The result is effective turnkey management of hazardous, toxic, and radioactive materials. To further meet the needs of its customers, IT has implemented a Total Quality Management (TQM) process. TQM focuses the company's ongoing quality assurance/quality control programs through continuous improvement. Through TQM quality teams, the company's associates actively participate in the ongoing achievement of quality.

NUCLEAR FUEL SERVICE
1219 Banner Hill Road, Erwin TN 37650. 423/743-6186. **Contact:** Human Resources. **Description:** Provides environmental cleanup and hazardous waste removal services. **NOTE:** Resumes can be sent to: Rhonda Bishop, Nuclear Fuel Service, 1205 Banner Hill Road, Erwin TN 37650. **Common positions include:** Accountant/Auditor; Chemical Engineer; Computer Programmer; Environmental Engineer; Process Engineer.

PAI CORPORATION
116 Milan Way, Oak Ridge TN 37830. 423/483-0666. **Fax:** 423/481-0003. **Contact:** Jeff Ginsburg, Deputy Office Manager. **Description:** This location provides technical and environmental support services to the Department of Energy; engineering, environmental, and research and development services to Martin Marietta Energy Systems, Inc.; and environmental restoration and management support to DOE/OR through Jacobs Engineering Group. Pai Corporation is an engineering, environmental, safety, health, quality assurance, and management consulting firm. The company's objective is to provide services to commercial and government programs that require expertise in science, technology, and regulations. Major multi-task programs are performed for approximately 20 organizations across the nation. Services range from providing environmental support services to the Defense Nuclear Energy to providing fire protection and life safety survey services to the Department of Justice's Federal Bureau of Prisons. **Corporate headquarters location:** This Location. **Other U.S. locations:** Livermore CA; Paducah KY; St. Charles MO; Albuquerque NM; Las Vegas NV; Aiken SC; Richland WA.

PRECIPITATOR SERVICES GROUP
P.O. Box 339, Elizabethton TN 37644. 423/543-7331. **Contact:** Teresa Lee Nidiffer, Personnel. **Description:** Precipitator Services Group, Inc. (PSG) is a manufacturer of air pollution control equipment. The company works on developing and manufacturing top-quality replacement parts and upgrade components. PSG maintains an inventory of many components and accessories ready for immediate shipment. The company also offers short lead times on most custom fabricated parts. The company manufactures a full line of components to meet the needs of all electrostatic precipitators, and the company's technical and engineering staff possesses experience in both American and European ESP designs. Replacement components and services include discharge electrodes, bottle weights, collecting plates, plate repair, rapper and rapper

accessories. Accessory components include high voltage components and bus ducts, high voltage frames and hanger assemblies, rapper trains, collecting plate support beams, spacer bars and assemblies, access doors and antisway assemblies. PSG's capabilities also extend beyond the manufacturing of standard replacement parts.

QUANTERRA ENVIRONMENTAL SERVICES

5815 Middlebrook Pike, Knoxville TN 37921. 423/588-6401. **Fax:** 423/584-4315. **Contact:** Human Resources. **Description:** In June 1994, Corning's Enseco division and IT Analytical Services, the two largest commercial environmental analytical companies in the world, merged to become Quanterra, a completely new, independent company. Quanterra provides a complete range of environmental testing services to private industry, engineering consultants, and government agencies in support of major federal and state environmental regulations. The company also possesses a variety of special analytical capabilities, including specializations in the following areas: Air Toxics; Field Analytical Services, Radiochemistry/Mixed Waste; and Advanced Technology. The company is owned jointly by Corning Incorporated and International Technology Corporation. The company's goal is to provide customers with the highest level of service in the environmental analytical testing industry. **Other U.S. locations:** CA; CO; FL; MO; NC; OH; TX; WA.

RADIAN CORPORATION

1093 Commerce Park Drive, Suite 100, Oak Ridge TN 37830. 423/483-9870. **Contact:** Laurie Easterling, Human Resource Manager. **Description:** Radian Corporation was founded in 1969 in Austin, Texas, by a group of scientists and engineers committed to developing creative solutions to challenging technical problems for government and industry. In addition to this facility, Radian has 22 additional U.S. offices and 12 international offices. Radian became part of The Hartford Steam Boiler Inspection and Insurance Company in 1975 as a wholly-owned subsidiary. Over 60 percent of the Radian staff, including top-level managers, hold degrees in science and engineering, and a large number hold advanced degrees. Most engineering disciplines are represented in the company's staff, as are most of the physical, biological, and social sciences. The diversity of the staff has also allowed Radian to expand from a singular focus on environmental control and energy technologies to the multidisciplinary services firm that it is today. This multidisciplinary culture allows the staff to focus on the diverse needs of a client's organization. The company does this by forming client teams to work closely with the organization in identifying and meeting their needs -- whether related to regulatory compliance, engineering, technology, or production. Specific technical services provided include: Regulatory Compliance Support, Site Investigation and Remediation, Air Pollution Controls, VOC and Air Toxics Control, Biotreatment, Waste Management, Ambient and Source Monitoring, Risk Management, Information Management, Project Chemistry, Specialty Chemicals, Remote Sensing Services, Materials and Machinery Analysis, and Electronic Services. **Common positions include:** Aerospace Engineer; Chemical Engineer; Chemist; Civil Engineer; Computer Scientist; Electrical/Electronics Engineer; Environmental Engineer; Geologist/Geophysicist; Industrial Hygienist;

Mechanical Engineer; Metallurgical Engineer; Meteorologist; Statistician; Toxicologist. **Corporate headquarters location:** Austin TX.

SCIENCE APPLICATIONS INTERNATIONAL CORPORATION
P.O. Box 2501, Oak Ridge TN 37831. 423/482-9031. **Contact:** Kathy Phillips, Human Resources Manager. **Description:** Offers engineering services, nuclear fuel cycle and waste storage analysis, technical information services, information systems, environmental analysis and modeling, program management, and document preparation.

SCIENTIFIC ECOLOGY GROUP, INC. (SEG)
P.O. Box 2530, Oak Ridge TN 37831. 423/481-0222. **Contact:** Joe Albence, Director of Human Resources. **Description:** Processes low-level radioactive waste.

SMURFIT RECYCLING COMPANY
1131 69 Agnes Place, Memphis TN 38104. 901/726-1600. **Contact:** Human Resources. **Description:** Smurfit Recycling brings more than 60 years experience in waste paper collection and recycling to its position as one of America's leading recyclers. Together, Smurfit's two recycling segments -- Smurfit Recycling and Pacific Recycling -- market more than four million tons of paper annually. Aluminum cans, plastic bottles, and glass are also reclaimed by the company's recycling operations. More than half of the paper the company collects is used by Jefferson Smurfit Corporation to manufacture and/or convert into a wide range of products, including boxboard, folding cartons, linerboard, medium, corrugated containers, newsprint, cylinderboard, tubes, cores, and partitions. The remainder is sold to customers in this country and abroad, where the company ranks as the largest U.S. exporter of waste paper. Overall, Smurfit Recycling serves more than 6,000 customer and community sources through nearly 50 plants and sales offices nationwide. These operations provide collection and marketing services for customized recycling programs designed to meet the specific needs of the company's commercial, municipal, private, and residential customers. On the international, national, and local levels, the company has the capacity and flexibility to handle the wide range of waste paper generated by such diverse businesses as grocery and retail chains, consumer and industrial products companies, printers, and publishers. The company also serves a number of urban and suburban communities and civic interest groups. Beyond full-service recycling, from collection and handling through marketing, Smurfit offers clients consultation in solid waste management, specialized office paper recycling programs, and collection and destruction of highly-sensitive documents, internal files, and records.

SMURFIT RECYCLING COMPANY
707 19th Avenue North, Nashville TN 37203. 615/329-4855. **Contact:** Mike Majino, Controller. **Description:** Smurfit Recycling brings more than 60 years experience in waste paper collection and recycling to its position as one of America's leading recyclers. Together, Smurfit's two recycling segments -- Smurfit Recycling and Pacific Recycling -- market more than four million tons of paper annually. Aluminum cans, plastic bottles, and glass are also reclaimed by the company's recycling operations. More than half of

the paper the company collects is used by Jefferson Smurfit Corporation to manufacture and/or convert into a wide range of products, including boxboard, folding cartons, linerboard, medium, corrugated containers, newsprint, cylinderboard, tubes, cores, and partitions. The remainder is sold to customers in this country and abroad, where the company ranks as the largest U.S. exporter of waste paper. Overall, Smurfit Recycling serves more than 6,000 customer and community sources through nearly 50 plants and sales offices nationwide. These operations provide collection and marketing services for customized recycling programs designed to meet the specific needs of the company's commercial, municipal, private, and residential customers. On the international, national, and local levels, the company has the capacity and flexibility to handle the wide range of waste paper generated by such diverse businesses as grocery and retail chains, consumer and industrial products companies, printers, and publishers. The company also serves a number of urban and suburban communities and civic interest groups. Beyond full-service recycling, from collection and handling through marketing, Smurfit offers clients consultation in solid waste management, specialized office paper recycling programs, and collection and destruction of highly sensitive documents, internal files, and records.

STEINER-LIFF METALS GROUP
P.O. Box 1182, Nashville TN 37202. 615/271-3300. **Contact:** Carl Macke, Director of Human Resources. **Description:** A recycling company which buys scrap metal and recycles it. **Number of employees nationwide:** 500.

U.S. ECOLOGY
109 Flint Road, Oak Ridge TN 37830-7033. 423/482-5532. **Contact:** Marcy Meldahl, Human Resources. **Description:** A recycling center.

WASTE MANAGEMENT OF NASHVILLE
1428 Antioch Pike, Nashville TN 37013. 615/831-9600. **Contact:** Kathy Tack, Human Resources Manager. **Description:** A waste disposal company that handles environmental concerns.

WASTE MANAGEMENT OF TENNESSEE
1428 Antioch Pike, Antioch TN 37013. 615/831-9600. **Contact:** Human Resources. **Description:** A waste disposal company that handles environmental concerns.

Note: Because addresses and telephone numbers of smaller companies change rapidly, we recommend you call each company to verify the information below before inquiring about job opportunities. Mass mailings are not recommended.

Additional employers with under 250 employees:

SANITARY SERVICES

BFI Waste Systems
115 Dean Dr,
Clarksville TN 37040.

Quadrex Recycle Center
109 Flint Rd, Oak Ridge TN 37830-7033. 423/482-5532.

For more information on career opportunities in environmental and waste management services:

Associations

AIR AND WASTE MANAGEMENT ASSOCIATION
One Gateway Center, Third Floor, Pittsburgh PA 15222. 412/232-3444. A nonprofit, technical and educational organization providing a neutral forum where all points of view of an environmental management issue can be addressed.

ASSOCIATION OF STATE & INTERSTATE WATER POLLUTION CONTROL ADMINISTRATORS
750 First Street NE, Suite 910, Washington DC 20002. 202/898-0905. Fax: 202/898-0929. A national, nonpartisan professional organization comprised of government officials. Members implement surface and groundwater protection programs throughout the nation.

ENVIRONMENTAL INDUSTRY ASSOCIATION
4301 Connecticut Avenue N, Suite 300, Washington DC 20008. 202/659-4613. Fax: 202/966-4818.

INSTITUTE OF CLEAN AIR COMPANIES
1707 L Street NW, Suite 570, Washington DC 20036. 202/457-0911-4201. A national association of companies involved in stationary source air pollution control.

U.S. ENVIRONMENTAL PROTECTION AGENCY
401 M Street SW, Washington DC 20460. 202/260-2090. Provides EPA background career information.

WATER ENVIRONMENT FEDERATION
601 Wythe Street, Alexandria VA 22314. 703/684-2400. Subscription to jobs newsletter required for career information.

Magazines

CAREERS AND THE ENGINEER
Adams Media Corporation, 260 Center Street, Holbrook MA 02343. 617/767-8100.

ENVIRONMENTAL CAREER OPPORTUNITIES
1776 I Street NW, Suite 710, Washington DC 20006. A publication that lists career opportunities in the environmental fields. $67 for 12 issues; $127 for 26 issues.

JOURNAL OF AIR AND WASTE MANAGEMENT ASSOCIATION
One Gateway Center, Third Floor, Pittsburgh PA 15222. 412/232-3444.

FABRICATED/PRIMARY METALS AND PRODUCTS

In 1995, the demand for steel dropped from 114 million to 110 million tons, and executives in the industry weren't expecting a turnaround in '96. While the price of structural beams rose, the price for flat-rolled steel, used in automobiles, for example, plummeted. Unfortunately, in early 1995, the industry was undergoing a boom in minimill-construction. These new mills may add more capacity to an already glutted market.

ALCOA (ALUMINUM COMPANY OF AMERICA)
SOUTH PLANT
300 North Hall Road, Alcoa TN 37701-2516. 423/977-2011. **Contact:** Anna Bright, Human Resources. **Description:** ALCOA provides aluminum fabricating, ingot, and can-recycling services.

ALLTRISTA ZINC PRODUCTS COMPANY
P.O. Box 1890, Greeneville TN 37744-1890. 423/639-8111. **Fax:** 423/639-3125. **Contact:** David Sarkozy, Director of Human Resources. **Description:** Manufactures solid zinc strip in a variety of alloys, which are rolled into master coils weighing up to 13,000 pounds each. Solid zinc strip is an economical, versatile metal that can be rolled and slit to customers' specifications; the manufacturing facility can produce coils with an inside diameter of up to 18 inches, and an outside diameter of up to 48 inches. The parent company, Alltrista Corporation, was spun off from Ball Corporation in April, 1993. Alltrista has interests in metal, plastics, consumer products, and industrial equipment. Alltrista Corporation has approximately 1,400 employees and operates 11 manufacturing facilities in the eastern third of the United States and Puerto Rico. Alltrista is traded on NASDAQ under the symbol of JARS. **Common positions include:** Accountant/Auditor; Blue-Collar Worker Supervisor; Chemical Engineer; Electrical/Electronics Engineer; General Manager; Industrial Engineer; Metallurgical Engineer; Quality Control Supervisor. **Corporate headquarters location:** Muncie IN. **Parent company:** Alltrista Corporation. **Operations at this facility include:** Manufacturing. **Number of employees at this location:** 300.

CARADON BETTER-BILT PRODUCTS COMPANY
704 12th Avenue, Smyrna TN 37167. 615/459-4161. **Contact:** Maribeth Sauls, Human Resources Manager. **Description:** Manufactures aluminum products.

CARGILL STEEL & WIRE
P.O. Box 18733, Memphis TN 38181-0733. 901/794-9910. **Fax:** 901/363-1398. **Contact:** Lionel Collins, Administrative Assistant. **Description:** This location produces steel and wire. Overall, the parent company, Cargill, with its subsidiaries and affiliates, is involved in nearly 50 individual lines of business. Cargill has over

130 years of service and international experience in commodity trading, handling, transporting, processing, and risk management, and employs more than 70,000 people in plants and offices all over the world. Cargill is a major trader of grains and oilseeds, as well as a marketer of many other agricultural and non-agricultural commodities. As a transporter, it uses a complex network of rail and road systems, inland waterways, and ocean-going routes, combining its own fleet and transportation services purchased from outside sources to find the most efficient and economical modes of transport to move bulk commodities from point of origin to point of consumption. As an agricultural supplier, Cargill is a leader in developing farm products and in supplying them to growers. Agricultural products include a wide variety of feed, seed, fertilizers, and other goods and services needed by producers worldwide. Cargill is also a leader in producing and marketing seed varieties and hybrids. Cargill Central Research, located at Cargill headquarters, is dedicated to developing new agricultural products to address the needs of customers around the world. Cargill also provides financial and technical services. Cargill's Financial Markets Division (FMD) supports Cargill and its subsidiaries with financial products and services that address the full spectrum of market conditions. These include financial instrument trading, emerging markets instrument trading, value investing, and money management. Cargill's worldwide food processing businesses supply products ranging from basic ingredients used in food production to recognized name brands. Cargill also operates a number of other industrial businesses. **Parent company:** Cargill.

CONLEY FROG & SWITCH COMPANY
387 East Bodley Avenue, Memphis TN 38109. 901/948-4591. **Contact:** Mr. Pat Riley, Industrial Relations Manager. **Description:** A manufacturer of railroad track accessories and commercial forgings for uses nationwide as well as in Canada. This facility deals only with steel and manganese. **Common positions include:** Accountant/Auditor; Administrator; Blue-Collar Worker Supervisor; Buyer; Draftsperson; Financial Analyst; Human Resources Specialist; Industrial Engineer; Manufacturer's/Wholesaler's Sales Rep.; Mechanical Engineer; Metallurgical Engineer; Operations/Production Manager; Purchasing Agent and Manager; Quality Control Supervisor; Systems Analyst. **Educational backgrounds include:** Business Administration; Computer Science; Engineering; Finance. **Benefits:** Life Insurance; Medical Insurance; Profit Sharing. **Corporate headquarters location:** This Location. **Operations at this facility include:** Administration; Manufacturing; Research and Development; Sales.

CRESSONA ALUMINUM COMPANY
P.O. Box 871, Elizabethton TN 37644. 423/543-3561. **Contact:** Mr. Aubrey Lee, Human Resources Manager. **Description:** An aluminum extrusion company.

DOEHLER-JARVIS INC.
Rufe Taylor Road, P.O. Box 1950, Greeneville TN 37744-1950. 423/639-1155. **Contact:** Russ Matthews, Human Resources Manager. **Description:** A producer of aluminum castings.

EKCO GLACO, LTD.
One Ekco Glaco Drive, Humboldt TN 38343. 901/784-7140.
Contact: Glenda Johnson, Human Resources Manager. **Description:**
Produces metal stampings. **Common positions include:**
Accountant/Auditor; Computer Programmer; Draftsperson;
Electrical/Electronics Engineer; General Manager; Human Resources
Specialist; Industrial Engineer; Industrial Production Manager;
Management Trainee; Manufacturer's/Wholesaler's Sales Rep.;
Marketing Specialist; Mechanical Engineer; Operations/Production
Manager; Purchasing Agent and Manager; Quality Control
Supervisor. **Educational backgrounds include:** Accounting; Business
Administration; Computer Science; Engineering; Finance; Marketing.
Benefits: Dental Insurance; Disability Coverage; Life Insurance;
Medical Insurance; Pension Plan; Tuition Assistance. **Corporate
headquarters location:** This Location. **Operations at this facility
include:** Manufacturing; Research and Development; Sales; Service.
Number of employees at this location: 200.

FLORIDA STEEL CORPORATION WEST
P.O. Box 3670, Jackson TN 38303. 901/424-5600. **Contact:** Bill
Kipp, Human Resources Manager. **Description:** Manufactures steel
industrial products such as rebar.

LINCOLN BRASS WORKS INC.
P.O. Box 748, Waynesboro TN 38485. 615/722-5422. **Contact:** Ed
Odoriso, Human Resources Manager. **Description:** Manufactures
brass products such as valves and other related items.

MAGOTTEAUX
P.O. Box 518, Pulaski TN 38478. 615/363-7471. **Contact:** Jeff
Wall, Personnel Director. **Description:** An iron foundry.

ORMET ALUMINUM MILL PRODUCTS CORPORATION
1100 Richmond, Jackson TN 38301. 901/424-2000. **Contact:** Don
Lubes, Human Resources. **Description:** Manufactures aluminum
products for industrial use.

PLANT MAINTENANCE SERVICE CORPORATION
P.O. Box 280883, Memphis TN 38168-0883. 901/353-9880. **Fax:**
901/353-0882. **Contact:** Mr. Harold Gilliland, Human Resources
Manager. **Description:** Engaged in metal plate fabrication for pressure
vessels, heat exchangers, process vessels, boiler repairs, and tanks.
Common positions include: Cost Estimator; Draftsperson; Industrial
Engineer; Machinist; Mechanical Engineer; Welder. **Benefits:** 401K;
Dental Insurance; Disability Coverage; Life Insurance; Medical
Insurance; Profit Sharing. **Corporate headquarters location:** This
Location. **Other U.S. locations:** Gulfport MS. **Operations at this
facility include:** Administration; Manufacturing; Sales. **Listed on:**
Privately held. **Number of employees at this location:** 300. **Number
of employees nationwide:** 400.

SOUTHERN FABRICATORS INC.
P.O. Box 18987, Memphis TN 38181. 901/363-1571. **Contact:**
Personnel. **Description:** Miscellaneous steel fabricators. **NOTE:** All
resumes must be accompanied by an application.

TRIDON INC.
P.O. Box 1600, Nashville TN 37202. **Contact:** Human Resources. **Description:** Manufactures metal hardware.

TRINITY OF NASHVILLE
P.O. Box 239, Nashville TN 37202. 615/244-2050. **Fax:** 615/726-5276. **Contact:** Susan Grubbs, Personnel. **Description:** Manufactures industrial structural metal products.

U.S. PIPE AND FOUNDRY COMPANY
P.O. Box 311, Chattanooga TN 37401. 423/752-3800. **Contact:** Human Resources. **Description:** A ductile iron foundry.

VAMISTER CORPORATION
144 Riverbend Drive, Sevierville TN 37876. 423/453-0001. **Contact:** John Farry, Vice President of Sales and Marketing. **Description:** Develops and manufacturers high-reliability, precision-metal-film, electrical resistors.

VESTAL MANUFACTURING
P.O. Box 420, Sweetwater TN 37874. 423/337-6125. **Contact:** Human Resources. **Description:** Manufactures a wide variety of cast iron and steel building materials. Vestal Manufacturing operates both a steel fabricating plant and a foundry.

WALKER DIE CASTING INC.
P.O. Box 1189, Lewisburg TN 37091. 615/359-6206. **Contact:** Randy Short, Personnel. **Description:** Manufactures aluminum castings.

Note: Because addresses and telephone numbers of smaller companies change rapidly, we recommend you call each company to verify the information below before inquiring about job opportunities. Mass mailings are not recommended.

Additional employers with under 250 employees:

WHOLESALE METALS SERVICE CENTERS AND OFFICES

Glazer Steel Corp.
P.O. Box 11486, Knoxville TN 37939-1486. 423/687-1251.

Crucible Service Center
501 Airpark Center Dr, Nashville TN 37217-2962. 615/361-6699.

Reynolds Aluminum Supply
1440 Poplar Ln, Nashville TN 37210-4580. 615/242-3405.

Siskin Steel & Supply Co.
4040 Jordonia Station Rd, Nashville TN 37218-2400. 615/242-4444.

William Bonnell Co.
54 Bonnell Ln, Gordonsville TN 38563-4600. 615/683-8291.

STEEL WORKS, BLAST FURNACES, AND ROLLING MILLS

Air Maze Corp.
P.O. Box 1270, Greeneville TN 37744-1270. 423/639-4154.

Allsteel Casegoods
71 Denton Fly Rd, Milan TN 38358-6288. 901/686-4100.

Anchor Wire Corp.
P.O. Box 268, Goodlettsville TN 37070-0268. 615/859-1306.

Bethlehem Steel Corporation
925 Crossover Ln, Memphis TN 38117-4906. 901/767-6292.

BTL Industries
P.O. Box 1752, Greeneville TN 37744-1752. 423/638-6171.

Ceco Entry Systems
1 Ceco Dr, Dickson
TN 37055-2769.
615/446-6220.

**Challenger Electrical
Equipment Corp.**
P.O. Box 428,
Portland TN 37148-
0428. 615/325-6800.

Cutler Hammer
3990 Old Tasso Rd
NE, Cleveland TN
37312-5827.
423/472-3305.

**Delfasco TN Division
of David B. Lilly**
P.O. Box 725,
Greeneville TN 37744-
0725. 423/639-6191.

**Harding Machine
Division Fluid Power**
228 Rush St,
Lexington TN 38351-
2241. 901/968-2513.

ITW Paslode
1211 Hope St,
Covington TN 38019-
1605. 901/476-3414.

**LTV Steel Tubular
Products**
641 Watson Branch
Dr, Franklin TN
37064-5133.
615/790-2920.

NKC of America Inc.
1584 E Brooks Rd,
Memphis TN 38116-
1988. 901/396-5353.

**Star Manufacturing
International**
P.O. Box 518,
Smithville TN 37166-
0518. 615/597-1561.

Tebco Fasteners
P.O. Box 12145,
Memphis TN 38182-
0145. 901/452-7491.

Thomas Industries Inc.
P.O. Box 489,
Dyersburg TN 38025-
0489. 901/286-4220.

TRW Fuji Valve Inc.
128 River Bend Dr,
Sevierville TN 37876-
1942. 423/453-0199.

**STEEL WIRE, NAILS,
AND SPIKES**

**Parthenon Metal
Works**
P.O. Box 307, La
Vergne TN 37086-
0307. 615/793-6801.

**Quality Dental
Products Inc.**
3111 Hanover Rd,
Johnson City TN
37604-1430.
423/282-1453.

**Stainless Metal
Products Inc.**
P.O. Box 22067,
Chattanooga TN
37422-2067.
423/892-3720.

**STEEL SHEET, STRIP,
AND BARS**

Alemite Corp.
167 Roweland Dr,
Johnson City TN
37601-3832.
423/928-8203.

Anderson Hickey
711 Sumrow St, Halls
TN 38040-1131.
901/836-7513.

**Clarksville Division
Metal Forge**
P.O. Box 3159,
Clarksville TN 37043-
3159. 615/552-4011.

**General Metal
Products Co.**
1641 N 9th Ave,
Humboldt TN 38343-
1715. 901/784-4811.

Kirsch Co.
1111 Hope St,
Covington TN 38019-
1603. 901/476-1111.

**Tsubaki Conveyor of
America**
138 Davis St, Portland

TN 37148-2000.
615/325-9221.

**STEEL PIPE AND
TUBES**

Form Rite Corp.
P.O. Box 309,
Surgoinsville TN
37873-0309.
423/345-2383.

**Nashville Wire
Products Display
Division**
1415 Elm Hill Pike,
Nashville TN 37210-
4532. 615/255-6331.

**IRON AND STEEL
FOUNDRIES**

TB Wood's Sons Co.
1230 S Manufacturers
Row, Trenton TN
38382-3637.
901/855-4117.

**Toyota TRW
Automotive Inc.**
5932 Commerce Blvd,
Morristown TN
37814-1051.
423/585-0999.

ALUMINUM

Norandal USA Inc.
1284 Northwood Dr,
Huntingdon TN
38344-2406.
901/986-5011.

**SMELTING AND
REFINING OF
NONFERROUS
METALS**

Refined Metals Corp.
257 W Mallory Ave,
Memphis TN 38109-
2222. 901/775-3770.

**NONFERROUS
ROLLING AND
DRAWING OF
METALS**

Parker Hannifin Corp.
100 Parker Rd,
Greenfield TN 38230-
9500. 901/235-3122.

Aluma-Form Inc.
3625 Old Getwell Rd,
Memphis TN 38118-
6074. 901/362-0100.

**Del-Met Tennessee
Inc.**
123 Kirby Dr, Portland
TN 37148-2004.
615/325-6741.

**Kolpak Manufacturing
Co.**
789 Peach St, Selmer
TN 38375-1246.
901/645-7955.

Alumax Emp Inc.
2404 Dr FE Wright Dr,
Jackson TN 38305-
7503. 901/424-0400.

**Assured Castings
Corp.**
300 Industrial Park Dr,
Rogersville TN 37857-
2121. 423/272-8911.

Ganton Technologies
1250 W Madison St,
Pulaski TN 38478-
2640. 615/363-8341.

**Tennalum Division
Kaiser Aluminum**
309 Industrial Dr,
Jackson TN 38301-
9616. 901/423-2811.

Abeco Diecasting Inc.
1424 Higgs Rd,
Lewisburg TN 37091-
4402. 615/359-4287.

Insteel Wire Products
P.O. Box 1916,
Gallatin TN 37066-
1916. 615/452-7615.

DIE-CASTINGS

**Harvard Industrial
Casting Products
Group of TN**
S Industrial Park,
Ripley TN 38063.
901/635-0771.

**METAL HEAT
TREATING**

**Universal Technologies
Inc.**
165 Alsonia St, Estill
Springs TN 37330-
3128. 615/649-5171.

**PRIMARY METAL
PRODUCTS**

Hoeganaes Corp.
1315 Airport Blvd,
Gallatin TN 37066-
3719. 615/451-2000.

**Hoover Precision
Products**
P.O. Box 500, Erwin
TN 37650-0500.
423/743-9121.

**Southern Foundry
Supply Inc.**
P.O. Box 6216,
Chattanooga TN
37401-6216.
423/756-6070.

Stackpole Ltd. USA
400 Dupree Ave,
Brownsville TN
38012. 901/772-
3780.

**FABRICATED
STRUCTURAL METAL
PRODUCTS**

Fischer Steel Corp.
3347 Pearson Rd,
Memphis TN 38118-
1632. 901/363-4986.

S&H Erectors Inc.
8427 Hixson Pike,
Hixson TN 37343-
1557. 423/842-3444.

Amtrol Inc.
P.O. Box 17385,
Nashville TN 37217-
0385. 615/641-7731.

First Thermal Systems
200 Compress St
#4756, Chattanooga
TN 37405-3764.
423/265-3441.

**Tennessee Metal
Specialty**
100 Rosser Wyatt Rd,
Huntingdon TN
38344. 901/986-
2244.

**A&S Building Systems
Inc.**
RR 1 Box 53, Caryville
TN 37714-9801.
423/426-2141.

**Hendrick
Manufacturing Co.**
8275 Tournament Dr,
Memphis TN 38125-
8899. 901/748-1010.

**SCREW MACHINE
PRODUCTS**

Greer Stop Nut Inc.
481 McNally Dr,
Nashville TN 37211-
3311. 615/832-8375.

METAL FORGINGS

Dixie Industries
3510 N Orchard Knob
Box 180600,
Chattanooga TN
37406-1301.
423/698-3323.

**Volvo Penta Marine
Products**
200 Robert Wallace
Dr, Lexington TN
38351-4701.
901/968-0151.

**Modern Forge of
Tennessee**
P.O. Box 100, Piney
Flats TN 37686-0100.
423/538-8185.

**CROWNS AND
CLOSURES**

Cap Snap Co.
408 Tilthammer Dr,
Kingsport TN 37660-
3542. 423/246-3732.

METAL STAMPINGS

**Aristocrat Stamping &
Manufacturing**
1540 Amherst Rd,

Knoxville TN 37909-
1203. 423/584-2009.

**Genco Stamping &
Manufacturing Co.**
P.O. Box 2009,
Cookeville TN 38502-
2009. 615/528-5574.

**General Metal
Products Co.**
523 N 22nd Ave,
Humboldt TN 38343-
3011. 901/784-4524.

STEEL SPRINGS

Lucerne Products Inc.
RR 1, Box 212, Bolivar

TN 38008-9408.
901/658-4771.

**FABRICATED WIRE
PRODUCTS**

**Feldkircher Wire
Fabricating Co.**
1015 W Kirkland Ave,
Nashville TN 37216-
3019. 615/262-0471.

Grisham Corp.
P.O. Box 549,
Arlington TN 38002-
0549. 901/867-8900.

**METAL FOIL AND
LEAF**

**Sonoco Products Co.
Inc.**
71 Wisteria St,
Jackson TN 38301-
6753. 901/424-3740.

**FABRICATED METAL
PRODUCTS**

Eureka Foundry Co.
P.O. Box 151,
Chattanooga TN
37401-0151.
423/267-3328.

For more information on career opportunities in the fabricated/primary metals and products industries:

Associations

**ASM INTERNATIONAL: THE
MATERIALS INFORMATION
SOCIETY**
Materials Park OH 44073.
800/336-5152. Gathers,
processes, and disseminates
technical information to foster the
understanding and application of
engineered materials.

**AMERICAN FOUNDRYMEN'S
SOCIETY**
505 State Street, Des Plaines IL
60016-847/824-0181.

AMERICAN WELDING SOCIETY
550 LeJeune Road NW, Miami FL
33126. 305/443-9353.

Directories

**DIRECTORY OF STEEL
FOUNDRIES IN THE UNITED**

STATES, CANADA, AND MEXICO
Steel Founder's Society of
America, 455 State Street, Des
Plaines IL 60016. 847/299-9160.

Magazines

AMERICAN METAL MARKET
25 7th Avenue, New York NY
10019. 212/887-8580.

IRON AGE NEW STEEL
191 South Gary, Carol Stream IL
60188. 708/462-2285.

IRON & STEEL ENGINEER
Association of Iron and Steel
Engineers, Three Gateway Center,
Suite 2350, Pittsburgh PA
15222. 412/281-6323.

MODERN METALS
625 North Michigan Avenue,
Suite 2500, Chicago IL 60611.
312/654-2300.

FINANCIAL SERVICES

You can't get much better than 1995. The stock market soared throughout the year, boosting business at brokerage houses. And, although the market isn't expected to be as hot in '96, it appears likely that the Federal Reserve will lower interest rates, putting the pieces into place for another solid year.

Jobseekers who have experience with mergers and acquisitions should benefit. At the same time, expect more consolidation among brokerage houses themselves. Analysts believe that the largest houses will get larger and the small boutique firms will continue to prosper, but the firms in the middle may get crunched.

AVCO FINANCIAL SERVICES, INC.
260 West Main Street, Suite 208, Hendersonville TN 37075. 615/822-9711. **Contact:** Human Resources. **Description:** Avco Financial Services, Inc., a wholly-owned subsidiary of Textron Inc., includes two groups: Finance and Insurance. The Finance Group offers secured and unsecured consumer loans, loans secured by real property, and purchases installment contracts through retail dealers, such as appliance and furniture stores, through 1,198 branch offices in seven countries around the world. This group also has Special Business Units, which include: Leasing, Revolving Credit, Military Loans, and the National Dealer Center. The Insurance Group, Avco Insurance Services, primarily sells credit life, credit disability, and involuntary unemployment insurance to customers of the Finance Group and to independent financial institutions, such as banks, credit unions, and savings and loans. Avco Insurance also offers collateral protection, personal lines auto, and renters' insurance, as well as other life insurance products and services to many of these same customers. **Corporate headquarters location:** Irvine CA.

AVCO FINANCIAL SERVICES, INC.
P.O. Box 485, Dyersburg TN 38025. 901/285-7030. **Contact:** Ron Hamblin, Manager. **Description:** Avco Financial Services, Inc., a wholly-owned subsidiary of Textron Inc., includes two groups: Finance and Insurance. The Finance Group offers secured and unsecured consumer loans, loans secured by real property, and purchases installment contracts through retail dealers, such as appliance and furniture stores, through 1,198 branch offices in seven countries around the world. This group also has Special Business Units, which include: Leasing, Revolving Credit, Military Loans, and the National Dealer Center. The Insurance Group, Avco Insurance Services, primarily sells credit life, credit disability, and involuntary unemployment insurance to customers of the Finance Group and to independent financial institutions, such as banks, credit unions, and savings and loans. Avco Insurance also offers collateral protection, personal lines auto, and renters' insurance, as well as other life insurance products and services to many of these same customers. **Corporate headquarters location:** Irvine CA.

J.C. BRADFORD & COMPANY
330 Commerce Street, Nashville TN 37201. 615/748-9000.
Contact: Human Resources. **Description:** A regional investment firm, founded in 1927, with offices in over 60 cities in the Southeast and Ohio. J.C. Bradford & Company specializes in services to individual investors such as retirement, college education, parental care, and capital preservation and cash flow. Investment solutions range from managed accounts and retirement plans to options, commodities, and stock portfolios. Bradford Asset Checking Account provides checking account privileges, an optional credit card, and a high level of account insurance. Tax-free bonds, government-backed securities, mutual funds, annuities, and limited partnerships are also offered. J.C. Bradford also offers services to emerging growth companies, including underwriting corporate securities, trading equity, and debt securities in secondary markets, mergers and acquisitions, and financing public debt for state and local governments. These services aid institutions as well as provide investment opportunities for individual clients. **Corporate headquarters location:** This Location. **Other U.S. locations:** CA; FL; GA; KY; LA; MA; MS; NC; NY; OH; SC; Chattanooga TN; Clarksville TN; Cookeville TN; Crossville TN; Jackson TN; Johnson City TN; Kingsport TN; Knoxville TN; Memphis TN; Murfreesboro TN; VA. **Listed on:** Privately held.

J.C. BRADFORD & COMPANY
701 Broad Street, Chattanooga TN 37402. 423/267-1813. **Contact:** Arlene Swallows. **Description:** A regional investment firm, founded in 1927, with offices in over 60 cities in the Southeast and Ohio. J.C. Bradford & Company specializes in services to individual investors such as retirement, college education, parental care, and capital preservation and cash flow. Investment solutions range from managed accounts and retirement plans to options, commodities, and stock portfolios. Bradford Asset Checking Account provides checking account privileges, an optional credit card, and a high level of account insurance. Tax-free bonds, government-backed securities, mutual funds, annuities, and limited partnerships are also offered. J.C. Bradford also offers services to emerging growth companies, including underwriting corporate securities, trading equity, and debt securities in secondary markets, mergers and acquisitions, and financing public debt for state and local governments. These services aid institutions as well as provide investment opportunities for individual clients. **Corporate headquarters location:** Nashville TN. **Other U.S. locations:** CA; FL; GA; KY; LA; MA; MS; NC; NY; OH; SC; Clarksville TN; Cookeville TN; Crossville TN; Jackson TN; Johnson City TN; Kingsport TN; Knoxville TN; Memphis TN; Murfreesboro TN; VA. **Listed on:** Privately held.

J.C. BRADFORD & COMPANY
One Park Place, Suite 102, 6148 Lee Highway, Chattanooga TN 37421. 423/892-4956. **Contact:** Ms. Jean Hatfield. **Description:** A regional investment firm, founded in 1927, with offices in over 60 cities in the Southeast and Ohio. J.C. Bradford & Company specializes in services to individual investors such as retirement, college education, parental care, and capital preservation and cash flow. Investment solutions range from managed accounts and retirement plans to options, commodities, and stock portfolios. Bradford Asset Checking Account provides checking account privileges, an optional credit card, and a high level of account

insurance. Tax-free bonds, government-backed securities, mutual funds, annuities, and limited partnerships are also offered. J.C. Bradford also offers services to emerging growth companies, including underwriting corporate securities, trading equity, and debt securities in secondary markets, mergers and acquisitions, and financing public debt for state and local governments. These services aid institutions as well as provide investment opportunities for individual clients. **Corporate headquarters location:** Nashville TN. **Other U.S. locations:** CA; FL; GA; KY; LA; MA; MS; NC; NY; OH; SC; Clarksville TN; Cookeville TN; Crossville TN; Jackson TN; Johnson City TN; Kingsport TN; Knoxville TN; Memphis TN; Murfreesboro TN; VA. **Listed on:** Privately held.

J.C. BRADFORD & COMPANY
P.O. Box 3945, Clarksville TN 37043. 615/552-1300. **Contact:** Human Resources. **Description:** A regional investment firm, founded in 1927, with offices in over 60 cities in the Southeast and Ohio. J.C. Bradford & Company specializes in services to individual investors such as retirement, college education, parental care, and capital preservation and cash flow. Investment solutions range from managed accounts and retirement plans to options, commodities, and stock portfolios. Bradford Asset Checking Account provides checking account privileges, an optional credit card, and a high level of account insurance. Tax-free bonds, government-backed securities, mutual funds, annuities, and limited partnerships are also offered. J.C. Bradford also offers services to emerging growth companies, including underwriting corporate securities, trading equity, and debt securities in secondary markets, mergers and acquisitions, and financing public debt for state and local governments. These services aid institutions as well as provide investment opportunities for individual clients. **Corporate headquarters location:** Nashville TN. **Other U.S. locations:** CA; FL; GA; KY; LA; MA; MS; NC; NY; OH; SC; Chattanooga TN; Cookeville TN; Crossville TN; Jackson TN; Johnson City TN; Kingsport TN; Knoxville TN; Memphis TN; Murfreesboro TN; VA. **Listed on:** Privately held.

J.C. BRADFORD & COMPANY
115 North Washington Avenue, Cookeville TN 38501. 615/528-5426. **Contact:** Human Resources. **Description:** A regional investment firm, founded in 1927, with offices in over 60 cities in the Southeast and Ohio. J.C. Bradford & Company specializes in services to individual investors such as retirement, college education, parental care, and capital preservation and cash flow. Investment solutions range from managed accounts and retirement plans to options, commodities, and stock portfolios. Bradford Asset Checking Account provides checking account privileges, an optional credit card, and a high level of account insurance. Tax-free bonds, government-backed securities, mutual funds, annuities, and limited partnerships are also offered. J.C. Bradford also offers services to emerging growth companies, including underwriting corporate securities, trading equity, and debt securities in secondary markets, mergers and acquisitions, and financing public debt for state and local governments. These services aid institutions as well as provide investment opportunities for individual clients. **Corporate headquarters location:** Nashville. **Other U.S. locations:** CA; FL; GA; KY; LA; MA; MS; NC; NY; OH; SC; Chattanooga TN; Clarksville TN;

Crossville TN; Jackson TN; Johnson City TN; Kingsport TN; Knoxville
TN; Memphis TN; Murfreesboro TN; VA. **Listed on:** Privately held.

J.C. BRADFORD & COMPANY
773 North Parkway, Jackson TN 38305. 901/664-4435. **Contact:**
Mike Tankersley, Office Manager. **Description:** A regional investment
firm, founded in 1927, with offices in over 60 cities in the Southeast
and Ohio. J.C. Bradford & Company specializes in services to
individual investors such as retirement, college education, parental
care, and capital preservation and cash flow. Investment solutions
range from managed accounts and retirement plans to options,
commodities, and stock portfolios. Bradford Asset Checking Account
provides checking account privileges, an optional credit card, and a
high level of account insurance. Tax-free bonds, government-backed
securities, mutual funds, annuities, and limited partnerships are also
offered. J.C. Bradford also offers services to emerging growth
companies, including underwriting corporate securities, trading
equity, and debt securities in secondary markets, mergers and
acquisitions, and financing public debt for state and local
governments. These services aid institutions as well as provide
investment opportunities for individual clients. **Corporate
headquarters location:** Nashville TN. **Other U.S. locations:** CA; FL;
GA; KY; LA; MA; MS; NC; NY; OH; SC; Chattanooga TN; Clarksville
TN; Cookeville TN; Crossville TN; Johnson City TN; Kingsport TN;
Knoxville TN; Memphis TN; Murfreesboro TN; VA. **Listed on:**
Privately held.

J.C. BRADFORD & COMPANY
P.O. Box 1469, Kingsport TN 37662. 423/246-7111. **Contact:**
Human Resources. **Description:** A regional investment firm, founded
in 1927, with offices in over 60 cities in the Southeast and Ohio.
J.C. Bradford & Company specializes in services to individual
investors such as retirement, college education, parental care, and
capital preservation and cash flow. Investment solutions range from
managed accounts and retirement plans to options, commodities,
and stock portfolios. Bradford Asset Checking Account provides
checking account privileges, an optional credit card, and a high level
of account insurance. Tax-free bonds, government-backed securities,
mutual funds, annuities, and limited partnerships are also offered.
J.C. Bradford also offers services to emerging growth companies,
including underwriting corporate securities, trading equity, and debt
securities in secondary markets, mergers and acquisitions, and
financing public debt for state and local governments. These services
aid institutions as well as provide investment opportunities for
individual clients. **NOTE:** Human Resources should be contacted at:
330 Commerce Street, Nashville TN 37201. **Corporate headquarters
location:** Nashville TN. **Other U.S. locations:** CA; FL; GA; KY; LA;
MA; MS; NC; NY; OH; SC; Chattanooga TN; Clarksville TN;
Cookeville TN; Crossville TN; Jackson TN; Johnson City TN;
Knoxville TN; Memphis TN; Murfreesboro TN; VA. **Listed on:**
Privately held.

J.C. BRADFORD & COMPANY
First Tennessee Plaza, Suite A, 800 South Jay Street, Knoxville TN
37929. 423/522-5183. **Contact:** Tom Filer. **Description:** A regional
investment firm, founded in 1927, with offices in over 60 cities in
the Southeast and Ohio. J.C. Bradford & Company specializes in

services to individual investors such as retirement, college education, parental care, and capital preservation and cash flow. Investment solutions range from managed accounts and retirement plans to options, commodities, and stock portfolios. Bradford Asset Checking Account provides checking account privileges, an optional credit card, and a high level of account insurance. Tax-free bonds, government-backed securities, mutual funds, annuities, and limited partnerships are also offered. J.C. Bradford also offers services to emerging growth companies, including underwriting corporate securities, trading equity, and debt securities in secondary markets, mergers and acquisitions, and financing public debt for state and local governments. These services aid institutions as well as provide investment opportunities for individual clients. **Corporate headquarters location:** Nashville TN. **Other U.S. locations:** CA; FL; GA; KY; LA; MA; MS; NC; NY; OH; SC; Chattanooga TN; Clarksville TN; Cookeville TN; Crossville TN; Jackson TN; Johnson City TN; Kingsport TN; Memphis TN; Murfreesboro TN; VA. **Listed on:** Privately held.

J.C. BRADFORD & COMPANY
P.O. Box 171840, Memphis TN 38187-1840. 901/761-3010. **Contact:** Ann Heffington or Jiles Coors. **Description:** A regional investment firm, founded in 1927, with offices in over 60 cities in the Southeast and Ohio. J.C. Bradford & Company specializes in services to individual investors such as retirement, college education, parental care, and capital preservation and cash flow. Investment solutions range from managed accounts and retirement plans to options, commodities, and stock portfolios. Bradford Asset Checking Account provides checking account privileges, an optional credit card, and a high level of account insurance. Tax-free bonds, government-backed securities, mutual funds, annuities, and limited partnerships are also offered. J.C. Bradford also offers services to emerging growth companies, including underwriting corporate securities, trading equity, and debt securities in secondary markets, mergers and acquisitions, and financing public debt for state and local governments. These services aid institutions as well as provide investment opportunities for individual clients. **NOTE:** For staff hiring for this location, contact Ann Heffington. For broker hiring for this location, contact Jiles Coors. **Corporate headquarters location:** Nashville TN. **Other U.S. locations:** CA; FL; GA; KY; LA; MA; MS; NC; NY; OH; SC; Chattanooga TN; Clarksville TN; Cookeville TN; Crossville TN; Jackson TN; Johnson City TN; Kingsport TN; Knoxville TN; Murfreesboro TN; VA. **Listed on:** Privately held.

J.C. BRADFORD & COMPANY
P.O. Box 607, Murfreesboro TN 37133-0607. 615/890-9000. **Contact:** Helen Colvin. **Description:** A regional investment firm, founded in 1927, with offices in over 60 cities in the Southeast and Ohio. J.C. Bradford & Company specializes in services to individual investors such as retirement, college education, parental care, and capital preservation and cash flow. Investment solutions range from managed accounts and retirement plans to options, commodities,

and stock portfolios. Bradford Asset Checking Account provides checking account privileges, an optional credit card, and a high level of account insurance. Tax-free bonds, government-backed securities, mutual funds, annuities, and limited partnerships are also offered. J.C. Bradford also offers services to emerging growth companies, including underwriting corporate securities, trading equity, and debt securities in secondary markets, mergers and acquisitions, and financing public debt for state and local governments. These services aid institutions as well as provide investment opportunities for individual clients. **Corporate headquarters location:** Nashville TN. **Other U.S. locations:** CA; FL; GA; KY; LA; MA; MS; NC; NY; OH; SC; Chattanooga TN; Clarksville TN; Cookeville TN; Crossville TN; Jackson TN; Johnson City TN; Kingsport TN; Knoxville TN; Memphis TN; VA. **Listed on:** Privately held.

CATERPILLAR FINANCIAL SERVICES CORPORATION
3322 West End Avenue, Nashville TN 37203. 615/386-5800. **Contact:** Human Resources. **Description:** Provides financial services.

FARM CREDIT SERVICES
MID AMERICA
P.O. Box 248, Selmer TN 38375-0248. 901/645-4015. **Contact:** Human Resources. **Description:** Farm Credit Services provides financial services through 46 branch offices in the United States. FCS provides long-, intermediate-, and short-term financing to agricultural producers, farm-related businesses, fishermen, part-time farmers, and country homeowners. Banks and related associations provide credit and credit-related services to, or for the benefit of, eligible borrowers for qualified agricultural purposes.

MERRILL LYNCH
101 South Highland Avenue, Jackson TN 38301. 901/422-6600. **Contact:** Mike Key, Manager. **Description:** A diversified financial services organization. The company is a major broker in securities, option contracts, commodities and financial futures contracts, and insurance. Merrill Lynch also deals with corporate and municipal securities and investment banking. **Corporate headquarters location:** New York NY.

MORGAN KEEGAN & COMPANY
Morgan Keegan Tower, 50 North Front Street, Memphis TN 38103. 901/524-4100. **Contact:** Jane Pienaar. **Description:** A holding company which, through its subsidiary, a regional securities broker-dealer, does business with individual clients in the southeastern U.S. and for institutional clients throughout the U.S. and abroad. Morgan Keegan & Company has 409 account executives in 23 offices in 10 states. **Number of employees nationwide:** 1,218.

WILLIS CORROON CORPORATION
26 Century Boulevard, Nashville TN 37214. 615/872-3000. **Contact:** Personnel. **Description:** A financial services and insurance company.

Note: Because addresses and telephone numbers of smaller companies change rapidly, we recommend you call each company to verify the information below before inquiring about job opportunities. Mass mailings are not recommended.

Additional employers with under 250 employees:

CREDIT AGENCIES AND INSTITUTIONS

Allied Credit Corp.
725 S Church St,
Murfreesboro TN
37130-4925.
615/896-2274.

Allied Credit Corp.
Green Village
Shopping Center,
Dyersburg TN 38024.
901/286-4011.

Allied Credit Corp.
5606 Nolensville Rd,
Nashville TN 37211-
6422. 615/834-1155.

Associates Financial Services
1567 N Eastman Rd,
Kingsport TN 37664-
2680. 423/246-1499.

City Finance Company
256 Poplar View
Pkwy, Collierville TN
38017-3112.
901/853-1037.

City Finance Company
813 S Garden St,
Columbia TN 38401-
3251. 615/388-8037.

Commercial Credit Plan Inc.
6518 Chapman Hwy,
Knoxville TN 37920-
6573. 423/579-5703.

First Capital Mortgage Corp.
Osborne Bldg,
Chattanooga TN
37411. 423/855-
7008.

Transouth Financial Services
Rt 4, Bradford Hicks
Dr, Livingston TN
38570. 615/823-
5661.

Fleet Funding
783 Old Hickory Blvd,
Brentwood TN 37027-
4508. 615/373-5050.

Gulf Pacific Mortgage
9724 Kingston Pike,
Knoxville TN 37922-
3347. 423/693-5555.

Mercury Finance Company
2902 Tazewell Pike,
Knoxville TN 37918-
1877. 423/689-7522.

National Mortgage Company
1770 Kirby Pkwy,
Suite 105, Memphis
TN 38138-7400.
901/754-8686.

Pioneer Credit Co.
904 Dupitt St, Athens
TN 37303-2465.
423/745-3760.

Security Finance Corp.
1004 Memorial Blvd,
Murfreesboro TN
37129-2407.
615/896-4000.

Security Financial & Mortgage
15 Century Blvd, Suite
101, Nashville TN
37214-3692.
615/391-5800.

Transouth Financial Corp.
525 W Market St,
Dyersburg TN 38024-
5001. 901/286-4971.

Tennessee Credit
595 Hillsboro Rd,
Franklin TN 37064-
2123. 615/791-7186.

American General Finance
5520 Old Hickory
Blvd, Hermitage TN
37076-2576.
615/889-0050.

Sunstar Acceptance Corporation
404 BNA Dr, Suite
302, Nashville TN
37217-2517.
615/360-3434.

First Merchants Acceptance
9041 Executive Park
Dr, Knoxville TN
37923-4621.
423/693-0741.

MORTGAGE BANKERS

Equity One Inc.
11 Northgate Park,
Suite 408,
Chattanooga TN
37415-6950.
423/875-3434.

Fleet Mortgage
5100 Poplar Ave
#2730, Memphis TN
38137-4002.
901/684-1509.

GMAC Mortgage Corp.
6799 Great Oaks Rd,
Suite 209, Memphis
TN 38138-2572.
901/754-4475.

Gulf Pacific Mortgage
5100 Poplar Ave,
Memphis TN 38137-
4002. 901/767-3400.

Leader Federal Mortgage
1 Burton Hills Blvd,
Nashville TN 37215-
6104. 615/665-1060.

Metropolitan Mortgage & Security Co.
446 Metroplex Dr,
Nashville TN 37211-
3139. 615/831-1554.

Singleton Mortgage Corp.
6254 Poplar Ave, Memphis TN 38119-4713. 901/761-1888.

SECURITY BROKERS AND DEALERS

AG Edwards & Sons Inc.
203 Broyles St, Suite 200, Johnson City TN 37601-2500. 423/245-1243.

Duncan-Williams Inc.
5860 Ridgeway Center Pkwy, Memphis TN 38120-4005. 901/761-6804.

Edward D. Jones & Co.
2020 Northpark Dr, Johnson City TN 37604-3127. 423/929-9093.

Edward D. Jones & Co.
106 Administration Rd, Oak Ridge TN 37830-6901. 423/483-3923.

JC Bradford & Co.
2000 Richard Jones Rd, Suite 100, Nashville TN 37215-2885. 615/383-3839.

JC Bradford & Co.
214 Mountcastle Dr, Johnson City TN 37601-2509. 423/928-7144.

Morgan Keegan & Co. Inc.
150 4th Ave N, Nashville TN 37219-2415. 615/255-0600.

Titan Value Equities
124 Timber Creek Dr, Arlington TN 38002.

Waterhouse Securities Inc.
315 Deaderick St, Nashville TN 37201-1114. 615/251-9522.

INVESTMENT ADVISORS

EP James Company Inc.
180 Market Place Blvd, Knoxville TN 37922-2337. 423/539-4350.

Raymond James & Associates Inc.
537 Market St, Suite 105, Chattanooga TN 37402-1225. 423/756-2371.

For more information on career opportunities in financial services:

Associations

FINANCIAL EXECUTIVES INSTITUTE
P.O. Box 1938, Morristown NJ 07962-1938. 201/898-4600. Fee and membership required. Publishes biennial member directory. Provides member referral service.

INSTITUTE OF FINANCIAL EDUCATION
111 East Wacker Drive, Chicago IL 60601. 312/946-8800. Offers career development program.

NATIONAL ASSOCIATION OF BUSINESS ECONOMISTS
1233 20th Street NW, Suite 505, Washington DC 20036. 202/463-6223. Bulletin board number: 216/241-6254. Newsletter and electronic bulletin board list job openings. Members can upload resumes and listed positions desired to bulletin board.

NATIONAL ASSOCIATION OF CREDIT MANAGEMENT
8815 Centre Park Drive, Suite 200, Columbia MD 21045-2158. 410/740-5560. Contact: Delores Richman. Publishes a business credit magazine.

NATIONAL ASSOCIATION OF REAL ESTATE INVESTMENT TRUSTS
1129 20th Street NW, Suite 305, Washington DC 20036. 202/785-8717. Contact: Donna Smith, Membership.

PUBLIC SECURITIES ASSOCIATION
40 Broad Street, 12th Floor, New York NY 10004. 212/809-7000. Contact: Caroline Binn x427. Publishes an annual report and several newsletters.

SECURITIES INDUSTRY ASSOCIATION
120 Broadway, 35th Floor New York NY 10271. 212/608-1500. Contact: Phil Williams/Membership. Publishes a security industry yearbook.

TREASURY MANAGEMENT ASSOCIATION
7315 Wisconsin Avenue, Suite 1250-W, Bethesda MD 20814. 301/907-2862.

<u>Directories</u>

DIRECTORY OF AMERICAN FINANCIAL INSTITUTIONS
Thomson Business Publications, 6195 Crooked Creek Road, Norcross GA 30092. 770/448-1011. Sales 800/321-3373.

MOODY'S BANK AND FINANCE MANUAL
Moody's Investor Service, 99 Church Street, New York NY 10007. 212/553-0300.

<u>Magazines</u>

BARRON'S: NATIONAL BUSINESS AND FINANCIAL WEEKLY
Dow Jones & Co., 200 Liberty Street, New York NY 10281. 212/416-2700.

FINANCIAL PLANNING
40 West 57th Street, 11th Floor, New York NY 10019. 212/765-5311.

FINANCIAL WORLD
Financial World Partners, 1328 Broadway, 3rd Floor, New York NY 10001. 212/594-5030.

INSTITUTIONAL INVESTOR
488 Madison Avenue, 12th Floor, New York NY 10022. 212/303-3300.

FOOD AND BEVERAGES/AGRICULTURE

Employment in food processing is expected to fall slightly through 2005. Although the industry's output should grow, increasing automation and productivity will mean food can be produced with fewer workers. However, some food processing industries are likely to remain fairly labor intensive. For example, meat packing and poultry processing are difficult to fully automate because each animal processed is different. Professional specialty occupations, although small in number, are also expected to grow. The growth of these occupations -- including engineers, systems analysts, and food scientists -- reflects the industry's emphasis on scientific research to improve food products and production processes. Demand for food scientists will also grow in response to expanding government inspection and regulation of food production.

Several factors may slow the decline in food processing employment. As consumers increasingly seek "ready-to-heat" foods, the food processing industry has introduced many new products. Many of these new goods, which require more processing than the items they are replacing, will help maintain the demand for food processors in the future. In addition, the food processing industry is taking advantage of new technology to perform much of the processing formerly done by retailers. One other factor that may help stem employment decline is growing international trade in food products. Food processing firms expect growing trade to provide new markets for their products. The emerging field of biotechnology and other new food science technologies may also provide new jobs.

BRACH & BROCK CONFECTIONS, INC.
P.O. Box 22427, Chattanooga TN 37422-2427. 423/899-1100. **Contact:** Mike Donilon, Vice President of Human Resources. **Description:** A candy and snack food manufacturer and marketer. **Common positions include:** Accountant/Auditor; Budget Analyst; Computer Programmer; Computer Systems Analyst; Customer Service Representative; Electrician; Financial Analyst; General Manager. **Educational backgrounds include:** Accounting; Computer Science; Engineering; Finance. **Benefits:** 401K; Disability Coverage; Employee Discounts; Life Insurance; Medical Insurance; Pension Plan; Savings Plan; Tuition Assistance. **Corporate headquarters location:** This Location. **Operations at this facility include:** Administration; Manufacturing; Research and Development; Sales; Service. **Listed on:** Privately held. **Number of employees at this location:** 1,000. **Number of employees nationwide:** 3,500.

BUSH BROTHERS & COMPANY
3885 Highway 411, Dandridge TN 37725. 423/509-2361. **Contact:** Dean Williams, Human Resources. **Description:** A food-processing plant specializing in canned vegetables. The primary product produced by Bush Brothers & Company is Bush's Baked Beans.

COLONIAL BAKING COMPANY
2407 Franklin Road, Nashville TN 37204. 615/297-5393. **Contact:** Human Resources. **Description:** A bread baking company.

CONWOOD CAPITAL CORPORATION
813 Rich Lake Boulevard, Memphis TN 38120. 901/761-2050. **Contact:** John Metz, Vice President of Administration/Personnel. **Description:** Manufactures smokeless tobacco products. Brand names include Kodiak and Levi Garrett.

COORS BREWING COMPANY
5151 East Raines, Memphis TN 38118. 901/375-2000. **Contact:** William Peters, Director of Human Resources. **Description:** A beer brewing plant. The parent company, Adolph Coors, is a holding company with subsidiaries which produce and distribute malt beverages such as beer. Coors Brewing is one of the world's largest brewing companies and the largest subsidiary of Adolph Coors Company. Through its ACX Technologies subsidiary, Adolph Coors Company also operates Golden Aluminum Company, Graphic Packaging Corporation, Coors BioTech Inc., Coors Energy Company, Golden Technologies Company, Inc., and Coors Ceramics.

CRESTAR FOODS INC.
750 Old Hickory Boulevard, Suite 250, Brentwood TN 37027. 615/371-0071. **Contact:** Jan Samuels, Human Resources Director. **Description:** A food manufacturer specializing in pizzas.

JIMMY DEAN FOODS
RUDY'S FARM COMPANY
8000 Centerview Parkway, Suite 400, Cordova TN 38018. 901/753-1600. **Contact:** Mr. Army Ward, Personnel Department. **Description:** A producer of a variety of processed meats. **Parent company:** Sara Lee Corporation is a diversified consumer products firm.

DELTA BEVERAGE GROUP, INC.
2221 Democrat Road, Memphis TN 38132. 901/344-7100. **Contact:** Raymond R. Stitle, Vice President of Human Resources. **Description:** A Pepsi-Cola and 7-Up bottling and sales company with operations throughout four states. **Common positions include:** Accountant/Auditor; Computer Programmer; Financial Analyst; Human Resources Specialist. **Educational backgrounds include:** Business Administration; Marketing. **Benefits:** 401K; Dental Insurance; Disability Coverage; Life Insurance; Medical Insurance; Tuition Assistance. **Corporate headquarters location:** This Location. **Other U.S. locations:** AK; LA; MI. **Operations at this facility include:** Manufacturing; Sales. **Listed on:** Privately held. **Number of employees at this location:** 1,500.

EAGLE SNACKS, INC.
P.O. Box 818, Fayetteville TN 37334. 615/433-3800. **Contact:** Joyce Gray, Employee Relations Manager. **Description:** Eagle Snacks, Inc., which began operations in 1979, produces and distributes a line of snack food items. The line of snack and nut items is distributed through a network of Anheuser-Busch wholesalers and independent distributors throughout the United States. The company produces a broad line of snack items including Thins and Ripples Potato Chips,

Crispy Cooked Potato Chips, Nacho Cheese and Ranch flavored Tortilla Thins, Restaurant Style and El Grande Style Tortilla Chips, Eagle Salsa and Bean Dip, and several other products. Eagle also markets nuts, including Honey Roast and Lightly Salted Peanuts, Mixed Nuts, and Fancy Cashews. **Corporate headquarters location:** St. Louis MO. **Parent company:** Anheuser-Busch Companies, Inc. (St. Louis MO).

FAST FOOD MERCHANDISERS, INC.
P.O. Box 277, Monterey TN 38574. 615/839-2273. **Contact:** Nancy Connelly, Human Resources Manager. **Description:** A fast food distribution company serving Hardee's Food Systems. Established in 1962, Fast Food Merchandisers was formed by Hardee's to keep up with the growing demand for the restaurant's products. The manufacturing and distribution group services nearly all of Hardee's restaurants from its three plants and 10 distribution facilities, which are located across the country. Hardee's Food Systems, Inc. is one of the largest fast-food hamburger restaurant companies in the world, operating over 4,000 restaurants in 40 states and 10 foreign countries. **Corporate headquarters location:** Rocky Mount NC.

FLEMING FOODS
500 South Cartwright Street, Goodlettsville TN 37072-1867. 615/859-4171. **Contact:** Mike Tate, Human Resources. **Description:** Fleming markets food and food-related products by servicing 2,900 supermarkets in 36 states in the U.S. and several foreign countries. With 32 computer-supported divisions, the company supplies retail customers with virtually every national brand grocery product as well as high-volume private label items. Fleming also provides a full line of perishables, including meats, dairy and delicatessen products, frozen foods, and fresh produce, along with a variety of general merchandise. The company offers its retailers a complete range of services, enabling them to compete more effectively. Fleming's distribution fleet consists of 1,700 tractors and 3,600 trailers. **Corporate headquarters location:** Oklahoma City OK. **Parent company:** Fleming Companies, Inc.

FLOWERS BAKING COMPANY
P.O. Box 1774, Morristown TN 37816. 423/586-2471. **Contact:** Dan Fisher, Human Resources Director. **Description:** Bakers of buns and rolls.

FLOWERS BAKING COMPANY
P.O. Box 495, Crossville TN 38557. 615/484-6101. **Contact:** Joan Crowell, Human Resources Director. **Description:** Bakers of sweet breads and rolls.

HERITAGE FARMS DAIRY
1100 New Salem Road, Murfreesboro TN 37129. 615/895-2790. **Contact:** Jeff Phillips, Human Resources Manager. **Description:** A milk-producing dairy farm.

HUNTS FOOD COMPANY
540 East Broadway, Newport TN 37821. 423/623-2333. **Contact:** Lisa Sweeney, Personnel Department. **Description:** A food processing company. Products processed at this location by Hunts Food Company include various bean and chili items, including Van Camps'

canned pork and beans, as well as specialty products such as Beanee Weenee canned beans and wieners. This location formerly operated as part of The Quaker Oats Company. **Corporate headquarters location:** Chicago IL. **Other U.S. locations:** Jackson TN. **Parent company:** ConAgra International.

KELLOGG COMPANY
P.O. Box 429, Rossville TN 38066. 901/853-6458. **Contact:** Human Resources. **Description:** Founded in 1906, Kellogg is a diversified international company specializing in the manufacturing and marketing of ready-to-eat cereals, as well as frozen waffles, toaster pastries, cereal bars, frozen pies, and other convenience foods. Kellogg products are manufactured in 18 countries in North America, Europe, Asia-Pacific, and Latin America, and are distributed in more than 150 countries. This location is also the headquarters of the Kellogg USA Convenience Foods Division, formed in 1993. This division's production facilities in California, Georgia, New Jersey, Pennsylvania, and Tennessee manufacture products such as Kellogg's Pop-Tarts toaster pastries, Eggo waffles, Kellogg's Nutri-Grain bars, Kellogg's Low Fat Granola bars, Kellogg's Croutettes stuffing mix, and Kellogg's Corn Flake Crumbs. **Corporate headquarters location:** Battle Creek MI. **Other U.S. locations:** Ontario, Canada; San Jose CA; San Leandro CA; Atlanta GA; Omaha NE; Blue Anchor NJ; Lancaster PA; Muncy PA; Pottstown PA; Memphis TN. **Listed on:** New York Stock Exchange.

KING COTTON
P.O. Box 13039, Memphis TN 38113. 901/942-3221. **Contact:** Sandy Peterson, Human Resources. **Description:** A distributor of processed meat goods. **Parent company:** Sara Lee Corporation is a diversified producer of consumer goods.

KRAFT FOODS INGREDIENTS CORPORATION
6410 Poplar Avenue, Memphis TN 38119. 901/766-2100. **Contact:** Vicky Odle, Human Resources Director. **Description:** Kraft Foods Ingredients Corporation manufactures private-label and industrial food products for sale to other food processing companies. Philip Morris Companies is a holding company whose principal wholly-owned subsidiaries are Philip Morris Inc. (Philip Morris U.S.A.), Philip Morris International Inc., Kraft Foods, Inc., Miller Brewing Company, and Philip Morris Capital Corporation. In the food industry, Kraft Foods, Inc. is one of the largest producers of packaged grocery products in North America. Major brands include Jell-O, Post, Kool-Aid, Crystal Light, Entenmann's, Miracle Whip, Stove Top, and Shake 'n' Bake. Kraft markets a number of products under the Kraft brand including natural and process cheeses and dry packaged dinners. The Oscar Mayer unit markets processed meats, poultry, lunch combinations, and pickles under the Oscar Mayer, Louis Rich, Lunchables, and Claussen brand names. Kraft is also one of the largest coffee companies with principal brands including Maxwell House, Sanka, Brim, and General Foods International Coffees. In the tobacco industry, Philip Morris U.S.A. and Philip Morris International together form one of the largest international cigarette operations in the world. U.S. brand names include Marlboro, Parliament, Virginia Slims, Benson & Hedges, and Merit. Miller Brewing Company brews brands names including Molsen Ice, Miller Genuine Draft, Miller High Life, Sharp's non-alcoholic, Red Dog, Miller Lite, Icehouse, Foster's

Lager, and Lowenbrau. Philip Morris Capital Corporation is engaged in financial services and real estate. **Corporate headquarters location:** Northfield IL. **Parent company:** Philip Morris Companies Inc. (New York). **Number of employees nationwide:** 155,000.

LEAF INC.
975 Kansas Street, P.O. Box 2038, Memphis TN 38101. 901/775-2960. **Contact:** Paul Solarski, Human Resources. **Description:** Manufactures chewing gum for baseball card packages.

McKEE FOODS CORPORATION
P.O. Box 750, Collegedale TN 37315. 423/238-7111. **Contact:** Human Resources. **Description:** Produces baked goods.

PEPSI-COLA OF NASHVILLE
715 Thompson Lane, P.O. Box 40968, Nashville TN 37204-0968. 615/383-7000. **Fax:** 615/269-7199. **Contact:** Mr. Lonnie E. Hillis, Human Resource Manager. **Description:** A distributor of soft drinks. The parent company, PepsiCo, Inc., operates on a worldwide basis within three industry segments: beverages, snack foods, and restaurants. The beverage segment primarily markets its brands worldwide, and manufactures concentrates for its brands for sale to franchised bottlers worldwide. The beverage segment also operates bottling plants and distribution facilities in the U.S. and in key international markets, and distributes ready-to-drink Lipton tea products under a joint venture agreement. In addition, under separate distribution and joint-venture agreements, the beverage segment distributes certain previously existing, as well as jointly developed, Ocean Spray juice products. **Common positions include:** Accountant/Auditor; Administrator; Advertising Clerk; Assistant Manager; Automotive Mechanic/Body Repairer; Blue-Collar Worker Supervisor; Computer Programmer; Customer Service Representative; Department Manager; Electrical/Electronics Engineer; General Manager; Human Resources Specialist; Industrial Engineer; Instructor/Trainer; Management Trainee; Operations/Production Manager; Quality Control Supervisor; Sales Associate; Transportation/Traffic Specialist. **Educational backgrounds include:** Accounting; Business Administration; Engineering; Liberal Arts; Marketing. **Benefits:** Dental Insurance; Disability Coverage; Employee Discounts; Life Insurance; Medical Insurance; Pension Plan; Profit Sharing; Tuition Assistance. **Corporate headquarters location:** This Location. **Parent company:** PepsiCo, Inc. **Operations at this facility include:** Administration; Manufacturing; Regional Headquarters; Sales. **Listed on:** New York Stock Exchange. **Number of employees at this location:** 579.

PRESIDENT BAKING BISHOP
1355 South Ocoee Street, P.O. Box 3720, Cleveland TN 37320. 423/472-1561. **Contact:** Joan Dalton, Personnel Manager. **Description:** A baking company. President Baking Bishop produces snack cakes, sold individually and in family packs. **Common positions include:** Accountant/Auditor; Claim Representative; Customer Service Representative; Electrical/Electronics Engineer; Food Scientist/Technologist; Human Resources Specialist; Manufacturer's/Wholesaler's Sales Rep.; Mechanical Engineer; Operations/Production Manager; Quality Control Supervisor; Transportation/Traffic Specialist. **Educational backgrounds include:**

Engineering; Mathematics. **Benefits:** Life Insurance; Medical Insurance. **Special Programs:** Training Programs. **Corporate headquarters location:** Atlanta GA. **Number of employees at this location:** 300.

PRESTO FOOD PRODUCTS, INC.
5885 Jetway Drive, Arlington TN 38002-9313. 901/867-2903. **Contact:** Human Resources. **Description:** Manufactures non-dairy whipped topping and coffee creamer.

PROCTER & GAMBLE MANUFACTURING
P.O. Box 2104, Jackson TN 38302. 901/423-7100. **Contact:** Mr. Terry Toteet, Human Resources Manager. **Description:** This location manufactures Pringles and Duncan Hines food products. Overall, Procter & Gamble manufactures over 300 laundry, cleaning, paper, beauty care, health care, food, and beverage products in more than 140 countries around the world. Laundry and household cleaning products include hard surface cleaners, such as Mr. Clean (introduced in 1959), and fabric conditioners, such as Bounce and Downy. Paper products include Pampers and Luvs diapers, Charmin bath tissue, and Bounty paper towels. Beauty products include Pantene Pro-V, the Vidal Sassoon hair care line, Cover Girl cosmetics, and Giorgio Beverly Hills fragrances. Health care products include Vicks brand cold remedies; Aleve, the first non-prescription version of Naprosyn; Didro-Kit therapy for osteoporosis; and Asacol, a treatment for ulcerative colitis. Food and beverage products include brand names such as Sunny Delight juice drink and Pringles potato chips. Other Procter & Gamble brands include Tide, Ariel, Crest, Crisco, and Max Factor. The company does extensive international business in Europe, Asia, Latin America, and Canada. Procter & Gamble's philosophy is built on building brand and consumer loyalty. In 1994, the company was awarded the Opportunity 2000 Award by the United States Department of Labor, a distinction recognizing the efforts of men and women throughout the organization to promote and advance employees of all origins and backgrounds. **NOTE:** Hiring is limited to entry-level positions and recruiting is centrally coordinated. **Corporate headquarters location:** Cincinnati OH.

PURITY DAIRIES INC.
P.O. Box 100957, Nashville TN 37224. 615/244-1900. **Contact:** Human Resources. **Description:** A dairy products manufacturer.

THE QUAKER OATS COMPANY
P.O. Box 2688, Jackson TN 38302. 901/426-6287. **Contact:** Human Resources. **Description:** This location produces a variety of frozen food products, including Sealtest ice cream and Aunt Jemima frozen breakfast products. Quaker Oats is a grocery product company with 81 percent of sales produced by brands holding the number-one or number-two positions in their respective categories. The Quaker Oats Company is best known for its Old Fashioned Quaker Oats. Other products include Quaker Chewy granola bars, rice cakes, Aunt Jemima products, Cycle pet food, pet treats such as Snausages and Pup-peroni, Celeste frozen pizza, Van Camp's canned beans, Wolf brand chili, Gatorade, Rice-A-Roni, Noodle Roni, and Near East rice products. **Corporate headquarters location:** Chicago IL.

C.B. RAGLAND COMPANY, INC.
P.O. Box 40587, Nashville TN 37204. 615/259-4622. **Contact:** Mrs. Ruby Vaughn, Director of Personnel. **Description:** A wholesale grocery products distributor.

RICH PRODUCTS CORPORATION
P.O. Box 248, Murfreesboro TN 37133. 615/890-4211. **Contact:** Mike Gallo, Human Resources Director. **Description:** Manufactures bread, rolls, sweet dough, pastries, and cookies. **Corporate headquarters location:** Buffalo NY.

MIKE ROSE FOODS INC.
189 Spence Lane, Nashville TN 37210. 615/889-8345. **Contact:** Jeannie Evenson, Human Resources Director. **Description:** A manufacturer of a variety of salad dressings.

THE J.M. SMUCKER COMPANY
P.O. Box 18498, Memphis TN 38181. 901/362-3550. **Contact:** Personnel Department. **Description:** Manufactures jellies, jams, pancake syrups, and ice cream toppings. **Common positions include:** Accountant/Auditor; Branch Manager; Customer Service Representative; Department Manager; Food Scientist/Technologist; Operations/Production Manager; Quality Control Supervisor. **Educational backgrounds include:** Accounting; Business Administration; Engineering. **Benefits:** Disability Coverage; Employee Discounts; Life Insurance; Medical Insurance; Pension Plan; Tuition Assistance. **Corporate headquarters location:** Orrville OH. **Operations at this facility include:** Manufacturing; Regional Headquarters; Sales. **Listed on:** New York Stock Exchange.

A.E. STALEY MANUFACTURING
198 Blair Bend Drive, Loudon TN 37774. 423/458-5681. **Contact:** Jennifer Ogle, Human Resources. **Description:** Manufacturers of corn syrup.

STANDARD CANDY COMPANY
715 Massman Drive, Nashville TN 37210. 615/889-6360. **Contact:** Gary Baker, Plant Manager. **Description:** A candy manufacturer.

TYSON FOODS INC.
P.O. Box 8, Shelbyville TN 37160. 615/684-8180. **Contact:** Don Smith, Personnel Manager. **Description:** This location is one of 48 poultry processing plants, engaged in chicken slaughtering, dressing, cutting, packaging, and de-boning. Tyson Foods is one of the world's largest fully-integrated producers, processors, and marketers of poultry-based food products. The company also produces other center-of-the-plate and convenience food items. Chicken continues to account for 75 percent of sales, and Tyson poultry production capacity is projected by the company to increase to approximately 37 million heads per week by the end of 1997. Familiar Tyson products include Tyson Holly Farms Fresh Chicken, Weaver, Louis Kemp Crab, Lobster Delights, Healthy Portion products, Beef Stir Fry, Crab Delights Stir Fry, Chicken Fried Rice Kits, Pork Chops with Cinnamon Apples, Salmon Grill Kits, Fish'n Chips Kits, and Rotisserie Chicken. **Corporate headquarters location:** Springdale AR. **Listed on:** NASDAQ.

UNITED FOODS INC.
10 Pictsweet Drive, Bells TN 38006. 901/422-7600. **Contact:** Human Resources. **Description:** A manufacturer of a variety of foods. This location manufactures frozen vegetables.

Note: Because addresses and telephone numbers of smaller companies change rapidly, we recommend you call each company to verify the information below before inquiring about job opportunities. Mass mailings are not recommended.

Additional employers with under 250 employees:

CORN

Master Mix Feeds
1200B Judd Rd, Chattanooga TN 37406-4711. 423/629-7341.

Tennessee Farmers Co-Op
4814 Co-Op Rd, Rockford TN 37853-3006. 423/577-1303.

HOGS

Fineberg Packing Co.
2875 Starling Pl, Memphis TN 38108-1727. 901/458-2622.

DAIRY FARMS

Mayfield Dairy Farms Industries
2115 N Thompson Ln, Murfreesboro TN 37129-6026. 615/849-3939.

ANIMAL SPECIALTY SERVICES

Fowlplay Farm Exotics
1100 Oak Plains Rd, Clarksville TN 37043-6906. 615/362-3687.

MEAT AND POULTRY PROCESSING

Byron's Inc.
349 W Main St, Gallatin TN 37066-3240. 615/452-4892.

Elm Hill Meats Inc.
1001 Elm Hill Rd, Lenoir City TN 37771-4339. 423/986-8005.

Kesterson Food Co. Inc.
211 Highway 69 N, Paris TN 38242-6592. 901/642-5031.

Lay Packing Co. Inc.
807 Campbell Ave, Knoxville TN 37915. 423/525-1918.

Pierre Frozen Foods
P.O. Box 55, Caryville TN 37714-0055. 423/562-8471.

Tennessee Cold & Dry Storage
1300 Market St, Chattanooga TN 37402-4446. 423/755-9000.

Zartic Inc.
P.O. Box 749, Chattanooga TN 37401-0749. 423/756-3435.

DAIRY PRODUCTS

Turner Dairies Inc.
653 Turner Ln, Covington TN 38019-4551. 901/476-2643.

PRESERVED FRUITS AND VEGETABLES

Arrow Industries Inc.
140 International Blvd, La Vergne TN 37086-3225. 615/793-7751.

GRAIN MILL PRODUCTS

PFB LP
P.O. Box 609, Jackson TN 38302-0609. 901/424-3535.

Planters Lifesavers
P.O. Box 22068, Chattanooga TN 37422-2068. 423/894-8420.

The White Lily Foods Co.
P.O. Box 871, Knoxville TN 37901-0871. 423/546-5511.

MacMillan Bloedel America
P.O. Box 22968, Nashville TN 37202-2968. 615/742-4100.

DOG AND CAT FOOD

Nutro Products Inc.
920 Artic Dr, Lebanon TN 37090-5300. 615/449-4996.

BAKERY PRODUCTS

Merita Bakery
1218 N Central St, Knoxville TN 37917-6311. 423/524-3631.

Rainbo Baking Co.
P.O. Box 2387, Johnson City TN 37605-2387. 423/928-1137.

Turnbull Cone Baking Co.
120 Parmenas Ln,
Chattanooga TN
37405-2623.
423/265-4553.

SUGAR AND CONFECTIONERY PRODUCTS

Bradley Candy Manufacturing
211 Babb Dr, Lebanon
TN 37087-2507.
615/444-8586.

FATS AND OILS

Hunt-Wesson Foods Inc.
P.O. Box 1759,
Memphis TN 38101-
1759. 901/726-6929.

Bunge Foods
P.O. Box 2309,
Chattanooga TN
37409-0309.
423/821-3511.

Southern Cotton Oil Co.
2782 Chelsea Ave,
Memphis TN 38108-
1705. 901/452-3151.

BEVERAGES

Brown Forman/Jack Daniels
110 21st Ave S,
Nashville TN 37203-
2416. 615/340-1000.

Coca Cola/Dr. Pepper Bottling Works
P.O. Box 1750,
Tullahoma TN 37388-
1750. 615/455-3466.

Land O' Sun Dairies Inc.
P.O. Box 1349,
Kingsport TN 37662-
1349. 423/245-5154.

FOOD PREPARATIONS

Flavorite Laboratories Inc.
P.O. Box 1315,

Memphis TN 38101-
1315. 6013933610.

Pet Inc./US Grocery Operators
1112 W Irish St,
Greeneville TN 37743-
5214. 423/638-3171.

FOOD WHOLESALE

D. Canale Food Services
7 W Georgia Ave,
Memphis TN 38103-
4729. 901/525-6811.

Institutional Wholesale Co.
25 S Whitney Ave,
Cookeville TN 38501-
3237. 615/526-9588.

Knott's Wholesale Foods
215 Sterling St,
Jackson TN 38301-
5825. 901/427-3022.

PAC Food Distributor
P.O. Box 30144,
Memphis TN 38130-
0144. 901/363-7810.

Charles Parks Co.
P.O. Box 119, Gallatin
TN 37066-0119.
615/452-2406.

Specialty Distribution Center
1717 JP Hennessey
Dr, La Vergne TN
37086-3526.
615/641-9821.

The HT Hackney Co.
342 Dale Ave,
Knoxville TN 37921-
6718. 423/525-9541.

The HT Hackney Co.
27 East Ave, Athens
TN 37303-1619.
423/745-2582.

Unijax Sloan
810 Cowan St Bldg,
Nashville TN 37207-
5600. 615/259-3000.

Unijax Sloan
1307 Karnes Ave,

Knoxville TN 37917-
2627. 423/688-8600.

Unijax Sloan
1310 E 14th St,
Chattanooga TN
37404-4244.
423/622-7795.

Smith & Woods
554 National Dr,
Maryville TN 37804-
5428. 423/970-2050.

Turner Dairies Inc.
2040 Madison Ave,
Memphis TN 38104-
2747. 901/726-5684.

Barber's Ice Cream
51 Oldham St,
Nashville TN 37213-
1108. 615/255-7431.

Frito-Lay Inc.
4016 Industry Dr,
Chattanooga TN
37416-3811.
423/894-3570.

Golden Flake Snack Foods
1576 Three Pl,
Memphis TN 38116-
3508. 901/346-7349.

Loggins Meat Co. Inc.
245 S Sussex Ln,
Cordova TN 38018-
8181. 901/755-6244.

Travis Meats Inc.
7210 Clinton Hwy,
Powell TN 37849-
5216. 423/938-9051.

Premapak Inc.
502 Swan Dr, Smyrna
TN 37167-2019.
615/223-0062.

Hostess Cake Co.
2612 Grandview Ave,
Nashville TN 37211-
2203. 615/254-3149.

LIVESTOCK

Bryan Food Buying Station
16620 Highway 196,
Arlington TN 38002.
901/867-3731.

Bryan Foods Inc.
9020 David Crockett
Hwy, Winchester TN
37398. 615/967-
3965.

**ALCOHOL
WHOLESALE**

Ajax Turner
1045 Visco Dr,
Nashville TN 37210-
2207. 615/244-2424.

Ajax Turner
801 Visco Dr,
Nashville TN 37210-
2149. 615/259-7533.

AS Barboro Inc.
4116 BFGoodrich
Blvd, Memphis TN
38118-6920.
901/795-5310.

**Athens Distributing
Co.**
1000 Herman St,
Nashville TN 37208-
3144. 615/254-0101.

**FARM SUPPLIES
WHOLESALE**

Terra International
1310 W Church St,
Alamo TN 38001.
901/696-4565.

**TOBACCO AND
TOBACCO PRODUCTS
WHOLESALE**

**Brown & Williamson
Tobbaco**
2106 N Roan St,
Johnson City TN
37601-2504.
423/282-5309.

Eli Witt Co.
4280 Concorde Rd,
Memphis TN 38118-
7401. 901/365-3939.

For more information on career opportunities in the food, beverage, and agriculture industries:

Associations

**AMERICAN ASSOCIATION OF
CEREAL CHEMISTS (AACC)**
3340 Pilot Knob Road, St. Paul
MN 55121. 612/454-7250.
Contact: Marla Meyers. Dedicated
to the dissemination of technical
information and continuing
education in cereal science.

**AMERICAN FROZEN FOOD
INSTITUTE**
1764 Old Meadow Lane, Suite
350. McLean VA 22102.
703/821-0770. A national trade
association representing the
interests of the frozen food
industry.

**AMERICAN SOCIETY OF
AGRICULTURAL ENGINEERS**
2950 Niles Road, St. Joseph MI
49085. 616/429-0300. Contact:
Julie Swim.

**AMERICAN SOCIETY OF
BREWING CHEMISTS
ASSOCIATION**
3340 Pilot Knob Road, St. Paul
MN 55121. 612/454-7250.
Founded in 1934 to improve and
bring uniformity to the brewing
industry on a technical level.

**CIES - THE FOOD BUSINESS
FORUM**
3800 Moore Plaza, Alexandria VA
22305. 703/549-4525. A global
food business network.

Membership is on a company
basis. Members learn how to
manage their businesses more
effectively and gain access to
information and contacts.

**DAIRY AND FOOD INDUSTRIES
SUPPLY ASSOCIATION (DFISA)**
1451 Dolly Madison Boulevard,
McLean VA 22101-3850.
703/761-2600. Contact: Dorothy
Brady. A trade association whose
members are suppliers to the
food, dairy, liquid processing, and
related industries.

**MASTER BREWERS
ASSOCIATION OF THE
AMERICAS (MBAA)**
2421 North Mayfair Road, Suite
310, Wauwatosa, WI 53226.
414/774-8558. Promotes,
advances, improves, and protects
the professional interests of brew
and malt house production and
technical personnel. Disseminates
technical and practical
information.

**NATIONAL AGRICULTURAL
CHEMICALS ASSOCIATION**
1156 15th Street NW, Suite 900,
Washington DC 20005. 202/296-
1585.

**NATIONAL BEER WHOLESALERS'
ASSOCIATION**
1100 South Washington Street,
Alexandria VA 22314-4494.

703/683-4300. Fax: 703/683-8965. Contact: Karen Craig.

NATIONAL FOOD PROCESSORS ASSOCIATION
1401 New York Avenue NW, Suite 400, Washington DC 20005. 202/639-5900. Contact: Ned Endler.

UNITED DAIRY INDUSTRY ASSOCIATION (UDIA)
10255 West Higgins Road, Suite 900, Rosemont IL 60018. 847/803-2000. A federation of state and regional dairy promotion organizations that develop and execute effective programs to increase consumer demand for U.S.-produced milk and dairy products.

Directories

FOOD ENGINEERING'S DIRECTORY OF U.S. FOOD PLANTS
Chilton Book Company, Chilton Way, Radnor PA 19089. 800/695-1214.

THOMAS FOOD INDUSTRY REGISTER
Thomas Publishing Company, Five Penn Plaza, New York NY 10001. 212/695-0500.

Magazines

BEVERAGE WORLD
Keller International Publishing Corporation. 150 Great Neck Road, Great Neck NY 11021. 516/829-9210.

FOOD PROCESSING
301 East Erie Street, Chicago IL 60611. 312/644-2020.

FROZEN FOOD AGE
Maclean Hunter Media, #4 Stamford Forum, Stamford CT 06901. 203/325-3500.

PREPARED FOODS
Gorman Publishing Company, 8750 West Bryn Mawr, Chicago IL 60631. 312/693-3200.

GOVERNMENT

While the federal government is still the nation's largest employer, the number of federal jobs is rapidly on the decline. Adding to this instability was the federal government's shut down on more than one occasion while the President and Congress were in budgetary deadlock. The decrease in Department of Defense employment that started with the collapse of the Soviet Union has only increased due to federal deficits. The Defense Department is expected to reduce its workforce through attrition over the next decade.

Employment in other executive agencies is also expected to fall. Many workers are being offered buyouts, early retirement, and other incentives to leave the federal government. Demand remains strong, however, for nurses and engineers.

The outlook for state and local government workers is somewhat better. While opportunities vary from one state to the next, the Bureau of Labor Statistics forecasts a 16 percent job rise through 2005. Adding to the demand is the rising need for services. Since the early '80s, the government has decentralized and states have assumed more responsibility for providing services. Many policy decisions have been shifted to individual state governments, which are increasingly dealing with transportation problems, health care issues, energy policies, and poverty.

Even so, future job growth may be slowed by budgetary constraints. Local governments are struggling to meet the demand for services because tax revenues and federal aid are declining. Many states have cut their workforces to reduce spending and keep budgets balanced.

CITY HALL
111 West Vine Street, Murfreesboro TN 37130. 615/893-5210. **Contact:** Human Resources. **Description:** Responsible for all functions of the city of Murfreesboro, such as the plan and design of city building structures and streets and the maintenance and control of the city budget. Offices at this location include the mayor's office, as well other city officials; Public Works Department; court; legal offices; tax collection; and recreation.

MEMPHIS AND SHELBY COUNTY HEALTH DEPARTMENT
814 Jefferson Avenue, Room 131, Memphis TN 38105. 901/576-7771. **Fax:** 901/576-7908. **Contact:** Charles Wolfe, Director of Human Resources. **Description:** Provides health-related services such as birth certificates, death certificates, and immunizations. The department also provides care for pediatric and chronically ill adults. **Common positions include:** Administrator; Chemist; Counselor; Dietician/Nutritionist; Human Resources Specialist; Nurse; Physician. **Educational backgrounds include:** Biology; Business Administration; Chemistry; Engineering; Geology. **Benefits:** Dental Insurance;

Disability Coverage; Life Insurance; Medical Insurance; Pension Plan; Tuition Assistance. **Corporate headquarters location:** This Location. **Operations at this facility include:** Administration; Health Care. **Number of employees nationwide: 797.**

Note: Because addresses and telephone numbers of smaller companies change rapidly, we recommend you call each company to verify the information below before inquiring about job opportunities. Mass mailings are not recommended.

Additional employers with under 250 employees:

EXECUTIVE, LEGISLATIVE, & GENERAL GOVT.

Patrol West Sector
6730 Charlotte Pike, Nashville TN 37209.

Tennessee Arts Commission
404 James Robertson

Pkwy, Nashville TN 37219. 615/741-1701.

REGULATORY ADMINISTRATION OF UTILITIES

Athens Utilities Board
100 New Englewood

Rd, Athens TN 37303-4707. 423/745-4501.

UNITED STATES POSTAL SERVICE

Kingsport Main Post Office
320 W Center St, Kingsport TN 37660-3658. 423/245-5111.

For more information about career opportunities in the government:

Directories

ACCESS...FCO ON-LINE
Federal Research Service, Inc., P.O. Box 1059, 243 Church Street, Vienna VA 22183-1059. 703/281-

0200. This is the online service of the *Federal Career Opportunities* publication. To join online, the cost is $25 for the set-up and $45 for one hour, payable by credit card over the phone.

HEALTH CARE: SERVICES, EQUIPMENT, AND PRODUCTS

With no time to worry about the failure of government-proposed health care reforms, the health care industry is surging ahead with its own solutions, pressured by a competitive marketplace to cut costs. HMOs and insurance providers are looking to nursing homes and home care companies as an alternative to long-term hospital stays, and shifting from inpatient to less expensive outpatient care. Hospitals are streamlining operations and consolidating, with cutback efforts targeting staff, as well as unnecessary tests and laboratory fees. Hospital cost-cutting has also hurt medical equipment suppliers, as many hospitals form networks to share expensive equipment.

Even so, from 1990 to 1995, the number of health care workers in the United States grew from 8.86 million 10.5 million. Despite pressure to cut back, the health care industry remains a growth area. As the elderly population continues to grow faster than the population as a whole and the survival rate of the severely ill continues to improve, the need for new workers will continue to increase, and the large employment base will create replacement needs.

ADVOCAT INC.
277 Mallory Station Road, Suite 130, Franklin TN 37067. 615/771-7575. **Contact:** Bob Rice, Director of Employee and Client Relations. **Description:** Advocat Inc. operates 86 long-term care facilities, including 66 nursing homes containing 7,440 licensed beds and 20 retirement centers containing 2,134 units as of December 31, 1994. The company owns two nursing homes, acts as lessee of 37 of the nursing homes it operates, and acts as manager of the remaining 27 nursing homes. The company acts as lessee of seven of the retirement centers that it operates and manager of the remaining 13 retirement centers. Seventeen of the company's 20 retirement centers are in Canada. The company's leased and managed homes provide a range of health care services to their residents. In addition to the nursing and social services usually provided in the long-term care facilities, the company offers a variety of rehabilitative, nutritional, respiratory, and other specialized ancillary services. The company operates facilities in Alabama, Arkansas, Florida, Kentucky, Ohio, Tennessee, Texas, West Virginia, and the Canadian provinces of Ontario and British Columbia.

AMERICAN HEALTHCORP
DIABETES TREATMENT CENTERS OF AMERICA
One Burton Hills Boulevard, Suite 300, Nashville TN 37215. 615/665-1122. **Contact:** Rita Sailer, Vice President, Human Resources. **Description:** American Healthcorp, through its wholly-owned subsidiary, Diabetes Treatment Centers of America, Inc. (DTCA), is one of the nation's leading providers of comprehensive diabetes treatment services to physicians and hospitals. These services are designed to increase the quality and lower the cost of

the treatment of patients with diabetes, a chronic, incurable disease. More than 12 million people are estimated to have diabetes in the United States. American Healthcorp created the business of hospital-based diabetes treatment centers 1984 and has 63 centers in operation. Through its majority ownership of Amsurg Corporation, the company develops, acquires, and manages physician practice-based ambulatory surgery practices. AmSurg has 10 surgery centers in operation. The company also wholly owns ArthritisCare Centers of America, which operates two comprehensive treatment centers for individuals with arthritis.

AMERICAN HOMEPATIENT, INC.
105 Reynold Drive, Franklin TN 37064. 615/794-3313. **Contact:** Ms. Sandy Irvin. **Description:** American HomePatient provides home health care products and services through 80 locations in 13 states in the southwestern and southeastern United States. The company is one of the nation's largest diversified home health care providers. The main services offered by American HomePatient include respiratory and infusion therapy, enteral and parenteral nutrition, and the rental and sale of medical equipment and related supplies for the home.

BAPTIST HOSPITAL
2000 Church Street, Nashville TN 37236. 615/329-5555. **Contact:** Rachel West, Assistant Vice President, Human Resources. **Description:** Baptist Hospital is a not-for-profit medical center that has served the Middle Tennessee region since 1919, consistently offering a wide range of programs and services to meet virtually all medical needs. In the past 10 years, Baptist has grown from a relatively small community hospital to a state-of-the-art regional medical center of more than 1 million square feet spanning more than six city blocks. With a growing medical staff of 900-plus physicians, the hospital's 3,300 employees care for more than 200,000 inpatient, outpatient, and Emergency Pavilion patients each year. Baptist is developing the Baptist Healthcare Group, similar to models such as the Mayo, Scripps, and Ochsner Clinic's structure, which is Tennessee's first integrated health care system designed to offer the highest quality care at the most cost-efficient prices. **Number of employees at this location:** 3,300.

BAPTIST HOSPITAL
137 Blount Avenue, Knoxville TN 37920. 423/632-5011. **Contact:** Scott Shaffer, Vice President of Human Resources. **Description:** Located in downtown Knoxville on the south bank of the Tennessee River, Baptist Hospital is a 438-bed acute care hospital serving as the central resources of The Baptist Health System of East Tennessee. Since opening in 1948, Baptist -- through its advanced diagnostic and innovative treatment capabilities -- has become a leader in a variety of specialties, including Cardiac Care; Eye Care; Cancer Care; Neurosciences; and Medical/Surgical. Baptist Hospital provides a comprehensive cardiac program which includes angioplasty, open heart surgery and cardiac rehabilitation. The Baptist Eye Institute is the region's first facility devoted exclusively to eye care. The Baptist Regional Cancer Center is accredited by the American College of Surgeons as a Comprehensive Community Cancer Center offering both inpatient and outpatient facilities. Other services provided include neorplogical services and neurosciences.

BAPTIST MEMORIAL HEALTH CARE SYSTEM

899 Madison Avenue, Memphis TN 38146. 901/227-5090. **Contact:** Human Resources Department. **Description:** The company is a health care group which runs 17 hospitals in Tennessee, Mississippi, and Arkansas. The hospitals range in size from 40-beds to 1,366-beds. The system was founded in 1912 when the Southern Baptist Conventions of the three states pooled their resources to "establish an organization to render quality health care to all in this area in keeping with the tenets of our church." Today, Baptist Memorial says it is striving for greater efficiency by developing an integrated delivery system -- a network of health care organizations and physicians who provide and coordinate the delivery of health care services -- while also working to contain the cost of health care.

BEHAVIORAL MEDICINE

612 West Due West Avenue, Madison TN 37115. 615/865-3385. **Contact:** Ms. Jan Dann, Nurse Manager. **Description:** A 28-bed psychiatric hospital.

BLOUNT MEMORIAL HOSPITAL

907 East Lamar Alexander Parkway, Maryville TN 37804-5193. 423/983-7211. **Contact:** Joe Hill, Director of Human Resources. **Description:** Blount Memorial Hospital is a fully accredited 334-bed acute care facility located five miles south of the Knoxville Metropolitan Airport. The hospital provides quality care and education in hospital, outpatient, worksite, and community settings. More than 220 physicians serve on active and courtesy staffs -- 93 members of active staff are in 27 areas of specialization. The hospital also has 330 RNs and 125 LPNs. Blount Memorial offers a 24-hour physician-staffed emergency department (a designated Level III Trauma Center); comprehensive therapeutic and diagnostic facilities; a state-of-the-art surgery center including eight new surgical suites, same-day surgery, and an intensive care unit; innovative industrial medicine and occupational health and employee assistance programs for business and industry; primary care and occupational health clinic network; a family birthing center; and alcohol, drug, and eating disorders treatments.

BRISTOL REGIONAL MEDICAL CENTER

One Medical Park Boulevard, Bristol TN 37620. 423/844-1121. **Contact:** Jim Minatra, Director of Human Resources. **Description:** Bristol Regional Medical Center is a 377-bed, not-for-profit regional referral center, which provides a vast array of medical services and resources for thousands of patients in Northeast Tennessee and Southwest Virginia, as well as areas of Kentucky, West Virginia, and North Carolina. The all-new Bristol Regional Medical Center, opened in January 1994, is based on the medical mall concept, which gives patients, visitors, and employees alike much easier access to services. Bristol has served the region since 1925, first as King's Mountain Memorial Hospital, then as Bristol Memorial Hospital, and finally as Bristol Regional Medical Center. Nearly 140 board-certified and/or board-eligible physicians are associated with BRMC. To complement the medical diversity of the physicians, BRMC employs some 1,500 health care professionals, and is licensed for 377 beds, 15 newborn bassinets, and emergency medical services. BMRC operating rooms include two dedicated to cystoscopy, one heart room, and seven multi-specialty rooms. Adjacent to the OR is a three-room endoscopy suite.

CTI PET SYSTEMS, INC.
810 Innovation Drive, Knoxville TN 37932. 423/966-7539. **Fax:** 423/966-8955. **Contact:** Karin Davies, Human Resources Manager. **Description:** CTI PET Systems, Inc. is a joint venture with Siemens Medical Systems, Inc., developing and manufacturing equipment used in Positron Emission Tomography (PET). PET is a non-invasive medical imaging technique that is able to detect abnormal functions of the body in its early stages, long before other conventional diagnostic techniques, by imaging biochemical and metabolic changes. PET analyzes this biomedical metabolic function or dysfunction both qualitatively and quantitatively. PET studies are useful in a wide range of brain, heart, and cancer studies, by measuring the blood flow and metabolic rate of a particular organ. It is used in cardiology for tissue viability and perfusion studies, in neurology for studying epilepsy and dementia, as well as other investigative brain studies, and in oncology for early tumor diagnosis, tumor grading, and extent of metastasis. **Common positions include:** Accountant/Auditor; Biomedical Engineer; Buyer; Chemical Engineer; Computer Systems Analyst; Designer; Electrical/Electronics Engineer; Human Resources Specialist; Mechanical Engineer; Software Engineer. **Benefits:** 401K; Dental Insurance; Disability Coverage; Life Insurance; Medical Insurance; Pension Plan; Savings Plan; Tuition Assistance. **Corporate headquarters location:** This Location. **Number of employees at this location:** 150.

CENTENNIAL MEDICAL CENTER
PARTHENON PAVILION
2401 Parman Place, Nashville TN 37203. 615/342-1400. **Contact:** Personnel. **Description:** Founded in 1971, Parthenon Pavilion is one of the oldest and largest full-service psychiatric facilities in Middle Tennessee. A 162-bed, fully-licensed and accredited hospital, the Pavilion offers a comprehensive program of mental health services for adolescents, adults, and the elderly. Patients at the Pavilion enjoy the benefits of specialized psychiatric care and the advantages of the extensive medical facilities of Centennial Medical Center. The Pavilion's continuum of care encompasses eight units, where treatment is tailored to the needs of people with various illnesses and in different age groups. The treatment process involves close collaboration among the patient, family, and the professional team representing many disciplines. At Parthenon Pavilion, patients and their families work together with one team of experts throughout the treatment process. The team includes a physician, primary nurse, social worker, and education therapist, when appropriate. Other specialists are available to contribute to the work of the team if needed. Directed by the physician, a primary nurse works closely with each patient on a daily basis and coordinates communication among team members. The Pavilion's medical staff includes over 60 physicians, each of whom must achieve board certification within three years of affiliation with Parthenon Pavilion. All members of the nursing staff undergo training in psychiatric nursing, and the majority are certified by the American Nurses Association as psychiatric/mental health nurses. Over 90 percent of the hospital's social service professionals are licensed clinical social workers.

CLARKSVILLE MEMORIAL HOSPITAL
1171 Madison Street, P.O. Box 3160, Clarksville TN 37043. 615/552-6622. **Contact:** Pete Napolitano, Vice President of Human Resources. **Description:** Clarksville Memorial Hospital provides family-centered, contemporary health care services for residents in north Tennessee and southern Kentucky. The hospital delivers customer-oriented, cost-effective, specialized care which enhances access, convenience, and wellness for residents of the service area.

COLUMBIA REGIONAL HOSPITAL
P.O. Box 3310, Jackson TN 38303. 901/661-2000. **Contact:** Carla Robbins, Human Resources. **Description:** Regional Hospital of Jackson opened its doors in March, 1977 under the name of Parkway Hospital, a General Care Corporation facility. Today, the hospital provides a number of health care services, including: critical care, radiology, surgery, cardiopulmonary/respiratory therapy, emergency care, physical therapy, nuclear medicine, outpatient surgery, ultrasound services, renal hemodialysis, and a computer tomography scanner. Other programs include a substance abuse and adolescent psychiatric unit, public education classes and programs, the Breast Diagnostic Center, the Sleep Disorders Laboratory, mobile lithotripsy, cardiac catheterization, opthalmic surgery, peripheral laser angioplasty, Holter monitoring, color-flow echo imaging; laser laparoscopic surgery, the Center for Women's Health, a dedicated pediatric unit, magnetic resonance imaging, and the Family Birth Center. Regional Hospital of Jackson has 166 beds, over 500 employees, more than 180 physicians on staff, and over 4,000 admissions a year.

COLUMBIA/HCA
One Park Plaza, Nashville TN 37203. 615/327-9551. **Contact:** Neil Hemphill, Vice President. **Description:** A national chain of over 200 hospitals and medical centers, Columbia/HCA (formerly Columbia Hospital Corporation) has been expanding since its start in the late 1980s, and now operates facilities from Alaska to Florida. Columbia purchased the HCA chain of hospitals in early 1994. Worldwide, the company employs over 130,000. **Corporate headquarters location:** This Location.

COLUMBIA/HCA INDIAN PATH PAVILION
2300 Pavilion Drive, Kingsport TN 37660. 423/378-7500. **Contact:** Patricia Blankenship, Assistant Director of Human Resources. **Description:** Indian Path Pavilion is a psychiatric health facility which is part of a regional medical center system serving the Tri-Cities area. The regional system also includes a 295-bed primary care medical-surgical hospital, and other local facilities. The regional group is part of the national chain of over 200 hospitals and medical centers, Columbia/HCA Healthcare Corporation. Columbia/HCA (formerly Columbia Hospital Corporation) has been expanding since its start in the late 1980s, and now operates facilities from Alaska to Florida. Columbia purchased the HCA chain of hospitals in early 1994, acquiring the Indian Path system in the process. **Parent company:** Columbia/HCA Healthcare Corporation (Nashville TN).

CROCKETT HOSPITAL
P.O. Box 847, Lawrenceburg TN 38464. 615/762-6571. **Contact:** Bob Augustine, Director of Human Resources. **Description:** A hospital.

EG&G ORTEC
100 Midland Road, Oak Ridge TN 37831. 423/482-4411. **Contact:** Cathy O'Connor, Human Resources. **Description:** Develops and manufactures a variety of laser-based medical equipment. The parent company designs and manufactures laboratory and field-test instruments and electronic and mechanical components for commercial customers. EG&G provides systems engineering, precision component manufacturing, and test-site operating and management services to many government agencies and laboratories. EG&G employs 34,000 people worldwide. **Parent company:** EG&G.

EAST TENNESSEE CHILDREN'S HOSPITAL
P.O. Box 15010, Knoxville TN 37901-5010. 423/541-8000. **Contact:** Paul Bates, Director of Human Resources. **Description:** As the only freestanding medical center in east Tennessee devoted solely to children, Children's Hospital of East Tennessee cares for some 60,000 children from east Tennessee, southeast Kentucky, southwest Virginia and western North Carolina. Children's Hospital is the region's leading pediatric referral center. The hospital actively recruits pediatric specialists in a variety of fields from across the nation. These subspecialists bring with them an intensive level of training in all fields of pediatric medicine and surgery, from allergy/immunology to urology. Services include the hospital's Pediatric Intensive Care Unit; the Neonatal Intensive Care Unit; the Pediatric Critical Care Transport Team and the Neonatal Transport Team; the Pediatric Emergency Department and Trauma Center; pediatric medical floors; outpatient clinics; pediatric surgical services; home health; children's rehabilitation center; Children's Hospital Intensive Psychiatric Services (CHIPS); the Child Life Department; Patient and Community Relations; Pastoral Care; Nutrition Services; and Social Work.

EASTWOOD MEDICAL CENTER
3000 Getwell Road, Memphis TN 38118. 901/369-8100. **Contact:** Human Resources. **Description:** Eastwood Medical Center is a 243-bed medical/surgical hospital. The Center offers a complete range of services including a 24-hour physician staffed emergency center, inpatient and outpatient health care, mental health services, and a treatment for chemical dependency for adults and adolescents. Eastwood provides both state-of-the-art technology and patient care over a wide range of hospital services. The Health Resource Center, located in the Eastwood Medical Office Building, was created to help educate and serve the community through a broad range of health-related events. The Resource Center, along with the staff of the Medical Center, offers free health seminars and free health screenings each month. **Parent company:** Regent Health Group, Inc.

ERLANGER MEDICAL CENTER
975 East Third Street, Chattanooga TN 37403-9975. 423/778-7000. **Contact:** Robert Terry, Senior Vice President, Human Resources. **Description:** Erlanger's commitment to the people of

Chattanooga began in 1891, when the Medical Center was a small public hospital -- the first one to serve the city. Throughout the past century, Erlanger has grown into an 811-bed teaching facility, providing almost every conceivable medical service and staffed with the region's top physicians and nurses. Erlanger is the third-largest hospital complex in Tennessee, the largest public hospital in the state, and Chattanooga's third-largest employer. Erlanger's facilities range from the region's only Level I Trauma Center to the James J. Fowle Regional Cancer Center; from the Willie D. Miller Eye Center to the T.C. Thompson Children's Hospital; from the Regional Heart Center and the Regional Women's Center to the hospital's affiliation with the Chattanooga Unit of the University of Tennessee College of Medicine; and from LIFE FORCE, the region's only air ambulance to the Regional Kidney Transplant Center, the region's first and only organ transplantation program.

FORT SANDERS HEALTH SYSTEM
1901 Clinch Avenue, Knoxville TN 37916. 423/541-1111. **Contact:** Human Resources. **Description:** The Fort Sanders Health System is a not-for-profit health care system that includes hospitals, physicians, clinics, and specialized health services stretching across East Tennessee. The system's specialty areas include cardiology, neurosciences, orthopedics, physical rehabilitation, oncology, and women's services (including perinatology). The system is comprised of the following affiliates: Fort Sanders Louden Medical Center; Fort Sanders Parkwest Medical Center; Fort Sanders Regional Medical Center (at this location); Fort Sanders Sevier Medical Center; Fort Sanders West; Maternity Center of East Tennessee; Patricia Neal Rehabilitation Center; and Thompson Cancer Survival Center. The system also has a presence in managed care and home health services through joint ownership (along with Methodist Medical Center of Oak Ridge) of the area's largest PPO, Preferred Health Partnership, with over 1,500 participating companies and 210,000 covered lives, and MedCenters HomeCare, a comprehensive home health company providing home infusion therapy, durable medical equipment, respiratory therapy and home health nursing. **NOTE:** For clinical positions, contact Mitzi Coker. For clerical positions, contact Sandra Billingsley. For housekeeping and other manual-type positions, contact Stacey Donald. **Corporate headquarters location:** This Location.

FORT SANDERS PARKWEST MEDICAL CENTER
9352 Parkwest Boulevard, Knoxville TN 37923. 423/693-5151. **Contact:** Human Resources. **Description:** Fort Sanders Parkwest Medical Center is a full-service general acute care hospital located in the heart of West Knox County, the area's fastest-growing community. The 325-bed medical center offers a complete array of state-of-the-art services including open heart surgery, neurosurgery, and laser surgery. Comprehensive emergency medical care is available 24 hours a day. A regional referral center, the hospital provides many highly specialized services such as cardiology, oncology, urology, orthopedics, and obstetrics and gynocology. The hospital also boasts a broad range of outpatient services, all designed with the convenience of the consumer uppermost in mind. From one-day surgery to outpatient testing, Fort Sanders Parkwest Medical Center provides the latest outpatient procedures backed by

the sophisticated services of a fully-equipped, modern medical center.

FORT SANDERS SEVIER MEDICAL CENTER

P.O. Box 8005, Sevierville TN 37864. 423/429-6100. **Contact:** Ms. Sandy Wilson, Human Resources. **Description:** Fort Sanders Sevier Medical Center is a rural health care facility, offering a wide range of medical and surgical specialties to residents of Sevier County. The hospital's medical staff includes specialists in a wide range of fields, including pediatrics, obstetrics and gynocology, cardiology, nephrology, and urology. The medical center consists of a 70-bed acute care hospital and an adjacent 54-bed nursing home providing skilled and intermediate care. Both facilities performed in the top 10 percent of health care facilities in the 1990 survey of the Joint Commission on Accreditation of Health Care Organizations. Fort Sanders Sevier Medical Center is an affiliate of the Fort Sanders Health System, a not-for-profit health care system headquartered in Knoxville, Tennessee. Fort Sanders Health System includes hospitals, physicians, clinics and specialized health services stretching across East Tennessee. The System's specialty areas include cardiology, neurosciences, orthopedics, physical rehabilitation, oncology, and women's services (including perinatology). In addition to Fort Sanders Sevier Medical Center, the System is comprised of the following affiliates: Fort Sanders Louden Medical Center; Fort Sanders Parkwest Medical Center; Fort Sanders Regional Medical Center; Fort Sanders West; Maternity Center of East Tennessee; Patricia Neal Rehabilitation Center; and Thompson Cancer Survival Center. The system also has a presence in managed care and home health services through joint ownership (along with Methodist Medical Center of Oak Ridge) of the area's largest PPO, Preferred Health Partnership, with over 1,500 participating companies and 210,000 covered lives, and MedCenters HomeCare, a comprehensive home health company providing home infusion therapy, durable medical equipment, respiratory therapy, and home health nursing.

HENRY COUNTY MEDICAL CENTER

P.O. Box 1030, Paris TN 38242. 901/644-8472. **Fax:** 901/644-8474. **Contact:** Ed Ledden, Human Resources Director. **Description:** A general acute care hospital and long-term service nursing home. **Common positions include:** Accountant/Auditor; Administrative Services Manager; Buyer; Clerical Supervisor; Clinical Lab Technician; Computer Programmer; Computer Systems Analyst; Customer Service Representative; Dietician/Nutritionist; EEG Technologist; EKG Technician; Electrician; Emergency Medical Technician; Human Resources Specialist; Medical Records Technician; Nuclear Medicine Technologist; Pharmacist; Physical Therapist; Public Relations Specialist; Purchasing Agent and Manager; Radiologic Technologist; Registered Nurse; Respiratory Therapist; Restaurant/Food Service Manager; Social Worker; Surgical Technician. **Educational backgrounds include:** Accounting. **Benefits:** 401K; Dental Insurance; Disability Coverage; Employee Discounts; Life Insurance; Medical Insurance; Tuition Assistance. **Corporate headquarters location:** This Location. **Operations at this facility include:** Administration. **Number of employees at this location:** 470.

HOLSTON VALLEY MEDICAL CENTER
130 West Ravine Road, Kingsport TN 37662. 423/224-4000.
Contact: Anna Borders, Human Resources Director. **Description:** A full-service medical center.

JOHNSON CITY MEDICAL CENTER
400 North State of Franklin Road, Johnson City TN 37604-6094. 423/461-6721. **Contact:** Personnel. **Description:** A 407-bed, not-for-profit, comprehensive teaching hospital, affiliated with the East Tennessee State University College of Medicine. Johnson City Medical Center Hospital is also a major medical referral center, serving Tennessee, Virginia, North Carolina, and Kentucky. The hospital's staff includes physicians with a wide array of specialties including allergy and immunology, adolescent medicine, anesthesiology, cardiology, dermatology, emergency medicine, endrocrinology, genetics, gynecology, infertility, neonatology, neurosurgery, orthopedics, pediatrics, psychiatry, radiology, and urology as well as numerous others. Johnson City Medical Center Hospital has also established heart, cancer treatment, breast care, wellness, surgery, sleep disorders, and maternal/infant centers.

LAUGHLIN MEMORIAL HOSPITAL
1420 Tusculun Boulevard, Greenville TN 37745. 423/639-6161. **Contact:** Noah Roark, Human Resources. **Description:** A 140-bed, all-private facilities hospital. The hospital added a radiology/oncology department at the start of 1995, and expanded its outpatient services.

LE BONHEUR CHILDREN'S MEDICAL CENTER
50 North Dunlap, Memphis TN 38103. 901/572-3000. **Contact:** Human Resources. **Description:** A licensed, fully-accredited 225-bed medical center, Le Bonheur Children's Medical Center is a pediatric specialty and subspecialty referral center for hundreds of physicians and nearly 1 million children. With a medical staff of 450, Le Bonheur serves more than 105,000 children and adolescents each year through inpatient care, 22 specialty clinics, and a fully staffed Emergency Department. Patients at Le Bonheur come from 90 counties in six states -- Tennessee, Mississippi, Arkansas, Missouri, Kentucky, and Alabama -- and represent a variety of acutely-ill and chronically-ill children, many with complex diagnostic and therapeutic problems. Each year, there are approximately 17,000 inpatient admissions and 33,000 visits to the Emergency Department. In 1994, Le Bonheur completed a $75 million Master Facility Plan which included the construction of a new West Patient Tower. In the new tower are three floors of patient rooms, two floors dedicated to the Crippled Children's Foundation Research Center, a new same-day surgery unit, and an atrium lobby complete with a new cafeteria, gift shop, and play areas for the patients. Other new or recently renovated facilities include a new 16,000 square foot Emergency Department, a new 18-bed Intensive Care Unit, a 12-bed Transitional Care Unit, a Physicians Office Building, and a new parking garage. Le Bonheur is also the pediatric teaching facility of the University of Tennessee, Memphis. Students in medicine, nursing, and other allied health fields receive training at Le Bonheur.

MAURY REGIONAL HOSPITAL
1224 Trotwood Avenue, Columbia TN 38401. 615/381-1111. **Contact:** Caroline Harrison, Human Resources. **Description:** Maury Regional Hospital is a non-profit community hospital, which is completely self-supporting, receiving no funding from county tax dollars. Maury Regional provides specialized services to an eight county area. With over 11,000 admissions per year, the facility is licensed for 275 beds. There are 100 physicians and 26 dentists affiliated with the hospital. Maury provides educational and training services on a regional basis for roughly 300 students through clinical affiliation with Columbia State Community College in the areas of lab, X-ray, Respiratory Care, and Registered Nursing. The hospital is twice the size of any other hospital between Nashville, TN and Huntsville, AL, and is the second-largest employer in Maury County. **Number of employees at this location:** 1,250.

MEDICAL CENTER OF MANCHESTER
P.O. Box 1409, Manchester TN 37355. 615/728-6354. **Fax:** 615/728-5420. **Contact:** Ms. Jean Alter, Payroll/Personnel Coordinator. **Description:** A general acute care hospital offering a wide range of medical, surgical, and psychiatric services. The hospital's units include a 24-hour emergency room, staffed by specially trained in-house doctors and nurses; an intensive care unit, providing care for critically-ill patients; and four modern surgical suites with a wide range of physicians/specialists credentialed to perform surgery. The hospital also runs the Center for Behavioral Medicine, which is designed to help those who can benefit from short term psychiatric care; a medical laboratory headed by a physician; a radiology department which houses ultrasound, CAT scanning, X-ray, and mammography equipment and also offers nuclear medicine diagnostic services; and two departments which offer physical therapy and respiratory therapy services. **Common positions include:** Clinical Lab Technician; Licensed Practical Nurse; Medical Records Technician; Pharmacist; Radiologic Technologist; Registered Nurse; Respiratory Therapist. **Educational backgrounds include:** Accounting; Biology; Business Administration; Chemistry. **Benefits:** 401K; Dental Insurance; Disability Coverage; Employee Discounts; Life Insurance; Medical Insurance. **Corporate headquarters location:** This Location. **Number of employees at this location:** 200.

MEMPHIS MENTAL HEALTH INSTITUTE
P.O. Box 40966, Memphis TN 38174-0966. 901/524-1272. **Contact:** Charles P. Radford, Personnel Director. **Description:** An institute of mental health. **Common positions include:** Accountant/Auditor; Administrator; Attorney; Dietician/Nutritionist; Human Resources Specialist; Instructor/Trainer; Psychiatrist; Purchasing Agent and Manager; Registered Nurse; Systems Analyst; Teacher. **Benefits:** Dental Insurance; Disability Coverage; Employee Discounts; Life Insurance; Medical Insurance; Pension Plan; Savings Plan; Tuition Assistance. **Corporate headquarters location:** Nashville TN. **Parent company:** State of Tennessee. **Operations at this facility include:** Administration; Research and Development; Service. **Number of employees nationwide:** 360.

METHODIST HEALTH SYSTEMS, INC.
1265 Union Avenue, Memphis TN 38104. 901/726-2300. **Contact:** Kathy Sullivan, Vice President of Human Resources. **Description:**

Methodist Health Systems is affiliated with the Mississippi, North Arkansas, and Memphis Conferences of the United Methodist Church. Methodist has grown steadily into a major regional network of health care facilities, where over 1,150 physicians represent all medical specialties and sub-specialties. An important part of that network is the 1,351-bed Methodist Hospitals of Memphis (MHM), the 12th-largest private hospital system in the United States. MHM is made up of three separate facilities located throughout the city: Methodist Central, Methodist North, and Methodist South. One of the first hospitals in the Mid-South to offer many non-traditional services such as home health care, treatment of eating disorders, and health and wellness programs for business and industry, Methodist Hospitals of Memphis remains one of the most progressive hospital systems in the region. **Corporate headquarters location:** 1211 Union Avenue, Suite 700, Memphis TN 38104.

MIDDLE TENNESSEE MEDICAL CENTER
400 North Highland Avenue, Murfreesboro TN 37130-3854. 615/849-4100. **Contact:** Paul Hilton, Vice President, Human Resources. **Description:** Middle Tennessee Medical Center's mission is to provide high-quality comprehensive health services, health education, and wellness programs on a cost-effective basis and in accordance with the precepts of the Baptist and Catholic faiths. Established in 1927, MTMC serves patients from throughout southern middle Tennessee. The hospital has been affiliated with Baptist and St. Thomas Hospitals since 1986.

NATIONAL HEALTHCARE, L.P. (NHC)
P.O. Box 1398, Murfreesboro TN 37133. 615/890-2020. **Contact:** Vice President of Personnel. **Description:** National HealthCare L.P., which prior to January 1, 1995 was named National HealthCorp L.P., is a long-term health care company that operates health care centers, managed care specialty units, retirement apartments, and homecare programs that include infusion therapy. NHC operates 96 long-term health care centers with a total of 12,308 beds. The 29 home care programs located in Tennessee and Florida offer nursing care and rehabilitative therapies to patients in their homes. NHC operates four retirement apartment complexes with a total of 387 units. The company was founded in 1971 and today employs more than 13,000 employees. **Number of employees nationwide:** 13,000.

NORTH PARK HOSPITAL
2051 Hammill Road, Chattanooga TN 37343. 423/870-1300. **Contact:** Jack Yankovich, Director, Human Resources. **Description:** North Park Hospital, a fully-accredited 83-bed, acute-care facility, offers a full range of patient services including: cardiopulmonary care, cosmetic surgery, diet counseling, 24-hour emergency treatment, outpatient and home heath care, laser surgery, gastrointestinal/pulmonary care, nuclear medicine, ophthalmology, physical therapy, physician referral, and radiology. As an affiliate of the hospital, Home Heath Care, provides high technology nursing, physical therapy, speech therapy, medical social services, and personal care 24 hours a day, seven days a week. **Common positions include:** Certified Occupational Therapy Assistant; Certified Physical Therapy Assistant; CT/MRI Technologist; Dietician/Nutritionist; EKG Technician; Health Care Administrator;

Nurse; Physical Therapist; Physician; Radiologic Technologist. **Number of employees at this location:** 650.

OMEGA HEALTH SYSTEMS, INC.

5100 Poplar Avenue, Suite 2100, Memphis TN 38137. 901/683-7868. **Contact:** Lori Jennings, Corporate Office Manager. **Description:** Omega Health Systems, Inc. is in the business of developing regional eye care delivery systems and operating and managing eye care centers from which opthalmologists provide medical and surgical care to patients having disorders of the eye. The company and its wholly-owned subsidiaries currently own 16 centers, including two ambulatory surgical centers adjacent to centers owned by the company. Omega Health Systems also provides management, marketing, and consulting services to five independent opthalmic practices pursuant to management agreements, and provides services in 21 satellite locations for a total of 44 locations in nine states and managed care operations in five states. Each of the centers provides medical and surgical support services for one or more opalmic practices pursuant to management agreements. The company's activities are restricted to providing support to medical professionals. The company does not provide medical care to patients. The company's centers and managed practices emphasize professional interrelationships between opthalmologists and optometrists for the co-management of patient care. The company also develops and administers managed eye care programs for health maintenance organizations and other third-party payers.

ORNDA HEALTHCORP

3401 West End Avenue, Suite 700, Nashville TN 37203. 615/383-8599. **Contact:** Jim Johnston, Vice President of Human Resources. **Description:** OrNda HealthCorp is a leading provider of health care services in the United States, delivering a broad range of inpatient and outpatient health care services principally through the operation of 46 hospitals located in urban and suburban communities in 15 states, primarily in Southern California, South Florida, and Arizona. The company's strategy is to increase revenues and market share growth by developing integrated health care delivery networks, vertically integrating, expanding outpatient services, being a low-cost provider and increasing specialty services. The company also intends to pursue strategic acquisitions of health care providers in geographic areas and with service capabilities that will facilitate the development of integrated networks. The company is the fifth largest investor-owned hospital management company in the country.

PHYCOR, INC.

30 Burton Hills Boulevard, Suite 400, Nashville TN 37215. 615/665-9066. **Contact:** Brandon Dyson, Director of Human Resources. **Description:** Operates multi-specialty medical clinics. PhyCor owns and operates 18 clinics in 11 states, and manages the operations of two additional clinics. The company has also entered into long-term agreements with the medical groups in these clinics, which, together with PhyCor, are positioning the clinics for health care reform. PhyCor believes that the decisions of physicians drive the cost and quality of medical care. The company also believes that primary-care-balanced, multi-specialty medical groups are the organizations

best positioned to impact physicians' decisions. It believes these organizations will become the core, and determine the success, of emerging competitive networks, which will be at the center of the reformed health care system. **Corporate headquarters location:** This Location.

QUORUM HEALTH GROUP, INC.
105 Continental Place, Brentwood TN 37027. 615/371-7979. **Contact:** Rhonda Morris, Human Resources. **Description:** Operates acute care hospitals through affiliates. As of June 30, 1994, Quorum owned 11 hospitals in Abeline and San Angelo, Texas; Dothan, Gadsen, and Enterprise, Alabama; Las Vegas, Nevada; Columbus, Ohio; Vicksburg, Mississippi; Paramount, California; and Macon, Georgia, where the company operates two hospitals. Quorum Health Resources, Inc., a subsidiary, is one of the nation's largest managers of acute care hospitals and also provides consulting services to hospitals throughout the country. Management contracts at the end of fiscal year 1994 totalled 262, and 115 consulting agreements were in place with additional hospital clients. The company had operations in 44 states and approximately 8,500 employees on June 30, 1994. **Corporate headquarters location:** This Location.

REGIONAL MEDICAL CENTER AT MEMPHIS
877 Jefferson Avenue, Memphis TN 38103. 901/545-7569. **Fax:** 901/545-8315. **Contact:** Vicky Tomlinson, Employment Manager. **Description:** A large health care center serving the mid-South region, with inpatient and outpatient facilities, Trauma Center, Burn/Wound Center, and Neo-Natal Center. **Common positions include:** Accountant/Auditor; Clinical Lab Technician; Computer Programmer; Computer Systems Analyst; Dietician/Nutritionist; Licensed Practical Nurse; Registered Nurse; Respiratory Therapist; Sociologist; Surgical Technician. **Educational backgrounds include:** Computer Science; Health Care. **Benefits:** Life Insurance; Medical Insurance; Savings Plan; Tuition Assistance. **Corporate headquarters location:** This Location. **Operations at this facility include:** Administration; Service. **Number of employees at this location:** 2,600.

REHABILITY CORPORATION
111 Westwood Place, Brentwood TN 37027. 615/377-2937. **Contact:** Human Resources. **Description:** Provides both outpatient and inpatient physical therapy. **Corporate headquarters location:** This Location.

REN CORPORATION-USA
6820 Charlotte Pike, Nashville TN 37209. 615/353-4200. **Contact:** Susan Presley, Director of Human Resources. **Description:** REN Corporation-USA provides renal dialysis services to patients suffering from chronic kidney failure, primarily in its freestanding outpatient dialysis centers known as REN centers. The corporation also provides dialysis in patients' homes or at hospitals on a contractual basis, urine and blood testing at its centers, and independent physicians at its clinical labs. **Number of employees nationwide:** 1,243.

RESPONSE ONCOLOGY
2001 Charlotte Avenue, Suite 100, Nashville TN 37203. 615/320-7300. **Fax:** 615/327-2722. **Contact:** Human Resources. **Description:** Provides advanced cancer treatments and related services, principally on an outpatient basis, through treatment centers owned and operated by the company. The centers, known as IMPACT Centers, are staffed by experienced oncology nurses, pharmacists, laboratory technologists, and other support personnel to deliver outpatient services under the direction of practicing oncologists. The primary treatments provided by the IMPACT Centers involve intensive levels of chemotherapy, supported by a combination of autologous peripheral blood stem cell products and bone marrow growth factors to support the patient's immune system. IMPACT Centers also provide home pharmacy services, such as pain medications, antibiotics, and nutritional support; outpatient infusional services; blood banking services; and specialized nursing and laboratory services for its patients. Response Oncology evaluates, adapts, and develops treatment programs for various types of cancer, but does not engage in basic research. **NOTE:** For information on professional hiring contact: Cindy Dill, Human Resources Manager, 1775 Moriah Woods Boulevard, Memphis TN 38117, 901/763-7020.

RESPONSE ONCOLOGY
1775 Moriah Woods Boulevard, Memphis TN 38117. 901/763-7020. **Contact:** Cindy Dill, Human Resources Manager. **Description:** Provides advanced cancer treatments and related services, principally on an outpatient basis, through treatment centers owned and operated by the company. The centers, known as IMPACT Centers, are staffed by experienced oncology nurses, pharmacists, laboratory technologists, and other support personnel to deliver outpatient services under the direction of practicing oncologists. The primary treatments provided by the IMPACT Centers involve intensive levels of chemotherapy, supported by a combination of autologous peripheral blood stem cell products and bone marrow growth factors to support the patient's immune system. IMPACT Centers also provide home pharmacy services, such as pain medications, antibiotics, and nutritional support; outpatient infusional services; blood banking services; and specialized nursing and laboratory services for its patients. Response Oncology evaluates, adapts, and develops treatment programs for various types of cancer, but does not engage in basic research.

ST. FRANCIS HOSPITAL
5959 Park Avenue, Memphis TN 38119. 901/765-1000. **Contact:** Human Resources Department. **Description:** A hospital facility offering a wide range of inpatient, outpatient, and home health services. St. Francis Hospital opened in December of 1974 to serve the growing needs of the Shelby County suburbs. Today it is a major medical complex serving the Mid-South with a complete range of services in a variety of specialties and sub-specialties. The fully-equipped hospital boasts a quality staff and is conveniently located in East Memphis near local doctors' office buildings, as well as Interstate 240 and other major roadways.

ST. JUDE CHILDREN'S RESEARCH HOSPITAL
332 North Lauderdale, Memphis TN 38105. 901/495-3300. **Contact:** Human Resources. **Description:** St. Jude Children's

Research Hospital is a nonprofit, non-sectarian institution. Its mission is to provide care for children with catastrophic illnesses, and to create new knowledge through research that will improve the outlook for these children. Laboratory research at St. Jude is directed toward understanding the molecular, genetic, and biochemical bases of childhood cancer and other catastrophic diseases, and elucidating the fundamental processes of normal cellular function. Clinical research efforts are aimed at understanding the mechanisms of disease, developing better diagnostic and therapeutic tools, and providing a bridge from the laboratory to the bedside. Education of new investigators and health care providers and dissemination of research findings to the international biomedical community are crucial to the hospital's mission. These efforts reach far beyond the confines of the hospital, with outreach/consultation programs designed to share the knowledge and skills gained at St. Jude with health care providers and researchers working in less advantageous settings.

SMITH & NEPHEW
1450 East Brooks Road, Memphis TN 38116. 901/396-2121. **Contact:** Human Resources. **Description:** Manufactures medical products.

SOFAMOR DANEK GROUP INC.
1800 Pyramid Place, Memphis TN 38132. 901/396-2695. **Contact:** Jack Young, Director of Human Resources. **Description:** Develops, manufactures, and markets spinal implant devices used in the surgical treatment of spinal degenerative diseases and deformities. These devices also increase stability during the healing of spinal trauma. The combination between Sofamor S.A. and Danek Group, Inc. was completed in June 1993, creating Sofamor Danek Group, Inc. Sofamor Danek's products are sold in over 45 countries. **Listed on:** New York Stock Exchange. **Number of employees nationwide:** 306.

SURGICAL CARE AFFILIATES
102 Woodmont Boulevard, Suite 610, Nashville TN 37205. 615/385-3541. **Contact:** Beth Allen, Director of Human Resources. **Description:** Develops, owns, and operates outpatient surgical care centers. **Number of employees nationwide:** 1,200.

TAKOMA ADVENTIST HOSPITAL
401 Takoma Avenue, Greeneville TN 37743. 423/639-3151. **Fax:** 423/636-2374. **Contact:** Donna Ward, Human Resources. **Description:** Takoma Adventist Hospital dates back to the 1920s. Since then, the hospital has expanded through five major building programs. Services include recovery care, such as Takoma's Transitional Care Center, its Physical Therapy Unit, and its Home Health Agency; specialized care, such as obstetrics/gynocology, urology, orthopedics, opthalmology, and oral and general surgery; diagnostic care, such as radiology and ultrasound mammography services; emergency care, including a 7-bed 24-hour unit; psychiatric care, including an 18-bed inpatient unit; maternal and child health care, including two birthing rooms and a nursery equipped to handle even premature deliveries; and community care, including Takoma's IndustriCare program, a comprehensive case management program available 24 hours a day.

TENNESSEE CHRISTIAN MEDICAL CENTER
500 Hospital Drive, Madison TN 37115. 615/865-2373. **Contact:**
Marcy Jones, Director of Human Resources. **Description:** A 309-bed
hospital with a 220 member medical staff and professional
employees. The facility serves roughly 35,000 patient visits per year,
providing outpatient and inpatient acute care as well as behavioral
and rehabilitation programs. Tennessee Christian is a not-for-profit
Christian institution and a member of the Adventist Health System, a
network of 500 health care facilities around the world. The facility's
85-year history has been marked by an approach to health that
balanced physical, mental, social, and spiritual well-being. Tennessee
Christian now marries that philosophy with state-of-the-art MRI, CAT
scan, and nuclear medicine technologies.

TENNESSEE REHABILITATION CENTER
460 Ninth Avenue, Smyrna TN 37167-2010. 615/459-6811.
Contact: Human Resources. Description: Rehabilitation center for
people with physical handicaps.

U.S. DEPARTMENT OF VETERANS AFFAIRS MEDICAL CENTER
1310 24th Avenue South, Nashville TN 37212. 615/327-4751.
Contact: William Hardwick, Personnel. **Description:** The U.S.
Department of Veterans Affairs (VA) was established March 15,
1989 to resume responsibility for providing federal benefits to
veterans and their dependents. Headed by the Secretary of Veterans
Affairs, VA is the second largest of the 14 cabinet departments and
operates nationwide programs of health care, assistance services,
and national cemeteries. The most visible of all VA benefits and
services is VA's health care system, the largest in the nation. From
54 hospitals in 1930, the VA health care system has grown to
include 171 medical centers; more than 364 outpatient, community,
and outreach clinics; 130 nursing home care units; and 37
domicilaries. VA operates at least one medical center in each of the
48 contiguous states, Puerto Rico, and the District of Columbia.
With approximately 76,000 medical center beds, VA treats nearly
one million patients in VA hospitals; 75,000 in nursing home care
units; and 25,000 in domicilaries. VA's outpatient clinics register
approximately 24 million visits per year. **Corporate headquarters
location:** Washington DC.

VANDERBILT UNIVERSITY MEDICAL CENTER
Box 7700, Station B, Nashville TN 37235. 615/322-8300. **Contact:**
Recruitment and Staffing. **Description:** The Medical Center is a
comprehensive health care facility which combines the education of
health professionals, patient care, and biomedical research. Through
its programs, it has become a major referral center for the Southeast
and the nation. The Medical Center can trace its roots back to the
mid-1800s. The School of Medicine began at the University of
Nashville in 1850, some 23 years before Vanderbilt University was
established. It became part of Vanderbilt in 1874 and awarded its
first Vanderbilt medical degrees to 61 graduates in 1875. Today, the
Medical Center is made up of The School of Medicine, The School of
Nursing, Vanderbilt University Hospital, The Vanderbilt Clinic,
Children's Hospital, Vanderbilt Psychiatric Hospital, and Vanderbilt
Stallworth Rehabilitation Hospital.

WILLIAMSON MEDICAL CENTER
P.O. Box 681600, Franklin TN 37068-1600. 615/791-2197. **Recorded Jobline:** 615/791-2117. **Contact:** Human Resources. **Description:** Williamson Medical Center offers comprehensive inpatient and outpatient services that are designed not only to provide convenient, quality services to patients, but to provide the technology, facilities, and personnel necessary to support the practice of the center's medical staff. Areas of specialty include the following: allergy; anesthesiology; cardiology; dermatology; emergency medicine; endocrinology; family practice; gastroenterology; general practice; internal medicine; neurology; obstetrics and gynecology; oncology; opthalmology; oral and maxillofacial surgery; orthodaedics and sports medicine; pathology; pediatrics; plastic surgery; psychiatry; pulmonary medicine; radiology; surgery; and urology.

Note: Because addresses and telephone numbers of smaller companies change rapidly, we recommend you call each company to verify the information below before inquiring about job opportunities. Mass mailings are not recommended.

Additional employers with under 250 employees:

MEDICAL EQUIPMENT AND SUPPLIES WHOLESALE

Mediquip Home Care Equipment
210 Jackson Ave, Memphis TN 38105-2730. 901/577-3092.

Health Effects Inc.
1296 N Highland Ave, Suite 14, Jackson TN 38301-4096. 901/427-2244.

MEDICAL EQUIPMENT RENTAL AND LEASING

Volunteer Surgical Inc.
144 College St, Gallatin TN 37066-2947. 615/259-2020.

DOCTORS' OFFICES AND CLINICS

Highland Rim Mental Health Center
712 N Main St, Shelbyville TN 37160-2828. 615/684-0522.

Plateau Mental Health Center
1200 S Willow Ave,
Cookeville TN 38506-4157. 615/432-4123.

Signature Health Alliance
P.O. Box 3818, Knoxville TN 37927-3818. 423/546-1893.

Deborah R. Distefano MD
1949 Gunbarrel Rd, Suite 300, Chattanooga TN 37421-3187. 2054953937.

Diagnostic Imaging Inc.
395 Wallace Rd, Suite 307, Nashville TN 37211-8024. 615/331-9373.

OFFICES AND CLINICS OF HEALTH PRACTITIONERS

Clarkrange Medical Clinic
Hwy 127 S, Clarkrange TN 38553. 615/863-5095.

Physiotherapy Associates
853 New Shackle
Island Rd, Hendersonvlle TN 37075-8808. 615/824-9715.

Physical Therapy Associates
1010 E 3rd St, Chattanooga TN 37403-2109. 423/265-6111.

Psychiatric Care Network
2401 Murphy Ave, Nashville TN 37203-1518. 615/385-5288.

Home Technology Healthcare
8630 Sparta Pike, Watertown TN 37184-1306. 615/237-3120.

NURSING AND PERSONAL CARE FACILITIES

Anderson Healthcare Inc.
791 Old Gray Station Rd, Gray TN 37615-3717. 423/477-7146.

Athens Health Care Center
1204 Frye St, Athens

TN 37303-3052.
423/745-0434.

**Baptist Convalescent
Center**
603 College St,
Newport TN 37821.
423/625-2195.

**Bells Nursing Home
Inc.**
Highway 79 &
Intersection 412, Bells
TN 38006. 901/663-
2335.

**Rockwood Health Care
Center**
5580 Roane State
Hwy, Rockwood TN
37854. 423/354-
3366.

**Brentwood Residential
Home**
1034 Waller Rd,
Brentwood TN 37027-
8325. 615/776-2587.

Briarwood Manor
41 Hospital Dr,
Lexington TN 38351-
1423. 901/968-6629.

**Brookhaven Health
Care Center**
421 E Stone Dr,
Kingsport TN 37660-
4058. 423/246-8934.

**Scott Health Care
Center**
2380 Buffalo Rd,
Lawrenceburg TN
38464-4809.
615/762-9418.

**Cedars Health Care
Center**
932 E Baddour Pkwy,
Lebanon TN 37087-
3707. 615/449-5170.

Clarksville Manor Inc.
2134 Old Ashland City
Rd, Clarksville TN
37043-4976.
615/552-9403.

**Southern TN Skilled
Facility**
629 Hospital Rd,
Winchester TN

37398-2407.
615/967-8249.

**Cookeville Health Care
Center**
815 Bunker Hill Rd,
Cookeville TN 38501-
3960. 615/528-5516.

**Cookeville Manor
Nursing Center**
215 W 6th St,
Cookeville TN 38501-
1723. 615/528-7466.

**Court Manor Nursing
Home**
1414 Court Ave,
Memphis TN 38104-
6395. 901/272-2494.

**Crestview Health Care
Center**
704 Dupree St,
Brownsville TN
38012-1707.
901/772-3356.

**Decatur County Manor
Inc.**
1051 Kentucky Ave,
Parsons TN 38363.
901/847-6371.

**Decatur Health Care
Nurse Home**
River Rd, Decatur TN
37322. 423/334-
3002.

**Dickson County
Nursing Home**
901 N Charlotte St,
Dickson TN 37055-
1010. 615/446-5171.

**Elderly Care Service
Inc.**
Warren Hollow Rd,
Shelbyville TN 37160.
615/684-4704.

**Emerald Hodgson
Hospital Skilled**
1260 University Ave,
Sewanee TN 37375-
2303. 615/598-5691.

**Fayetteville Health
Care Center**
4081 Thornton Taylor
Pkwy, Fayetteville TN

37334-2674.
615/433-9973.

**Franklin Health Care
Center**
216 Fairground St,
Franklin TN 37064-
3531. 615/790-0154.

**Franklin Manor
Nursing Center**
1501 Columbia Ave,
Franklin TN 37064-
3810. 615/794-2624.

**Graceland Nursing
Center**
1250 Farrow Rd,
Memphis TN 38116-
7116. 901/332-7290.

**Greeneville West
Health Care Center**
210 Holt Ct,
Greeneville TN 37743-
3004. 423/639-0213.

**Hancock Manor
Nursing Home**
E Main, Sneedville TN
37869. 423/733-
4783.

**Hartsville
Convalescent Center**
649 McMurry Blvd,
Hartsville TN 37074-
1915. 615/374-2167.

**Hendersonville Nurse
Home**
672 W Main St,
Hendersonvlle TN
37075-2879.
615/824-8301.

**Heritage Manor
Nursing Home**
708 Dwight Ave,
Chattanooga TN
37406-3499.
423/622-4301.

**Heritage Manor of
Rogersville**
Highway 70 11 W
Bypass, Rogersville TN
37857. 423/272-
3099.

**Hidden Acres Nursing
Center**
904 Hidden Acres

Ave, Mount Pleasant TN 38474-1097. 615/379-5502.

Hillhaven Convalescent Center
118 Halliburton St, Ripley TN 38063-2011. 901/635-5180.

Hillhaven Convalescent Center
700 Nuckolls Rd, Bolivar TN 38008-1531. 901/658-4707.

Hillview Health Care Center
2710 Trotwood Ave, Columbia TN 38401-4903. 615/388-7182.

River Park Health Care Center
1306 Katie St, Nashville TN 37207-5318. 615/228-3494.

John M. Reed Nursing Home
124 John M Reed Nursing Home R, Limestone TN 37681. 423/257-6122.

Kirby Pines Manor
3535 Kirby Rd, Memphis TN 38115-4232. 901/365-3665.

Royal Care
Erin Knight Rd, Erin TN 37061. 615/289-4141.

Life Care Center Elizabethton
1641 19E Byp #19-E, Elizabethton TN 37643-4646. 423/542-4133.

Life Care Center of Church Hill
701 W Main Blvd, Church Hill TN 37642-3915. 423/357-7178.

Oakwood Manor
1636 Woodlawn Ave, Dyersburg TN 38024-2026. 901/285-6400.

Life Care Center Redbank
1020 Runyan Dr, Chattanooga TN 37405-1200. 423/877-1155.

Lincoln Skilled Care Center
501 Amana Ave, Fayetteville TN 37334-3365. 615/433-3075.

Loudon Healthcare Center
1520 Grove St, Loudon TN 37774-1575. 423/458-5436.

Ave Maria Home
2805 Charles Bryan Rd, Memphis TN 38134-4756. 901/386-3211.

Mariner Health Care of Lebanon
731 Castle Heights Ct, Lebanon TN 37087-2646. 615/444-4319.

Quality Care Center of Memphis
1755 Eldridge Ave, Memphis TN 38108-1115. 901/278-3840.

Meadowbrook Nursing Home
1245 E College St, Pulaski TN 38478-4541. 615/363-7548.

Merihil Health Care Center
1653 Mooresville Hwy, Lewisburg TN 37091-2005. 615/359-4506.

Mission Convalescent Home
118 Glass St, Jackson TN 38301-4625. 901/424-2951.

Mountain City Health Care
919 Memorial Park Dr, Mountain City TN 37683. 423/727-7800.

Mountain View Health Care
155 Davis Rd, La Follette TN 37766-3114. 423/562-0760.

National Healthcare Center
374 Brink St, Lawrenceburg TN 38464-3244. 615/762-6548.

Northhaven Health Care Center
3300 N Broadway St, Knoxville TN 37917-2733. 423/689-2052.

Scott County Nursing Home
Hwy 27, Oneida TN 37841. 423/569-8382.

Oakwood Health Care Center
244 Oakwood Dr, Lewisburg TN 37091-3153. 615/359-3563.

Resthaven Nursing Center
300 N Bellevue Blvd, Memphis TN 38105-4397. 901/726-9786.

Park Rest Hardin County Health Center
410 Shelby Dr, Savannah TN 38372-2312. 901/925-1181.

Pheo Medical Center
1169 Cross Creek Dr, Franklin TN 37067-4035. 615/790-0665.

Pickett County Nursing Home
129 Hillcrest Dr, Byrdstown TN 38549-2326. 615/864-3162.

Pine Ridge Care Center
1200 Spruce Ln, Elizabethton TN 37643-4301.

Pulaski Health Care Center
993 E College St,
Pulaski TN 38478-
4432. 615/363-3572.

Weston Place
2900 Lake Brook Blvd,
Knoxville TN 37909-
1177. 423/531-9935.

Quality Care Nursing Home
932 E Baddour Pkwy,
Lebanon TN 37087-
3707. 615/444-1836.

Vanco Manor Convalescent Center
813 S Dickerson Rd,
Goodlettsville TN
37072-1707.
615/859-6600.

Richland Place Inc.
504 Elmington Ave,
Nashville TN 37205-
2508. 615/292-4900.

Rosewood Manor Inc.
1400 Rosewood Dr,
Columbia TN 38401-
4878. 615/388-6573.

Westwood Health Care Center
W Main St,
Decaturville TN
38329. 901/852-
3591.

Whitehaven Manor
1076 Chambliss Rd,
Memphis TN 38116-
6381. 901/396-8470.

Wood Presbyterian Home
322 Highway 68,
Sweetwater TN
37874-1903.
423/337-5326.

West TN Skilled Nurse Center
670 Skyline Dr,
Jackson TN 38301-
3923. 901/425-6226.

Spring Meadows Health Care Center
220 Highway 76,
Clarksville TN 37043-
4102. 615/552-0181.

Sunny Point Health Care Center
825 Fisher Ave,
Smithville TN 37166-
2140. 615/597-4284.

Union City Manor Nursing Center
1630 E Reelfoot Ave,
Union City TN 38261-
6021. 901/885-8095.

McMinnville Memorial Nurse Home
P.O. Box 410, Etowah
TN 37331-0410.
423/263-3646.

Oak Manor Healthcare Center
150 Oak Manor Rd,
McKenzie TN 38201-
8846. 901/352-5317.

Life Care Center
P.O. Box 518,
Ducktown TN 37326-
0518. 423/496-3245.

Clay County Manor
RR 3 Box 201A,
Celina TN 38551-
9803. 615/243-3130.

St. Barnabas Nursing Home
300 W 6th St,
Chattanooga TN
37402-1112.
423/267-3764.

Windsor House
3425 Knight Rd,
Whites Creek TN
37189-9189.
615/876-2754.

Wharton Nursing Home
P.O. Box 168,
Pleasant Hill TN
38578-0168.
615/277-3511.

Southern TN Medical Center
629 Hospital Rd,
Winchester TN
37398-2407.
615/967-8240.

Hillview Nursing Home
P.O. Box 769,
Dresden TN 38225-
0769. 901/364-3886.

Bledsoe County Nursing Home
122 Wheelertown Rd
Hwy 30 W, Pikeville
TN 37367. 423/447-
6811.

Cane Creek Rehabilitation Complex
180 Mount Pelia Rd,
Martin TN 38237-
3812. 901/587-4231.

South Pittsburg Hospital
P.O. Box 349, S
Pittsburg TN 37380-
0349. 423/837-6781.

Sweetwater Hospital
304 Wright St,
Sweetwater TN
37874-2837.
423/337-6171.

Lewisburg Community Hospital
P.O. Box 1609,
Lewisburg TN 37091-
0609. 615/359-6241.

HOSPITALS AND MEDICAL CENTERS

Cleveland Community Hospital
2800 Westside Dr
NW, Cleveland TN
37312-3599.
423/339-4100.

Copper Basin Medical Center
P.O. Box 990,
Copperhill TN 37317-
0990. 423/496-5511.

Harriman City Hospital
P.O. Box 489,
Harriman TN 37748-
0489. 423/882-1323.

Highland Hospital
105 Redbud Dr,
Portland TN 37148-
1673. 615/325-7301.

Indian Path Pavilion
2300 Pavilion Dr,
Kingsport TN 37660-
4622. 423/378-7500.

**Jackson County
Hospital**
P.O. Box 36,
Gainesboro TN 38562-
0036. 615/268-0211.

Midsouth Hospital
135 N Pauline St,
Memphis TN 38105-
4619. 901/527-5211.

**Moccasin Bend Mental
Health Institute**
100 Moccasin Bend
Rd, Chattanooga TN
37405-4415.
423/265-2271.

**Nashville
Rehabilitation Hospital**
610 Gallatin Rd,
Nashville TN 37206-
3225. 615/226-4330.

Peninsula Hospital
Jones Bend Road,
Louisville TN 37777.
423/970-9800.

**Perry Memorial
Hospital**
RR 10 Box 8, Linden
TN 37096-9100.
615/589-2121.

Scott County Hospital
P.O. Box 4939,
Oneida TN 37841-
4939. 423/569-8521.

**Smith County
Memorial Hospital**
158 Hospital Dr,
Carthage TN 37030-
1096. 615/735-1560.

**Wayne County
General Hospital**
P.O. Box 580,
Waynesboro TN
38485-0580.
615/722-5411.

**W. Tennessee
Behavioral Center**
238 Summar Dr,
Jackson TN 38301-
3906. 901/935-8200.

**White County
Community Hospital**
401 Sewell Dr, Sparta
TN 38583-1223.
615/738-9211.

**Psychiatric Center at
Harton Regional
Medical**
1801 N Jackson St,
Tullahoma TN 37388-
2201. 615/455-4537.

**Geriatric Psychiatry
Care Unit**
324 Doolittle Rd,
Woodbury TN 37190-
1139. 615/563-4062.

**HOME HEALTH CARE
SERVICES**

A Plus Homecare Inc.
356 24th Ave N,
Nashville TN 37203-
1514. 615/320-9840.

**ABC Home Health
Services**
6011 Trotwood Ave,
Columbia TN 38401-
5087. 615/381-6296.

Bedford Home Health
140 Dover St,
Shelbyville TN 37160-
2776. 615/685-5330.

C&M Home Health
41 Federal Dr,
Jackson TN 38305-
3906. 901/664-5585.

**Country Home Health
Inc.**
RR 1, Box 386-A,
Sardis TN 38371-
9801. 901/687-3208.

**Elk Valley Home
Health Care**
131 W End Ave,
Centerville TN 37033-
1328. 615/729-3538.

**Girling Health Care
Inc.**
4709 Papermill Rd,
Suite 102, Knoxville
TN 37909-1900.
423/947-4600.

**Homebound Medical
Systems**
6402 E Brainerd Rd,
Chattanooga TN
37421-3940.
423/899-7256.

**Homecare Health
Services**
104 Court St, Camden
TN 38320. 615/289-
4236.

**Homeward Bound
Home Health**
P.O. Box 276,
Livingston TN 38570-
0276. 615/823-2050.

Housecall Health Care
4263 Highway 411,
Madisonville TN
37354-1571.
423/442-3712.

Hug Center
5805 Lee Hwy, Suite
303, Chattanooga TN
37421-3546.
423/892-2583.

Interim Healthcare
1635 Western Ave,
Knoxville TN 37921-
6700. 423/522-3707.

Interim Healthcare
3319 W End Ave,
Nashville TN 37203-
1059. 615/386-9295.

**Knoxville Home
Therapeutics**
1508 Coleman Rd
#108, Knoxville TN
37909-3808.
423/584-1501.

**MedCorp. Inc.
Regional Health Care**
72 Stonebridge Blvd,
Suite 3, Jackson TN
38305-2038.
901/688-2818.

Medshares Home Care
716 W Main St,
Livingston TN 38570-
1720. 615/823-6850.

Medshares Home Care
105 Walker Hill Cir,

Crossville TN 38555-5440. 615/484-5655.

Pro Care Home Health Service
P.O. Box 32, McKenzie TN 38201-0032. 901/352-7721.

Pulaski Homecare
600 E College St, Pulaski TN 38478-4407. 615/363-0703.

Rescare
196 Carriage House Dr, Jackson TN 38305-3903. 901/664-2264.

Rescare Home Health Inc.
510 N Maney Ave, Murfreesboro TN 37130-2923. 615/893-4496.

Springfield Homecare
2100 Park Plaza Dr, Springfield TN 37172-3937. 615/384-0687.

Sumner Home Health Services
704 S Broadway, Portland TN 37148-1674. 615/325-3395.

Super Home Health Care
701 N State of Franklin Rd, Johnson City TN 37604-3669. 423/928-8011.

Super Home Health Care
306 W Main St, Woodbury TN 37190-1125. 615/563-2506.

Superior Home Health Care
6080 Shallowford Rd, Suite 108, Chattanooga TN 37421-7201. 423/892-0043.

Superior Home Health Care
4007 Keith St NW,

Cleveland TN 37312-4361. 423/476-7400.

Superior Home Health Care
108 E Court Sq, Trenton TN 38382-1862. 901/855-9353.

UTMC Knoxville Home Health Hospice
220 Sutherland Ave, Knoxville TN 37919. 423/544-6200.

Valley Home Health Care Inc.
401 Betsy Pack Dr, Jasper TN 37347-3319. 423/942-3462.

Your Home Visiting Nurse Service
5703-A N Broadway, Knoxville TN 37918. 423/688-4227.

KIDNEY DIALYSIS CENTERS

Dialysis Clinic Inc.
6104 N Mack Smith Rd, East Ridge TN 37412-3985. 423/894-8133.

SPECIALTY OUTPATIENT FACILITIES

Adolescent Rebos
539 S Old Kentucky Rd, Cookeville TN 38501-4351. 615/528-2712.

Baptist Recovery Center
899 Madison Ave, Memphis TN 38103-3405. 901/227-4357.

Cumberland Heights Alcohol & Drug
145 Thompson Ln, Nashville TN 37211-2411. 615/333-3971.

Central Appalachia Service
2301 E Center St, Kingsport TN 37664-2701. 423/247-4000.

Hiwassee Mental Health Center
2650 Executive Park NW, Cleveland TN 37312-2746. 423/479-4170.

Liberty Academy
1457 W Morris Blvd, Morristown TN 37813-2828. 423/581-8930.

Youth Villages Inc.
P.O. Box D, Eads TN 38028-0217. 901/867-8832.

Volunteer Rescue Squad
Nankipoo Rd, Halls TN 38040. 901/836-5077.

Montgomery County Rescue Squad
Ft Campbell Blvd, Clarksville TN 37042. 615/645-2646.

HEALTH AND ALLIED SERVICES

International Health Inc.
516 Chestnut St, Suite B, Chattanooga TN 37402-4906. 423/265-2898.

Nabi Biomedical Center
1021 McCallie Ave, Chattanooga TN 37403-2814. 423/756-0930.

Med Lab Inc.
1211 Union Ave, Suite 200, Memphis TN 38104-6654. 901/726-7253.

Tennessee Donor Services
308 15th Ave N, Nashville TN 37203-2910. 615/327-2247.

RESIDENTIAL CARE

Kelly Miller Smith Towers
2136 Cliff Dr,
Nashville TN 37218-2833. 615/254-6505.

Lakeshore Retirement & Nurse
3025 Fernbrook Ln,
Nashville TN 37214-1623. 615/885-2320.

Maplewood Village
400 Meadow Ln,
Somerville TN 38068-9776. 901/465-9711.

Trezevant Manor
177 N Highland St,
Memphis TN 38111-4747. 901/325-4000.

Wesley Homes Inc.
850 Highway 51 By-Pass N, Dyersburg TN 38024. 901/285-7622.

Wesley Madison Towers
383 Madison Ave,
Memphis TN 38103-3223. 901/521-0003.

Windlands Retirement Community
3800 Sam Boney Dr,
Nashville TN 37211-3756. 615/834-1951.

MEDICAL EQUIPMENT

Cardio-Systems
6164 E Shelby Dr,
Memphis TN 38141-7701. 901/362-7227.

Williams Optical Lab Inc.
P.O. Box 1246,
Nashville TN 37202-1246. 615/256-6631.

For more information on career opportunities in the health care industry:

Associations

ACCREDITING COMMISSION ON EDUCATION FOR HEALTH SERVICES ADMINISTRATION
1911 North Fort Myer Drive,
Suite 503, Arlington VA 22209.
703/524-0511.

AMERICAN ACADEMY OF FAMILY PHYSICIANS
8880 Ward Parkway, Kansas City MO 64114. 816/333-9700.
Promotes continuing education for family physicians.

AMERICAN ACADEMY OF PHYSICIAN ASSISTANTS
950 North Washington Street,
Alexandria VA 22314. 703/836-2272. Promotes the use of physician assistants.

AMERICAN ASSOCIATION FOR CLINICAL CHEMISTRY
2101 Lovely Street NW, Suite 202, Washington, DC 20037-1526. 202/857-0717. A nonprofit association for clinical, chemical, medical, and technical doctors.

AMERICAN ASSOCIATION FOR RESPIRATORY CARE
11030 Ables Lane, Dallas TX 75229-4593. 214/243-2272.
Promotes the art and science of respiratory care, while focusing on the needs of the patients.

AMERICAN ASSOCIATION OF COLLEGES OF OSTEOPATHIC MEDICINE
6110 Executive Boulevard, Suite 405, Rockville MD 20852.
301/468-2037. Provides applications processing services for colleges of osteopathic medicine.

AMERICAN ASSOCIATION OF COLLEGES OF PODIATRIC MEDICINE
1350 Piccard Drive, Suite 322, Rockville MD 20850. 301/990-7400. Provides applications processing services for colleges of podiatric medicine.

AMERICAN ASSOCIATION OF DENTAL SCHOOLS
1625 Massachusetts Avenue NW, Washington DC 20036-2212.
202/667-9433. Fax: 202/667-0642. E-mail address:
aads@aads.jhu.edu. Represents all 54 of the dental schools in the U.S. as well as individual members. Goals of the organization include the expansion of postdoctoral training and increasing the number of women and minorities in the dental field.

AMERICAN ASSOCIATION OF HEALTHCARE CONSULTANTS
11208 Waples Mill Road, Suite 109, Fairfax VA 22030.
703/691-2242.

AMERICAN ASSOCIATION OF HOMES AND SERVICES FOR THE AGING
901 E Street NW, Suite 500, Washington DC 20004-2037. 202/783-2242.

AMERICAN ASSOCIATION OF MEDICAL ASSISTANTS
20 North Wacker Drive, Suite 1575, Chicago IL 60606. 312/899-1500.

AMERICAN ASSOCIATION OF NURSE ANESTHETISTS
222 South Prospect Avenue, Park Ridge IL 60068-4001. 847/692-7050.

AMERICAN CHIROPRACTIC ASSOCIATION
1701 Clarendon Boulevard, Arlington VA 22209. 703/276-8800. A national, nonprofit professional membership organization. Provides educational services (through films, booklets, texts, and kits), regional seminars and workshops, and major health and education activities to provide information on public health, safety, physical fitness, and disease prevention.

AMERICAN COLLEGE OF HEALTHCARE ADMINISTRATORS
325 South Patrick Street, Alexandria VA 22314. 703/549-5822. A professional membership society for individual long-term care professionals. Sponsors educational programs, supports research, and produces a number of publications, including the *Journal of Long-Term Care Administration* and *The Long-Term Care Administrator*.

AMERICAN COLLEGE OF HEALTHCARE EXECUTIVES
One North Franklin, Suite 1700, Chicago IL 60606-3491. 312/424-2800. Offers credentialing and educational programs. Publishes *Hospital & Health Services Administration* (a journal), and *Healthcare Executive* (a magazine).

AMERICAN COLLEGE OF MEDICAL PRACTICE EXECUTIVES
104 Inverness Terrace, East Englewood CO 80112-5306. 303/397-7869.

AMERICAN COLLEGE OF PHYSICIAN EXECUTIVES
4890 West Kennedy Boulevard, Suite 200, Tampa FL 33609-2575. 813/287-2000.

AMERICAN DENTAL ASSOCIATION
211 East Chicago Avenue, Chicago IL 60611. 312/440-2500.

AMERICAN DENTAL HYGIENISTS ASSOCIATION
Division of Professional Development, 444 North Michigan Avenue, Suite 3400, Chicago IL 60611. 312/440-8900.

AMERICAN DIETETIC ASSOCIATION
216 West Jackson Boulevard, Chicago IL 60606-6995. 312/899-0040 or 800/877-1600. Promotes optimal nutrition to improve public health and well-being.

AMERICAN HEALTH INFORMATION MANAGEMENT ASSOCIATION
919 North Michigan Avenue, Suite 1400, Chicago IL 60611. 312/787-2672.

AMERICAN HOSPITAL ASSOCIATION
One North Franklin Street, Suite 2700, Chicago IL 60606. 312/422-3000.

AMERICAN MEDICAL ASSOCIATION
515 North State Street, Chicago IL 60610. 312/464-5000. An organization for medical doctors.

AMERICAN MEDICAL TECHNOLOGISTS
710 Higgins Road, Park Ridge IL 60068. 847/823-5169.

AMERICAN NURSES ASSOCIATION
600 Maryland Avenue SW, Suite 100W, Washington DC 20024-2571. 202/554-4444.

AMERICAN OCCUPATIONAL THERAPY ASSOCIATION
4720 Montgomery Lane,
Bethesda MD 20824-1220.
301/652-2682. 800/377-8555.
Fax: 301/652-7711.

AMERICAN OPTOMETRIC ASSOCIATION
243 North Lindbergh Boulevard,
St. Louis MO 63141. 314/991-
4100. Offers publications,
discounts, and insurance
programs for members.

AMERICAN ORGANIZATION OF NURSE EXECUTIVES
One North Franklin Street, Suite
3400, Chicago IL 60606.
312/422-2800.

AMERICAN PHYSICAL THERAPY ASSOCIATION
1111 North Fairfax Street,
Alexandria VA 22314. 703/684-
2782. Small fee required for
information.

AMERICAN PUBLIC HEALTH ASSOCIATION
1015 15th Street NW, Suite 300,
Washington DC 20005. 202/789-
5600.

AMERICAN VETERINARY MEDICAL ASSOCIATION
1931 North Meacham Road, Suite
100, Schaumburg IL 60173-
4360. 847/925-8070. Provides a
forum for the discussion of issues
of importance to the veterinary
profession, and for the
development of official positions.

ASSOCIATION OF MENTAL HEALTH ADMINISTRATORS
60 Revere Drive, Suite 500,
Northbrook IL 60062. 847/480-
9626.

ASSOCIATION OF UNIVERSITY PROGRAMS IN HEALTH ADMINISTRATION
1911 North Fort Myer Drive,
Suite 503, Arlington VA 22209.
703/524-5500.

GROUP HEALTH ASSOCIATION OF AMERICA, INC.
1129 20th Street NW, Suite 600,
Washington DC 20036. 202/778-
3200.

HEALTHCARE FINANCIAL MANAGEMENT ASSOCIATION
Two Westbrook Corporate
Center, Suite 700, Westchester IL
60154. 708/531-9600.

NATIONAL MEDICAL ASSOCIATION
1012 Tenth Street NW,
Washington DC 20001. 202/347-
1895.

Magazines

AMERICAN JOURNAL OF NURSING
555 West 57th Street, New York
NY 10019. Publishes five
editions: Hospital, Critical Care,
Continuing Care, Regular, and
Nurse Practitioner. Accredited as
a provider of continuing education
in nursing by the American Nurses
Credentialing Center.

AMERICAN MEDICAL NEWS
American Medical Association,
515 North State Street, Chicago
IL 60605. 312/464-5000.

CHANGING MEDICAL MARKETS
Theta Corporation, Theta Building,
Middlefield CT 06455. 860/349-
1054.

HEALTH CARE EXECUTIVE
American College of Health Care
Executives, One North Franklin,
Suite 1700, Chicago IL 60606.
312/424-2800.

MODERN HEALTHCARE
Crain Communications, 740 North
Rush Street, Chicago IL 60611.
312/649-5374.

NURSEFAX
Springhouse Corporation, 1111
Bethlehem Pike, P.O. Box 908,
Springhouse PA 19477. 215/646-
8700. This is a jobline service
designed to be used in
conjunction with *Nursing*
magazine. Please call to obtain a
copy of the magazine or the
Nursing directory.

HOTELS AND RESTAURANTS

Job opportunities in the restaurant industry are plentiful. A number of trends will boost job growth, including population growth, rising incomes, and more dual-income families. Some demand will be met through labor saving innovations like salad bars, untended meal stations, automated beverage stations, and central kitchens that serve a number of establishments in the same restaurant chain. In the fast-food sector, use of labor-saving technology is essential to remain competitive. Since the most time-consuming transaction at drive-in windows is making change, some restaurants are experimenting with debit and credit cards to reduce transaction time. However, despite labor-saving innovations, the increased demand for services will increase the need for workers.

Jobs in hotels, motels, and other lodging places will be plentiful throughout the next decade. Driving the growth will be many of the same trends affecting the restaurant industry, as well as low-cost airfares and foreign tourism in the U.S. Another hot trend: legalized gambling. The hotel and motel industry invests heavily in the gaming industry, and that has further fueled job growth. This growth will continue as hotels increasingly attract families by offering relatively inexpensive casino vacation packages.

The greatest growth is in all-suite properties and budget motels. Since they don't have restaurants, dining rooms, lounges, or kitchens, these properties offer few jobs for food and beverage workers, but jobs should be available for managers and assistant managers. The trend toward chain-affiliated lodging places should provide managers with opportunities for advancement into general manager positions and corporate administrative jobs.

BACK YARD BURGERS, INC.
2768 Colony Park Drive, Memphis TN 38118. 901/367-0888. **Contact:** H. Ray Jones, Vice President of Human Resources. **Description:** Back Yard Burgers operates and franchises quick-service restaurants that specialize in charbroiled, fresh food. According to the company, Back Yard Burgers strives to offer the same high-quality ingredients and special care typified by outdoor grilling in the back yard. Its menu features gourmet hamburgers, chicken sandwiches and other sandwich items, name brand condiments and beverages, as well as hand-dipped milkshakes, fresh-squeezed lemonade, and fresh-baked cobblers. The company's strategy is to meet consumer interest in off-premises consumption of restaurant food. Depending on markets and locations, Back Yard Burger has a unit format that enables it to pair single or double drive through service with in-store dining. **Corporate headquarters location:** This Location.

CRACKER BARREL OLD COUNTRY STORE, INC.
P.O. Box 787, Lebanon TN 37088-0787. 615/444-5533. **Contact:** Ms. Pat Williams, Supervisor of Recruiting. **Description:** Cracker Barrel Old Country Store, Inc. owns and operates over 150 full-

service country store restaurants with gift shops, located in the southeastern and midwestern portions of the United States.

EMBASSY SUITES-MEMPHIS
1022 South Shady Grove Road, Memphis TN 38120. 901/684-1777. **Contact:** Dean Grillo, General Manager. **Description:** A 200-suite, upscale hotel. Features include Frank Grisanti's Restaurant, room services, non-smoking floors, handicapped access, six conference suites, dual-line phones with voice messaging, remote-controlled cable TV, indoor pool, whirlpool, and sauna.

FAMILY INNS OF AMERICA
P.O. Box 10, Pigeon Forge TN 37868-0010. 423/453-4988. **Contact:** Lonna Hubbs, Personnel Manager. **Description:** Family Inns of America operates hotels and motels which provide lodging, food, and beverages for the general public. **Common positions include:** Accountant/Auditor; Hotel Manager/Assistant Manager; Management Trainee. **Educational backgrounds include:** Accounting; Business Administration; Finance; Marketing. **Benefits:** Bonus Award/Plan; Medical Insurance. **Special Programs:** Internships; Training Programs. **Corporate headquarters location:** This Location. **Operations at this facility include:** Regional Headquarters.

GIVEN ENTERPRISES
3640 Win Place Road, Memphis TN 38118. 901/363-0500. **Contact:** Frank Wood, Owner. **Description:** This location is the corporate headquarters for Given Enterprises, which owns and operates four restaurants in Mississippi under the names Shoney's and Captain D. These full-service, family-style restaurants are generally open 18 hours a day, seven days a week. Shoney's offers breakfast, lunch, and dinner. Captain D's restaurants specialize in seafood. Most Captain D's locations include drive-through, take-out service.

HARRAH'S ENTERTAINMENT
1023 Cherry Road, Memphis TN 38117. 901/762-8600. **Contact:** Ben Peternell, Vice President of Human Resources. **Description:** Harrah's Entertainment is a casino entertainment business. Properties include 12 casino properties, 11 of which operate under the name Harrah's, located in Colorado, Illinois, Mississippi, New Jersey, and Nevada. While most locations are land-based, there are riverboat/dockside locations in Joliet IL, Tunica MS, and Vicksburg MS. Extensive expansion in New Orleans, North Kansas City, Shreveport, St. Louis, and Phoenix is planned or under development. According to management, Harrah's promotes employee empowerment, with all employees making decisions and assuming responsibilities in fast-paced environments. **Corporate headquarters location:** This Location. **Other U.S. locations:** Black Hawk CO; Central City CO; Joliet IL; St. Louis MO; Tunica MS; Vicksburg MS; Atlantic City NJ; Las Vegas NV. **Number of employees nationwide:** 25,000.

HOLIDAY INN CHATTANOOGA CHOO CHOO
1400 Market Street, Chattanooga TN 37402. 423/266-5000. **Fax:** 423/756-2420. **Contact:** Vivian Cobb, Human Resources Director. **Description:** A hotel and tourist attraction. **Common positions include:** Assistant Manager; Bank Teller; Cashier; Chef/Cook/Kitchen Worker; Customer Service Representative; Department Manager;

Electrician; Employment Interviewer; Food and Beverage Service Worker; General Manager; Hotel Manager/Assistant Manager; Hotel/Motel Clerk; Human Resources Specialist; Landscape Architect; Marketing/Advertising/PR Manager; Payroll Clerk; Public Relations Specialist; Receptionist; Restaurant/Food Service Manager; Retail Sales Worker; Secretary; Services Sales Representative; Typist/Word Processor. **Educational backgrounds include:** Accounting; Business Administration; Communications; Marketing. **Benefits:** Dental Insurance; Employee Discounts; Medical Insurance; Savings Plan. **Special Programs:** Internships. **Corporate headquarters location:** This Location. **Operations at this facility include:** Sales; Service. **Number of employees at this location:** 400.

KRYSTAL COMPANY

The Krystal Building, One Union Square, Chattanooga TN 37402. 615/757-1550. **Contact:** Larry Reeher, Vice President of Human Resources. **Description:** The Krystal Company develops, operates, and franchises full-size Krystal and smaller double drive-through Krystal Kwik quick-service hamburger restaurants, featuring quality food, clean facilities, moderate prices, and quick and efficient service. The company has been in the fast food restaurant business since 1932, making it among the oldest fast food restaurant chains in the country. As of January 1, 1995, the company owned 242 Krystal restaurants and 10 Krystal Kwik restaurants. The company began franchising Krystal Kwik restaurants in 1990 and Kyrstal restaurants in 1991. Franchisees owned 28 Crystal restaurants and 37 Krystal Kwik restaurants at January 1, 1995. At the end of the 1994 fiscal year, a total of 317 company owned and franchised restaurants were located in 12 states, primarily in the southeastern United States.

LOGAN'S ROADHOUSE, INC.

565 Marriott Drive, Suite 490, Nashville TN 37214. 615/885-9056. **Contact:** Human Resources. **Description:** Logan's Roadhouse, Inc. operates eight company-owned Logan's Roadhouse restaurants that feature steaks, ribs, chicken, and seafood dishes in a distinctive atmosphere reminiscent of an American roadhouse. The Logan's Roadhouse concept is designed to appeal to a broad range of customers by offering generous portions of moderately priced, high-quality food in a very casual, relaxed dining environment that is lively and entertaining. The restaurants are open seven days a week for lunch and dinner and offer full bar service. The Logan's Roadhouse menu is designed to appeal to a wide variety of tastes, emphasizing extra-aged, hand-cut USDA choice steaks and signature dishes such as fried green tomatoes, baked sweet potatoes, and made-from-scratch yeast rolls. Prices range from $3.50 to $6.95 for lunch items and from $6.95 to $16.95 for dinner entrees. The average check per customer, including beverages, is approximately $8.50 for lunch and $11.50 for dinner. The lively, country honky-tonk atmosphere of Logan's Roadhouse restaurants is designed to appeal to families, couples, single adults, and business persons. The company's spacious restaurants are constructed of rough-hewn cedar siding in combination with banks of corrugated metal outlined in red neon. Interiors are decorated with murals depicting scenes from American roadhouses of the 1940s and 1950s, concrete and wooden planked floors and neon signs and feature Wurlitzer jukeboxes playing country hits. The restaurants also feature a display cooking grill and

an old-fashioned meat counter displaying steaks, ribs, seafood, and salads, and include a spacious, comfortable bar area with a large-screen television. The company's target markets, primarily in the Southeast and southern Midwest, are mid-sized metropolitan markets with attractive demographics and smaller markets where the appeal of the company's concept, together with fewer competing casual dining restaurants, provides an attractive opportunity for the company.

NASHVILLE COUNTRY CLUB, INC.

402 Heritage Plantation Way, Hickory Valley TN 38042. 901/764-2300. **Contact:** Jock Weaver, President. **Description:** Nashville Country Club, Inc. owns and operates The Nashville Country Club restaurant, a casual dining restaurant which serves moderately priced American-style food and beverages and features country music and its associated culture as its basic theme. As of late 1995, the company was considering opening additional restaurants in Los Angeles and London. The Nashville Country Club restaurant concept is based upon the popularity and appeal of Country Music and the culture and lifestyle that it represents, and is designed to provide customers with an opportunity to dine in an environment that enables them to experience the look, sound, feel and excitement of the country music segment of the entertainment industry. Management creates this environment primarily through the use of prerecorded traditional and contemporary country music, a decor that will feature country music memorabilia, collectibles and art, and by developing a reputation for attracting country music entertainers or music industry professionals. It is not expected that the company's restaurants will feature live musical performances or a dance floor.

O'CHARLEY'S INC.

P.O. Box 291809, 3038 Sidco Drive, Nashville TN 37229. 615/256-8500. **Contact:** Carol Arrowood, Human Resources Supervisor. **Description:** O'Charley's operates and franchises 60 full-service restaurants in 10 states in the Southeast and Midwest. Menu items are prepared on-site according to original recipes, using fresh ingredients. The typical restaurant in the chain seats 220 people, and does 33 percent of its business in lunch traffic and 67 percent in dinner service. The menu is moderately priced, with the average price for a meal running $8.11 at lunchtime and $11.80 for dinner. The company offers certain incentive programs, including "Express Lunches" and "Kids Eat Free." **Common positions include:** Restaurant/Food Service Manager. **Educational backgrounds include:** Business Administration. **Benefits:** 401K; Dental Insurance; Disability Coverage; Employee Discounts; Life Insurance; Medical Insurance. **Corporate headquarters location:** This Location. **Listed on:** NASDAQ. **Number of employees at this location:** 175. **Number of employees nationwide:** 5,000.

ROBERT ORR/SYSCO FOOD SERVICES COMPANY

P.O. Box 305137, Nashville TN 37230. 615/350-7100. **Contact:** Dorothy Merkle, Vice President of Human Resources. **Description:** The company markets and distributes a wide variety of foods and food-related items to restaurants and similar businesses. The company started in 1859 when Robert Orr, an Irish immigrant, established a provisions business, selling dried rations to the Union and Confederate Armies. In 1972 the company merged with Systems and Services Company (SYSCO), the national food service marketer and distributor. Now the company is one of the largest food service companies in America. In addition to foods, the company also sells kitchen equipment, paper supplies, utensils, and furniture for dining rooms. The company has more than 15,000 items available for customers to put on their menus, including fresh seafood, produce, and high-quality meats. **Parent company:** SYSCO Corporation.

ROBERT ORR/SYSCO FOOD SERVICES COMPANY
1539 Amherst Road, Knoxville TN 37909. 423/588-5726. **Contact:** Mr. Putty Mosier, Vice President of Sales, Eastern Region. **Description:** The company markets and distributes a wide variety of foods and food-related items to restaurants and similar businesses. The company started in 1859 when Robert Orr, an Irish immigrant, established a provisions business, selling dried rations to the Union and Confederate Armies. In 1972 the company merged with Systems and Services Company (SYSCO), the national food service marketer and distributor. Now the company is one of the largest food service companies in America. In addition to foods, Robert Orr/SYSCO also sells kitchen equipment, paper supplies, utensils, and furniture for dining rooms. The company has more than 15,000 items available for customers to put on their menus, including fresh seafood, produce, and high quality meats. **Corporate headquarters location:** Nashville TN.

PANCHO'S MEXICAN FOODS
2881 Lamar Avenue, Memphis TN 38114. 901/744-3900. **Contact:** Pamela Wallace, Director of Human Resources. **Description:** A restaurant with a primarily Mexican menu. **Common positions include:** Industrial Production Manager; Operations/Production Manager; Services Sales Representative. **Benefits:** Dental Insurance; Employee Discounts; Life Insurance; Medical Insurance. **Special Programs:** Training Programs. **Corporate headquarters location:** This Location.

PERKINS FAMILY RESTAURANTS, L.P.
6075 Poplar Avenue, Suite 800, Memphis TN 38119. 901/766-6400. **Contact:** Teresa Hester, Manager of Corporate Human Resources. **Description:** A restaurant chain with locations throughout the United States and Canada. Most of the restaurant locations also include a retail bakery where Perkins' pastries and desserts are sold for carry-out. There are over 400 restaurants in the chain, with 127 owned by the company and 298 franchised. To maintain a checks and balances system with the franchisees, Perkins holds quarterly Franchise Advisory Council Meetings, regular Quality Circle meetings with top management and franchisees, and a Franchise Business Conference every year and a half. Systemwide sales in 1993 reached $587 million. Designed to appeal to a wide cross-section of consumers, Perkins provides table service dining for the entire family at moderate prices. A broad menu features signature items for every meal occasion. **Corporate headquarters location:** This Location.

THE PROMUS HOTEL CORPORATION
850 Ridge Lake Boulevard, Suite 400, Memphis TN 38120. 901/680-7200. **Contact:** Human Resources. **Description:** Operates

several chains of hotels. **Corporate headquarters location:** This Location. **Other U.S. locations:** Memphis TN.

SHOLODGE, INC.
217 West Main Street, Gallatin TN 37066. 615/452-7200. **Fax:** 615/452-7332. **Contact:** Jim Grout, Executive Vice President of Human Resources. **Description:** ShoLodge is the exclusive franchisor of Shoney's Inns, a chain of 63 motels located throughout the Southeast. The company owns and operates 22 of these locations, and manages four of the remaining 41 franchises. The company is also a developer and manager of AmeriSuites hotels, constructing lodging facilities for itself and others. Additionally, ShoLodge owns and operates eight restaurants, two under the name Shoney's, and six under the name Captain D's Seafood Restaurants. Shoney's are full-service, family-style restaurants generally open 18 hours a day, seven days a week. Shoney's offers breakfast, lunch, and dinner. Captain D's are also full-service restaurants, specializing in seafood. Most Captain D's locations include drive-through, take-out service. The company owns and operates inns in Alabama, Delaware, Florida, Georgia, Louisiana, Mississippi, Missouri, Tennessee, Texas, and Virginia. The company's stock is traded under the symbol LODG. **Corporate headquarters location:** This Location. **Listed on:** NASDAQ.

SHONEY'S
1717 Elm Hill Pike, Suite A4, Nashville TN 37210. 615/231-2395. **Contact:** Tara Lepley, Vice President, Human Resources. **Description:** Shoney's are full-service, family-style restaurants generally open 18 hours a day, seven days a week. Shoney's offers breakfast, lunch, and dinner.

SOUTHDOWN CORPORATION
500 Wilson Pike Circle, Suite 100, Brentwood TN 37027. 615/371-8150. **Contact:** Julia Douglas, Director of Human Resources. **Description:** Southdown Corporation is one of the largest franchisee companies in the Southeast, operating 28 Burger King restaurants.

SOUTHERN HOSPITALITY CORPORATION
P.O. Box 48, Nashville TN 37202. 615/399-9700. **Fax:** 615/399-3373. **Contact:** Dale Bruner, Director of Training. **Description:** Southern Hospitality Corporation is an operator of Wendy's fast-food franchises. **Common positions include:** Assistant Manager; General Manager; Management Trainee; Operations/Production Manager; Restaurant/Food Service Manager. **Benefits:** 401K; Credit Union; Dental Insurance; Disability Coverage; Employee Discounts; Life Insurance; Medical Insurance; Tuition Assistance. **Other U.S. locations:** Nationwide. **Parent company:** Davco Restaurants Inc. **Number of employees at this location:** 1,000.

TPI RESTAURANTS, INC.
2158 Union Avenue, Memphis TN 38104. 901/725-6400. **Contact:** Human Resources. **Description:** As part of TPI Enterprises, the company is one of the largest restaurant franchisees in the nation, and the largest franchisee of Shoney's, Inc. The company is present in 11 states, operating nearly 200 Shoney's and 67 Captain D's Seafood Restaurants. TPI's Shoney's are competitors in the full-service, family-style restaurant market, offering a complete dining

experience. They are generally open 18 hours a day, seven days a week, offering breakfast, lunch, and dinner. Captain D's are fast-service restaurants, specializing in seafood meals. Captain D's locations generally include a drive-through take-out service. **Corporate headquarters location:** West Palm Beach FL. **Parent company:** TPI Enterprises, Inc.

TOMKATS, INC.
408 Broadway, Nashville TN 37203. 615/256-9596. **Contact:** Lisa Gillian, Human Resources Department. **Description:** A catering company supplying food service to directors, actors, and crews on more than 70 movie sets.

Note: Because addresses and telephone numbers of smaller companies change rapidly, we recommend you call each company to verify the information below before inquiring about job opportunities. Mass mailings are not recommended.

Additional employers with under 250 employees:

EATING PLACES

Air Host Inc.
1355 Lynnfield Rd, Memphis TN 38119-5883. 901/767-3463.

Applebee's
584 Carriage House Dr, Jackson TN 38305-2222. 901/661-9950.

Applebee's
2400 Elliston Pl, Nashville TN 37203-1729. 615/329-2306.

Asia Chinese Restaurant
129 N Lowry St, Smyrna TN 37167-2560. 615/223-0509.

Bangkok Oriental Restaurant
3279-B Ft Campbell Blvd, Clarksville TN 37042. 615/431-3804.

Belair Grill
9117 Executive Park Dr, Knoxville TN 37923-4509. 423/694-0606.

Big River Grill & Brewing Works
222 Broad St, Chattanooga TN 37402-1009. 423/267-2739.

Bristol Bar & Grille
113 Church Street Mall, Nashville TN 37219-2501. 615/255-7007.

Burger King
2011 8th Ave S, Nashville TN 37204-2201. 615/383-6317.

Cancun Mexican Restaurant
108 E Court St, Covington TN 38019-2506. 901/476-8222.

Chili's Grill & Bar
2322 W End Ave, Nashville TN 37203-1708. 615/327-1588.

City Cafe
203 E Main St, Rutherford TN 38369-9799. 901/665-7508.

Cooker Bar & Grille
2609 W End Ave, Nashville TN 37203-1424. 615/327-2925.

Cooker Bar & Grille
1211 Murfreesboro Pike, Nashville TN 37217-2432. 615/361-4747.

Cooker Bar & Grille
6120 Poplar Ave, Memphis TN 38119. 901/685-2800.

Cosimo's Pizza
1000 Two Mile Pkwy, Goodlettsville TN 37072-2402. 615/851-0906.

Richard's Bar-B-Q
413 W Jackson St, Bolivar TN 38008-2009. 901/658-7652.

Damon's The Place For Ribs
1640 Parkway, Sevierville TN 37862-2850. 423/428-6200.

Depot Restaurant
111 N Railroad St, Selmer TN 38375-1735. 901/645-6626.

Domino's Pizza
1495 Madison St, Clarksville TN 37040-3845. 615/552-0030.

Ryan's Family Steakhouse
1829 Old Fort Pkwy, Murfreesboro TN 37129-3364. 615/895-4272.

EW James & Sons
Hwy 64 E,

Waynesboro TN
38485. 615/722-5456.

EW James & Sons
556 E Main St,
Hohenwald TN 38462-2006. 615/796-2420.

Golden Panda
2005 N Locust Ave,
Lawrenceburg TN
38464-2337.
615/762-5888.

Grady's American Grill
1914 N Roan St,
Johnson City TN
37601-3116.
423/282-2722.

Grady's Goodtimes
318 N Peters Rd,
Knoxville TN 37922-2330. 423/694-4663.

Grady's Goodtimes
2020 Hamilton Place
Blvd, Chattanooga TN
37421-6034.
423/894-4663.

Hardee's
255 S Lowry St,
Smyrna TN 37167-3007. 615/459-9668.

Hardee's of Dickson
211 Henslee Dr,
Dickson TN 37055-2090. 615/441-1157.

Hardee's of Gallatin
452 E Main St,
Gallatin TN 37066-2913. 615/451-4931.

**Hardee's of
Huntingdon**
690 E Main St,
Huntingdon TN
38344-3306.
901/986-0255.

Hardee's of Knoxville
5310 Kingston Pike,
Knoxville TN 37919-5027. 423/584-1387.

Hardee's of Selmer
619 Mulberry St,
Selmer TN 38375-2321. 901/645-5342.

Hardee's Restaurant
784 W Poplar Ave,
Collierville TN 38017-2544. 901/853-3137.

Hardee's of Springfield
2002 Memorial Blvd,
Springfield TN 37172-3914. 615/384-2969.

**Hardee's of
Jamestown**
554 N Main St,
Jamestown TN
38556-3736.
615/879-4369.

Hardee's of Nashville
110 Haywood Ln,
Antioch TN 37013-3320. 615/333-9193.

**Helen's Breakfast
Shop**
725 Cornersville Rd,
Lewisburg TN 37091-4114. 615/359-3699.

**Indian Hills Restaurant
& Lounge**
405 Calumet Trce,
Murfreesboro TN
37130-6354.
615/896-1045.

J. Alexander's
73 White Bridge Rd,
Nashville TN 37205-1444. 615/352-0981.

**Kentucky Fried
Chicken**
314 Long Hollow Pike,
Goodlettsville TN
37072-1876.
615/859-2903.

**Lee's Famous Recipe
Chicken**
2526 Franklin Rd,
Nashville TN 37204-2714. 615/292-8408.

**Lee's Famous Recipe
Chicken**
3127 Dickerson Rd,
Nashville TN 37207-2903. 615/226-5532.

**Little Caesar's Pizza
Pizza**
4230 Harding Rd,
Nashville TN 37205-2013. 615/383-0900.

**Little Caesar's Pizza
Pizza**
1404 McGavock Pike,
Nashville TN 37216-3209. 615/226-2900.

**Little Caesar's Pizza
Pizza**
7091 Old Harding Rd,
Nashville TN 37221-2829. 615/646-5300.

**Logan's Roadhouse
Restaurant**
3072 Wilma Rudolph
Blvd, Clarksville TN
37040-5005.
615/645-8333.

**Lone Star Steakhouse
& Saloon**
1805 N Roan St,
Johnson City TN
37601-3105.
423/929-3136.

**Long John Silvers
Seafood**
1682 Memorial Blvd,
Murfreesboro TN
37129-2104.
615/895-1800.

**Long John Silvers
Seafood**
870 S Jefferson Ave,
Cookeville TN 38501-4031. 615/528-2215.

Louis Chez
100 E Vine St,
Murfreesboro TN
37130-3734.
615/893-6050.

**Mama Grazie's Italian
Kitchen**
3420 Plaza Ave,
Memphis TN 38111-4614. 901/454-4800.

**Market Street
Performance Hall**
221 Market St,
Chattanooga TN
37402-1020.
423/267-2498.

McDonald's Restaurant
313 W Main St,
Waverly TN 37185-1548. 615/296-3311.

McDonald's Restaurant
4500 N Lee Hwy,
Cleveland TN 37312-4039. 423/339-5898.

McDonald's Restaurant
Hwy 11 W, Kingsport TN 37660. 423/246-7911.

McDonald's Restaurant
674 N Germantown Pkwy, Cordova TN 38018-6210.
901/757-1989.

Michael's Pizza
2124 Dover Rd,
Woodlawn TN 37191-9000. 615/553-7800.

Mick's at Oak Court Mall
4465 Poplar Ave,
Memphis TN 38117-3739. 901/763-1850.

Toddle House Restaurants
740 W Poplar Ave,
Collierville TN 38017-2544. 901/853-8030.

Top Dining Inc.
1501 Bluff City Hwy,
Bristol TN 37620-6018. 423/764-1916.

Nashville Palace
2400 Music Valley Dr,
Nashville TN 37214-1001. 615/885-1540.

Ober Gatlinburg Restaurant & Lounge
1339 Ski Mountain Rd, Gatlinburg TN 37738. 423/436-5423.

Olive Garden Italian Restaurant
7206 Kingston Pike,
Knoxville TN 37919-5601. 423/584-7300.

Outback Steakhouse
1560 Gallatin Rd N,
Madison TN 37115-2124. 615/868-0477.

Ruby Tuesday Restaurant
Hickory Hollow Parkway, Antioch TN 37013. 615/731-8144.

Ryan's Family Steak House
2404 Memorial Blvd,
Kingsport TN 37664-3343. 423/245-5178.

Papa John's Pizza
4230 Summer Ave,
Memphis TN 38122-4044. 901/680-0700.

Papa John's Pizza
903 Gallatin Rd S #A,
Madison TN 37115-4603. 615/865-1234.

Papa John's Pizza
226 E Broadway,
Gallatin TN 37066-2728. 615/230-7272.

Papa John's Pizza
2557 Murfreesboro Pike, Nashville TN 37217-3547.
615/399-7272.

Ryan's Family Steakhouse
6105 Stage Rd,
Memphis TN 38134-8313. 901/373-3870.

Petro's Chili & Chips
Stones River Mall,
Murfreesboro TN 37129. 615/890-2812.

Piccadilly Cafeteria
721 Madison Square Shop Ctr, Madison TN 37115-4041.
615/860-1129.

Piccadilly Cafeteria
The Mall At Johnson City, Johnson City TN 37601. 423/282-4327.

Piccadilly Cafeteria
Fort Henry Mall,
Kingsport TN 37664. 423/246-7001.

Piccadilly Classic American Cook
874 Murfreesboro Pike, Nashville TN 37217-1148.
615/367-4640.

Pizza Hut
382 Sumner Hall Dr,
Gallatin TN 37066-3129. 615/452-6500.

Po' Folks
1128 Murfreesboro Pike, Nashville TN 37217-2213.
615/361-8200.

Ponderosa Steakhouse
2112 Memorial Blvd,
Springfield TN 37172-3916. 615/384-6604.

Ponderosa Steakhouse
321 W Trinity Ln,
Nashville TN 37207-4939. 615/228-5206.

Red Lobster Restaurants
8040 Kingston Pike,
Knoxville TN 37919-5524. 423/693-4651.

Waffle House
119 Cedar Ln #A,
Knoxville TN 37912-3506. 423/688-6385.

Rolyat's
107 W Latta Ln,
Somerville TN 38068-1301. 901/465-8424.

Taco Bell
2000 N Roan St,
Johnson City TN 37601-3120.
423/282-8612.

Taco Pronto
2629 Westpark Dr,
Murfreesboro TN 37129-3217.
615/893-0605.

Smoky Mountain Brewing
424 S Gay St,
Knoxville TN 37902-1103. 423/673-8400.

S&S Cafeteria
4619 American Way,
Memphis TN 38118-8403. 901/363-2553.

Scotto Pizza
Governors Square Mall, Clarksville TN 37040. 615/648-1329.

Uncle Bud's Catfish
714 Stewarts Ferry Pike, Nashville TN 37214-2633.
615/872-7700.

Wendy's Old Fashioned Hamburgers
241 S Lowry St,
Smyrna TN 37167-3007. 615/459-9579.

Waffle House
2210 Old Fort Pkwy,
Murfreesboro TN 37129-6911.
615/893-3057.

Mrs. Winners Chicken & Biscuits
1904 W End Ave,
Nashville TN 37203-2309. 615/320-1348.

Mrs. Winners Chicken & Biscuits
735 NW Broad St,
Murfreesboro TN 37129-2705.
615/893-1841.

Domino's Pizza
2113 Murfreesboro Pike, Nashville TN 37217-3310.
615/360-3030.

Banjo Mountain Enterprises
729 Fowler Ford Rd,
Portland TN 37148-1944. 615/325-5642.

D'Lisi Pizza
648 Lafayette Rd,

Clarksville TN 37042-5354. 615/552-0240.

DRINKING PLACES

Tradesmen Tavern
104 W Northfield Blvd, Murfreesboro TN 37129-1561.
615/896-4072.

Members Only Club
2446 Martin Luther King Jr Ave, Knoxville TN 37915-1633.
423/673-9834.

Jim's Pub
3758 Highway 209 N,
Ripley TN 38063-7128. 901/635-7456.

Red Lion Lounge
1360 Fort Campbell Blvd, Clarksville TN 37042-4049.
615/551-8999.

Cracker Box Lounge
477 Turkey Hill Rd,
Ripley TN 38063-5625. 901/635-2466.

HOTELS AND MOTELS

Wilson Inn Nashville
600 Ermac Dr,
Nashville TN 37214-5002. 615/889-4466.

Courtyard by Marriott
103 Eastpark Dr,
Brentwood TN 37027-7505. 615/371-9200.

Rivermont
293 Parkway,
Gatlinburg TN 37738-5150. 423/430-7220.

Hampton Inn
5630 Franklin Pike Cir,
Brentwood TN 37027-4324. 615/373-2212.

Hampton Inn
1919 W End Ave,
Nashville TN 37203-2335. 615/329-1144.

Holiday Inn Cedar Bluff
9128 Executive Park Dr, Knoxville TN 37923-4508.
423/693-1101.

Holiday Inn-Express
Hwy 96 & I-65,
Franklin TN 37064.
615/794-7591.

Holiday Inn-Sycamore View
6101 Shelby Oaks Dr,
Memphis TN 38134-7400. 901/388-7050.

Holiday Inn
Hwy 51 Bypass & 78 Hwy, Dyersburg TN 38024. 901/285-8601.

Red Roof Inn Inc.
209 Advantage Pl,
Knoxville TN 37922-2336. 423/691-1664.

Hampton Inn
2350 Elm Hill Pike,
Nashville TN 37214-5119. 615/871-0222.

Breckenridge Lake
Simonton Rd,
Crossville TN 38555.
615/788-6751.

Outdoor Resorts of America
2400 Crestmoor Rd,
Suite 200, Nashville TN 37215-2032.
615/244-5237.

Twin Mountain Cabin Rentals
739 Wears Valley Rd,
Sevierville TN 37862-7701. 423/429-8222.

Motel 6
1360 Springbrook Ave, Memphis TN 38116-1820.
901/396-3620.

Ramada Inn Airport
733 Briley Pkwy,
Nashville TN 37217-1301. 615/361-5900.

For more information on career opportunities in hotels and restaurants:

Associations

AMERICAN HOTEL AND MOTEL ASSOCIATION
1201 New York Avenue NW, Suite 600, Washington DC 20005-3931. 202/289-3100. Provides lobbying services and educational programs, maintains and disseminates industry data, and produces a variety of publications.

THE EDUCATIONAL FOUNDATION OF THE NATIONAL RESTAURANT ASSOCIATION
250 South Wacker Drive, 14th Floor, Chicago IL 60606. 312/715-1010. Offers educational products, including textbooks, manuals, instruction guides, manager and employee training programs, videos, and certification programs.

NATIONAL RESTAURANT ASSOCIATION
1200 17th Street NW, Washington DC 20036. 202/331-5900. Provides a number of services, including government lobbying, communications, research, and information, and operates the Educational Foundation (see separate address).

Directories

DIRECTORY OF CHAIN RESTAURANT OPERATORS
Business Guides, Inc., Lebhar-Friedman, Inc., 3922 Coconut Palm Drive, Tampa FL 33619-8321. 813/664-6700.

DIRECTORY OF HIGH-VOLUME INDEPENDENT RESTAURANTS
Lebhar-Friedman, Inc., 3922 Coconut Palm Drive, Tampa FL 33619-8321. 813/664-6700.

Magazines

CORNELL HOTEL AND RESTAURANT ADMINISTRATION QUARTERLY
Cornell University School of Hotel Administration, Statler Hall, Ithaca NY 14853-6902. 607/255-9393.

HOTEL AND MOTEL MANAGEMENT
120 West 2nd Street, Duluth MN 55802. 218.

INNKEEPING WORLD
Box 84108, Seattle WA 98124. 206/362-7125.

NATION'S RESTAURANT NEWS
Lebhar-Friedman, Inc., 3922 Coconut Palm Drive, Tampa, FL 33619. 813/664-6700.

INSURANCE

What's the job outlook in insurance? That depends on which industry segment you're looking at. Health insurers, who have avoided any Washington-based reforms, are reaping record profits, while property-casualty and life insurers are still struggling. The industry has been consolidating with major mergers, and that's likely to continue in 1996. Under pressure from low returns, and a growing number of environmental claims, the property-casualty industry needs to cut overhead. In many cases, that also means jobs.

The picture in health insurance is much brighter. By moving more and more consumers into managed care, insurers are benefiting from the economies of scale. Many of the biggest players in the insurance industry have moved into managed care. Metropolitan Life and Travelers Corporation, for example, combined health insurance operations into Metra Health in order to compete with leaders like CIGNA, Aetna, and Prudential.

AMERICAN GENERAL LIFE AND ACCIDENT INSURANCE COMPANY
2125 American General Center, Nashville TN 37250. 615/749-2088. **Contact:** Lisa Tunstall, Employment Counselor. **Description:** Engaged in individual life and health insurance sales and service. Number of employees: 1,150 in the home office; 7,500 in field sales. **Common positions include:** Accountant/Auditor; Actuary; Attorney; Claim Representative; Consultant; Customer Service Representative; Financial Analyst; Instructor/Trainer; Insurance Agent/Broker; Marketing Specialist; Operations/Production Manager; Services Sales Representative; Systems Analyst; Teacher. **Educational backgrounds include:** Accounting; Business Administration; Finance; Marketing; Mathematics. **Benefits:** Dental Insurance; Disability Coverage; Employee Discounts; Life Insurance; Medical Insurance; Pension Plan; Profit Sharing; Savings Plan; Tuition Assistance. **Special Programs:** Internships; Training Programs. **Parent company:** American General Corporation. **Operations at this facility include:** Administration; Sales; Service. **Listed on:** New York Stock Exchange.

AVCO FINANCIAL SERVICES, INC.
260 West Main Street, Suite 208, Hendersonville TN 37075. 615/822-9711. **Contact:** Human Resources. **Description:** Avco Financial Services, Inc., a wholly-owned subsidiary of Textron Inc., includes two groups: Finance and Insurance. The Finance Group offers secured and unsecured consumer loans, loans secured by real property, and purchases installment contracts through retail dealers, such as appliance and furniture stores, through 1,198 branch offices in seven countries around the world. This group also has Special Business Units, which include: Leasing, Revolving Credit, Military Loans and the National Dealer Center. The Insurance Group, Avco Insurance Services, primarily sells credit life, credit disability, and involuntary unemployment insurance to customers of the Finance Group and to independent financial institutions, such as banks, credit unions, and savings and loans. Avco Insurance also offers collateral protection, personal lines auto, and renters' insurance, as well as

other life insurance products and services to many of these same customers. **Corporate headquarters location:** Irvine CA.

AVCO FINANCIAL SERVICES, INC.

P.O. Box 485, Dyersburg TN 38025. 901/285-7030. **Contact:** Ron Hamblin, Manager. **Description:** Avco Financial Services, Inc., a wholly-owned subsidiary of Textron Inc., includes two groups: Finance and Insurance. The Finance Group offers secured and unsecured consumer loans, loans secured by real property, and purchases installment contracts through retail dealers, such as appliance and furniture stores, through 1,198 branch offices in seven countries around the world. This group also has Special Business Units, which include: Leasing, Revolving Credit, Military Loans and the National Dealer Center. The Insurance Group, Avco Insurance Services, primarily sells credit life, credit disability, and involuntary unemployment insurance to customers of the Finance Group and to independent financial institutions, such as banks, credit unions, and savings and loans. Avco Insurance also offers collateral protection, personal lines auto, and renters' insurance, as well as other life insurance products and services to many of these same customers. **Corporate headquarters location:** Irvine CA.

COVENTRY CORPORATION

53 Century Boulevard, Suite 250, Nashville TN 37214. 615/391-2440. **Contact:** Carol Woods, Office Supervisor. **Description:** Coventry Corporation is a managed health care company that provides comprehensive health care services through three market-leading regional health maintenance organizations (HMOs) located in Pennsylvania and Missouri. **Number of employees nationwide:** 2,000.

HAULERS INSURANCE COMPANY, INC.

P.O. Box 270, Columbia TN 38402. 615/381-5406. **Contact:** Duane Leach, Controller. **Description:** Haulers Insurance Company, Inc. writes policies covering both personal auto and professional auto insurance.

LAWYERS TITLE INSURANCE CORPORATION

6363 Poplar Avenue, Suite 108, Memphis TN 38119. 901/685-2500. **Contact:** Human Resources. **Description:** Lawyers Title Insurance Corporation provides title insurance and other real estate-related services on commercial and residential transactions in the United States, Canada, the Bahama Islands, Puerto Rico, and the U.S. Virgin Islands. Lawyers Title Insurance Corporation also provides search and examination services and closing services for a broad-based customer group that includes lenders, developers, real estate brokers, attorneys, and home buyers. This location covers Alabama, Arkansas, Georgia, Louisiana, Mississippi, and Tennessee. Subsidiaries include: Datatrace Information Services Company, Inc. (Richmond VA), which markets automated public record information for public and private use; Genesis Data Systems, Inc. (Englewood CO), which develops and markets computer software tailored specifically to the title industry; and Lawyers Title Exchange Company, which operates out of 10 of Lawyers Title Insurance Corporation's regional offices, and functions as an intermediary for individual and corporate investors interested in pursuing tax-free property exchanges under Section 1031 of the Internal Revenue Code. **Corporate headquarters location:** Richmond VA. **Other U.S.**

locations: Pasadena CA; Tampa FL; Chicago IL; Boston MA; Troy MI; White Plains NY; Westerville OH; Dallas TX. **Parent company:** Lawyers Title Corporation. **Listed on:** NASDAQ.

LAMAR MCKENZIE
STATE FARM INSURANCE AGENCY

P.O. Box 1016, Cleveland TN 37364. 423/479-8643. **Contact:** Lamar McKenzie, Agent. **Description:** Sells and services State Farm Insurance products to individuals and small businesses. **Common positions include:** Customer Service Representative; Insurance Agent/Broker; Marketing Specialist; Services Sales Representative. **Educational backgrounds include:** Business Administration; Marketing; Sales. **Benefits:** Dental Insurance; Disability Coverage; Life Insurance; Medical Insurance; Profit Sharing. **Special Programs:** Training Programs. **Number of employees at this location:** 6.

PERMANENT GENERAL COMPANIES, INC.

P.O. Box 110656, Nashville TN 37222-0656. 615/242-1961. **Contact:** Human Resources. **Description:** A non-standard automobile insurance carrier doing business in Tennessee and Ohio. **Common positions include:** Adjuster; Computer Programmer; Customer Service Representative; Underwriter/Assistant Underwriter. **Educational backgrounds include:** Business Administration; Computer Science. **Benefits:** Dental Insurance; Disability Coverage; Life Insurance; Medical Insurance; Profit Sharing; Savings Plan; Tuition Assistance. **Special Programs:** Training Programs. **Other U.S. locations:** Cleveland OH; Knoxville TN; Memphis TN. **Parent company:** Ingram Industries, Inc. **Number of employees at this location:** 130.

PROVIDENT LIFE AND ACCIDENT INSURANCE COMPANY
PROVIDENT LIFE CAPITAL CORPORATION

One Fountain Square, Chattanooga TN 37402. 615/755-3073. **Fax:** 615/755-7013. **Recorded Jobline:** 617/755-8507. **Contact:** Nicole Gaines, Employment Consultant. **Description:** Nationwide marketer of life and health insurance, employing approximately 5,000 people throughout the U.S. and Canada. **Common positions include:** Accountant/Auditor; Actuary; Adjuster; Claim Representative; Computer Programmer; Underwriter/Assistant Underwriter. **Educational backgrounds include:** Accounting; Business Administration; Computer Science; Economics; Finance; Liberal Arts; Marketing; Mathematics. **Benefits:** 401K; Dental Insurance; Disability Coverage; Employee Discounts; Life Insurance; Medical Insurance; Pension Plan; Tuition Assistance. **Special Programs:** Internships. **Corporate headquarters location:** This Location. **Other U.S. locations:** Nationwide. **Subsidiaries include:** Provident Healthcare Plans. **Parent company:** Provident Life and Accident Insurance Company of America. **Listed on:** New York Stock Exchange. **Number of employees at this location:** 2,399. **Number of employees nationwide:** 4,300.

SEDGWICK, INC.

Box 171377, Memphis TN 38187-1377. 901/761-1550. **Contact:** Ian Robb, Director of Human Resources. **Description:** Sedgwick, Inc. is an international insurance broker engaged in insurance booking, risk management, and benefits consulting. **Common positions include:** Actuary; Claim Representative; Customer Service Representative; Insurance Agent/Broker. **Educational backgrounds**

include: Business Administration; Finance. **Benefits:** Dental Insurance; Life Insurance; Medical Insurance; Pension Plan; Savings Plan. **Special Programs:** Internships; Training Programs. **Corporate headquarters location:** New York NY. **Parent company:** Sedgwick Group, plc. **Operations at this facility include:** Administration; Sales; Service. **Listed on:** London Stock Exchange.

TENNESSEE HEALTH CARE NETWORK (CARECHOICE)
BLUE CROSS BLUE SHIELD OF TENNESSEE
801 Pine Street, Chattanooga TN 37402. 615/755-5600. **Contact:** Leigh Winston, Recruiter. **Description:** Tennessee Health Care Network, a wholly-owned subsidiary of Blue Cross and Blue Shield of Tennessee, is a health maintenance organization operating under the CareChoice trademark. CareChoice serves a total of 2.3 million Tennesseans. More than 100,000 of those customers had no health coverage prior to 1994. As of late 1994, CareChoice served 21,309 members and their families in 56 of the state's 95 counties. The CareChoice network of health care providers added 202 primary care physicians and 518 specialists during their first nine months of 1994. As of October, 1994, the network included 519 primary care physicians, and 2,180 specialists. CareChoice's parent company, Blue Cross and Blue Shield of Tennessee, has served Tennessee since 1945. Blue Cross and Blue Shield of Tennessee is an independent licensee of the Blue Cross and Blue Shield Association.

Note: Because addresses and telephone numbers of smaller companies change rapidly, we recommend you call each company to verify the information below before inquiring about job opportunities. Mass mailings are not recommended.

Additional employers with under 250 employees:

INSURANCE COMPANIES

Tennessee Farmers Life Reassurance
P.O. Box 307, Columbia TN 38402-0307. 615/388-7872.

Milligan Reynolds Guaranty Title
2115 Stein Dr, Chattanooga TN 37421-7200. 423/855-9035.

Merastar Insurance Co.
537 Market St, Suite 301, Chattanooga TN 37402-1225. 423/266-2886.

For more information on career opportunities in insurance:

Associations

ALLIANCE OF AMERICAN INSURERS
1501 Woodfield Road, Suite 400 West, Schaumburg IL 60173-4980. 847/330-8500.

HEALTH INSURANCE ASSOCIATION OF AMERICA
555 13th Street North, Suite 600E, Washington DC 20004. 202/824-1600.

INSURANCE INFORMATION INSTITUTE
110 William Street, 24th Floor, New York NY 10038. 212/669-9200. Provides informational products on property and casualty insurance.

SOCIETY OF ACTUARIES
475 North Martingale Road, Suite 800, Schaumburg IL 60173-2226. 847/706-3500.

Directories

INSURANCE ALMANAC
Underwriter Printing and
Publishing Company, 50 East
Palisade Avenue, Englewood NJ
07631. 201/569-8808.
Hardcover annual, 639 pages,
$115. Available at libraries.

INSURANCE MARKET PLACE
Rough Notes Company, Inc., P.O.
Box 564, Indianapolis IN 46206.
317/634-1541.

**INSURANCE PHONE BOOK AND
DIRECTORY**
Reed Reference Publishing, 121
Chanlon Road, New Providence
NJ 07974. 800/521-8110.
$89.95, new editions available
every other year. Also available at
libraries.

**NATIONAL DIRECTORY OF
HEALTH MAINTENANCE
ORGANIZATIONS**
Group Health Association of
America, 1129 20th Street NW,
Suite 600, Washington DC
20036. 202/778-3200.

Magazines

BEST'S REVIEW
A.M. Best Company, A.M. Best
Road, Oldwick NJ 08858-9988.
908/439-2200. Monthly.

INSURANCE JOURNAL
Wells Publishing, 9191 Towne
Centre Drive, Suite 550, San
Diego, CA 92122-1231 619/455-
7717. A biweekly magazine
covering the insurance industry.
Subscription: $78 per year, $3 for
a single issue.

INSURANCE TIMES
M & S Communications, 20 Park
Plaza, Suite 1101, Boston MA
02116. 617/292-7117. A
regional biweekly insurance
newspaper for insurance
professionals.

LEGAL SERVICES

The number of people working in the legal services field has exploded since the early '70s. According to a 1969 survey by the Bureau of Labor Statistics (BLS), there were 387,000 workers in legal services. Today, that number is well over 1 million. The glut of lawyers has led to tremendous competition in the legal profession. Law firms are laying off associates and firing unproductive partners. Graduates of prestigious law schools face tough competition for jobs, but for the top graduates, the offers will be there. According to Jon Sargent, an economist for the Office of Economic Growth at the BLS, some jobseekers looking to break into this industry may need to look outside the mainstream legal services industry: nonprofit companies, government positions, or law firms in smaller communities.

Paralegals have carved out a niche for themselves and continue to be the fastest-growing profession in legal services. "Paralegals have become a cost-effective way to provide legal services in many cases," says Sargent, referring to the realization by many employers that paralegals can do many of the same jobs as associates, at a much lower cost.

BAKER, DONELSON, BEARMAN AND CALDWELL
1700 Nashville City Center, 511 Union Street, P.O. Box 190613, Nashville TN 37219. 615/726-5600. **Contact:** Human Resources. **Description:** A legal services firm.

GIBSON AND GREGORY
Suite 600, Noel Place, 200 4th Avenue North, Nashville TN 37219. 615/242-7700. **Contact:** Office Manager. **Description:** Specializes in general law, excluding divorce and criminal defense.

MILLER & MARTIN
832 Georgia Avenue, Suite 1000, Chattanooga TN 37402-2289. 615/756-6600. **Contact:** Betsy Farrar, Office Manager. **Description:** Specializes in real estate, tax, and litigation law.

ORTALE, KELLEY, HERBERT AND CRAWFORD
P.O. Box 198985, Nashville TN 37219. 615/256-9999. **Contact:** Roseanne Hurst, Office Manager. **Description:** Specializes in civil litigation.

Note: Because addresses and telephone numbers of smaller companies change rapidly, we recommend you call each company to verify the information below before inquiring about job opportunities. Mass mailings are not recommended.

Additional employers with under 250 employees:

LEGAL SERVICES

Burch Porter & Johnson
130 Court Ave,
Memphis TN 38103-
2288. 901/523-2311.

Manier Herod Hollabaugh
150 4th Ave N,
Nashville TN 37219-
2415. 615/244-0030.

Leitner Warner Moffitt
Pioneer Bank Bldg,
Chattanooga TN
37402. 423/265-
0214.

For more information on career opportunities in legal services:

Associations

AMERICAN BAR ASSOCIATION
750 North Lake Shore Drive,
Chicago IL 60611. 312/988-
5000.

FEDERAL BAR ASSOCIATION
1815 H. Street NW, Suite 408,
Washington DC 20006-3697.
202/638-0252.

NATIONAL ASSOCIATION OF LEGAL ASSISTANTS
1516 South Boston, Suite 200,
Tulsa OK 74119-4013. 918/587-
6828. An educational association.
Offers the National Voluntary

Association Exam. Memberships
are available.

NATIONAL FEDERATION OF PARALEGAL ASSOCIATIONS
P.O. Box 33108, Kansas City MO
64114-0108. 816/941-4000.
World Wide Web address:
http:/www.paralegals.org. Offers
magazines, seminars, and Internet
job listings.

NATIONAL PARALEGAL ASSOCIATION
P.O. Box 629, 6186 Honey
Hollow Road, Doylestown PA
18901. 215/297-8333.

MANUFACTURING AND WHOLESALING: MISCELLANEOUS CONSUMER

The consumer goods manufacturing industry is more than just one industry. To generally forecast about the entire range of companies that make products for consumers is risky, since so much can differ from one segment to the next. In fact, many consumer manufacturers are listed under more specific categories in this book.

With that said, some general statements can be made about the outlook for this gigantic field. Over the long term, many analysts are optimistic. An improved economy, as well as an aging baby boom generation with growing disposable income, should provide stimulus for increases in personal durables. Continued growth in international trade should also point to a favorable long-term outlook for household consumer durables.

U.S. exports of household durables should also expand as trade barriers drop. The North American Free Trade Agreement (NAFTA), passed in early 1994, will give U.S. manufacturers even greater access to what is already the second-largest export market for U.S. household durables. Other trade agreements may follow with several Latin American countries. Potential markets in Eastern Europe and independent states of the former Soviet Union may also open.

ALADDIN INDUSTRIES INC.
703 Murfreesboro Road, Nashville TN 37210. 615/748-3000. **Contact:** Tom Bryant, Director of Human Resources. **Description:** Manufactures a variety of consumer products including thermos bottles, lamps, coolers, and lunch boxes.

ANCHOR ADVANCED PRODUCTS COMPANY
209 East Desota Avenue, Morristown TN 37815. 423/585-1800. **Contact:** Human Resources. **Description:** Produces a variety of blow-molded products, including cosmetic brushes and toothbrushes.

AQUA GLASS CORPORATION
P.O. Box 412, Adamsville TN 38310. 901/632-0911. **Contact:** Human Resources. **Description:** Manufactures bathtubs.

AVERY DENNISON CORPORATION
2110 West Avenue North, Crossville TN 38557. 615/484-6131. **Contact:** Human Resources. **Description:** A manufacturing plant for the nationally-recognized corporation, which is a leader in pressure-sensitive adhesives, office products, labels, tags, retail systems, and specialty chemicals. The company specializes in producing a wide variety of labels, especially clear labels, for use in packaging products ranging from apparel to motor oil to liquid soap to automobiles. Labels are marketed under the Avery and Fasson brand names. The company also uses its expertise in labeling to produce

product identification and control systems. In addition to its operations within the United States, Avery Dennison operates plants in international markets as well. **Corporate headquarters location:** Pasadena CA.

BATESVILLE CASKET COMPANY
175 Monogard Drive, Manchester TN 37355. 615/728-2231. **Contact:** Human Resources. **Description:** A manufacturing plant for a leading producer of protective metal and hardwood burial caskets. The company also manufactures a line of cremation urns and caskets. Products are marketed to licensed funeral directors operating licensed funeral homes in North America and selected export markets. In hopes of strengthening communications with customers, the company has opened a new Customer Business Center at its headquarters. The company is now offering a new line of cremation urns and services, called Options, which the company states is a total system approach for marketing cremation products through funeral homes. Batesville is also offering caskets with Kente fabric, a distinctively designed material that recognizes the heritage of African-Americans. **Corporate headquarters location:** Batesville IN. **Parent company:** Hillenbrand Industries.

BERKLINE CORPORATION
P.O. Box 6003, Morristown TN 37815. 423/585-1500. **Contact:** Carolyn Vaughn, Human Resources. **Description:** A furniture manufacturer.

BIKE ATHLETIC COMPANY
2801 Red Dog Drive, Knoxville TN 37901. 423/546-4703. **Contact:** Human Resources. **Description:** Bike Athletic Company is a sporting goods manufacturer. Products include athletic shorts, pants, T-shirts, tank tops, pullover jerseys, button front jerseys, Portex practice jerseys, replica football jerseys, youth jerseys, button front vests, youth and adult fleece pants, fleece crewnecks, mock turtlenecks, hooded vests, hooded pullovers, lycra pants, soft collar shirts, spandex shorts, workout shorts, supporters, and cups.

BROTHER INDUSTRIES (U.S.A.), INC.
2950 Brother Boulevard, Bartlett TN 38133. 901/377-7777. **Contact:** Human Resources. **Description:** A manufacturer of typewriters and other office equipment. **Common positions include:** Data Processor; Manufacturing Engineer; Mechanical Engineer.

BUSHLINE INC.
P.O. Box 527, 707 Industrial Park Drive, New Tazewell TN 37825. 423/626-5246. **Contact:** Linda Cochrane, Personnel Director. **Description:** A furniture manufacturer. Products include living room sets, chairs, tables, and dinette sets.

CHATTEM, INC.
1715 West 38th Street, Chattanooga TN 37409. 423/821-7571. **Contact:** Matthew Brown, Personnel Director. **Description:** Chattem, Inc. and its wholly owned subsidiaries are primarily engaged in manufacturing and marketing branded consumer products and specialty chemicals. The consumer products are sold nationwide and in many international markets, primarily through independent and chain drug stores, drug wholesalers, mass merchandisers and food

stores. Specialty chemicals are sold primarily to other manufacturing companies. Chattem, Inc. operates through the following divisions: Chattem Consumer Products, which include over the counter pharmaceuticals, cosmetics and toiletries; Chattem Chemicals, which include aluminum hydroxides, aluminum derivitives, glycine, and new product development operations; and Chattem International, which directs the international sales of Chattem Consumer Products. **Corporate headquarters location:** This Location.

CLEVELAND CHAIR COMPANY
P.O. Box 159, Cleveland TN 37364. 615/476-8544. **Contact:** Tommy Arthur, Personnel. **Description:** Manufactures chairs.

CRESCENT MANUFACTURING COMPANY
P.O. Box 1438, Gallatin TN 37066. 615/452-1671. **Contact:** Dennis Condra, Human Resources Director. **Description:** Manufactures living room and dining room furniture.

DAY RUNNER INC.
1293 Heil Quaker Boulevard #C, LaVergne TN 37086-3516. 615/793-2785. **Contact:** Human Resources. **Description:** A distribution center for Day Runner organizers and planners.

DURACELL INTERNATIONAL, INC.
P.O. Box 3390, Cleveland TN 37320. 423/478-6000. **Contact:** Larry Hillard, Human Resources Manager. **Description:** Duracell is a maker of a line of batteries sold worldwide under the Duracell trademark. The company also markets and distributes its products, with extensive operations in the U.S., Europe, Mexico, South America, the Middle East, and the Pacific Rim. Battery types include alkaline, which accounts for most of the company's business, and zinc, rechargeable, and lithium. The company also manufactures batteries used in hearing aids, and photographic and communications equipment. A subsidiary conducts marketing operations for a line of lighting products under the Durabeam name. Duracell employs 7,700 people worldwide. Manufacturing facilities are located in the United States, Canada, Mexico, the U.K., and Belgium. The company also plans to build manufacturing plants in China and India.

ENGLAND CORSAIR UPHOLSTERY
402 Old Knoxville Highway, New Tazewell TN 37825. 423/626-5211. **Contact:** Mike Ayers, Human Resources Director. **Description:** England Corsair Upholstery manufactures upholstered living room furniture.

FRANKLIN FURNITURE CORPORATION
300 Baileyton Road, Greeneville TN 37743. 423/639-6102. **Contact:** Human Resources. **Description:** Franklin Furniture Corporation manufactures dining room furniture.

FRIGIDAIRE COMPANY RANGE PRODUCTS
P.O. Box 10, 202 Hicks Street, Athens TN 37303. 615/745-4332. **Contact:** Cathy Barnes, Human Resources. **Description:** Manufactures oven ranges. The parent company has four business areas: Household Appliances, Commercial Appliances, Outdoor Products, and Industrial Products. The main operation in Household Appliances is white goods, which account for 70 percent of sales.

Other operations include floor-care products, absorption refrigerators for caravans and hotel rooms, room air-conditioners, and sewing machines, as well as kitchen and bathroom cabinets. The main operations in Commercial Appliances are food-service equipment for restaurants and institutions, and equipment for such applications as apartment-house laundry rooms and commercial laundries. These product areas account for almost 75 percent of sales. Other operations include refrigeration equipment and freezers for shops and supermarkets, as well as vacuum cleaners and wet/dry cleaners for commercial use. Outdoor Products include garden equipment, chain saws, and other equipment for forestry operations. Garden equipment refers to portable products such as lawn trimmers and leaf blowers, as well as lawn mowers and garden tractors. Industrial Products comprise the Group's second largest business area. Over 40 percent of sales consist of profiles and other half-finished goods in aluminum, manufactured by Granges. Other main operations include car safety belts and other products for personal safety in cars as well as materials-handling equipment. **Corporate headquarters location:** Dublin OH. **Other U.S. locations:** Springfield TN. **Parent company:** AB Electrolux.

FRIGIDAIRE COMPANY RANGE PRODUCTS
1100 Industrial Drive, Springfield TN 37172. 615/384-2431. **Contact:** Bob Lipscomb, Human Resources Director. **Description:** Manufactures oven ranges. A.B. Electrolux, the parent company, has four business areas: Household Appliances, Commercial Appliances, Outdoor Products, and Industrial Products. The main operation in Household Appliances is white goods, which account for 70 percent of sales. Other operations include floor-care products, absorption refrigerators for caravans and hotel rooms, room air-conditioners, and sewing machines, as well as kitchen and bathroom cabinets. The main operations in Commercial Appliances are food-service equipment for restaurants and institutions, and equipment for such applications as apartment-house laundry rooms and commercial laundries. These product areas account for almost 75 percent of sales. Other operations include refrigeration equipment and freezers for shops and supermarkets, as well as vacuum cleaners and wet/dry cleaners for commercial use. Outdoor Products include garden equipment, chain saws, and other equipment for forestry operations. Garden equipment refers to portable products such as lawn trimmers and leaf blowers, as well as lawn mowers and garden tractors. Industrial Products comprise the Group's second largest business area. Over 40 percent of sales consist of profiles and other half-finished goods in aluminum, manufactured by Granges. Other main operations include car safety belts and other products for personal safety in cars as well as materials-handling equipment. **Corporate headquarters location:** Dublin OH. **Other U.S. locations:** Athens TN. **Parent company:** AB Electrolux.

GIBSON USA
WORLD HEADQUARTERS
1818 Elm Hill Pike, Nashville TN 37210. 615/871-4500. **Contact:** Carl Hansen, Human Resources Director. **Description:** A manufacturer and distributor of electric and acoustic guitars, other musical instruments, and accessories. **Common positions include:** Accountant/Auditor; Blue-Collar Worker Supervisor; Buyer; Computer Programmer; Credit Manager; Customer Service Representative;

Electrical/Electronics Engineer; Financial Analyst; General Manager; Mechanical Engineer; Operations/Production Manager; Quality Control Supervisor. **Educational backgrounds include:** Accounting; Business Administration; Communications; Computer Science; Engineering; Finance; Marketing. **Benefits:** 401K; Dental Insurance; Employee Discounts; Life Insurance; Medical Insurance; Profit Sharing; Savings Plan; Tuition Assistance. **Corporate headquarters location:** This Location. **Other U.S. locations:** Huntington Beach CA; Oakland CA; Elgin IL; Bozeman MT. **Listed on:** Privately held.

HART'S FURNITURE
141 Eastley Street, Collierville TN 38017. 901/853-8595. **Contact:** Marcy Hiers, Human Resources. **Description:** Hart's Furniture manufactures bedroom and dining room furniture.

HUNTER FAN COMPANY
P.O. Box 14775, Memphis TN 38114. 901/743-1360. **Contact:** Human Resources. **Description:** A manufacturer of ceiling fans, mechanical and programmable thermostats, decorative lighting, and air purifiers.

KIMBERLY-CLARK CORPORATION
5600 Kimberly Way, Loudon TN 37774. 615/988-7000. **Contact:** Maryann Burout, Human Resources Team Leader. **Description:** Engaged in the manufacturing and marketing throughout the world of a wide range of products for personal, business, and industrial uses. Most products are made from natural and synthetic fibers using advanced technologies in absorbency, fibers, and nonwovens. Well-known brands include Kleenex facial and bathroom tissue, Huggies diapers and baby wipes, Pull-Ups training pants, Kotex and New Freedom feminine care products, Depend and Poise incontinence care products, Hi-Dri household towels, Kimguard sterile wrap, Kimwipes industrial wipers, and Classic business and correspondence papers.

LASKO METAL PRODUCTS INC.
P.O. Box 130, Franklin TN 37065. 615/794-2531. **Contact:** Human Resources. **Description:** Manufactures household electric fans.

LE-AL-CO (LEBANON ALUMINUM PRODUCTS, INC.)
P.O. Box 519, Lebanon TN 37087-0519. 615/444-3812. **Contact:** Bob Merrill, Personnel Manager. **Description:** Manufactures a broad selection of aluminum window and door products. Products include aluminum storm doors, solid wood core storm doors with magnetic seal, premium full view doors, sliding glass doors, thermal break windows, horizontal sliding windows, and single hung windows.

MAYTAG CLEVELAND COOKING PRODUCTS
740 King Edward Avenue, Cleveland TN 37311. 615/478-4291. **Fax:** 615/478-4237. **Contact:** Bob Barton, Director, Salary Administration. **Description:** A manufacturer of gas and electric ranges. **Common positions include:** Accountant/Auditor; Buyer; Ceramics Engineer; Chemical Engineer; Claim Representative; Clerical Supervisor; Computer Systems Analyst; Designer; Draftsperson; Electrical/Electronics Engineer; Electrician; Financial Analyst; General Manager; Health Services Manager; Human Resources Specialist; Industrial Engineer; Industrial Production Manager; Licensed Practical

Nurse; Management Trainee; Materials Engineer; Mechanical Engineer; Metallurgical Engineer; Operations/Production Manager; Public Relations Specialist; Purchasing Agent and Manager; Quality Control Supervisor; Registered Nurse; Technical Writer/Editor. **Educational backgrounds include:** Accounting; Business Administration; Computer Science; Engineering; Finance. **Benefits:** 401K; Dental Insurance; Disability Coverage; Employee Discounts; Life Insurance; Medical Insurance; Pension Plan; Tuition Assistance. **Special Programs:** Internships. **Corporate headquarters location:** Newton IA. **Other U.S. locations:** Galesburg IL; Indianapolis IN; North Canton OH; Jackson TN. **Subsidiaries include:** Hoover and Dixie NARCO. **Parent company:** Maytag Corporation is comprised of 14 companies with primary emphasis in the major home appliance field. Maytag also manufactures soft drink vending machines, currency-changers, furnaces, air-conditioners, ventilation systems, and heating elements. **Operations at this facility include:** Administration; Manufacturing; Research and Development. **Listed on:** New York Stock Exchange. **Number of employees at this location:** 1,900. **Number of employees nationwide:** 18,000.

MECO CORPORATION
1500 Industrial Road, Greeneville TN 37745. 423/639-1171. **Contact:** Dominic Jackson, Director of Human Resources. **Description:** Manufactures folding tubular steel furniture such as chairs, card tables, and banquet tables. Meco Corporation also manufactures electric and charcoal grills.

MURRAY, INC.
Hannon Drive, Lawrenceburg TN 38464. 615/762-0100. **Fax:** 615/762-0104. **Contact:** Human Resources. **Description:** Murray Outdoor Products, Inc. is a manufacturer of lawn mowers, bicycles, snowblowers, and edgers. Customers include major discounters, such as Wal-Mart, Kmart, and Home Depot. **Common positions include:** Accountant/Auditor; Blue-Collar Worker Supervisor; Ceramics Engineer; Computer Programmer; Computer Systems Analyst; Designer; Draftsperson; Electrical/Electronics Engineer; Human Resources Specialist; Industrial Engineer; Industrial Production Manager; Materials Engineer; Mechanical Engineer; Metallurgical Engineer; Purchasing Agent and Manager; Quality Control Supervisor; Registered Nurse. **Educational backgrounds include:** Accounting; Computer Science; Engineering. **Benefits:** Dental Insurance; Life Insurance; Medical Insurance. **Corporate headquarters location:** Brentwood TN. **Other U.S. locations:** Jackson TN; McKenzie TN. **Operations at this facility include:** Administration; Manufacturing; Regional Headquarters; Service. **Listed on:** NASDAQ. **Number of employees at this location:** 3,600. **Number of employees nationwide:** 5,600.

MURRAY, INC.
210 American Drive, Jackson TN 38301. 901/422-1690. **Contact:** Bart Freeman, Human Resources Director. **Description:** Murray Outdoor Products, Inc. is a manufacturer of lawn mowers, bicycles, snowblowers, and edgers. Customers include major discounters, such as Wal-Mart, Kmart, and Home Depot. **Corporate headquarters location:** Brentwood TN. **Other U.S. locations:** Lawrenceburg TN; McKenzie TN. **Listed on:** NASDAQ. **Number of employees nationwide:** 5,600.

MURRAY, INC.
1165 Airport Road, McKenzie TN 38201. 901/352-7961. **Contact:** Human Resources. **Description:** Murray Outdoor Products, Inc. is a manufacturer of lawn mowers, bicycles, snowblowers, and edgers. Customers include major discounters, such as Wal-Mart, Kmart, and Home Depot. **NOTE:** For information on professional hiring, please contact Murray's Jackson, Tennessee location (Mr. Bart Freeman, Human Resources, Murray, Inc., 210 American Drive, Jackson, TN 38303). **Corporate headquarters location:** Brentwood TN. **Other U.S. locations:** Lawrenceburg TN; Jackson TN. **Listed on:** NASDAQ. **Number of employees nationwide:** 5,600.

ORGILL BROTHERS & COMPANY
P.O. Box 140, Memphis TN 38101. 901/948-3381. **Contact:** Mary K. Allen, Human Resources Director. **Description:** A hardware distributor. The company was founded in 1847 by Joseph and William Orgill and operated mainly as a hardware retailer until the turn of the century, when Orgill's focus changed to wholesale. In recent decades, Orgill expanded its geographic presence by acquiring other hardware distributors -- with four such mergers since 1970. The result was an increased sales force and wider customer base. Orgill is still a family-owned business, owned by a fifth generation member of the Orgill Brothers family through the West Union Corporation. Other businesses are owned and managed by West Union, with Orgill Brothers representing the largest division. **Parent company:** West Union Corporation. **Listed on:** Privately held. **Number of employees at this location:** 300.

PELIKAN INC.
P.O. Box 3000, Franklin TN 37068. 615/794-9000. **Contact:** Dave Luther, Vice President of Human Resources. **Description:** Manufactures typewriter and computer ribbon. The company also operates a toner developer location in Derry, Pennsylvania.

PHILIPS CONSUMER ELECTRONICS CORPORATION
One Philips Drive, P.O. Box 14810, Knoxville TN 37914. 423/521-4316. **Fax:** 423/521-4586. **Contact:** Human Resources Manager. **Description:** An audio, video, and television equipment manufacturer specializing in engineering design and development for Magnavox, Philips, and audio-video products. **Common positions include:** Accountant/Auditor; Buyer; Computer Programmer; Computer Systems Analyst; Electrical/Electronics Engineer. **Educational backgrounds include:** Computer Science; Engineering; Finance; Marketing. **Benefits:** 401K; Dental Insurance; Life Insurance; Medical Insurance; Pension Plan; Profit Sharing. **Parent company:** Philips Electronics North America. **Operations at this facility include:** Administration; Divisional Headquarters. **Number of employees at this location:** 800. **Number of employees nationwide:** 5,000.

PIONEER AIR SYSTEMS, INC.
210 Flatfork Road, Wartburg TN 37887. 423/346-6693. **Contact:** Patricia Abbott, Human Resources Director. **Description:** A manufacturer of refrigerator and regenerative dryers.

PORTER CABLE CORPORATION
P.O. Box 2468, Jackson TN 38302. 901/668-8600. **Contact:** Tom Bridges, Vice President of Human Resources. **Description:** Manufactures portable power tools.

RUBBERMAID OFFICE PRODUCTS
1427 William Blount Drive, Maryville TN 37801. 423/977-5477. **Fax:** 423/977-6849. **Contact:** Sheri Tiernan, Division Recruiter. **Description:** Manufacturers of a wide variety of consumer products including office accessories, office furnishings, and filing systems. **Common positions include:** Accountant/Auditor; Buyer; Customer Service Representative; Designer; Education Administrator; Financial Manager; General Manager; Human Resources Specialist; Industrial Production Manager; Operations/Production Manager; Purchasing Agent and Manager; Quality Control Supervisor; Transportation/Traffic Specialist. **Educational backgrounds include:** Accounting; Art/Design; Business Administration; Engineering; Marketing. **Benefits:** Dental Insurance; Disability Coverage; Employee Discounts; Life Insurance; Medical Insurance; Pension Plan; Profit Sharing; Savings Plan; Tuition Assistance. **Special Programs:** Internships. **Parent company:** Rubbermaid Incorporated. **Operations at this facility include:** Administration; Distribution; Divisional Headquarters; Manufacturing; Research and Development; Sales. **Listed on:** New York Stock Exchange. **Number of employees at this location:** 400. **Number of employees nationwide:** 500.

SAMSONITE FURNITURE COMPANY
P.O. Box 189, Murfreesboro TN 37133-0189. 615/893-0300. **Contact:** Richard Slicker, Director of Personnel. **Description:** Manufactures patio and folding furniture as well as office furniture. **Common positions include:** Accountant/Auditor; Administrator; Advertising Clerk; Blue-Collar Worker Supervisor; Buyer; Computer Programmer; Credit Manager; Customer Service Representative; Department Manager; Draftsperson; Electrical/Electronics Engineer; General Manager; Human Resources Specialist; Industrial Engineer; Manufacturer's/Wholesaler's Sales Rep.; Marketing Specialist; Mechanical Engineer; Operations/Production Manager; Public Relations Specialist; Purchasing Agent and Manager; Quality Control Supervisor; Statistician; Systems Analyst. **Educational backgrounds include:** Accounting; Business Administration; Computer Science; Engineering; Finance; Marketing. **Benefits:** Dental Insurance; Employee Discounts; Life Insurance; Medical Insurance; Pension Plan; Profit Sharing; Tuition Assistance. **Corporate headquarters location:** This Location. **Parent company:** Beatrice Company.

SANFORD BEROL CORPORATION
P.O. Box 470, Shelbyville TN 37160-0470. **Contact:** Blake Clayton, Human Resources Manager. **Description:** Sanford Berol manufactures writing instruments, such as pens, pencils, markers, and erasers. The company also manufactures a variety of other office supplies including stamp pads, magnetic clips, address books, pencil sharpeners, scissors, staple removers, calculators, thumb tacks, labels, paper clips, binder clips, reinforcements, erasers, rubber bands, and rulers. **Common positions include:** Accountant/Auditor; Blue-Collar Worker Supervisor; Buyer; Chemical Engineer; Chemist; Clerical Supervisor; Computer Programmer; Computer Systems Analyst; Electrical/Electronics Engineer; Electrician; Financial Analyst;

Human Resources Specialist; Industrial Engineer; Management Trainee; Mechanical Engineer; Operations/Production Manager; Production Manager; Purchasing Agent and Manager; Quality Control Supervisor; Registered Nurse. **Educational backgrounds include:** Accounting; Business Administration; Chemistry; Economics; Engineering. **Benefits:** 401K; Dental Insurance; Disability Coverage; Life Insurance; Medical Insurance; Pension Plan; Tuition Assistance. **Corporate headquarters location:** Brentwood TN. **Other U.S. locations:** San Fernando CA; Rockford IL; Georgetown KY. **Operations at this facility include:** Administration; Manufacturing; Research and Development. **Listed on:** Privately held. **Number of employees at this location:** 850. **Number of employees nationwide:** 1,000.

SANFORD BEROL CORPORATION
105 West Park Drive, Brentwood TN 37027. 615/371-1199. **Contact:** Carol McDaniel, Human Resources. **Description:** Sanford Berol manufactures writing instruments, such as pens, pencils, markers, and erasers. The company also manufactures a variety of other office supplies including stamp pads, magnetic clips, address books, pencil sharpeners, scissors, staple removers, calculators, thumb tacks, labels, paper clips, binder clips, reinforcements, erasers, rubber bands, and rulers. **Corporate headquarters location:** This Location. **Other U.S. locations:** San Fernando CA; Rockford IL; Georgetown KY. **Listed on:** Privately held. **Number of employees nationwide:** 1,000.

SNAP-ON, INC.
2195 Stateline Road, Elizabethton TN 37643-4636. 423/543-5771. **Contact:** Thomas Langwell, Plant Manager. **Description:** Formerly Snap-On Tools Corporation, this company makes and distributes tools, storage units, and diagnostic equipment for professional repair, maintenance, and industrial use. Tools include a line of over 14,000 tools, tool chests, custom tools, and diagnostic equipment. Products are supplied through over 5,000 independent dealers and franchises and more than 500 sales representatives.

SPRINGS INDUSTRIES, INC.
BATH FASHION DIVISION
P.O. Box 516, Nashville TN 37202. 615/350-7400. **Fax:** 615/350-7428. **Contact:** Diana Berry, Specialist, Human Resources. **Description:** The Bath Fashion Division manufactures and distributes bath rugs, area rugs, shower curtains, and other bath fashion products. Primary customers are various retailers. Overall, Springs Industries is a producer of home furnishings, finished fabrics, and other fabrics for industrial uses. Products include bedroom accessories, bath products, novelties, window treatments, and specialty fabrics for the clothes manufacturing, home furnishing, home sewing, sporting goods, and fire-retardant industries. **Common positions include:** Accountant/Auditor; Blue-Collar Worker Supervisor; General Manager; Human Resources Specialist; Industrial Engineer; Industrial Production Manager; Operations/Production Manager; Quality Control Supervisor. **Educational backgrounds include:** Accounting; Business Administration; Engineering. **Benefits:** 401K; Dental Insurance; Disability Coverage; Life Insurance; Medical Insurance; Pension Plan; Profit Sharing; Savings Plan; Tuition Assistance. **Corporate headquarters location:** Fort Mill SC. **Other**

U.S. locations: Nationwide. **Operations at this facility include:** Administration; Manufacturing. **Listed on:** New York Stock Exchange. **Number of employees at this location:** 700.

THE STANLEY WORKS
STANLEY TOOLS
1200 Stanley Boulevard, Shelbyville TN 37160. 615/684-6980. **Contact:** Ted Ellis, Director of Human Resources. **Description:** The Stanley Works is a worldwide producer of tools, hardware, and specialty hardware for home improvement, consumer, industrial, and professional use. The company operates 114 manufacturing and major distribution facilities in 18 countries covering every major region of the world. Operating as a division of Stanley Works, Stanley Tools manufactures consumer tools, such as carpenters' hand tools, tool boxes, paint preparation and application tools, masonry tools, and agricultural tools. In addition to Stanley Tools, Stanley Works operates 10 other business units. Stanley Mechanics Tools manufactures mechanics' hand tools, air tools, electronic diagnostic tools, and tool boxes. Stanley Vidmar manufactures cabinets, racks, and engineered handling systems for inventory control, storage, and retrieval. Mail Media manufactures custom-designed precision tool kits and safety products. Stanley Fastening Systems manufactures pneumatic nailers and staplers, fasteners, and office products. Stanley Air Tools manufactures torque-controlled fastening tools for vehicle assembly. Stanley Hydraulic Tools produces mounted and hand-held hydraulic beakers, shears, crushers, and specialty tools. Stanley Hardware produces consumer, residential, and architectural hardware; closet doors; organizers; mirrored doors; and decorative wall mirrors. Stanley Acmetrack manufactures bi-fold and sliding closet doors and closet organizing systems. Stanley Door Systems manufactures residential garage and entry doors, garage door openers, and home automation products. Stanley Access Technologies produces power-operated doors, gates, sensors, and parking systems. **Corporate headquarters location:** New Britain CT.

STERLING KINKEAD
P.O. Box 769, Union City TN 38261. 901/885-1200. **Contact:** Personnel. **Description:** Manufactures shower doors and tub doors.

SUNBEAM-OSTER HOUSEHOLD PRODUCTS
150 Cadillac Lane, McMinnville TN 37110. 615/668-4121. **Contact:** Anzena Montandon, Personnel Assistant. **Description:** Sunbeam-Oster Household Products manufactures, engineers, and markets clippers and blades for the professional, personal, and animal grooming markets worldwide. **Common positions include:** Accountant/Auditor; Administrator; Blue-Collar Worker Supervisor; Buyer; Commercial Artist; Credit Manager; Customer Service Representative; Department Manager; Draftsperson; Electrical/Electronics Engineer; Financial Analyst; Human Resources Specialist; Industrial Engineer; Industrial Production Manager; Manufacturer's/Wholesaler's Sales Rep.; Mechanical Engineer; Operations/Production Manager; Purchasing Agent and Manager; Quality Control Supervisor; Systems Analyst. **Benefits:** Dental Insurance; Disability Coverage; Life Insurance; Medical Insurance; Pension Plan; Profit Sharing; Savings Plan; Tuition Assistance. **Corporate headquarters location:** Providence RI. **Parent company:**

Sunbeam-Oster Corporation is a designer, manufacturer, and marketer of consumer products. The company is divided into four business groups: Outdoor Products, Household Products, Specialty Products, and International. Outdoor Products include propane, natural gas, electric, and charcoal barbecue grills; aluminum lawn and patio furniture and related accessories; and wrought iron and wood furniture. The company is estimated to have a 50 percent market share in grills and aluminum furniture. Household Products include electric and conventional blankets, comforters, heated throws, heating pads, bath scales, health-monitoring systems, vaporizers, humidifiers, irons, steamers, and dental and hair care products. Small kitchen appliances include stand mixers, hand mixers, blenders, food processors, juice extractors, toasters, can openers, waffle makers, and other culinary accessories. Sunbeam also produces barber and beauty products, personal care products, and pet and large animal products, as well as clocks, timers, thermometers, and weather instruments. The company operates in over 60 countries through its international unit, primarily throughout Latin America and Canada, with manufacturing facilities in Mexico and Venzuela. International sales consist primarily of small appliances. **Operations at this facility include:** Administration; Divisional Headquarters; Manufacturing. **Listed on:** New York Stock Exchange.

SUPERIOR FIREPLACE COMPANY
503 East Realfoot Avenue, Union City TN 38261. 901/885-7621. **Contact:** Dale Hamiliton, Personnel Manager. **Description:** Manufactures fireplaces, woodburning stoves, and gas stoves.

TOSHIBA AMERICA CONSUMER PRODUCTS
1420 Toshiba Drive, Lebanon TN 37087. 615/444-8501. **Contact:** Leonard Tyree, Human Resources. **Description:** A consumer electronics manufacturer.

VAUGHAN FURNITURE/EMPIRE DIVISION
P.O. Box 3590-CRS, Johnson City TN 37602. 423/926-3107. **Contact:** Henry Harris, Plant Supervisor. **Description:** A furniture manufacturer.

WORTH, INC.
P.O. Box 88104, Tullahoma TN 37388. 615/455-0691. **Contact:** Bill Keene, Human Resources Director. **Description:** The company is a manufacturer of sporting goods equipment. Primary products include batting gloves, baseball bats, baseball gloves, sporting bags designed for different sports, baseballs, softballs, and other sporting accessories.

Note: Because addresses and telephone numbers of smaller companies change rapidly, we recommend you call each company to verify the information below before inquiring about job opportunities. Mass mailings are not recommended.

Additional employers with under 250 employees:

WOOD KITCHEN CABINETS

Scepter Hardwoods
P.O. Box 6368, Sparta
TN 38583-6368.
615/738-5264.

COSMETICS AND RELATED PRODUCTS

Heavenly Scents
4500 Bonnie Brae Dr,
Millington TN 38053-
8112. 901/873-4500.

HOUSEHOLD FURNITURE

Five Rivers Craft Inc.
Indl Pk, Dandridge TN
37725. 423/397-
3986.

Southern Wood Products Inc.
RR 10 Box 241,
Sparta TN 38583-
9810. 615/738-5299.

Walnut Grove Furniture Manufacturing
305 Jackson St,
Savannah TN 38372-
2150. 901/925-7047.

Young's Furniture Manufacturing Co.
1701 Needmore Rd,
Whitesburg TN
37891-9209.
423/235-6548.

Charisma Chairs Division Flexsteel
P.O. Box 386,
Sweetwater TN
37874-0386.
423/337-6694.

Cooke Manufacturing
P.O. Box 4230,
Cleveland TN 37320-
4230. 423/476-5536.

Mill Business Furniture
205 Mill Dr, Cookeville
TN 38501-2157.
615/526-9745.

PFC Inc.
3036 Congress Pkwy
NW, Athens TN
37303-2800.
423/745-9127.

MISC. FURNITURE AND FIXTURES

Home Fashions Innovative Resources
3970 Delp St,
Memphis TN 38118-
6124. 901/795-0071.

SAW BLADES AND HAND SAWS

Sandvic Windsor Corp.
RR 1, Milan TN
38358-9801.
901/686-9023.

HOUSEHOLD APPLIANCES

Black & Decker Co.
191 Polk Ave,
Nashville TN 37210-
4629. 615/726-8555.

Electrolux Corp.
340 Industrial Park Rd,
Piney Flats TN 37686-
4449. 423/538-3610.

Gem Products Inc.
1903 W Polymer Dr,
Chattanooga TN
37421-2204.
423/954-3318.

HOUSEHOLD AUDIO AND VIDEO EQUIPMENT

Electro-Voice Inc.
366 Industrial Rd,
Newport TN 37821-
8104. 423/623-2356.

Mystery Electronics
6438 Morton Rd,
Greenbrier TN 37073-
4713. 615/643-8460.

BATTERIES

Enpak Inc.
1699 Airways Blvd,
Memphis TN 38114-
4717. 901/458-8553.

MUSICAL INSTRUMENTS

Mapes Piano String Co.
P.O. Box 700,
Elizabethton TN
37644-0700.
423/543-3195.

TOYS AND SPORTING GOODS

Educational Insights
2206 Oakland Pkwy,
Columbia TN 38401-
6533. 615/381-9066.

MPG LP
106 Western Dr,
Portland TN 37148-
2017. 615/325-5800.

Parris Manufacturing Co.
P.O. Box 338,
Savannah TN 38372-
0338. 901/925-3918.

OFFICE AND ART SUPPLIES

Economy Pen & Pencil Co.
710 Blue Ribbon
Pkwy, Shelbyville TN
37160-3013.
615/684-5434.

Nu-Kote International Inc.
136 Davis St, Portland TN 37148-2000. 615/325-5707.

FASTENERS, BUTTONS, NEEDLES, AND PINS

Henry I. Siegel Co. Inc.
P.O. Box 98, Saltillo TN 38370-0098. 901/687-3211.

Stitches Inc.
150 Old Barton Rd, Red Boiling Springs TN 37150-3352. 615/699-2283.

WHOLESALE FURNITURE AND HOME FURNISHINGS

McQuiddy Office Designers
110 7th Ave N, Nashville TN 37203-3704. 615/256-5643.

Steelcase Inc.
906 Briarwood Crest,

Nashville TN 37221-4351. 615/373-5816.

RA Siegel Co.
415 Brick Church Park Dr, Nashville TN 37207-3218. 615/228-9001.

Fred's Wholesale Carpet Sales
222 W Bockman Way, Sparta TN 38583-1922. 615/836-2230.

WHOLESALE OF ELECTRICAL APPLIANCES, TELEVISIONS, AND RADIOS

Audiovox South Corp.
6555 Quince Rd, Memphis TN 38119-8259. 901/754-7233.

HARDWARE WHOLESALE

House Hasson Hardware Co.
3125 Water Plant Rd, Knoxville TN 37914-6640. 423/525-0471.

Lewis Supply Company
913 Myatt Industrial Dr, Madison TN 37115-2429. 615/865-4797.

SPORTING AND RECREATIONAL GOODS AND SUPPLIES WHOLESALE

Adams USA Inc.
203 S Chestnut St, Monterey TN 38574-1464. 615/839-3116.

PAPER AND OFFICE SUPPLIES WHOLESALE

Athens Paper Co. Inc.
1898 Elm Tree Dr, Nashville TN 37210-3727. 615/889-7900.

Atlantic Envelope Co.
423 E Depot Ave, Knoxville TN 37917-7608. 423/525-4957.

For more information on career opportunities in consumer manufacturing and wholesaling:

Associations

ASSOCIATION FOR MANUFACTURING TECHNOLOGY
7901 Westpark Drive, McLean VA 22102. 703/893-2900. Offers research services.

ASSOCIATION OF HOME APPLIANCE MANUFACTURERS
20 North Wacker Drive, Chicago IL 60606. 312/984-5800.

NATIONAL ASSOCIATION OF MANUFACTURERS
1331 Pennsylvania Avenue NW, Suite 1500, Washington DC 20004. 202/637-3000. A lobbying association for manufacturers.

NATIONAL HOUSEWARES MANUFACTURERS ASSOCIATION
6400 Schafer Court, Suite 650,

Rosemont IL 60018. 847/292-4200. Offers shipping discounts and other services.

SOCIETY OF MANUFACTURING ENGINEERS
P.O. Box 930, One SME Drive, Dearborn MI 48121. 313/271-1500. Offers educational events and educational materials on manufacturing.

Directories

APPLIANCE MANUFACTURER ANNUAL DIRECTORY
Appliance Manufacturer, 5900 Harper Road, Suite 105, Solon OH 44139. 216/349-3060. $25.00.

HOUSEHOLD AND PERSONAL PRODUCTS INDUSTRY BUYERS GUIDE
Rodman Publishing Group, 17

South Franklin Turnpike, Ramsey
NJ 07446. 201/825-2552.
$12.00.

Magazines

APPLIANCE
1110 Jorie Boulevard, Oak Brook
IL 60522-9019. 708/990-3484.
Monthly. $70.00 for a one-year
subscription.

COSMETICS INSIDERS REPORT
Advanstar Communications, 131
West 1st Street, Duluth MN
55802. 800/346-0085. $189.00
for a one year subscription; 24
issues annually. Features timely
articles on cosmetics marketing
and research.

MANUFACTURING AND WHOLESALING: MISCELLANEOUS INDUSTRIAL

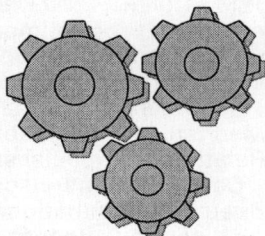

New investments by American businesses have generated much of the U.S. economy's expansion in recent years. That's good news for machinery manufacturers, who have been very busy. Through October 1995, the manufacturing of machinery and equipment was up about 12 percent over the previous year.

Employment in the wholesale trade sector is also closely tied to the growth of the economy. However, industry trends will change a good portion of the composition and nature of wholesale trade employment. Consolidation of the industry into fewer firms and the spread of new technology should slow growth in some occupations, but many new jobs will be created in others as firms provide a growing array of support services. In addition, these trends will change the role of many other workers.

Heightened competition and pressure to lower operating costs should continue to force distributors to merge with or acquire other firms. The resulting consolidation of wholesale trade among fewer, larger firms will reduce the demands for some workers as merged companies eliminate duplicated staff. Consolidation and greater competition among wholesale trade firms, however, will lead more firms to expand customer service, increasing the demand for these types of workers. Clerks or sales workers will advance to many of these new customer service or marketing jobs, and new workers may be needed for financial, logistical, technical, or advertising positions.

AZO INC.
4445 Malone Road, P.O. Box 181070, Memphis TN 38118. 901/794-9480. **Fax:** 901/794-9934. **Contact:** Mr. Van Kent, Human Resources Director. **Description:** AZO is a producer of enclosed materials handling systems. AZO's high-tech materials handling provides an automated ingredient call-off as well as access to production data throughout production. The computerized intelligence identifies ingredients and manages inventory, formulas, material flow lines, and production orders. Because an AZO system is enclosed, operators have no contact with ingredients, making the product pick-up, the feeding of mixers and processing machines, and the metering of minor ingredients dust free.

THE ALPHA CORPORATION OF TENNESSEE
P.O. Box 670, Collierville TN 38027-0670. 901/853-2450. **Contact:** Hazel Somogyi, Director of Human Resources. **Description:** The Alpha Corporation of Tennessee operates in two divisions under the names Glasteel, Inc. and Glasteel Industrial Laminates. Glasteel, Inc. manufactures fiberglass panels and Glasteel Industrial Laminates manufactures electronic circuit boards.

AMANA REFRIGERATION INC.
1810 Wilson Parkway, Fayetteville TN 37334-3559. **Contact:** Larry Gerst, Manager of Human Resources. **Description:** Amana Refrigeration Inc. designs, develops, manufactures, and sells HVAC (heating, ventilation, and air-conditioning) products. **Common positions include:** Accountant/Auditor; Blue-Collar Worker Supervisor; Branch Manager; Buyer; Computer Programmer; Computer Systems Analyst; Credit Manager; Customer Service Representative; Designer; Draftsperson; Economist/Market Research Analyst; Electrical/Electronics Engineer; Electrician; Human Resources Specialist; Industrial Engineer; Mechanical Engineer; Operations/Production Manager; Public Relations Specialist; Purchasing Agent and Manager; Quality Control Supervisor; Technical Writer/Editor; Transportation/Traffic Specialist. **Educational backgrounds include:** Business Administration; Engineering. **Benefits:** 401K; Dental Insurance; Disability Coverage; Employee Discounts; Life Insurance; Medical Insurance; Pension Plan; Tuition Assistance. **Corporate headquarters location:** Amana IA. **Other U.S. locations:** Nationwide. **Parent company:** Raytheon. **Operations at this facility include:** Administration; Divisional Headquarters; Manufacturing; Research and Development; Sales; Service. **Listed on:** New York Stock Exchange. **Number of employees at this location:** 1,000.

AMERICAN NATIONAL CAN COMPANY
P.O. Box 747, Shelbyville TN 37160. 615/684-4161. **Contact:** Bill Matos, Human Resources Manager. **Description:** American National Can manufactures a variety of container products as a unit of the packaging firm. American National Can is 67 percent owned by Pechiney, a diversified international corporation that has operations in packaging, aluminum, turbine components, and related industrial sectors.

AMERICAN WATER HEATER GROUP
P.O. Box 1378, Johnson City TN 37605-1378. 423/928-6411. **Contact:** Peter Sage, Human Resources Director. **Description:** Manufactures water heaters.

AQUA-CHEM, INC.
3001 East John Sevier Highway, Knoxville TN 37914. 423/544-2065. **Contact:** Gail Wesline, Human Resources Manager. **Description:** A manufacturer of water purification and desalination systems. **Corporate headquarters location:** Milwaukee WI.

ASTEC INDUSTRIES, INC.
4101 Jerome Avenue, Chattanooga TN 37407. 423/867-4210. **Contact:** Ms. Lois Wallace, Personnel Manager. **Description:** Manufactures asphalt production equipment. Subsidiary operations manufacture all processing equipment needed to process quarry rock into asphalt pavement, place it on the road, and then recycle the pavement into new roads.

CAMCAR TEXTRON
TOWNSEND ENGINEERED PRODUCTS
P.O. Box 856, Spencer TN 38585. 615/946-2291. **Contact:** Ralph Northcut, Human Resources Director. **Description:** Manufactures small fasteners and studs. **Corporate headquarters location:** Providence RI.

CARRIER CORPORATION
97 South Byhalia Road, Collierville TN 38017. 901/854-3000.
Contact: Anne Bazydlo, Manager of Human Resources. **Description:**
A commercial manufacturer of HVAC (heating, ventilation, and air-
conditioning) equipment. **Corporate headquarters location:** Hartford
CT. **Parent company:** United Technologies Corporation provides high-
technology products and support services to customers in the
aerospace, building, military, and automotive industries worldwide.
Products include large jet engines, temperature control systems,
elevators and escalators, helicopters, and flight systems. The
company markets its products under a variety of brand names
including Carrier, Hamilton Standard, Otis, Pratt & Whitney, and
Sikorsky. Production facilities are located in the U.S., Latin America,
Mexico, Canada, Australia, Europe and Asia.

CARRIER CORPORATION
P.O. Box 104, McMinnville TN 37110. 615/668-2811. **Contact:** Bill
Patterson, Manager of Human Resources. **Description:** A commercial
manufacturer of HVAC (heating, ventilation, and air-conditioning)
equipment. **Corporate headquarters location:** Hartford CT. **Parent
company:** United Technologies Corporation provides high-technology
products and support services to customers in the aerospace,
building, military, and automotive industries worldwide. Products
include large jet engines, temperature control systems, elevators and
escalators, helicopters, and flight systems. The company markets its
products under a variety of brand names including Carrier, Hamilton
Standard, Otis, Pratt & Whitney, and Sikorsky. Production facilities
are located in the U.S., Latin America, Mexico, Canada, Australia,
Europe and Asia.

DACCO INC.
P.O. Box 2789, 741 Dacco Drive, Cookeville TN 38502. 615/528-
7581. **Fax:** 615/528-9777. **Contact:** Ralph Gann, Plant Manager.
Description: Manufactures industrial machinery and equipment.

DIESEL RECON COMPANY
5765 Summer Tree Drive, Memphis TN 38134. 901/320-3200.
Contact: Kim Warentte, Vice President of Human Resources.
Description: Manufactures engines.

DOVER ELEVATOR SYSTEMS INC.
P.O. Box 370, Middleton TN 38052. 901/376-8444. **Contact:** Mrs.
Ossie Gunn, Personnel Manager. **Description:** Manufactures
elevators.

DOVER ELEVATOR SYSTEMS INC.
P.O. Box 2177, Memphis TN 38101. 901/377-1993. **Contact:** David
Hage, Human Resources Director. **Description:** Manufactures
elevators.

THE DURIRON COMPANY INC.
P.O. Box 2609, Cookeville TN 38502. 615/432-4021. **Contact:**
Randy Boyd, Director of Human Resources. **Description:**
Manufactures valves for the chemical and petroleum industries.

EXCEL SYSTEMS INC.
P.O. Box 669, Pikeville TN 37367. 423/447-6861. **Fax:** 423/447-2736. **Contact:** Charles Reed, Human Resource Manager. **Description:** Manufacturers of manual and electric window lift systems. **Common positions include:** Accountant/Auditor; Blue-Collar Worker Supervisor; Buyer; Designer; Draftsperson; Electrical/Electronics Engineer; Electrician; General Manager; Human Resources Specialist; Industrial Engineer; Industrial Production Manager; Management Trainee; Mechanical Engineer; Operations/Production Manager; Purchasing Agent and Manager; Quality Control Supervisor; Statistician. **Educational backgrounds include:** Accounting; Business Administration; Engineering; Finance. **Benefits:** 401K; Dental Insurance; Disability Coverage; Life Insurance; Medical Insurance; Pension Plan; Profit Sharing; Tuition Assistance. **Corporate headquarters location:** Elkhart IN. **Parent company:** Excel Industries. **Operations at this facility include:** Manufacturing. **Listed on:** New York Stock Exchange. **Number of employees at this location:** 365.

FAYETTE TUBULAR PRODUCTS
P.O. Box 100, Livingston TN 38570. 615/823-1284. **Contact:** Bill Faris, Plant Manager. **Description:** Manufactures air-conditioner hoses.

FLEETGUARD INC.
402 BNA Drive, Suite 500, Nashville TN 37217. 615/367-0040. **Contact:** Ms. Darnella Mosley, Human Resources Manager. **Description:** Manufactures heavy-duty industrial air and fuel filters.

GENERAL ELECTRIC COMPANY
P.O. Box 389, Selmer TN 38375. 901/645-6121. **Contact:** Becky Johnson, Human Resources Director. **Description:** This location manufactures for Busway, the company's switchgear operations. Overall, General Electric operates in the following areas: aircraft engines (jet engines, replacement parts, and repair services for commercial, military, executive, and commuter aircraft); appliances; broadcasting (NBC); industrial (lighting products, electrical distribution and control equipment, transportation systems products, electric motors and related products, a broad range of electrical and electronic industrial automation products, and a network of electrical supply houses); materials (plastics, ABS resins, silicones, superabrasives, and laminates); power systems (products for the generation, transmission, and distribution of electricity); technical products and systems (medical systems and equipment, as well as a full range of computer-based information and data interchange services for both internal use and external commercial and industrial customers); and capital services (consumer services, financing, specialty insurance, and Kidder, Peabody investment bank and securities broker). **Corporate headquarters location:** Fairfield CT.

GRAPHIC PACKAGING CORPORATION
2006 Liberty Avenue, Lawrenceburg TN 38464. 615/762-6486. **Contact:** Human Resources. **Description:** Produces composite packaging.

HECKETHORN MANUFACTURING COMPANY
P.O. Box 310, Dyersburg TN 38025. 901/285-3310. **Contact:** Jerald Hamm, Director of Personnel. **Description:** Heckethorn Manufacturing Company is a manufacturer of precision products, components, and assemblies for government as well as for the automotive and trucking industries and their aftermarkets. One of the company's products, the Hecco Dyna-Grip exhaust clamp, is designed to withstand exhaust system clamping problems on rigid or flexible tubing by using positive locking bead seal. The exhaust clamp can withstand over 3,000 pounds compression or tension without tubing movement, at as high as 1,500 degrees Fahrenheit.

HURD CORPORATION
503 Bohannon Avenue, Greeneville TN 37745. **Fax:** 423/639-0266. **Contact:** Cindy Payne, Human Resources Director. **Description:** Manufactures lock sets for industrial and automotive customers such as Steelcase, Tri-Mark, and Ford Motor Company. **Common positions include:** Accountant/Auditor; Advertising Clerk; Blue-Collar Worker Supervisor; Buyer; Civil Engineer; Computer Programmer; Computer Systems Analyst; Cost Estimator; Customer Service Representative; Designer; Draftsperson; Electrician; Financial Analyst; General Manager; Human Resources Specialist; Industrial Engineer; Management Trainee; Materials Engineer; Mechanical Engineer; Medical Records Technician; Operations/Production Manager; Purchasing Agent and Manager; Quality Control Supervisor. **Educational backgrounds include:** Accounting; Business Administration; Engineering; Finance; Marketing. **Benefits:** 401K; Dental Insurance; Life Insurance; Medical Insurance; Tuition Assistance. **Corporate headquarters location:** Upland IN. **Parent company:** Avis Industrial Corporation. **Operations at this facility include:** Administration; Manufacturing; Sales. **Listed on:** Privately held. **Number of employees at this location:** 1,075.

INSITUFORM TECHNOLOGIES INC.
1770 Kirby Parkway, Suite 300, Memphis TN 38138. 901/759-7473. **Contact:** Ann Hutcherson, Human Resources Manager. **Description:** Insituform Technologies is a developer and marketer of trenchless pipeline rehabilitation technologies for municipalities and industrial markets. Product developments include NuPipe Process, PRI's diameter reduction techniques for the oil and gas transmission market, and Insituform lateral and accelerated curing technologies. Insituform's revenues include product sales of material and equipment to licensees, construction revenues from trenchless installation and non-trenchless contracting activities, and royalty income and initial license fees received from licensees for the use of the company's trenchless rehabilitation process. Construction contract revenue is generated by the company's wholly-owned subsidiaries, Insituform Southwest, Insituform New England, Insituform Gulf South, Insituform Midwest, IGL Canada Limited, Insituform Permaline Limited, and NuPipe Limited.

INTER-CITY PRODUCTS CORPORATION U.S.A.
1136 Heil-Quaker Boulevard, La Vergne TN 37086. 615/793-0450. **Contact:** Ralph Shimbaum, Human Resources Director. **Description:** Manufactures central heating and air-conditioning units.

INTERNATIONAL SPECIALTY SUPPLY
820 East 20th Street, Cookeville TN 38501. 615/526-1106. **Fax:** 615/526-8338. **Contact:** Diane Boatman, Human Resources Director. **Description:** A designer and manufacturer of hydroponic equipment (farm equipment). International Specialty Supply is also engaged in freezing vegetables and making water reclamation equipment. **Common positions include:** Accountant/Auditor; Biological Scientist/Biochemist; Chemical Engineer; Electrical/Electronics Engineer; Mechanical Engineer; Production Manager; Production Worker; Purchasing Agent and Manager; Sales Representative; Warehouse/Distribution Worker; Welder. **Number of employees at this location:** 75.

JEFFREY CHAIN CORPORATION
2307 Maden Drive, Morristown TN 37813. 423/586-1951. **Contact:** Maxine Shackelford, Vice President of Human Resources. **Description:** Supplies engineered chain products to a variety of customers. **Common positions include:** Accountant/Auditor; Buyer; Computer Programmer; Customer Service Representative; Draftsperson; Human Resources Specialist; Industrial Engineer; Mechanical Engineer; Metallurgical Engineer; Production Manager; Purchasing Agent and Manager. **Educational backgrounds include:** Accounting; Business Administration; Communications; Computer Science; Engineering; Finance. **Benefits:** 401K; Dental Insurance; Disability Coverage; Life Insurance; Medical Insurance; Profit Sharing; Tuition Assistance. **Corporate headquarters location:** This Location. **Parent company:** Guardian Development (Fairway, KS). **Operations at this facility include:** Administration; Divisional Headquarters; Manufacturing; Research and Development; Sales; Service.

KENNAMETAL INC.
128 Roweland Drive, Johnson City TN 37601. 615/928-7251. **Contact:** Doug Killian, Human Resources Director. **Description:** This location manufactures carbide cutting-tools. Overall, the company manufactures, purchases, and distributes a broad range of tools, tooling systems, supplies, and services for the metalworking, mining, and highway construction industries. Kennametal specializes in developing and manufacturing metalcutting tools and wear-resistant parts using a specialized type of powder metallurgy. The company's metalcutting tools are made of cemented carbides, ceramics, cermets, and other hard materials. Kennametal manufactures a complete line of toolholders and toolholding systems by machining and fabricating steel bars and other metal alloys. The company's mining and construction cutting tools are tipped with cemented carbide and are used for underground coal mining and highway construction, repair, and maintenance. Metallurgical products consist of powders made from ore concentrates, compounds, and secondary materials. International locations include Canada, China, England, Germany, and The Netherlands. **Corporate headquarters location:** Latrobe PA. **Other U.S. locations:** Troy MI; Henderson NC; Roanoke Rapids NC; Fallon NV; Orwell OH; Solon OH; Bedford PA; New Market VA. **Listed on:** New York Stock Exchange.

KINGSTON COMPANY
P.O. Box 170, Miller Road, Smithville TN 37166. 615/597-4096. **Contact:** Marie Johnson, Human Resources Director. **Description:** Manufactures motors and generators.

KOMATSU DRESSER COMPANY
CHATTANOOGA MANUFACTURING OPERATION
409 Single Mountain Road, P.O. Box 168, Chattanooga TN 37401-0168. 423/267-1066. **Fax:** 423/267-1131. **Contact:** Ed Jones, Personnel Manager. **Description:** Manufactures construction equipment. This location has over 380,000 square feet of manufacturing and office space on 47 acres, with a wide array of robotics, CNC machinery, and assembly and finishing processes. The facility uses a material management system with a real-time information system, a material movement tracking system, and a flexible, efficient material flow system. Products manufactured at this facility include hydraulic excavators and wheel loaders. **Special Programs:** Training Programs. **Corporate headquarters location:** Lincolnshire IL. **Other U.S. locations:** Hayward CA; Norcross GA; Libertyville IL; Peoria IL; Galion OH. **Parent company:** Komatsu Ltd. (Tokyo, Japan) is a diversified company manufacturing and selling construction equipment, industrial machinery, components, and other products, while diversifying into other manufacturing markets, electronics, civil engineering and architectural construction, computer software, real estate, and trading. Other U.S. subsidiaries and affiliated companies include: Komatsu America Corporation (Miami FL); Cummins Komatsu Engine Company (Seymour IN); Komatsu America Industries Corporation (Wood Dale IL); Danly-Komatsu L.P. (Chicago IL); and Komatsu Cutting Technologies, Inc. (Medford MA). Komatsu Ltd. also has subsidiaries and affiliates in Mexico, Brazil, Belgium, United Kingdom, Germany, France, Indonesia, Singapore, India, Thailand, Malaysia, Philippines, Australia, Hong Kong, China, Canada, Italy, Russia, Turkey, Iran, Saudi Arabia, Pakistan, Vietnam, and South Africa. **Listed on:** Frankfurt Stock Exchange; Tokyo Stock Exchange.

LOCKHEED MARTIN ENERGY SYSTEMS, INC.
P.O. Box 2009, Oak Ridge TN 37831. 423/574-1642. **Contact:** R. Mack Wilson, Vice President of Human Resources. **Description:** Lockheed Martin Corporation is comprised of several divisions known as the Space Group, Electronics Group, Energy Group, Information Group, Materials, Services, Sandia National Laboratories, and Technology Operations. As part of the Energy Group, Lockheed Martin Energy Systems is managing contractor for Department of Energy research and development, manufacturing technology, and environmental management operations in three states. Energy Systems provides expertise in advanced materials and ceramics, robotics, instrumentation and control technologies, environmental protection and waste management, and high-precision manufacturing. The Oak Ridge Centers for Defense and Manufacturing Technology at Y-12 also operate technology transfer programs to help small businesses solve technical problems through use of the Center's Expertise in materials science, measurement science, and state-of-the-art manufacturing processes. Energy Systems also manages an extensive environmental and waste management program at five Department of Energy sites. The Oak Ridge Center for Environmental Technology works with the private

sector, academia, and government to accelerate the development, demonstration, and commercialization of environmental technologies. **Corporate headquarters location:** Bethesda MD. **Parent company:** Lockheed Martin Corporation. **Number of employees at this location:** 15,000.

MODINE MANUFACTURING COMPANY
5050 South National Drive, Knoxville TN 37914. 423/546-5920. **Contact:** Robert Kiluffe, Director of Personnel. **Description:** Modine Manufacturing Company is an independent, worldwide leader in heat-transfer technology, serving vehicular (passenger car, van, truck, off-highway equipment, earth moving equipment, construction equipment, and agricultural equipment), industrial (a mixed category of OEM customers, including the makers of engines, air compressors, refrigeration equipment, and hydraulic-pneumatic devices), commercial, and building/HVAC (heating, ventilating, and air conditioning) markets. Modine Manufacturing Company develops, manufactures, and markets heat exchangers for use in various OEM applications for sale to the automotive aftermarket (as replacement parts) and to a wide array of building markets. The company's major products include radiators, oil coolers, vehicular air-conditioning condensers and evaporators, building/HVAC products, charge-air coolers, and radiator cores. Modine Manufacturing Company's largest single market in sales revenues is the aftermarket, which is mostly made up of replacement radiators for passenger cars. The company has the ability to supply products from multiple sources among more than 50 locations in 13 countries worldwide. Nine countries include at least one wholly-owned Modine facility with manufacturing operations. In addition, complete heat-transfer technical centers are in operation both in North America and in Europe, with research and development, engineering, prototype, and various testing capabilities. **Corporate headquarters location:** Racine WI. **International subsidiaries include:** Langerer & Reich (L&R); and the remainder of Austria Warmetauscher GmbH (AWG), which was formerly a 50 percent joint venture.

MOHAN INTERNATIONAL, INC.
P.O. Box 550, Paris TN 38242. 901/642-4251. **Fax:** 901/642-4262. **Contact:** Michelle Donoho, Director of Human Resources. **Description:** Mohan International is a manufacturer of Campbell Rhea brand laboratory furniture. Founded in 1951 by Mr. Campbell Rhea, the company has become one of the leading casework companies in the nation. The company's primary markets are elementary, middle, and high schools, and universities and research facilities. Campbell Rhea products are made exclusively from red oak.

MUELLER COMPANY
1401 Mueller Avenue, Chattanooga TN 37406. 423/698-8811. **Contact:** George Mathis, Director of Human Resources. **Description:** Manufactures water and gas valve products.

NIPPONDENSO TENNESSEE
1720 Robert C. Jackson Drive, Maryville TN 37801. 423/982-7000. **Contact:** Marlene Langley, Human Resources. **Description:** Nippondenso Tennessee manufactures meters and electronics. U.S. parent company is Nippondenso America, Inc. Established in December, 1985. Nippondenso America, Inc. is the regional

headquarters in the U.S. of Nippondenso Company, Ltd. (Kariya, Japan). Its business is the sale of air conditioners, electrical automotive equipment, heaters, radiators, instrument clusters, and automotive electronic products; and engineering services, design, testing, and R&D. The parent company is one of the world's largest suppliers of automotive components. It supplies automakers with components and systems that keep costs down, keep quality and performance up, and satisfy increasingly demanding expectations in regard to safety and the environment. The company supplies those components and systems to nearly all the world's automakers, including the Big Three U.S. automakers as well as most of the Japanese and European automakers. It makes its products at 34 plants in 13 nations. Nippondenso leads advances in automotive electronics, as well as in systems for electronic fuel injection, braking control, and navigation. It also is a leader in car air-conditioners, fuel pumps, radiators, and other components. Diversified products include hand-held bar-code readers, factory automation systems, and portable telephones. Car air-conditioners and heaters are the biggest product sector for Nippondenso, which is one of the world's largest manufacturers of those products.

OXFORD INSTRUMENTS, INC.
P.O. Box 2560, Oak Ridge TN 37831. 423/483-8405. **Contact:** Kim Flisnik, Human Resources Manager. **Description:** A manufacturer of nuclear instrumentation modules, detectors, counters, and high-purity, detector-grade germanium materials for environmental and health science uses.

PATHWAY BELLOWS, INC.
115 Franklin Road, P.O. Box 3027, Oak Ridge TN 37831. 423/483-7444. **Contact:** Janet Byrne, Human Resources. **Description:** Pathway is a designer and manufacturer of high quality metal and fabric expansion joints. The company also performs planned and emergency on-site expansion joint analysis, repair and original installation. The company has performed its services in all parts of the world, including Algeria, Indonesia, Korea, Japan, United Kingdom, Germany, Holland, Spain, Brazil, Venezuela, New Zealand, Singapore, Canada, and Mexico. Pathway performs extensive on-site service throughout the United States and has vast experience with nuclear generating plants, refineries, fossil generating plants, gas turbine installations, and central steam systems. The company maintains a 48-hour design and manufacturing capability and 24-hour on-site service crew to ensure swift repair or turnaround.

PEN HOLDINGS, INC.
P.O. Box 2128, Brentwood TN 37024-2128. 615/371-7330. **Contact:** Candace Herzog, Director of Personnel. **Description:** A diversified corporation involved in energy, high-tech, and international trade.

PLASTI-LINE, INC.
P.O. Box 59043, Knoxville TN 37950. 423/938-1511. **Fax:** 423/947-8565. **Contact:** Julie A. Glibbery, Human Resources Manager. **Description:** Plasti-Line, Inc. provides products and services to corporate identities and retail stores, including manufacturing and distributing large, illuminated plastic signs. **Common positions include:** Blue-Collar Worker Supervisor; Buyer;

258/The Tennessee JobBank

Customer Service Representative; Designer; Draftsperson; Industrial Engineer; Industrial Production Manager; Mechanical Engineer; Purchasing Agent and Manager. **Benefits:** 401K; Disability Coverage; Life Insurance; Medical Insurance; Profit Sharing; Savings Plan. **Corporate headquarters location:** This Location. **Other U.S. locations:** Fontana CA; Florence KY. **Listed on:** NASDAQ. **Number of employees at this location:** 600. **Number of employees nationwide:** 800.

PRECISION TUBULAR HEATER CORPORATION
111 Alpha Drive, Franklin TN 37064. **Contact:** Ms. Alma Miller, Human Resources Director. **Description:** Manufactures heating elements for small appliances.

REXNORD CORPORATION
LINK BELT BEARING OPERATION
P.O. Box 330, Clinton TN 37716. 423/457-4780. **Contact:** Tom Plachinski, Human Resources Director. **Description:** Manufactures ball bearings.

ROCKWELL AUTOMATION
DODGE BEARING PLANT
Reliance Road at West Main, Rogersville TN 37857. 423/272-2686. **Contact:** Alex Masotti, Human Resources Manager. **Description:** Manufactures industrial bearings.

W.J. SAVAGE COMPANY
One Hopkins Avenue, P.O. Box 157, Knoxville TN 37901. 423/637-9441. **Contact:** Robert Klingerman, President. **Description:** W.J. Savage Company is a manufacturer of industrial saws.

STATE INDUSTRIES, INC.
500 Bypass Road, Ashland City TN 37015. 615/792-4371. **Contact:** Greg Bates, Director of Human Resources. **Description:** Manufactures water heaters.

STEWARD INC.
P.O. Box 510, East 36th Street, Chattanooga TN 37401. 423/867-4100. **Fax:** 423/867-4102. **Contact:** Pam Stevens, Personnel. **Description:** Steward is a producer of ferrite and related materials used in the copier, electronics, automotive, and military industries. Established in 1876, Steward has two facilities in Chattanooga with over 150,000 square feet and 300 employees. The company manufactures EMI shielding components, wide band transformer and filter toroids, copier developer materials, and iron silicide powders. Steward's nickel ferrite parts are used in the suppression of electromagnetic interference known as EMI. Suppression of EMI is a major concern in the transmission, reception, and processing of electronic intelligence. Steward offers a family of ferrites whose compositions differ to allow the user to select the most optimum type for application. Steward's ferrite teroid materials range in initial permeabilities from 16 up to 10,000. These products are found in pulse transformers and data line and power filters. Steward manufactures carrier bead ferrite materials used to formulate developers for both mono and dual component xerographic applications. Steward's carrier bead powders are shipped in volume to copy machine manufacturers. Steward also offers a selection of

fine powders for attenuation and absorption of EMI. Steward's iron silicide powder provides solutions for many problems experienced with standard radar absorbing materials and has characteristics for numerous metallurgical uses as well. Steward's iron silicide is oxidation resistant, erosion resistant, chemical resistant, and available in numerous particle sizes.

SUBURBAN MANUFACTURING COMPANY
P.O. Box 399, Dayton TN 37321. 423/775-2131. **Contact:** Yvonne Creasman, Personnel Manager. **Description:** Manufactures heating equipment.

TPI CORPORATION
P.O. Box 4973, Johnson City TN 37602-4973. 423/477-4131. **Contact:** Lance Lucas, Director of Human Resources. **Description:** Manufactures electric heating and air ventilation products. **Common positions include:** Accountant/Auditor; Blue-Collar Worker Supervisor; Buyer; Credit Manager; Customer Service Representative; Draftsperson; Electrical/Electronics Engineer; Electrician; Human Resources Specialist; Industrial Engineer; Industrial Production Manager; Manufacturer's/Wholesaler's Sales Rep.; Mechanical Engineer; Purchasing Agent and Manager; Quality Control Supervisor. **Educational backgrounds include:** Business Administration; Engineering. **Benefits:** 401K; Disability Coverage; Life Insurance. **Corporate headquarters location:** This Location. **Other U.S. locations:** Nationwide. **Subsidiaries include:** Fostoria Industries and Columbus Electric. **Operations at this facility include:** Administration; Manufacturing; Research and Development; Sales; Service. **Listed on:** Privately held. **Number of employees at this location:** 425.

TELEDYNE LAARS STILLMAN
1011 Volunteer Drive, Cookeville TN 38501. 615/526-3351. **Contact:** Priscilla Cox, Director of Human Resources. **Description:** Manufactures heating elements for domestic electric ranges.

THE TORRINGTON COMPANY
P.O. Box 597, Kathleen Drive, Pulaski TN 38478. 615/363-7661. **Contact:** Don Haney, Director of Human Resources. **Description:** The firm designs, develops, manufactures, and markets anti-friction bearings. The Torrington Company also produces universal joints and precision components and assemblies. The company is located throughout the U.S., Germany, Australia, Brazil, Canada, England, and Japan. **Corporate headquarters location:** Torrington CT. **Parent company:** Ingersoll-Rand. **Number of employees nationwide:** 10,500.

TUTCO INC.
500 Gould Drive, Cookeville TN 38501. 615/432-4141. **Contact:** Human Resources. **Description:** Manufactures industrial products.

UNDERWOOD AIR SYSTEMS INC.
2713 Larmon Drive, Nashville TN 37204-2822. 615/383-8479. **Contact:** Human Resources. **Description:** Sells products that circulate air.

WEST UNION CORPORATION
35 Union Avenue, Third Floor, Memphis TN 38103. 901/529-5700. **Contact:** Human Resources. **Description:** A holding company. Divisions include hardware distribution, and aluminum door and window manufacturing.

WIS-CON TOTAL POWER CORPORATION
P.O. Box 181160, Memphis TN 38181-1160. 901/365-3600. **Fax:** 901/369-4056. **Contact:** Len Gilley, Director of Human Resources. **Description:** Wis-Con Total Power manufactures, markets, and distributes industrial engines to a global marketplace. Products range from three to 80 horsepowered engines powered by gasoline, natural gas, LPG, and diesel fuels. Currently two product families are manufactured domestically and are distributed worldwide. Two other product families are imported for marketing and distribution into North America and Europe. **Common positions include:** Accountant/Auditor; Advertising Clerk; Branch Manager; Buyer; Clerical Supervisor; Computer Programmer; Computer Systems Analyst; Credit Manager; Customer Service Representative; Draftsperson; Economist/Market Research Analyst; Electrical/Electronics Engineer; Emergency Medical Technician; Financial Analyst; General Manager; Human Resources Specialist; Industrial Engineer; Manufacturer's/Wholesaler's Sales Rep.; Mechanical Engineer; Purchasing Agent and Manager; Quality Control Supervisor. **Educational backgrounds include:** Accounting; Art/Design; Business Administration; Communications; Computer Science; Engineering; Finance; Marketing. **Benefits:** 401K; Dental Insurance; Disability Coverage; Life Insurance; Medical Insurance; Tuition Assistance. **Special Programs:** Internships. **Corporate headquarters location:** This Location. **Other U.S. locations:** Minneapolis MN; Salt Lake City UT; Fredricksburg VA; Milwaukee WI. **Operations at this facility include:** Administration; Manufacturing; Research and Development; Sales; Service. **Listed on:** Privately held. **Number of employees at this location:** 100. **Number of employees nationwide:** 360.

WRIGHT INDUSTRIES INC.
P.O. Box 17914, Nashville TN 37217. 615/361-6600. **Contact:** Human Resources. **Description:** Wright Industries designs and builds custom automated assembly equipment (non-metal-cutting) and large metal-working dies. The company is also involved in precision-machine work. **Corporate headquarters location:** This Location. **Other U.S. locations:** Gilbert AZ.

WYNN'S PRECISION INC.
104 Hartman Drive, Lebanon TN 37087. 615/444-0191. **Contact:** Human Resources. **Description:** Produces O-rings, gaskets, and seals.

ZELLWEGER USTER, INC.
456 Troy Circle, Knoxville TN 37919. 615/588-9716. **Contact:** Human Resources. **Description:** Manufactures fiber-testing equipment for the textile industry.

Note: Because addresses and telephone numbers of smaller companies change rapidly, we recommend you call each company to verify the information below before inquiring about job opportunities. Mass mailings are not recommended.

Additional employers with under 250 employees:

FABRICATED PIPE AND PIPE FITTINGS

Grinnell Corp.
2010 Old Jackson Rd,
Henderson TN 38340-
3645. 901/989-3551.

MOTORS AND GENERATORS

Jakel Inc.
P.O. Box 218, Ramer
TN 38367-0218.
901/645-6193.

COMMERCIAL FURNITURE AND FIXTURES

Fulmarque Inc.
1815 Blythe Ave SE,
Cleveland TN 37311-
3052. 423/476-3249.

Sandusky Cabinets Inc.
P.O. Box 125,
Millington TN 38083-
0125. 901/872-0188.

Volunteer Fabricators
Back Valley Rd,
Sneedville TN 37869.
423/733-2218.

Lamsteel Corp. of America
409 McMurry Blvd,
Hartsville TN 37074-
1213. 615/374-2261.

Unarco Material Handling
701 16th Ave E,
Springfield TN 37172-
3305. 615/384-3531.

PACKAGING PAPER AND PLASTICS FILM

Interstate Packaging
2285 Highway 47 N,
White Bluff TN
37187-4111.
615/797-9000.

Paramount Packaging
720 Eagle Blvd,

Shelbyville TN 37160-
7260. 615/685-9800.

Riviana Foods Inc.
P.O. Box 369,
Memphis TN 38101-
0369. 901/948-8556.

GASKETS, PACKING, AND SEALING DEVICES

Indian Head Industries Detroit Gasket
810 Thinwood Dr,
Newport TN 37821-
8036. 423/623-2366.

Rayloc Division of Genuine Parts
2860 Horn Lake Rd,
Memphis TN 38109-
2709. 901/785-0862.

METAL HARDWARE

Marshall Manufacturing Corp.
P.O. Box 1729,
Lewisburg TN 37091-
0729. 615/359-2573.

HEATING EQUIPMENT

United States Stove Co.
P.O. Box 151, S
Pittsburg TN 37380-
0151. 423/837-2100.

MISC. PIPE FITTINGS AND/OR VALVES

Manchester Tank & Equipment
285 Davis Rd,
Crossville TN 38555-
4062. 615/484-5163.

CONVEYORS AND CONVEYING EQUIPMENT

Automated Conveyor Systems Inc.
P.O. Box 130,
Memphis TN 38101-
0130. 5017325050.

Dynasteel Corp.
P.O. Box 27640,
Memphis TN 38167-
0640. 901/358-6231.

Southern Systems Inc.
4101 Viscount Ave,
Memphis TN 38118-
6106. 901/362-7340.

METAL CUTTING OR FORMING TOOLS

Fleetline Products Inc.
2410 Industrial Dr,
Springfield TN 37172-
5013. 615/384-4338.

METALWORKING MACHINERY

Powermatic
607 Morrison St,
McMinnville TN
37110-3097.
615/473-5551.

TEXTILE MACHINERY

Card-Monroe Co.
4936 Adams Rd,
Hixson TN 37343-
4010. 423/842-3312.

Tuftco Corp.
P.O. Box 3009,
Chattanooga TN
37404-0009.
423/698-8601.

WOODWORKING MACHINERY

Corley Manufacturing Co.
P.O. Box 471,
Chattanooga TN
37401-0471.
423/698-0284.

FOOD PRODUCTS MACHINERY

Kay's of Knoxville
3600 Pleasant Ridge
Rd, Knoxville TN
37921-1737.
423/525-7331.

Lockwood Greene Engineers
P.O. Box 171098, Nashville TN 37217-8098. 615/831-9055.

Procon Products
910 Ridgely Rd, Murfreesboro TN 37129-2734. 615/890-5710.

Campbell-Hausfeld Co.
85 Athens Dr, Mount Juliet TN 37122-3681. 615/758-5615.

FANS, BLOWERS, AND AIR PURIFICATION EQUIPMENT

Steelcraft Corp.
P.O. Box 12748, Memphis TN 38182-0748. 901/452-5200.

VENDING MACHINES

Cavalier Corp.
1105 E 10th St, Chattanooga TN 37403-3005. 423/267-6671.

COMMERCIAL LAUNDRY, DRY-CLEANING, AND PRESSING MACHINES

Forenta LP
P.O. Box 607, Morristown TN 37815-0607. 423/586-5370.

AIR-CONDITIONING, HEATING, AND REFRIGERATION EQUIPMENT

Dole Refrigerating Co.
1420 Higgs Rd, Lewisburg TN 37091. 615/359-6211.

Witt
P.O. Box 580, Collierville TN 38027-0580. 901/853-2770.

SERVICE INDUSTRY MACHINERY

United Service Equipment
P.O. Box 428, Murfreesboro TN 37133-0428. 615/893-8432.

ENGINE PARTS

Holley Performance Products
509 Industrial Dr, Springfield TN 37172-3324. 615/384-0700.

MEASURING AND CONTROLLING EQUIPMENT

Collegedale Casework Inc.
P.O. Box 810, Collegedale TN 37315-0810. 423/238-4131.

Cubic Precision Systems Division
1300 Cedar Ln, Tullahoma TN 37388-2247. 615/455-2437.

OFFICE EQUIPMENT WHOLESALE

Knoxville Xerographics Inc.
5710 Kingston Pike, Knoxville TN 37919-6323. 423/584-3600.

COMMERCIAL EQUIPMENT WHOLESALE

Microfoam Inc.
1480 Gould Dr, Cookeville TN 38506-4152. 615/432-4042.

WHOLESALE COAL, MINERALS, AND ORES

Alley-Cassetty Coal Co. Inc.
2 Oldham St, Nashville TN 37213-1107. 615/244-7077.

INDUSTRIAL MACHINERY AND EQUIPMENT WHOLESALE

Cameron & Barkley Company
3012 Industrial Pkwy E, Knoxville TN 37921-1710. 423/524-1206.

Power Equipment Co.
1877 Air Lane Dr, Nashville TN 37210-3811. 615/871-0900.

Power Equipment Co.
P.O. Box 2311, Knoxville TN 37901-2311. 423/577-5563.

Holston Gases
1306 Lebanon Rd, Nashville TN 37210-3006. 615/256-1120.

Stowers Machinery Corp.
6301 Rutledge Pike, Knoxville TN 37924-1654. 423/546-1414.

Utility Supply & Equipment Corp.
5275 Raleigh, Memphis TN 38134. 901/377-0621.

Tru Part
1890 Elm Tree Dr, Nashville TN 37210-3727. 615/889-8360.

Bearings & Drives Inc.
3012 Freeman St, Chattanooga TN 37406-3029. 423/624-8333.

Cummins Mid-South Inc.
1784 E Brooks Rd, Memphis TN 38116-3694. 901/345-1784.

Heavy Machines Inc.
4087 Viscount Ave, Memphis TN 38118-6106. 901/366-2200.

Industrial Gas and Supply Co.
518 Alabama St,
Bristol TN 37620-2307. 423/968-1536.

Rodem Inc.
128 Commerce Dr,
Hendersonvlle TN 37075-2859.
615/824-8812.

PCI Group
744 Cowan St,
Nashville TN 37207-5624. 615/242-1857.

WC Forklift
4099 Highway 11 E,
Bluff City TN 37618-2452. 423/538-3500.

Storage Specialist Inc.
477 N Main St,
Collierville TN 38017-2315. 901/853-1001.

Fontaine
508 Expressway Park Dr, Nashville TN 37210-2818.
615/244-9200.

Day International Printing Products
1412 Antioch Pke,
Nashville TN 37211.
615/781-8064.

Package Supply & Equipment
459 Harding Industrial Dr, Nashville TN 37211-3105.
615/333-7415.

Superior Container Service
7917 Old Lee Hwy,
Ooltewah TN 37363-8401. 423/892-6067.

Motion Industries
1420 Morgan Rd,
Dyersburg TN 38024-2339. 901/287-0234.

Tebco Threaded Fasteners
665 Scott St,
Memphis TN 38112-2231. 901/454-0902.

The Fastener House
2800 Foster Ave,
Nashville TN 37210-5310. 615/331-5556.

Fastenal Company
5227 N Middlebrook Pke, Knoxville TN 37921. 423/588-1529.

Consolidated Ceramic Products
16 Brushwood Cv,
Jackson TN 38305-8762. 901/668-7319.

Ripley Industries Inc.
342 New Byhalia Rd,
Collierville TN 38017-3706. 901/853-2237.

Cookeville Welding Supply
1981 N Willow Ave,
Cookeville TN 38501-1172. 615/528-3378.

Airco Selox Inc.
2300 Sycamore Dr,
Knoxville TN 37921-1749. 423/524-2783.

BOC/Airco Gases
201 Skyline Cir,
Dickson TN 37055-2562. 615/446-9353.

Air Products and Chemicals
1651 Highway 51 By-Pass N, Dyersburg TN 38024. 901/286-6550.

Sally Beauty Supply
1612 Fort Campbell Blvd, Clarksville TN 37042-3554.
615/648-8634.

Sally Beauty Supply
144 S Gallatin Pke S,
Madison TN 37115.
615/868-7255.

Grinnell Fire Protection Systems
207 N Holly St,
Chattanooga TN 37404-2531.
423/698-4418.

SCRAP AND WASTE MATERIALS WHOLESALE

Imco Recycling Inc.
P.O. Box 268,
Rockwood TN 37854-0268. 423/354-3626.

L&S Metals & Processing Inc.
P.O. Box 1058,
Columbia TN 38402-1058. 615/388-8784.

Sonoco Products Co. Inc.
766 Industrial Rd,
Newport TN 37821-8112. 423/623-8611.

For more information on career opportunities in industrial manufacturing and wholesaling:

Associations

APPLIANCE PARTS DISTRIBUTORS ASSOCIATION
228 East Baltimore Street, Detroit MI 48202. 313/875-8455. An association for wholesale distributors of appliance parts.

ASSOCIATION FOR MANUFACTURING TECHNOLOGY
7901 Westpark Drive, McLean VA 22102. 703/893-2900. A trade association.

INSTITUTE OF INDUSTRIAL ENGINEERS
25 Technology Park, Norcross GA 30092. 770/449-0460.

A nonprofit organization with 27,000 members. Conducts seminars and offers reduced rates on its books and publications.

NATIONAL ASSOCIATION OF MANUFACTURERS
1331 Pennsylvania Avenue NW, Suite 1500, Washington DC 20004. 202/637-3000. A lobbying association.

NATIONAL SCREW MACHINE PRODUCTS ASSOCIATION
6700 West Snowville Road, Brecksville OH 44141. 216/526-0300. Provides resource information.

NATIONAL TOOLING AND MACHINING ASSOCIATION
9300 Livingston Road, Fort Washington MD 20744. 301/248-1250. Reports on wages and operating expenses. Produces monthly newsletters. Offers legal advice.

SOCIETY OF MANUFACTURING ENGINEERS
P.O. Box 930, One SME Drive, Dearborn MI 48121. 313/271-1500. Offers educational events and educational materials on manufacturing.

Special Programs

BUREAU OF APPRENTICESHIP AND TRAINING
U.S. Department of Labor, 200 Constitution Avenue NW, Washington, DC 20210. 202/219-6540.

MINING/GAS/PETROLEUM/ENERGY RELATED

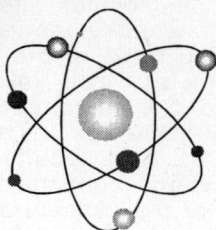

The energy industry just isn't what it used to be. In recent years, energy companies have been restructuring their operations in order to insure solid cash flows even in an era of low prices. Smaller, independent companies are now able to finance new production and land purchases with cash generated from stock sales.

Even so, jobseekers can't expect increased production to lead to much employment growth. Layoffs are expected to continue, but advanced technologies used by the energy industry continue to crop up, and jobseekers with engineering backgrounds should watch for energy-related, high-tech jobs.

In mining, earnings are much higher than average, but technological innovations, international competition, and environmental regulation will reduce employment. Best bets in the mining industry are for scientific technicians, professional specialty workers (such as geologists), and truck drivers.

ASARCO INC.
P.O. Box 460, Strawberry Plains TN 37871. 615/933-0858. **Contact:** Human Resources. **Description:** Asarco is one of the world's leading producers of nonferrous metals, principally copper, lead, zinc and silver, from its own mines and through interest in Southern Peru Copper Corporation. Asarco also produces specialty chemicals and construction aggregates and provides environmental services. Asarco operates mines in the United States, Peru, Australia and Mexico. Asarco's copper operations consist of its Mission and Ray mines in Arizona, smelters in Hayden, Arizona and El Paso, Texas and a refinery in Amarillo, Texas. In Missouri, the company operates an integrated lead circuit consisting of West Fork and Sweetwater mines which provide over 90 percent of the feed for the nearby Glover smelter and refinery. The Tennessee mines division accounted for 57 percent of the zinc concentrates produced by the company. The remaining 43 percent is produced as a co-product at the West Fork and Sweetwater lead mines in Missouri and at the Leadville (Colorado) mine. American Limestone Company is a wholly-owned subsidiary which operates in the southeastern United States and produces construction aggregates, ready-mixed concrete, and agricultural limestone. **NOTE:** All hiring for this facility is done through the Tennessee Job Service.

SAVAGE ZINC INC.
P.O. Box 1104, Clarksville TN 37041-1104. 615/552-4200. **Contact:** Emily Boyd, Industrial Relations Supervisor. **Description:** This location is a refinery. Formerly Union Mines Inc., Savage Zinc was purchased by Savage Resources Unlimited in 1994 and is one of the lowest-cost zinc producers in the world. Savage Zinc is comprised of four zinc mines and three concentrators, which supply the electrolytic zinc refinery at this location. The refinery also

produces and sells sulfuric acid, cadmium, and germanium bearing residues. The mines derive additional revenue from the sale of coarse limestone used in civil works and carbonate tailings for use as agricultural lime. The main mining operation is located near Gordonsville, where the Gordonsville-Elmwood-Stonewall-Cumberland complex currently produces around 1.6 mtpa of ore at an average grade of 3.2 percent zinc. The Idol Mine at Cinch Valley produces about 402,000 tpa at an average grade of 3.0 percent zinc and the Jefferson City Mine produces about 480,000 tpa at the same average grade. The concentrators at each of these locations produced around 105,000 tons of high-grade, low-iron concentrate with a zinc content of about 64 percent. The rest of the concentrate supply to the refinery is provided from Asarco's mines in eastern Tennessee. **Other U.S. locations:** Cumberland TN; Elmwood TN; Gordonsville TN; Jefferson City TN; Stonewall TN. **Parent company:** Savage Resources Limited (Sydney, Australia). **Number of employees at this location:** 670.

SAVAGE ZINC INC.
P.O. Box 359, Gordonsville TN 38563. 615/863-6411. **Contact:** James White, Industrial Relations Supervisor. **Description:** Formerly Union Mines Inc., Savage Zinc was purchased by Savage Resources Unlimited in 1994 and is one of the lowest cost zinc producers in the world. Savage Zinc is comprised of four zinc mines and three concentrators, which supply the electrolytic zinc refinery in Clarksville. The refinery also produces and sells sulfuric acid, cadmium, and germanium bearing residues. The mines derive additional revenue from the sale of coarse limestone used in civil works and carbonate tailings for use as agricultural lime. This location is the main mining operation. The Gordonsville-Elmwood-Stonewall-Cumberland complex currently produces around 1.6 mtpa of ore at an average grade of 3.2 percent zinc. The Idol Mine at Cinch Valley produces about 402,000 tpa at an average grade of 3.0 percent zinc and the Jefferson City Mine produces about 480,000 tpa at the same average grade. The concentrators at each of these locations produced around 105,000 tons of high-grade, low-iron concentrate with a zinc content of about 64 percent. The rest of the concentrate supply to the refinery is provided from Asarco's mines in eastern Tennessee. **Other U.S. locations:** Cumberland TN; Elmwood TN; Clarksville TN; Jefferson City TN; Stonewall TN. **Parent company:** Savage Resources Limited (Sydney, Australia).

SPECTRUM ACQUISITIONS, INC.
100 Industrial Drive, Selmer TN 38375. 901/645-4937. **Contact:** Personnel Department. **Description:** A blender and manufacturer of oil products.

SUN COAL COMPANY
P.O. Box 10388, Knoxville TN 37919. 423/558-0300. **Contact:** Karen Free, Human Resources. **Description:** A coal mining company.

TECHNOLOGY FOR ENERGY CORPORATION
P.O. Box 22996, Knoxville TN 37933. 423/966-5856. **Contact:** Jennifer Myers, Human Resources. **Description:** Technology for Energy Corporation is a supplier of high-tech engineering products and services for the energy-production industry.

Note: Because addresses and telephone numbers of smaller companies change rapidly, we recommend you call each company to verify the information below before inquiring about job opportunities. Mass mailings are not recommended.

Additional employers with under 250 employees:

PETROLEUM AND PETROLEUM PRODUCTS WHOLESALE

United Cities Propane Gas
956 S Highland Ave, Jackson TN 38301-7304. 901/424-4561.

Beach Oil Company Inc.
631 Highway 76, Clarksville TN 37043-5392. 615/358-9303.

Service Petroleum Inc.
514 Mulberry St, Nashville TN 37203-4636. 615/256-2713.

ORE MINING

Chemetals Inc.
795 Foote Ln, New Johsonvle TN 37134.

COAL MINING

Beech Grove Processing Co.
211 S Main Ave, Lake City TN 37769-2205. 423/426-7464.

Cross Mountain Coal Inc.
522 Cross Mountain Coal Rd, Lake City TN 37769. 423/426-9796.

Pen Coal Corp.
5110 Maryland Way, Brentwood TN 37027-7508. 615/371-7330.

ANTHRACITE MINING

UCAR Carbon Co. Inc.
P.O. Box 513, Columbia TN 38402-0513. 615/388-1410.

PETROLEUM REFINING

Lehman-Roberts Co.
P.O. Box 1603, Memphis TN 38101-1603. 901/774-4000.

Lojac Enterprises Inc.
3552 Hermitage Industrial Dr, Hermitage TN 37076-3411. 615/889-4046.

Mapco Petroleum Inc.
P.O. Box 2930, Memphis TN 38101-2930. 901/774-3100.

LUBRICATING OILS AND GREASES

Spectrum Acquisitions Inc.
100 Industrial Dr, Selmer TN 38375. 901/645-4937.

For more information on career opportunities in the mining, gas, petroleum and energy industries:

Associations

AMERICAN ASSOCIATION OF PETROLEUM GEOLOGISTS
P.O. Box 979, Tulsa OK 7410-0979. 918/584-2555. International headquarters for petroleum geologists.

AMERICAN GEOLOGICAL INSTITUTE
4220 King Street, Alexandria VA 22302-1507. 703/379-2480. Scholarships available. Publishes monthly *Geotimes*. Offers job listings.

AMERICAN NUCLEAR SOCIETY
555 North Kensington Avenue, La Grange Park IL 60525. 708/352-6611. Offers educational services.

AMERICAN PETROLEUM INSTITUTE
1220 L Street NW, Suite 900, Washington DC 20005. 202/682-8000. A trade association.

GEOLOGICAL SOCIETY OF AMERICA
3300 Penrose Place, P.O. Box 9140, Boulder CO 80301. 303/447-2020. Membership of over 17,000. Offers sales items and publications. Also conducts society meetings.

SOCIETY OF EXPLORATION GEOPHYSICISTS
P.O. Box 702740, Tulsa OK 74170-2740. 918/493-3516. A membership association. Offers publications.

Directories

**BROWN'S DIRECTORY OF
NORTH AMERICAN AND
INTERNATIONAL GAS
COMPANIES**
Advanstar Communications, 7500
Old Oak Boulevard, Cleveland OH
44130. 800/225-4569.

**NATIONAL PETROLEUM NEWS
FACT BOOK**
Adams/Hunter Publishing
Company, 2101 South Arlington
Heights Road, Suite 150,
Arlington Heights IL 60005-4142.
847/427-9512.

OIL AND GAS DIRECTORY
Geophysical Directory, Inc., P.O.
Box 130508, Houston TX 77219.
713/529-8789.

Magazines

AMERICAN GAS MONTHLY
1515 Wilson Boulevard, Arlington
VA 22209. 703/841-8686.

GAS INDUSTRIES
Gas Industries News, Inc., 6300
North River Road, Suite 505,
Rosemont IL 60018. 312/693-
3682.

NATIONAL PETROLEUM NEWS
Adams/Hunter Publishing
Company, 2101 South Arlington
Heights Road, Suite 150,
Arlington Heights IL 60005-4142.
847/427-9512.

OIL AND GAS JOURNAL
PennWell Publishing Company,
1421 South Sheridan Road, P.O.
Box 1260. Tulsa OK 74101.
918/835-3161.

PAPER AND WOOD PRODUCTS

The year 1995 was a dramatic one for the paper industry. Prices jumped higher and faster than they had at any time since World War II. According to Dean Witter, profits were up an astounding 180 percent during the year at the nation's 19 largest paper and paperboard companies.

By mid-1995, however, customers had begun to hoard paper, forcing prices back down. Luckily, even as profits soared in the early part of the year, the industry played its hand conservatively by resisting the impulse to expand capacity. Analysts expect prices to continue to stay down during 1996. That means that jobseekers shouldn't anticipate a major increase in industry hiring.

One hot trend, however, may provide opportunity. Environmental concerns should give the paper packaging segment an advantage over plastics, as companies move to become "green." The industry hopes to recycle at least half of the paper it produces by the turn of the century. Minimills, which convert cardboard into pulp, are springing up nationwide. Among the industry's recycling leaders: Weyerhaeuser and Boise Cascade.

BOWATER NEWSPRINT
CALHOUN OPERATION
5020 Highway 11 South, Calhoun TN 37309. 615/336-2211. **Contact:** Mr. Darryl Douglas, Human Resource Manager. **Description:** A producer of world-traded wood fiber products, including virgin and recycled-content newsprint and directory papers, coated publication and book papers, groundwood specialties, market pulp, and lumber. Bowater is also a leading converter of communication papers for use in computers and other business applications. As one of five pulp and paper products mills, this location manufactures and recycles newsprint, and produces bleached kraft market pulps. All mills are supported by over 4 million acres of forestland. Bowater also operates eight continuous-feed paper plants where communication papers are converted, and dimension lumber is produced at three saw mills. Computer and other business papers are marketed through 30 distribution centers. **Corporate headquarters location:** Greenville SC. **Parent company:** Bowater, Inc. **Other locations:** Nova Scotia, Canada; East Millinocket ME; Millinocket ME; Catawba SC. **Number of employees at this location:** 1,460.

BRUCE HARDWOOD FLOOR COMPANY
P.O. Box 1334, Jackson TN 38302. 901/422-7700. **Contact:** Jeff Cummings, Personnel Manager. **Description:** Manufactures hardwood flooring.

BRUCE HARDWOOD FLOOR COMPANY
5400 Centennial Boulevard, Nashville TN 37209. 615/350-8060. **Contact:** Human Resources. **Description:** Manufactures hardwood flooring.

HARTCO FLOORING COMPANY

300 South Main Street, P.O. Box 4009, Oneida TN 37841. 615/569-8526. **Fax:** 615/569-9124. **Contact:** Joan M. Clark, Director of Employment and Training. **Description:** Hartco Flooring Company manufactures hardwood flooring. **Common positions include:** Accountant/Auditor; Blue-Collar Worker Supervisor; Chemical Engineer; Electrical/Electronics Engineer; Electrician; General Manager; Industrial Engineer; Management Trainee; Mechanical Engineer. **Educational backgrounds include:** Accounting; Business Administration; Engineering. **Benefits:** 401K; Cafeteria Plan; Dental Insurance; Disability Coverage; Employee Discounts; Life Insurance; Medical Insurance; Prescription Drugs; Profit Sharing; Tuition Assistance. **Corporate headquarters location:** This Location. **Other U.S. locations:** Somerset KY. **Operations at this facility include:** Administration; Divisional Headquarters; Manufacturing; Sales. **Listed on:** New York Stock Exchange. **Number of employees at this location:** 800.

INTERNATIONAL PAPER COMPANY

6400 Poplar Avenue, Memphis TN 38197. 901/763-6000. **Fax:** 901/763-6140. **Contact:** Edna Macklin, Supervisor, Staffing and Development. **Description:** One of the world's largest forest products companies, with 72,500 employees in over 300 locations worldwide. International Paper is a manufacturer of pulp and paper, packaging, and wood products as well as a range of specialty products. Millions of acres of timberland are controlled by International Paper, making it one of the largest private landowners in the United States. The company is organized into five business segments, including: 1) Printing Papers, in which principal products include uncoated papers, coated papers, bristles, and pulp; 2) Packaging, which includes industrial packaging, consumer packaging, and kraft and specialty papers; 3) Distribution, which includes sales of printing papers, graphic arts equipment and supplies, packaging materials, industrial supplies, and office products; 4) Specialty Products, which includes imaging products, specialty panels, nonwovens, chemicals, and minerals; and 5) Forest Products, including logs and wood products. **Common positions include:** Accountant/Auditor; Administrative Worker/Clerk; Buyer; Computer Programmer; Computer Systems Analyst; Customer Service Representative; Receptionist; Secretary; Typist/Word Processor. **Educational backgrounds include:** Accounting; Business Administration; Computer Science; Finance. **Benefits:** Dental Insurance; Disability Coverage; Life Insurance; Medical Insurance; Pension Plan; Profit Sharing; Savings Plan. **Corporate headquarters location:** Purchase NY. **Operations at this facility include:** Administration. **Number of employees at this location:** 2,000. **Number of employees nationwide:** 72,500.

JEFFERSON SMURFIT CORPORATION U.S.
CORRUGATED CONTAINERS

1720 Ninth Avenue, P.O. Box 307, Humboldt TN 38343. 901/784-1500. **Contact:** Human Resources. **Description:** Corrugated shipping containers represent Jefferson Smurfit's largest business segment. The container division, which operates 56 plants in the U.S., Mexico, and Puerto Rico, ranks second in U.S. production of corrugated containers and, as a part of Smurfit Group, first in the world. When it comes to recycled material usage, JSC is also an industry leader in environmental responsibility. According to the company, its average recycled content significantly exceeds both the company's nearest competitor and the industry average. In addition, JSC is the premier converter of corrugated containers made from 100 percent recycled medium and liner, both supplied by Smurfit mills. The company's strategically located plants convert more than 27 billion square feet of high-quality corrugated containers and specialty applications designed to protect, ship, store, and merchandise customers' products as economically as possible. JSC's corrugated capabilities provide an extensive variety of performance materials, as well as a wide range of graphically enhanced containers and point-of-purchase displays. Jefferson Smurfit Corporation U.S. also provides value-added support to its customers through such diverse services as graphic and structural design, mechanical packaging, custom packaging, and a safe-transit certified testing center.

JEFFERSON SMURFIT CORPORATION U.S.
CORRUGATED CONTAINERS
4512 Anderson Road NE, Knoxville TN 37918. 423/687-6551. **Contact:** Human Resources. **Description:** A customer service and sales facility for Jefferson Smurfit Corporation's corrugated containers division. Corrugated shipping containers represent Jefferson Smurfit Corporation U.S.' largest business segment. The container division, which operates 56 plants in the U.S., Mexico, and Puerto Rico, ranks second in U.S. production of corrugated containers and, as a part of Smurfit Group, first in the world. When it comes to recycled material usage, JSC is also an industry leader in environmental responsibility. According to the company, its average recycled content significantly exceeds both the company's nearest competitor and the industry average. In addition, JSC is the premier converter of corrugated containers made from 100 percent recycled medium and liner, both supplied by Smurfit mills. The company's strategically located plants convert more than 27 billion square feet of high-quality corrugated containers and specialty applications designed to protect, ship, store, and merchandise our customers' products as economically as possible. JSC's corrugated capabilities provide an extensive variety of performance materials, as well as a wide range of graphically enhanced containers and point-of-purchase displays. The company also provides value-added support to its customers through such diverse services as graphic and structural design, mechanical packaging, custom packaging, and a safe-transit certified testing center.

MEMPHIS HARDWOOD FLOORING
1551 North Thomas Street, Memphis TN 38107. 901/526-7306. **Contact:** Fred Day, Controller. **Description:** Manufactures hardwood flooring.

STONE CONTAINER CORPORATION
P.O. Box 23330, Nashville TN 37202-3330. 615/256-8965. **Contact:** Joanne Justice, Controller. **Description:** A multi-national paper and packaging company with annual sales of approximately $5.7 billion. Its primary businesses are paperboard and paper packaging, and white paper and pulp operations. Paperboard and paper packaging is composed primarily of facilities which produce and sell containerboard and corrugated containers for manufacturers

of consumable and durable goods and other manufacturers of corrugated containers; boxboard, folding cartons, and other products for manufacturers of consumable goods, especially food, beverage, and tobacco products, and for other box manufacturers; and kraft paper and bags and sacks for supermarket chains and other retailers of consumable products, as well as for the food, agricultural, chemical, and cement industries. White paper and pulp operations produce and sell newsprint for newspaper publishers and commercial printers; uncoated groundwood paper for producers of advertising materials, magazines, directories, and computer papers; and market pulp for manufacturers of paper products, including fine papers, photographic papers, tissue, and newsprint. Other operations consist primarily of wood products operations which produce and sell lumber, plywood, and veneer for the construction and furniture industries. Including its subsidiaries and affiliates, Stone maintains nearly 200 manufacturing facilities and sales offices in North America, Latin America, Europe, and the Far East.

TENNECO PACKAGING
P.O. Box 33, Counce TN 38326-0033. 901/689-3111. **Contact:** Human Resource Manager. **Description:** Tenneco Packaging is a worldwide manufacturer of paper and paper products. The parent company, Tenneco Gas Company, is a holding company with subsidiaries which are engaged in the following types of activities: transporting and selling natural gas; mining and selling minerals; and manufacturing industrial products.

TENSION ENVELOPE CORPORATION
P.O. Box 30114, Memphis TN 38130-0114. 901/743-3300. **Contact:** Human Resources. **Description:** A manufacturer of paper envelopes.

VOLUNTEER LUMBER COMPANY
8000 East Brainerd Road, Chattanooga TN 37421-3205. 423/892-9040. **Contact:** Human Resources. **Description:** A lumber company.

WERTHAN PACKAGING INC.
P.O. Box 1310, Nashville TN 37202. 615/259-9331. **Contact:** Sue Daniels, Human Resources. **Description:** Werthan Packaging Inc. manufactures paper bags.

WILLAMETTE INDUSTRIES, INC.
100 Clinchfield Street, Kingsport TN 37660. 615/247-7111. **Contact:** Rich Polinske, Human Resources Manager. **Description:** Willamette Industries was founded in 1906 as the Willamette Valley Lumber Company in Dallas, Oregon. In 1967, Willamette Valley and several related firms merged to form Willamette Industries, Inc. Willamette Industries is a diversified, integrated forest products company with 90 plants and mills manufacturing containerboard, bag paper, fine paper, bleached hardwood market pulp, specialty printing papers, corrugated containers, business forms, cut sheet paper, paper bags, inks, lumber, plywood, particleboard, medium-density fiberboard, laminated beams, and value-added wood products. The company owns or controls 1,235,000 acres of forests. According to the company, Willamette's strengths are its vertical integration, its geographically-diverse, modern, fiber- and energy-efficient facilities, its concentration on a focused, related

product range, its balance among building materials, white paper and brown paper manufacturing and an organizational structure that the company feels encourages teamwork as well as individual initiative.

Note: Because addresses and telephone numbers of smaller companies change rapidly, we recommend you call each company to verify the information below before inquiring about job opportunities. Mass mailings are not recommended.

Additional employers with under 250 employees:

LUMBER AND WOOD WHOLESALE

Tennessee Building Products
P.O. Box 100926, Nashville TN 37224-0926. 615/259-4677.

Whitson Lumber Co.
5701 California Ave, Nashville TN 37209-1416. 615/350-7260.

Townsend Supply Co.
120 Johnson St, Jackson TN 38301-5917. 901/424-4300.

Warren Brothers Sash & Door
700 Massman Dr, Nashville TN 37210-3724. 615/885-0355.

Builder Specialty Inc. Memphis
9575 Macon Rd, Cordova TN 38018-6551. 901/757-1300.

Addison Corporation
2924 Sidco Dr, Nashville TN 37204-3710. 615/255-2617.

Tech Building Products
218 River Hills Dr, Nashville TN 37210-2392. 615/889-3091.

INDUSTRIAL PAPER AND RELATED PRODUCTS WHOLESALE

Presstock Store
1906 Church St, Nashville TN 37203-2204. 615/329-3482.

Zellerbach-A Mead Company
566 Mainstream Dr, Nashville TN 37228-1202. 615/259-9575.

Bemis Company Inc.
8000 Centerview Pkwy, Suite 101, Cordova TN 38018-4227. 901/759-3300.

Southern Standard Cartons
860 Ten Oaks Dr, Collierville TN 38017-1673. 901/854-1371.

LOGGING

Hassess & Hughes Lumber
P.O. Box 68, Collinwood TN 38450-0068. 615/724-9191.

WOOD MILLS

Aristokraft
P.O. Box 2539, Crossville TN 38557-2539. 615/456-1802.

Central Woodwork Inc.
3620 Regal Blvd, Memphis TN 38118-6116. 901/363-4141.

Cherokee Wood Preservers
P.O. Box 68, Mosheim TN 37818-0068. 423/422-6011.

Cumberland Lumber & Manufacturing
202 Red Rd, McMinnville TN 37110-1710. 615/473-9542.

Dyer Fruit Box Manufacturing Co.
130 Parkview Dr, Dyer TN 38330-1612. 901/692-2241.

Futuristic Inc.
P.O. Box 10, Bean Station TN 37708-0010. 423/235-6271.

Gordon's Inc.
P.O. Box 1676, Johnson City TN 37605-1676. 423/928-2191.

Gulf Lumber Co-TN
6311 Centennial Blvd, Nashville TN 37209-1101. 615/350-8282.

JR Moon Pencil Co.
P.O. Box 1309, Lewisburg TN 37091-0309. 615/359-1501.

Lafayette Manufacturing Co.
915 Red Boiling Springs Rd, Lafayette TN 37083-1321. 615/666-2165.

Norris Inc.
P.O. Box 99, Bean Station TN 37708-0099. 423/993-3343.

Oakwood Furniture Manufacturing
623 Straight Creek Rd, New Tazewell TN 37825-6408. 423/626-8201.

The Delfield Co.
1 Delfield Dr, Covington TN 38019-3406. 901/476-1225.

United Cabinet Corp. dba Kabinart
P.O. Box 110774,
Nashville TN 37222-
0774. 615/833-1961.

Walter Dimension Lumber
P.O. Box 843,
Jamestown TN
38556-0843.
615/879-8151.

Averitt Lumber Co.
310 Dover Rd,
Clarksville TN 37042-
4158. 615/647-8394.

Cortrim Hardwood Parts Co.
P.O. Box 919, Bristol
TN 37621-0919.
423/764-6127.

Desoto Hardwood Flooring
P.O. Box 40895,
Memphis TN 38174-
0895. 901/774-9672.

McMinnville Manufacturing Co.
215 S Chancery St,
McMinnville TN
37110-3208.
615/473-2131.

Sequatchie Handle Works
P O Box 140,
Sequatchie TN 37374.
423/942-5901.

Woodcraft Inc.
P.O. Box 1819,
Morristown TN
37816-1819.
423/581-5413.

MILLWORK, PLYWOOD, AND STRUCTURAL MEMBERS

Cumberland Hardwood
RR 10, Sparta TN
38583-9810.
615/738-5264.

Memphis Folding Stairs Inc.
P.O. Box 12305,
Memphis TN 38182-
0305. 901/458-1161.

Giles Industries of Tazewell
P.O. Box 750, New
Tazewell TN 37825-
0750. 423/626-7243.

Silver Furniture Co.
P.O. Box 3820,
Knoxville TN 37927-
3820. 423/637-4541.

Triangle Pacific Corp.
1007 Trade St,
Morristown TN
37813-5739.
423/586-7233.

Stewart Furniture Custom Woodworking
P.O. Box 1698,
Morristown TN
37816-1698.
423/581-0185.

WOOD BOXES AND SHOOK

North American Container
2180 Pulaski Hwy,
Lawrenceburg TN
38464-7422.
615/762-5817.

Tuscarora Inc.
P.O. Box 1236,
Greeneville TN 37744-
1236. 423/638-1205.

WOOD PRODUCTS

Pioneer Plastics Corp.
P.O. Box 1973,
Morristown TN
37816-1973.
423/587-1842.

Burroughs Ross Colville Co.
301 Depot St,
McMinnville TN
37110-3226.
615/473-2111.

Turner Day & Woolworth Handle
205 N Webb Ave,
Crossville TN 38555-
4675. 615/484-8491.

PAPER MILLS

Viskase Corp.
106 Blair Bend Dr,
Loudon TN 37774-
6562. 423/458-2071.

Ahlstrom Filtration Inc.
P.O. Box 2009,
Chattanooga TN
37409-0009.
423/821-4090.

American Greetings Corp.
601 Oak St, Lafayette
TN 37083-1307.
615/666-4607.

Arcade Inc.
1815 E Main St,
Chattanooga TN
37404-5041.
423/624-3301.

Atlantic Envelope Co.
P.O. Box 888,
Nashville TN 37202-
0888. 615/244-1071.

Georgia Pacific Corp.
P.O. Box 161134,
Memphis TN 38186-
1134. 901/346-8500.

Lithographics Inc.
1835 Air Lane Dr,
Nashville TN 37210-
3838. 615/889-1200.

McQuiddy Printing Co.
P.O. Box 292107,
Nashville TN 37229-
2107. 615/366-6565.

Nashville Electragraphics Nec
1504 Elm Hill Pike,
Nashville TN 37210-
3602. 615/367-9110.

Press Inc.
P.O. Box 1717,
Johnson City TN
37605-1717.
423/929-3111.

School Calendar Co.
P.O. Box 280,
Morristown TN
37815-0280.
423/581-4250.

The Robinette Co.
P.O. Box 3567, Bristol
TN 37625-3567.
423/968-7800.

**Chattanooga
Paperboard**
P.O. Box 431,
Chattanooga TN
37401-0431.
423/267-3801.

Clark Container Inc.
P.O. Box 160, Lyles
TN 37098-0160.
615/670-4400.

**Container Corp. of
America**
4512 Anderson Rd,
Knoxville TN 37918-
2713. 423/687-6551.

Custom Packaging Inc.
P.O. Box 1028,
Lebanon TN 37088-
1028. 615/444-6025.

Mill Division
P.O. Box 4068,
Chattanooga TN
37405-0068.
423/266-7381.

**Three Star Packaging
& Distribution**
407 N Irish St,
Greeneville TN 37745-
3328. 423/636-1958.

**PAPERBOARD
CONTAINERS AND
BOXES**

**Rock-Tenn Co. Folding
Division**
P.O. Box 51810,
Knoxville TN 37950-
1810. 423/524-1281.

**Container Corp. of
America**
2101 Rossville Ave,
Chattanooga TN
37408-2146.
423/265-8244.

**Model Box Inc. of
America**
1310 E 13th St,
Chattanooga TN
37404-4221.
423/622-0805.

**New Tech Packaging
Inc.**
2718 Pershing Ave,
Memphis TN 38112-
1954. 901/324-5553.

Rock-Tenn Co.
525 W 19th St,
Chattanooga TN
37408-1006.
423/756-0036.

Rock-Tenn Co.
410 Wilson Ave,
Tullahoma TN 37388-
3358. 615/455-8520.

St. Joe Container Co.
1700 S 3rd St,
Memphis TN 38109-
7712. 901/948-7761.

**Westvaco Container
Division**
P.O. Box 196,
Cleveland TN 37364-
0196. 423/472-3323.

**Weyerhaeuser Paper
Co.**
1170 N Manassas St,
Memphis TN 38107-
1911. 901/525-5511.

**McCowat-Mercer
Press Inc.**
P.O. Box 818,
Jackson TN 38302-
0818. 901/427-3376.

**Westvaco Folding
Carton Division**
P.O. Box 3780,
Cleveland TN 37320-
3780. 423/479-9783.

**COATED AND
LAMINATED PAPER**

John Deal Co.
P.O. Box 198, Mount
Juliet TN 37122-
0198. 615/758-5913.

**Thilmany Division of
International Paper**
2530 Westcott Blvd,
Knoxville TN 37931-
3100. 423/694-5400.

PAPER BAGS

Bemis Co. Inc.
1975 Latham St,
Memphis TN 38106-
7102. 901/775-2530.

**Shippers Paper
Products Co.**
1203 N Main St,
Mount Pleasant TN
38474-1072.
615/379-7731.

**DIE-CUT PAPER AND
PAPER PRODUCTS**

Inland Container Corp.
P.O. Box 911,
Elizabethton TN
37644-0911.
423/542-2112.

James River Corp.
119 Spicer Dr,
Gordonsville TN
38563-2143.
615/683-6352.

**Southern Champion
Tray Co.**
210 Compress St,
Chattanooga TN
37405-3764.
423/756-5121.

**CONVERTED PAPER
AND PAPERBOARD
PRODUCTS**

**Inland Container
Corporation**
P.O. Box 299, New
Johsonvle TN 37134-
0299. 615/535-2161.

For more information on career opportunities in the paper and wood products industries:

Associations

AMERICAN FOREST AND PAPER ASSOCIATION
1111 19th Street NW, Suite 700, Washington DC 20036. 202/463-2700. A lobbying group that conducts informational gatherings.

AMERICAN FOREST AND PAPER ASSOCIATION
260 Madison Avenue, New York NY 10016. 212/340-0600. Headquartered in Washington DC. A lobbying group that conducts informational gatherings.

FOREST PRODUCTS SOCIETY
2801 Marshall Court, Madison WI 53705-2295. 608/231-1361. An international, nonprofit, educational association that provides an information network for all segments of the forest products industry. Offers employment referral service.

NATIONAL PAPER TRADE ASSOCIATION
111 Great Neck Road, Great Neck NY 11021. 516/829-3070. Offers management services to wholesalers. Offers books, seminars, and research services.

PAPERBOARD PACKAGING COUNCIL
888 17th Street NW, Suite 900, Washington DC 20006. 202/289-4100. Offers statistical and lobbying services.

TECHNICAL ASSOCIATION OF THE PULP AND PAPER INDUSTRY
P.O. Box 105113, Atlanta GA 30348. 404/446-1400. Nonprofit. Offers conferences and education.

Directories

DIRECTORY OF THE FOREST PRODUCTS INDUSTRY
Miller Freeman Publications, Inc., 600 Harrison Street, San Francisco CA 94107. 415/905-2200.

LOCKWOOD-POST'S DIRECTORY OF THE PAPER AND ALLIED TRADES
Miller Freeman Publications, Inc., 600 Harrison Street, San Francisco CA 94107. 415/905-2200.

POST'S PULP AND PAPER DIRECTORY
Miller Freeman Publications, Inc., 600 Harrison Street, San Francisco CA 94107. 415/905-2200.

Magazines

PAPERBOARD PACKAGING
Advanstar Communications, 131 West First Street, Duluth MN 55802. 218/723-9200.

PULP AND PAPER WEEK
Miller Freeman Publications, Inc., 600 Harrison Street, San Francisco CA 94107. 415/905-2200.

WOOD TECHNOLOGIES
Miller Freeman Publications, Inc., 600 Harrison Street, San Francisco CA 94107. 415/905-2200.

PRINTING AND PUBLISHING

The big news in publishing in 1995 was the paper shortage. Paper costs account for 30 to 40 percent of the manufacturing costs of a book. Many companies compensated for the rising costs by stockpiling paper, designing books more tightly, lowering paper grades, and increasing book prices. The paper pinch also affected the magazine and newspaper industries. Newsprint prices rose more than 30 percent from early 1994 to early 1995. Magazines became noticeably shorter. One good sign for newspapers and magazines: As the economy improves, companies will increase their print advertising budgets. And, with a presidential election and a Summer Olympics on the calendar in '96, spending for advertising will increase.

Another way some publishers are balancing their books against the paper crunch is by looking to electronic media, a competitive and rapidly expanding medium. Many book publishers are offering CD-ROM versions of popular books, especially educational, reference, and children's books. Also, books-on-tape are growing in popularity. Magazines and newspapers also are joining the electronic bandwagon -- many periodicals and newspapers are now available online.

Book printing and distribution are also evolving. Traditionally, long print runs were necessary to keep costs down. But thanks to new digital presses that don't use plates, books can now be printed and distributed in small batches according to demand. Instead of printing and then distributing, publishers can now distribute and then print. Publishers will be able to use many small presses across the country, instead of one or two strategically placed large presses. The result: increased demand for computer-savvy printing professionals and dramatic cuts in shipping and warehousing.

AMERICAN GREETINGS CORPORATION
P.O. Box 528, Ripley TN 38063-7362. 901/635-3000. **Contact:** Human Resources. **Description:** Manufactures greeting cards.

HOLLISTON MILLS INC.
Highway 11 West, Kingsport TN 37662. 615/357-6141. **Contact:** Nancy Smith, Human Resources Director. **Description:** Manufactures book covers.

JOSTENS INC.
P.O. Box 208, Shelbyville, TN 37160-2133. 615/684-5290. **Contact:** Human Resources. **Description:** Printer of high school and college graduation announcements.

KNOXVILLE NEWS-SENTINEL COMPANY
P.O. Box 59038, Knoxville TN 37950-9038. 615/521-8109. **Fax:** 615/521-1793. **Contact:** Human Resources Department. **Description:** A newspaper publisher. **Common positions include:** Computer Programmer; Customer Service Representative; Editor; Electrician;

General Manager; Librarian; Purchasing Agent and Manager; Reporter. **Educational backgrounds include:** Accounting; Art/Design; Communications; Computer Science. **Benefits:** 401K; Dental Insurance; Disability Coverage; Life Insurance; Medical Insurance; Pension Plan; Savings Plan; Tuition Assistance. **Special Programs:** Internships. **Corporate headquarters location:** Cincinnati OH. **Operations at this facility include:** Administration; Sales; Service. **Number of employees at this location:** 570.

NASHVILLE BANNER
1100 Broadway, Nashville TN 37203. 615/259-8800. **Fax:** 615/259-8890. **Contact:** Mr. Pat Embry, Managing Editor. **Description:** A newspaper.

THOMAS NELSON INC.
Nelson Place at Elm Hill Pike, Nashville TN 37214-1000. 615/889-9000. **Recorded Jobline:** 615/889-9000x1430. **Contact:** Rusty Faulks, Director, Human Resources. **Description:** Founded in 1798, Thomas Nelson Inc. is believed to be the world's leading publisher of Bibles, and one of the world's leading independent publishers of Christian and inspirational books. The company also sells gift and stationery products and develops and markets Christmas and Christian music and video products. **Number of employees nationwide:** 1,100.

PRO LINE STORAGE CORP.
P.O. Box 449, Brownsville TN 38012-0449. 901/772-2500. **Contact:** Human Resources. **Description:** Manufactures supplies for photo albums, film processing, and the printing industry.

RAND-MCNALLY BOOK SERVICES GROUP
NASHVILLE DIVISION
418 Harding Industrial Drive, Nashville TN 37211. 615/834-7600. **Fax:** 615/331-7833. **Contact:** Human Resources. **Description:** Rand-McNally Book Services Group is engaged in book binding and loose-leaf packaging. It is one of the nation's largest trade binderies, using advanced bindery technology and machines. The bindery operations handle books of all sizes to produce books for the pocket or the coffee table. Binding styles include Smyth sewn, side sewn, center sewn, Wire-O, plastic comb, and spiral. The loose-leaf operations handle a wide variety of styles and materials -- square, round, or brass corners, turned edge, vinyl heatseal, custom index tabs, and covers from polyethylene to cow-hide leather. Projects range from manufacturing binders, slipcases, and angle boxes for computer software companies to teachers' resource kits for textbook publishers. The bindery at Nashville, one of the country's largest trade binderies, uses the most advanced bindery technology available, including Wire-O binding and Otabind. **Number of employees at this location:** 435.

SULLIVAN GRAPHICS
100 Winners Circle, Brentwood TN 37027. 615/377-0377. **Contact:** Lance Ikard, Vice President of Human Resources. **Description:** A printing company.

TAP PUBLISHING COMPANY

P.O. Box 509, Crossville TN 38557-0509. 615/484-5137. **Contact:** Human Resources. **Description:** Publishes trade journals in the areas of aviation, construction equipment, the oil and gas industry, and amateur radio operation.

THE UNITED METHODIST PUBLISHING HOUSE

201 Eighth Avenue South, P.O. Box 801, Nashville TN 37202. 615/749-6535. **Fax:** 615/749-6366. **Contact:** Cindy Knight, Employment Manager. **Description:** The oldest and largest general agency of The United Methodist Church. The publishing house began in Philadelphia in 1789 and opened publishing operations in Nashville in 1854. As the United Methodist Church's official publisher, the publishing house develops, produces, and distributes books for home, church, and official denominational church school curriculum. **NOTE:** The company offers a wide variety of multimedia resources and opportunities. United Methodist is seeking applicants with a variety of skills, training, experience, and interests. **Common positions include:** Accountant/Auditor; Advertising Clerk; Cashier; Computer Operator; Computer Programmer; Customer Service Representative; Editor; Employment Interviewer; Management Trainee; Market Research Analyst; Receptionist; Secretary; Systems Analyst; Typist/Word Processor. **Benefits:** Dental Insurance; Disability Coverage; Employee Discounts; Life Insurance; Medical Insurance; Pension Plan; Savings Plan; Tuition Assistance. **Special Programs:** Internships. **Corporate headquarters location:** This Location. **Number of employees at this location:** 850. **Number of employees nationwide:** 1,200.

WORLD COLOR PRESS

P.O. Box 927, Covington TN 38019. 901/476-0495. **Contact:** Tony Paul, Human Resource Director. **Description:** A magazine printer. **Corporate headquarters location:** This Location.

Note: Because addresses and telephone numbers of smaller companies change rapidly, we recommend you call each company to verify the information below before inquiring about job opportunities. Mass mailings are not recommended.

Additional employers with under 250 employees:

BOOKS, PERIODICALS, AND NEWSPAPERS WHOLESALE

Spring Arbor Distributors
RR 7, Newport TN 37821-9807. 423/625-0305.

Melton Book Company Inc.
P.O. Box 140990, Nashville TN 37214-0990. 615/391-3917.

Austin Periodical Services
499 Merritt Ave, Nashville TN 37203-5306. 615/242-7603.

NEWSPAPERS: PUBLISHING AND/OR PRINTING

Brentwood Journal
750 Old Hickory Blvd, Suite 150, Brentwood TN 37027-4502. 615/373-0445.

Kingsport Publishing Corp.
P.O. Box 479, Kingsport TN 37662-0479. 423/246-8121.

Kingsport Times-News
P.O. Box 479, Elizabethton TN 37643. 423/543-3303.

Mid-South Publishing Inc.
P.O. Box 68, Murfreesboro TN

37133-0068.
615/893-5860.

The Jackson Sun Inc.
P.O. Box 1059,
Jackson TN 38302-
1059. 901/427-3333.

USA Today
P.O. Box 1059,
Jackson TN 38302-
1059. 901/423-1010.

**PERIODICALS:
PUBLISHING AND/OR
PRINTING**

Cash Box Magazine
50 Music Sq W,
Nashville TN 37203-
3212. 615/329-2898.

**BOOKS: PUBLISHING
AND/OR PRINTING**

**Fundcraft Publishing
Co.**
410 US Highway 72
W, Collierville TN
38017-2804.
901/853-7070.

**Arcata
Graphics/Sherwood**
2400 Sherwood Rd,
Kingsport TN 37664-
3704. 423/378-1202.

MISC. PUBLISHING

**The Benson Music
Group Inc.**
365 Great Circle Rd,
Nashville TN 37228-
1703. 615/742-6800.

**Horipro Entertainment
Group**
1819 Broadway,
Nashville TN 37203-
2711. 615/329-0890.

Easychair Music Co.
509 Dupont Ave,
Madison TN 37115-
3348. 615/255-3577.

**COMMERCIAL
PRINTING**

Ambrose Printing Co.
210 Cumberland Bnd,
Nashville TN 37228-
1804. 615/256-1151.

B&M Printing Co.
2500 Lamar Ave,
Memphis TN 38114-
4347. 901/743-4444.

**Quebecor Printing
Memphis**
P.O. Box 16037,
Memphis TN 38186-
0037. 901/332-6391.

**RR Donnelley & Sons
Co.**
109 Westpark Dr,
Suite 480, Brentwood
TN 37027-5032.
615/371-2100.

**Southeastern Color
Graph**
P.O. Box 4975,
Johnson City TN
37602-4975.
423/282-9111.

Starr/Toof Printing Co.
670 S Cooper St,
Memphis TN 38104-
5353. 901/274-3632.

Screen Graphics Inc.
285 Union Ave,
Memphis TN 38103-
5200. 901/527-9400.

20/20 Design Inc.
6257 Highway 76 E,
Springfield TN 37172-
6325. 615/384-1359.

**BLANK BOOKS AND
BOOKBINDING**

Deluxe Check Printers
P.O. Box 138,
Memphis TN 38101-
0138. 901/795-5513.

Dickinson Press Inc.
49 Ashington Ln,
Brentwood TN 37027-
4367. 615/373-9773.

**PHOTOGRAPHIC
EQUIPMENT AND
SUPPLIES**

American Components
931 Mill St, Dandridge
TN 37725-4809.
423/397-0177.

**COMMERCIAL ART
AND GRAPHIC
DESIGN**

**Genigraphics
Corporation**
4155 Willow Lake
Blvd, Memphis TN
38118-7028.
901/795-6431.

NEWS SYNDICATES

Associated Press
1100 Broadway,
Nashville TN 37203-
3116. 615/244-2205.

**PHOTO FINISHING
LABORATORIES**

**Meteor Photo &
Imaging Co.**
9941 Sierra Vista Ln,
Knoxville TN 37922-
5736. 423/966-3896.

Meteor Photo Imaging
8724 Magnolia Bloom
Cv, Cordova TN
38018-6163.
901/753-8519.

Wolf Camera & Video
5252 Hickory Hollow
Pkwy, Antioch TN
37013. 615/731-
2306.

Wolf Camera & Video
7850 Poplar Ave,
Suite 6, Memphis TN
38138-5000.
901/753-4756.

For more information on career opportunities in printing and publishing:

Associations

AMERICAN BOOKSELLERS ASSOCIATION
828 South Broadway, Tarrytown NY 10591. 914/591-2665.

AMERICAN INSTITUTE OF GRAPHIC ARTS
919 3rd Avenue, 22nd Floor, New York NY 10003-3004. 212/807-1990. A 36-chapter, nationwide organization sponsoring programs and events for graphic designers and related professionals.

AMERICAN SOCIETY OF NEWSPAPER EDITORS
P.O. Box 4090, Reston VA 22090-1700. 703/648-1144.

ASSOCIATION OF GRAPHIC ARTS
330 7th Avenue, 9th Floor, New York NY 10001-5010. 212/279-2100. Offers educational classes and seminars.

BINDING INDUSTRIES OF AMERICA
70 East Lake Street, Suite 300, Chicago IL 60601. 312/372-7606. Offers credit collection, government affairs, and educational services.

THE DOW JONES NEWSPAPER FUND
P.O. Box 300, Princeton NJ 08543-0300. 609/520-4000.

GRAPHIC ARTISTS GUILD
11 West 20th Street, 8th Floor, New York NY 10011. 212/463-7730. A union for artists.

INTERNATIONAL GRAPHIC ARTS EDUCATION ASSOCIATION
4615 Forbes Avenue, Pittsburgh PA 15213. 412/682-5170.

MAGAZINE PUBLISHERS ASSOCIATION
919 Third Avenue, 22nd Floor, New York NY 10022. 212/752-0055. A membership association.

NATIONAL ASSOCIATION OF PRINTERS AND LITHOGRAPHERS
780 Pallisade Avenue, Teaneck NJ 07666. 201/342-0700. Membership. Offers consulting services and a publication.

NATIONAL NEWSPAPER ASSOCIATION
1525 Wilson Boulevard, Arlington VA 22209. 703/907-7900.

NATIONAL PRESS CLUB
529 14th St. NW, 13th Floor, Washington DC 20045. 202/662-7500. Offers professional seminars and career services; conference facilities; and members-only restaurants and a health club.

NEWSPAPER ASSOCIATION OF AMERICA
Newspaper Center, 11600 Sunrise Valley Drive, Reston VA 22091. 703/648-1000. The technology department publishes marketing research.

THE NEWSPAPER GUILD
Research and Information Department, 8611 2nd Avenue, Silver Spring MD 20910. 301/585-2990. A trade union.

PRINTING INDUSTRIES OF AMERICA
100 Dangerfield Road, Alexandria VA 22314. 703/519-8100. Members are offered publications, insurance, and political action.

TECHNICAL ASSOCIATION OF THE GRAPHIC ARTS
68 Lomb memorial Drive, Rochester NY 14623. 716/475-7470. Conducts an annual conference and offers newsletters.

WRITERS GUILD OF AMERICA WEST
8955 Beverly Boulevard, West Hollywood CA 90048. 310/550-1000. A membership association which registers scripts.

Directories

EDITOR & PUBLISHER INTERNATIONAL YEARBOOK
Editor & Publisher Company Inc., 11 West 19th Street, New York NY 10011. 212/675-4380.

$100.00. Offers newspapers to editors in both the United States and foreign countries.

GRAPHIC ARTS BLUE BOOK
A.F. Lewis & Company, 245 Fifth Avenue, New York NY 10016. 212/679-0770. $80.00. Manufacturers and dealers.

JOURNALISM CAREER AND SCHOLARSHIP GUIDE
The Dow Jones Newspaper Fund, P.O. Box 300, Princeton NJ 08543-0300. 609/520-4000.

Magazines

AIGA JOURNAL
American Institute of Graphic Arts, 164 Third Avenue, New York NY 10010. 212/752-0813. $21.50. A 56-page quarterly magazine dealing with contemporary issues.

EDITOR AND PUBLISHER
Editor & Publisher Company Inc., 164 Third Avenue, New York NY 10010. 212/807-1990.

GRAPHIC ARTS MONTHLY
249 West 49th Street, New York NY 10011. 212/463-6836.

GRAPHIS
141 Lexington Avenue, New York NY 10016. 212/532-9387. $89.00. Magazine covers

portfolios, articles, designers, advertising, and photos.

PRINT
104 Fifth Avenue, 19th Floor New York NY 10011. 212/463-0600. Offers a graphic design magazine. $55.00 for subscription.

PUBLISHER'S WEEKLY
249 West 17th Street, New York NY 10011. Weekly publication for book publishers and sellers.

Special Book and Magazine Programs

THE NEW YORK UNIVERSITY SUMMER PUBLISHING PROGRAM
48 Cooper Square, Room 108, New York NY 10003. 212/998-7219.

THE RADCLIFFE PUBLISHING COURSE
77 Brattle Street, Cambridge MA 02138. 617/495-8678.

RICE UNIVERSITY PUBLISHING PROGRAM
Office of Continuing Studies, P.O. Box 1892, Houston TX 77251-1892. 713/520-6022.

UNIVERSITY OF DENVER PUBLISHING INSTITUTE
2075 South University Boulevard, #D-114, Denver CO 80208. 303/871-4868.

REAL ESTATE

Rising interest rates in early 1995 caused housing starts to drop and sales of existing single-family homes to moderately decline. However, by mid-summer, rates began falling once more. Solid opportunities for jobseekers are available for those looking to enter the real estate field. Occupancy will go up in the office sector, as few new office properties are being built. Apartment construction, on the other hand, is on the rise. Commercial property sales will help maintain employment opportunities for real estate agents, brokers, and appraisers. The number of job openings in these occupations is expected to match the number of openings for most other careers nationwide. The majority of these openings, however, will be replacement positions, as agents return or leave the field, rather than new positions.

Property and real estate managers will have even greater opportunities to find employment, as more openings appear for these positions than for other occupations. The people with the most qualified backgrounds for these jobs will be those with college degrees in business administration and other related studies.

ALLEN & O'HARA, INC.
3385 Airways Boulevard, Third Floor, Memphis TN 38116. 901/345-7620. **Contact:** Susan Arrison, Vice President of Human Resources. **Description:** Founded in 1952, the company is involved in property management, construction, and real estate development. Allen & O'Hara has been managing hotel property since 1961, dealing primarily with major franchise hotels. The company has taken that experience a step further, started its own venture, and is now one of the largest owners/managers of student housing facilities in the U.S. The construction segment of the company operates as a general contractor. The company oversees the whole job, "from design/build services, through cost estimating, to project management." Finally, Allen & O'Hara uses its knowledge of property management and construction to benefit its real estate development sector. The company believes this experience helps in market research, economic analysis, site selection and "all the factors necessary to assure a successful new development." **Corporate headquarters location:** This Location.

BELZ ENTERPRISES
530 Oak Court Drive, Suite 300, Memphis TN 38117. 901/767-4780. **Contact:** Irvin Scopp, Director of Human Resources. **Description:** A real estate development and management company.

COOPER COMPANIES
1407 Union Avenue, Suite 400, Memphis TN 38104. 901/725-9631. **Contact:** Pace Cooper, President. **Description:** Provides property management and real estate services, as well as operates several hotels.

CRYE-LEIKE
5111 Maryland Way, Brentwood TN 37027. 615/373-2044. **Contact:** Suzanne Worley, Human Resources. **Description:** A full-service real estate firm with 10 offices across the state.

KEMMONS WILSON, INC.
1629 Winchester Road, Memphis TN 38116. 901/346-8803. **Contact:** Vicky Bradley, Human Resources Manager. **Description:** Involved in the development and management of hotels and real estate, banking, manufacturing, and other businesses. **Listed on:** Privately held. **Number of employees at this location:** 600. **Number of employees nationwide:** 2,700.

NATIONAL HEALTH INVESTORS, INC.
City Center, 100 Vine Street, Murfreesboro TN 37130. 615/890-9100. **Contact:** Human Resources. **Description:** National Health Investors, Inc. is a real estate investment trust which specializes in the purchase and leaseback of health care real estate and in the making of mortgage loans to health care operators. Revenue comes principally from rent and interest earned. NHI, which began operations in October 1991, owns or mortgages 176 properties in 25 states.

SCHATTEN PROPERTIES
1617 Hayes Street, Nashville TN 37203. 615/329-3011. **Contact:** Lynn Holt, Controller. **Description:** A property management firm.

Note: Because addresses and telephone numbers of smaller companies change rapidly, we recommend you call each company to verify the information below before inquiring about job opportunities. Mass mailings are not recommended.

Additional employers with under 250 employees:

REAL ESTATE OPERATORS

The Forum
6750 Poplar Ave, Memphis TN 38138-7424. 901/756-2911.

Stones River Mall
1720 Old Fort Pkwy, Murfreesboro TN 37129-3382. 615/896-4486.

Bartlett Heights Apartments
6130 Bartlett View Ln, Memphis TN 38134-8365. 901/388-6901.

Brentridge Apartments
1500 Brentridge Dr, Antioch TN 37013-3775. 615/331-0163.

Brentwood Highlands Apartments
249 Plum Nelly Cir, Brentwood TN 37027-4621. 615/373-5415.

Briar Club Apartments
6355 Briar Patch Ln, Memphis TN 38115-4116. 901/363-6865.

Broadway Towers Apartments
1508 McCroskey Ave, Knoxville TN 37917-4750. 423/524-4092.

Burning Tree Apartments
Burning Tree Dr, Hermitage TN 37076. 615/883-5884.

Cantebury Apartments
1001 Meadowview

Cv, Covington TN 38019-3429. 901/475-1371.

Countryside Apartments
6934 Country Manor Dr, Memphis TN 38133-8810. 901/377-4025.

Glen Townhomes
6081 Highway 70, Memphis TN 38134. 901/382-2994.

Greenbrook Apartments
1400 Greenbrook Pkwy, Memphis TN 38134-7836. 901/386-1991.

Hickory Forest Apartments
500 Ocala Dr,
Nashville TN 37211-
6352. 615/833-5095.

Johnathan's Ridge
820 Red Hill Dr,
Louisville TN 37777-
5347. 423/981-1729.

Kensington Place Apartments
Tenn Ave N, Parsons
TN 38363. 901/847-
7817.

Landings at Winchester
6787 S Landing Way,
Memphis TN 38115-
4375. 901/795-6395.

Lexington Garden
335 Forrest Park Rd,
Madison TN 37115-
3873. 615/865-8266.

Millwood Manor Apartments
305 Millwood Dr,
Nashville TN 37217.
615/360-6637.

Monticello Apartments
3250 Kirby Pkwy,
Memphis TN 38115-
3703. 901/366-1999.

Sunflower Apartments
4619 Sunflower Rd,
Knoxville TN 37909-
1427. 423/584-5796.

Villager Condominiums
1014 N Tennessee
Blvd, Murfreesboro TN
37130-2654.
615/890-5531.

Westboro Apartments
3101 W End Ave,
Nashville TN 37203-
1375. 615/297-2276.

Woodmont Towers
1550 N Parkway,
Memphis TN 38112-
4900. 901/272-2127.

REAL ESTATE AGENTS AND MANAGERS

Shular Companies
2708 Parkway, Pigeon
Forge TN 37863-
3212. 423/428-4949.

Century 21 Riverview Realty
312 W Main St,
Waverly TN 37185-
1513. 615/296-4005.

George W. Hussey & Co. Realty
515 Two Mile Pkwy,

Goodlettsville TN
37072-2011.
615/859-9310.

Phillips Builders Inc.
2910 Kraft Dr,
Nashville TN 37204-
3619. 615/244-9600.

Roy H. Adams Rentals
2523 Syon Dr,
Memphis TN 38119-
7440. 901/761-4123.

First Management Services
333 Union St,
Nashville TN 37201-
1413. 615/244-8060.

LAND SUBDIVIDERS AND DEVELOPERS

Hollis Management Group
5819 Old Harding Rd,
Nashville TN 37205-
3619. 615/352-7604.

Tayloe-Turley Development
985 Reddoch Cv,
Memphis TN 38119-
3614. 901/767-3424.

The Stellar Companies Inc.
900 S Gay St,
Knoxville TN 37902.

For more information on career opportunities in real estate:

Associations

INSTITUTE OF REAL ESTATE MANAGEMENT
430 North Michigan Avenue, P.O. Box 109025, Chicago IL 60610-9025. 312/661-1930. Dedicated to educating and identifying real estate managers who are committed to meeting the needs of real estate owners and investors.

INTERNATIONAL ASSOCIATION OF CORPORATE REAL ESTATE EXECUTIVES
440 Columbia Drive, Suite 100,

West Palm Beach FL 33409. 407/683-8111. An international association of real estate brokers.

Magazines

JOURNAL OF PROPERTY MANAGEMENT
Institute of Real Estate Management, 430 North Michigan Avenue, Chicago IL 60610. 312/661-1930.

NATIONAL REAL ESTATE INVESTOR
6151 Powers Ferry Road, Atlanta GA 30339. 404/955-2500.

RETAIL

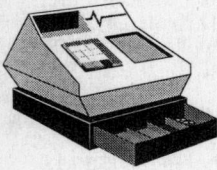

The '90s have been turbulent times for the retail industry. During the early years of the decade, the industry struggled as the national economy remained mired in recession. Now that the recession has technically been over for several years, one would think that shoppers would be flocking back to stores. Think again.

During 1995, sales rose by only 4.5 percent, and analysts expected about the same for '96. During 1995 alone, 15,000 retailers filed for Chapter 11 bankruptcy. Many of them, according to Business Week, were regional chains with outdated stores and merchandise.

The problem is simple: Consumers just aren't spending like they used to, and when customers insist on cut-rate bargains, only the giants, like Wal-Mart and Target, can survive. And not even all of them are safe from the threat of red ink. Kmart, the nation's third-largest chain, is closing 70 stores; while Bradlees and Ames are both having financial problems of their own.

AUTOZONE, INC.
123 South Front Street, Memphis TN 38103. 901/495-6500. **Contact:** Mr. William Poynter, Recruiting. **Description:** Autozone is a do-it-yourself retail auto parts chain specializing in foreign and domestic parts. **Common positions include:** Retail Executive; Retail Manager; Retail Sales Worker. **Benefits:** Dental Insurance; Disability Coverage; Employee Discounts; Life Insurance; Medical Insurance; Pension Plan; Stock Option. **Corporate headquarters location:** This Location. **Listed on:** New York Stock Exchange. **Number of employees at this location:** 850. **Number of employees nationwide:** 17,400.

CATHERINE'S STORES CORPORATION
3742 Lamar Avenue, Memphis TN 38118. 901/363-3900. **Contact:** Betty Jewett, Vice President of Human Resources. **Description:** Catherine's Stores Corporation is a specialty retailer of women's large-size clothing and accessories, operating 375 stores in 37 states. The company operates four store concepts. The Catherine's division emphasizes both career and casual fashions, and has 169 locations in 30 states. Added Dimensions, which has 85 stores in 15 states, focuses on career-oriented fashions that appeal to the over 35-years-old customer. PS Plus Sizes, Plus Savings is the corporation's "value oriented" division, focusing on affordable career and casual merchandise in its 87 locations. The Answer, which has 34 stores in 11 states, is also a "value oriented" store, but appeals to more career-minded customers. **Common positions include:** Accountant/Auditor; Advertising Clerk; Buyer; Clerical Supervisor; Credit Manager; Customer Service Representative; Economist/Market Research Analyst; Human Resources Specialist; Property and Real Estate Manager; Public Relations Specialist; Technical Writer/Editor. **Educational backgrounds include:** Accounting; Communications; Computer Science; Finance; Marketing. **Benefits:** 401K; Disability Coverage; Employee Discounts; Life Insurance; Medical Insurance; Profit Sharing. **Corporate headquarters location:** This Location. **Other**

U.S. locations: Nationwide. **Operations at this facility include:** Administration. **Listed on:** American Stock Exchange. **Number of employees at this location:** 450. **Number of employees nationwide:** 3,800.

DOLLAR GENERAL CORPORATION
104 Woodmont Boulevard, Suite 300, Nashville TN 37205. 615/783-2000. **Contact:** Ken Pynes. **Description:** Dollar General Corporation operates a chain of more than 2,059 general merchandise stores that feature quality merchandise at everyday low prices and serve low-, middle-, and fixed-income families. All of the company's stores are located in the United States, predominately in small towns in 24 midwestern and southeastern states. During 1995, Dollar General achieved its fourth consecutive year of double digit same-store sales growth, record sales, and record net income. In 1995, the company reinforced its accelerated growth plan by increasing the rate of store expansion, constructing a third distribution center and continuing to introduce appropriate information technology. **Corporate headquarters location:** This Location. **Number of employees nationwide:** 10,300.

FRED'S INC.
4300 New Getwell Road, Memphis TN 38118. 901/365-8880. **Contact:** Human Resources. **Description:** Fred's, Inc., founded in 1947, operates 170 discount general merchandise stores in nine states in the southeastern United States. The company also markets goods and services to 37 franchised stores. Fred's stores stock over 12,000 frequently purchased items that address the everyday needs of its customers, including nationally recognized brand name products, proprietary Fred's label products, and lower-priced off-brand products.

FREE SERVICE TIRE COMPANY
P.O. Box 1637, Johnson City TN 37605. 423/928-6476. **Fax:** 423/461-1617. **Contact:** Ginny Edmondson, Personnel Assistant. **Description:** Engaged in the retail and wholesale of tires and related products and the retail sale of automotive repair services. **Common positions include:** Automotive Mechanic/Body Repairer; Clerk; Credit Clerk and Authorizer; Management Trainee; Manufacturer's/Wholesaler's Sales Rep.; Store Manager. **Educational backgrounds include:** Business Administration. **Benefits:** Disability Coverage; Employee Discounts; Life Insurance; Medical Insurance; Profit Sharing. **Corporate headquarters location:** This Location. **Operations at this facility include:** Administration; Sales; Service. **Listed on:** Privately held. **Number of employees at this location:** 205.

GOODY'S FAMILY CLOTHING
400 Goody's Lane, Knoxville TN 37922-1900. 423/966-2000. **Contact:** Hazel Moxim, Human Resources. **Description:** Goody's Family Clothing, Inc. is a retailer of moderately priced fashion apparel for women, men and children. The company operates more than 170 stores in the southeastern and midwestern United States. Most of its stores are located in communities with populations of less than 75,000. **Corporate headquarters location:** This Location. **Other U.S. locations:** AL; AR; FL; GA; IL; IN; KY; MS; NC; OH; SC; TN; VA; WV. **Number of employees nationwide:** 4,337.

THE PATY COMPANY

P.O. Box 250, Piney Flats TN 37686. 423/538-8101. **Contact:** JoAnne Paty. **Description:** The Paty Company operates Paty Building Centers, a chain of family-owned home improvement supply stores. The company was founded in 1932 when the first store was opened in Elizabethton, TN. There are now nine locations spread throughout Tennessee, Virginia, and North Carolina. To service these stores, a 38-acre complex housing the corporate headquarters, a distribution warehouse, and a truss and pre-hung door manufacturing plant was built at this location. Paty also operates a lumber distribution yard, located on the East Tennessee Railway. The company stocks more than 15,000 items of materials and tools for building, maintaining, improving, decorating, and landscaping homes and other residential structures. **Other U.S. locations:** Asheville NC; Elizabethton TN; Greeneville TN; Johnson City TN; Kingsport TN; Morristown TN; Bristol VA; Duffield VA.

SERVICE MERCHANDISE COMPANY, INC.

P.O. Box 24600, Nashville TN 37202-4600. 615/660-3441. **Contact:** Deborah Daniel, Director, Human Resources. **Description:** Owns general merchandise retail stores with locations in 37 states, as well as catalog operations. The company sells a variety of products, including jewelry, cameras, toys, housewares, electronics, small appliances, and sporting goods. Service Merchandise operates 406 catalog showrooms and has distribution centers in Nevada, New York, Florida, Tennessee, and Texas. **Common positions include:** Accountant/Auditor; Aircraft Mechanic/Engine Specialist; Architect; Attorney; Bindery Worker; Budget Analyst; Buyer; CADD Operator; Claim Representative; Computer Operator; Computer Programmer; Computer Systems Analyst; Construction Contractor and Manager; Credit Manager; Employment Interviewer; Financial Manager; Graphic Artist; Human Resources Specialist; Industrial Engineer; Market Research Analyst; Printing Press Operator; Receptionist; Retail Sales Worker; Secretary; Stock Clerk; Store Manager; Systems Analyst; Travel Agent; Wholesale and Retail Buyer. **Educational backgrounds include:** Accounting; Art/Design; Business Administration; Computer Science; Marketing. **Benefits:** Dental Insurance; Disability Coverage; Employee Discounts; Life Insurance; Medical Insurance; Pension Plan; Profit Sharing; Savings Plan; Tuition Assistance. **Special Programs:** Internships. **Corporate headquarters location:** This Location. **Listed on:** New York Stock Exchange. **Number of employees at this location:** 1,400. **Number of employees nationwide:** 26,000.

TRACTOR SUPPLY COMPANY

320 Plus Park Boulevard, Nashville TN 37217. 615/366-4600. **Contact:** Brad Shramek, Director of Human Resources. **Description:** Since its founding as a mail-order tractor parts business in 1938, Tractor Supply Company has grown to be one of the largest operators of retail farm stores in America, with over 160 stores in 22 states. The company supplies the daily farming and maintenance needs of its target customers: hobby, part-time, and full-time farmers, as well as suburban customers, contractors, and tradesmen. Tractor Supply Company stores typically range in size from 10,000 to 12,500 square feet of inside selling space and use at least as many square feet of outside selling space. An average store displays a comprehensive selection of over 12,000 different products,

including farm maintenance products (fencing, tractor parts and accessories, agricultural spraying equipment, and tillage parts); animal products (specialty feeds, supplements, medicines, veterinary supplies, and livestock feeders); general maintenance products (air compressors, welders, generators, pumps, plumbing, and tools); lawn and garden products (riding mowers, tillers, and fertilizers); light truck equipment; and work clothing. The stores are located in rural communities and in outlying areas of large cities where farming is a significant factor in the local economy. Tractor Supply Company has been a public company since February 1994. Its stock is traded on the NASDAQ Stock Market under the symbol TSCO. **Corporate headquarters location:** This Location. **Number of employees nationwide:** 2,200.

IRA A. WATSON COMPANY
P.O. Box 22900, Knoxville TN 37933-0900. 423/690-6000. **Fax:** 423/691-5448. **Contact:** Bruce Kratz, Director Human Resources. **Description:** A value-priced family department store. **Common positions include:** Accountant/Auditor; Advertising Clerk; Buyer; Computer Programmer; Computer Systems Analyst; General Manager; Management Trainee; Wholesale and Retail Buyer. **Educational backgrounds include:** Accounting; Business Administration; Computer Science; Marketing. **Benefits:** 401K; Disability Coverage; Employee Discounts; Life Insurance; Medical Insurance; Tuition Assistance. **Corporate headquarters location:** This Location. **Other U.S. locations:** AL; IN; KY; MO; NC; SC; VA; WV. **Operations at this facility include:** Administration; Divisional Headquarters. **Listed on:** Privately held. **Number of employees at this location:** 170. **Number of employees nationwide:** 1,200.

WILLIAMS-SONOMA, INC.
4300 Concorde Road, Memphis TN 38118. 901/795-2625. **Contact:** Ben Bradley, Human Resources Director. **Description:** A retailer of cookware, serving equipment, and other specialty items. Products are sold both through retail stores and mail-order catalogs with the following brand names: Williams-Sonoma, Hold Everything, Gardener's Eden, Pottery Barn, and Chambers. This location is the company's distribution center. As such, it distributes merchandise to 300 stores and fulfills over 3 million packages generated from over 150 million catalog mailings a year.

Note: Because addresses and telephone numbers of smaller companies change rapidly, we recommend you call each company to verify the information below before inquiring about job opportunities. Mass mailings are not recommended.

Additional employers with under 250 employees:

VIDEO TAPE RENTAL

Blockbuster Video
6515 Poplar Ave, Memphis TN 38119-4873. 901/685-5322.

Blockbuster Video
2317 Murfreesboro Pike, Nashville TN 37217-3314. 615/361-8811.

Tower Records-Video Books
2400 W End Ave, Nashville TN 37203-1710. 615/327-3722.

Video Checkout
2405 Lebanon Rd, Nashville TN 37214-2412. 615/391-5424.

RETAIL LUMBER AND BUILDING MATERIALS

Lowe's of Tullahoma
2201 N Jackson St,

Tullahoma TN 37388-
2209. 615/455-1950.

Lowe's
7309 Chapman Hwy,
Knoxville TN 37920-
6611. 423/573-0031.

Lowe's Home Centers
5428 Highway 153,
Hixson TN 37343-
3721. 423/870-3214.

Lowe's of Clarksville
2710 Wilma Rudolph
Blvd, Clarksville TN
37040-5837.
615/648-4711.

**Lowe's of Johnson
City Inc.**
2805 N Roan St,
Johnson City TN
37601-1505.
423/282-8292.

Lowe's of Gallatin
450 Red River Rd,
Gallatin TN 37066-
3118. 615/452-2830.

Lowe's of Madison
10 Campbell Rd,
Madison TN 37115-
2655. 615/868-9810.

Lowe's of Crossville
Hwy 127 S, Crossville
TN 38555. 615/484-
1500.

CPI
621 E Old Hickory
Blvd, Madison TN
37115-3827.
615/865-0595.

United States Brick
830 Germantown
Pkwy, Cordova TN
38018. 901/755-
4041.

Home Depot Inc.
8101 Moores Ln,
Brentwood TN 37027-
8005. 615/370-0730.

Home Depot Inc.
4710 Centerline Dr,
Knoxville TN 37917-
1401. 423/637-9600.

**Huttig-Memphis Sash
& Door**
3886 Air Park St,
Memphis TN 38118-
6008. 901/795-3163.

**Pella Window & Door
Co.**
245 Sycamore St,
Jackson TN 38301-
6833. 901/423-4125.

Cayson Inc.
5869 US Highway 51
N, Millington TN
38053-8345.
901/353-1658.

Amarr Garage Doors
654 Eastern Star Rd,
Kingsport TN 37663-
3268. 423/349-7441.

Boral Bricks
1066 N Hollywood St,
Memphis TN 38108-
3202. 901/324-7134.

**Champion Concrete
Inc.**
2626 Zion Rd,
Columbia TN 38401-
6052. 615/381-7900.

Fencemaster
15 Bell Camp Rd,
Jackson TN 38301-
3632. 901/427-0492.

**PAINT, GLASS, AND
WALLPAPER STORES**

ACI Distribution
3808 Amnicola Hwy,
Chattanooga TN
37406-1003.
423/624-8814.

Glass Repair Service
7612 Nolensville Rd,
Nolensville TN 37135-
9458. 615/776-2029.

M&J Glass
202 Providence Blvd,
Clarksville TN 37042-
4324. 615/647-7290.

Safelite Auto Glass
6025 Knight Arnold
Road Ext, Memphis
TN 38115-3316.
901/362-9001.

Painter's Supply
C-3 New Smithville
Hwy, McMinnville TN
37110. 615/668-
7445.

The United Paint Place
6115 Stage Rd,
Bartlett TN 38134-
8313. 901/373-9301.

HARDWARE STORES

**Ace Hardware of
Ooltewah**
9231 Lee Hwy,
Ooltewah TN 37363-
8785. 423/238-6061.

**RETAIL NURSERIES
AND GARDEN
SUPPLY STORES**

**A-1 Underground
Sprinkling**
2901 Silverdale Rd,
Chattanooga TN
37421-1048.
423/499-0407.

**Pryor Implement
Company**
2321 US Highway 45
Byp S, Trenton TN
38382-4302.
901/855-2123.

**Lauderdale Farmers
Co-Op**
225 N Front, Halls TN
38040. 901/836-
5912.

**MOBILE HOME
DEALERS**

**Oakwood Mobile
Homes Inc.**
6401 Clinton Hwy,
Knoxville TN 37912-
1112. 423/947-5216.

**DEPARTMENT
STORES**

Kmart Stores
2288 Gunbarrel Rd,
Chattanooga TN
37421-2609.
423/855-7970.

Wal-Mart Discount Cities
354 Frey St, Ashland City TN 37015-1734. 615/792-7782.

Wal-Mart Discount Cities
100 S Dupree St, Brownsville TN 38012-3217. 901/772-9551.

Wal-Mart Discount Cities
US Hwy 27, Oneida TN 37841. 423/569-6228.

Wal-Mart Discount Cities
242 Cumberland Crossing, La Follette TN 37766. 423/566-5318.

Dillard Department Stores
3360 Austin Peay Hwy, Memphis TN 38128-3802. 901/377-4020.

Dillard Department Stores
3000 N Mall Rd, Knoxville TN 37924-2009. 423/524-6040.

Dillard Department Stores
5248 Hickory Hollow Pkwy, Antioch TN 37013-3004. 615/731-6600.

Dillard Department Stores
1796 Galleria Blvd, Franklin TN 37067-1601. 615/771-7101.

Dollar General Store
122 US Highway 77 E, Newbern TN 38059-1153. 901/627-3366.

Dollar General Store
730 Lynn Garden Dr, Kingsport TN 37660-5608. 423/245-8100.

Target Stores
18 Northgate Park, Chattanooga TN 37415-6948. 423/875-3100.

Target Stores
8040 Ray Mears Blvd, Knoxville TN 37919-5480. 423/693-2203.

Target Stores
1251 Wesley Dr, Memphis TN 38116-6425. 901/332-2270.

Factory Outlet
404 Highway 52 E, Portland TN 37148-1441. 615/325-4215.

Windsor Shirt
2655 Teaster Ln, Pigeon Forge TN 37863-3278. 423/429-1886.

London Fog Factory Store
Outlets Limited Mall, Murfreesboro TN 37129. 615/895-4473.

Belz Factory Outlet World
2655 Teaster Ln, Pigeon Forge TN 37863-3278. 423/453-3503.

Leather Loft
Belz Factory Outlet Mall, Pigeon Forge TN 37863. 423/428-3688.

Old Time Pottery Inc.
P.O. Box 1838, Murfreesboro TN 37133-1838. 615/890-2100.

Potters Discount Supply
Pine Haven, Jamestown TN 38556. 615/879-4566.

Belk Department Store
2021 N Highland Old Hickory Ma, Jackson TN 38305. 901/668-1414.

Uptons
50 Old Hickory Blvd, Jackson TN 38305-2599. 901/423-0387.

Parisian Inc.
2000 Hamilton Place Blvd, Chattanooga TN 37421-6000. 423/855-7710.

Proffitt's
Hamilton Place Mall, Chattanooga TN 37421. 423/899-3148.

Goldsmith's Department Store
1300 E Shelby Dr, Memphis TN 38116-7124. 901/348-1271.

VARIETY STORES

C'Ville Sales
1815 Highway 100, Centerville TN 37033-9427. 615/729-9563.

Dollar General Stores
166 W Main St, Camden TN 38320-1786. 901/584-4603.

Dollar Tree
Northgate Mall, Chattanooga TN 37415. 423/875-0263.

Everything's A Dollar
1631 Gallatin Rd N, Madison TN 37115-2151. 615/868-8873.

Everything's A Dollar
253 N Seven Oaks Dr, Knoxville TN 37922-2371. 423/693-0216.

Fred's Discount Store
333 S Main St, McKenzie TN 38201-2607. 901/352-5721.

Only One Dollar
East Towne Mall, Knoxville TN 37924. 423/974-9158.

MISC. GENERAL MERCHANDISE STORES

Maybery's Mercantile & Salvage
25 Pike Hill Rd,
McMinnville TN
37110-1017.
615/473-1055.

GROCERY AND CONVENIENCE STORES

Piggly Wiggly Supermarket
211 Waverly Plz,
Waverly TN 37185-
1533. 615/296-7781.

HG Hill Stores Inc.
235 Franklin Rd,
Brentwood TN 37027-
5214. 615/377-3506.

Big John's Household
101 Litton Rd, Oneida
TN 37841-3017.
423/569-6355.

Brass Lantern Market
2290 Pulaski Hwy,
Lawrenceburg TN
38464-7423.
615/762-8134.

Roadrunner Markets Inc.
853 Old State Route
34, Jonesborough TN
37659-6060.
423/753-5601.

Save A Lot Discount Food Store
17 N Maple St,
Hohenwald TN 38462-
1416. 615/796-2333.

C Mart
2919 Bloomingdale
Pike, Kingsport TN
37660-1958.
423/288-8202.

C Mart
4001 Memorial Blvd,
Kingsport TN 37664-
2837. 423/246-6746.

Celina Save-A-Lot
5290 Burkesville Hwy,
Celina TN 38551-
5288. 615/243-2357.

Compton's Foodland
2900 W End Ave,
Nashville TN 37203-
1316. 615/327-4187.

Cooke's Food Store
3430 Keith St NW,
Cleveland TN 37312-
3720. 423/472-5034.

The Red Food Stores
Highway 27, Soddy
Daisy TN 37379.
423/332-3413.

Crook's Supermarkets Inc.
2711 Franklin Rd,
Nashville TN 37204-
3009. 615/383-2794.

Delta Express
111 Luyben Hills Rd,
Kingston Springs TN
37082-8904.
615/952-9437.

Kwik Sak Inc.
611 W Main St,
Gallatin TN 37066-
5417. 615/452-7480.

EW James and Sons Supermarket
310 E Main St,
Huntingdon TN
38344-4209.
901/986-3744.

EW James and Sons Supermarket
677 W Church St,
Lexington TN 38351-
1711. 901/968-8375.

Weigel's Farm Stores
411 E Summit Hill Dr,
Knoxville TN 37915-
1028. 423/522-9179.

Favorite Market
8107 Standifer Gap
Rd, Chattanooga TN
37421-1223.
423/892-6502.

Favorite Market
1322 Smithville Hwy,
McMinnville TN
37110-1401.
615/473-6427.

Food City
East Gate Plaza,
Rogersville TN 37857.
423/272-2745.

Food Country USA
6766 W Andrew
Johnson Hwy,
Mosheim TN 37818-
3836. 423/422-9088.

Food Lion Inc.
860 N Ellington Pkwy,
Lewisburg TN 37091-
2225. 615/359-7672.

Food Lion Inc.
1141 Volunteer Pkwy,
Bristol TN 37620-
4619. 423/764-4188.

Food Lion Inc.
691 Emory Valley Rd,
Oak Ridge TN 37830-
7752. 423/483-8515.

Food Lion Inc.
1237 Huntsville Hwy,
Fayetteville TN
37334-3617.
615/433-4496.

Food Rite Supermarket
290 S Walnut Bend
Rd, Suite 6, Cordova
TN 38018-7280.
901/756-9986.

Food Max
4976 Highway 58,
Chattanooga TN
37416-1878.
423/892-7552.

Foodmax
4670 Lebanon Rd,
Hermitage TN 37076-
1314. 615/391-3495.

Foodmax
5527 Edmondson
Pike, Nashville TN
37211-5808.
615/834-0056.

Front Runner Market
1101 S Willow Ave,
Cookeville TN 38501-
4156. 615/526-2886.

Gene Stimson's Inc.
1355 Lynnfield Rd,
Suite 194, Memphis
TN 38119-5883.
901/761-2906.

Mapco Express
6193 Mount Moriah
Road Ext, Memphis
TN 38115-2748.
901/368-0344.

Mapco Express
2201 Whites Creek
Pike, Nashville TN
37207-4831.
615/227-1383.

Mapco Express
585 Stewarts Ferry
Pike, Nashville TN
37214-3414.
615/889-1556.

Mapco Express
3410 W End Ave,
Nashville TN 37203-
1036. 615/385-2919.

Mapco Express
1500 Lebanon Rd,
Nashville TN 37210-
3203. 615/889-8762.

Mapco Express
1507 21st Ave S,
Nashville TN 37212-
3101. 615/329-2003.

Mapco Express
8009 Moores Ln,
Brentwood TN 37027-
8005. 615/370-3304.

HG Hill Stores Inc.
213 W Main St,
Hendersonvlle TN
37075-3306.
615/824-3188.

Hartsville Foodtown
102 McMurry Blvd,
Hartsville TN 37074-
1108. 615/374-2208.

Hays Foods
419 E College St,
Jackson TN 38301-
6321. 901/422-6432.

**Henning Dillard
Grocery**
743 Williams Switch

Rd, Ripley TN 38063-
7807. 901/635-9936.

Houchens Market
511 S Broadway,
Portland TN 37148-
1506. 615/325-4104.

Jim Dandy Market
1011 Cherry Ave,
Nashville TN 37203-
4752. 615/256-3680.

Jim Dandy Market
728 Memorial Blvd,
Murfreesboro TN
37129-2731.
615/895-4110.

Jim Dandy Market
1883 Almaville Rd,
Smyrna TN 37167-
5765. 615/355-1024.

Kroger Co.
201 Forks of The
River Pkwy, Sevierville
TN 37862. 423/428-
1544.

Kroger Co.
4501 Asheville Hwy,
Knoxville TN 37914-
3607. 423/546-4728.

Kroger Food Stores
9050 US Highway 64,
Arlington TN 38002-
9711. 901/371-0405.

**Par Mart Convenience
Store**
3701 Nolensville Rd,
Nashville TN 37211-
3301. 615/333-1608.

Kwik Sak
904 SE Broad St,
Murfreesboro TN
37130-5065.
615/896-9861.

Lakeview Market
7114 Highway 49 E,
Springfield TN 37172-
6628. 615/382-1338.

Red Food Stores
1715 W Broadway
Ave, Maryville TN
37801-5509.
423/981-4310.

Save-A-Lot
102 E Main St,
Livingston TN 38570-
1928. 615/823-1072.

Save-A-Lot
407 Mulberry St,
Selmer TN 38375-
2307. 901/645-7215.

Piggly Wiggly
378 S Bells St, Alamo
TN 38001-1927.
901/696-5951.

Megamarket
940 W Poplar Ave,
Collierville TN 38017-
2546. 901/854-0632.

Megamarket
1627 Poplar Ave,
Memphis TN 38104-
2568. 901/725-6861.

Mr. Zip Inc. of Tenn
9091 Hiwassee St
NW, Charleston TN
37310. 423/336-
5946.

Wholesale Food Outlet
316 W Old Andrew
Johnson Hwy,
Jefferson Cty TN
37760-5200.
423/475-1023.

Warehouse Foods
805 Pennell Ln,
Dyersburg TN 38024-
1612. 901/285-7011.

Super Valu
270 E Court Ave,
Selmer TN 38375-
2304. 901/645-3244.

The Red Food Stores
6723 Ringgold Rd,
East Ridge TN 37412-
4229. 423/855-3010.

**Creech Quesnel
Supermarkets**
3485 Poplar Ave,
Suite 232, Memphis
TN 38111-4633.
901/458-5201.

**Par Mart Convenience
Store**
150 Franklin Rd,

Nashville TN 37201.
615/373-3425.

Raceway Food Mart
943 Louisville Hwy,
Goodlettsville TN
37072-1106.
615/859-4505.

C Mart
1001 S Roan St,
Johnson City TN
37601-6835.
423/929-1829.

Delta Express NBR
2732 York Rd,
Pleasant View TN
37146-9070.
615/746-8325.

Hunter's Market
1505 Verona Caney
Rd, Lewisburg TN
37091-6401.
615/270-6656.

**Speedway
Convenience Store**
3710 Gallatin Rd,
Nashville TN 37216-
2608. 615/227-0884.

Starmart
723 Lafayette Rd, Red
Boiling Springs TN
37150-2016.
615/699-3479.

Minit Mart
1008 N Washington
Ave, Cookeville TN
38501-1834.
615/526-9366.

Bull Markets Inc.
510 US Highway 51
S, Covington TN
38019-2426.
901/476-8348.

**Appco Convenience
Center**
149 S Broadway St,
Johnson City TN
37601-4958.
423/929-9211.

Volunteer Market
609 Beersheba St,
McMinnville TN
37110-2733.
615/473-4184.

Food Lion
4707 Dayton Blvd,
Chattanooga TN
37415-2103.
423/870-3555.

Red Food Store
130 The Acres,
Lewisburg TN 37091.
615/359-7209.

MISC. FOOD STORES

**Honeybaked Ham
Company**
5017 Hixson Pike,
Hixson TN 37343-
3952. 423/875-5300.

Southern Milk Sales
1155 Haley Rd,
Murfreesboro TN
37129-4950.
615/893-5426.

RETAIL BAKERIES

Colonial Bakery Store
1217 Congress Pkwy
NW, Athens TN
37303-4906.
423/745-4860.

**Colonial Baking Co.
Thrift Store**
2010 Wilma Rudolph
Blvd, Clarksville TN
37040-6620.
615/647-2596.

**Dolly Madison Thrift
Store**
1649 S Lee Hwy,
Cleveland TN 37311-
7325. 423/559-0917.

Flowers Thrift Store
400 Belmont Ave,
Shelbyville TN 37160-
4002. 615/684-9477.

Good Earth Bread Co.
6803 Mundel Rd,
Knoxville TN 37918-
9744. 423/689-0956.

AUTO DEALERS

**Kenworth of
Tennessee Inc.**
Spence Lane At I-40,
Nashville TN 37210.
615/366-5454.

**Mark Hoppe Chevy
Pontiac Buick**
17455 US Highway
64, Somerville TN
38068-6162.
901/465-3501.

**Tom Bannen
Chevrolet-Geo**
2340 Gallatin Rd N,
Madison TN 37115-
2008. 615/851-8022.

**Bill Heard Chevrolet
Geo Inc.**
5333 Hickory Hollow
Pkwy, Antioch TN
37013-3109.
615/731-3000.

**Hippodrome Dodge
Inc.**
1212 Broadway,
Nashville TN 37203-
3118. 615/248-5100.

Bell Ford
5500 Charlotte Pike,
Nashville TN 37209-
3211. 615/297-4111.

Crown Ford
646 Thompson Ln,
Nashville TN 37204-
3638. 615/244-3615.

Schilling Jeep Eagle
5390 Fox Plaza Dr,
Memphis TN 38115-
1502. 901/366-7222.

**Beaman Lincoln-
Mercury Inc.**
2300 Franklin Rd,
Nashville TN 37204-
2225. 615/383-8080.

Lexus of Kingsport
2527 E Stone Dr,
Kingsport TN 37660-
5858. 423/224-2270.

Lexus of Nashville
1514 Gallatin Rd N,
Madison TN 37115-
2117. 615/868-4400.

**Peterbilt of Nashville
Inc.**
115 Haywood Ln,
Nashville TN 37211.
615/833-6050.

Peterbilt of Knoxville Inc.
5218 Rutledge Pike, Knoxville TN 37924-2753. 423/546-9553.

Filmar Racing Enterprises
2602 Westwood Dr, Nashville TN 37204-2710. 615/386-9636.

Anderson Imports
128 W Stone Dr, Kingsport TN 37660-3221. 423/247-4135.

Dixie Auto Sales
1928 Highway 46 S, Dickson TN 37055-2754. 615/446-1121.

Sunbelt Truck Center
I-40 Exit 212, Nashville TN 37210. 615/244-8900.

CONSUMER SUPPLY STORES

All Things Audio
1712 W End Ave, Nashville TN 37203-2602. 615/329-3551.

Advance Auto Parts
1121 Volunteer Pkwy, Bristol TN 37620-4619. 423/764-4147.

Genuine Parts Co.
801 E Georgia Ave, Memphis TN 38126-4107. 901/774-1121.

Chief Auto Parts
1397 Jackson Ave, Memphis TN 38107-4431. 901/276-7091.

DPI Auto Parts
192 Washington St, Collierville TN 38017-2621. 901/853-6422.

Duraliner of Nashville
85 Cleveland St, Nashville TN 37207-5426. 615/262-0100.

Progressive Custom Wheels
819 Cowan St, Nashville TN 37207-5623. 615/726-0092.

KSG Industries Inc.
1418 Antioch Pke, Nashville TN 37211. 615/832-7562.

Motor Supply Company
922 N Central St, Knoxville TN 37917-6408. 423/524-0345.

NTW
5174 American Way, Memphis TN 38115-1500. 901/363-0090.

Universal Tire Inc.
5407 Middlebrook Pike, Knoxville TN 37921-5977. 423/588-5165.

NTW
5065 Covington Way, Memphis TN 38134-5653. 901/382-3332.

Sears Roebuck and Co.
2011 N Roan St, Johnson City TN 37601-3130. 423/282-2331.

Universal Tire Inc.
1201 Demonbreun St, Nashville TN 37203-3109. 615/244-9611.

Tire Warehouse
485 Craighead St, Nashville TN 37204-2333. 615/298-2729.

Brad Ragan Tire & Appliance
806 US Highway 51 N, Covington TN 38019-2039. 901/476-0097.

APPAREL AND ACCESSORY STORES

Memphis Group
3900 Willow Lake Blvd, Memphis TN 38118-7019. 901/362-8600.

Aviall Inc.
5851 Advantage Cv, Memphis TN 38141-8212. 901/362-6710.

University Trailer Sales
1610 US Highway 72, Collierville TN 38017-5508. 901/854-1176.

Boot Country
5360 Hickory Hollow Pkwy, Antioch TN 37013-3128. 615/731-7722.

Britches Great Outdoors
The Mall At Green Hills, Nashville TN 37215. 615/269-0043.

County Seat
1000 Two Mile Pkwy, Goodlettsville TN 37072-2402. 615/859-7237.

County Seat Stores
Hickory Hollow Mall, Antioch TN 37013. 615/731-5065.

Gentlemen's Wear-House
3536 Canada Rd, Arlington TN 38002-9722. 901/388-7090.

Gus Mayer Shoe Salon
2159 Green Hills Village Dr, Nashville TN 37215-2601. 615/383-4771.

Lansky's Big & Tall
169 S 2nd St, Memphis TN 38103-3709. 901/366-4200.

Lottie's Shoes
8025 Kingston Pike, Knoxville TN 37919-5556. 423/690-7501.

Rack Room Shoes
3536 Canada Rd, Arlington TN 38002-9722. 901/377-1166.

The Sansabelt Shop
Mall of Memphis,

Memphis TN 38118.
901/366-0377.

The Shoe Show
1720 Old Fort Pkwy,
Murfreesboro TN
37129-3382.
615/890-5036.

Webster Men's Wear
2100 Hamilton Place
Blvd, Chattanooga TN
37421. 423/892-
9549.

Added Dimensions
5252 Hickory Hollow
Pkwy, Antioch TN
37013. 615/731-
6440.

Added Dimensions
East Towne Mall,
Knoxville TN 37924.
423/522-3710.

Holliday Fashions
1223 E Shelby Dr,
Memphis TN 38116-
7123. 901/345-2818.

Lerner Shops
925 Bell Rd, Antioch
TN 37013-3103.
615/731-3253.

Maurice's
1410 Sparta St,
McMinnville TN
37110-1367.
615/473-4362.

Northern Reflections
2011 N Roan St,
Johnson City TN
37601-3130.
423/283-0227.

One Price Clothing
3049 Dickerson Rd,
Suite 106, Nashville
TN 37207-2968.
615/227-3407.

Rave
1000 Two Mile Pkwy,
Goodlettsville TN
37072-2402.
615/859-6592.

Rave
3032 N Mall Rd #B,

Knoxville TN 37924-
2057. 423/522-4871.

Simply 6
5450 Highway 153,
Hixson TN 37343-
3791. 423/870-3970.

Simply 6
110 S Dupree St,
Brownsville TN
38012-3217.
901/772-6477.

Sizes Unlimited
1745 Galleria Blvd,
Franklin TN 37067-
1624. 615/771-7082.

Stuarts/Stuarts Plus
3078 Village Shops
Dr, Memphis TN
38138-7900.
901/759-0144.

**The Body Shop for
Women**
3013 N Mall Rd,
Knoxville TN 37924-
2010. 423/521-7089.

The Finer Things
120 Franklin St,
Clarksville TN 37040-
3459. 615/551-9801.

The Gap
1800 Galleria Blvd,
Franklin TN 37067-
1605. 615/771-7315.

**Wearhouse of
Fashions**
6166 Macon Rd,
Memphis TN 38134-
7502. 901/386-7661.

Topkapi
2126 Abbott Martin
Rd, Nashville TN
37215-2617.
615/383-6589.

What's Hot
2055 West St, Suite
12, Memphis TN
38138-0809.
901/755-4179.

Tanner Companies Inc.
Warehouse Row 1110
Market St,
Chattanooga TN

37402. 423/265-
6702.

The Men's Wearhouse
7686 Poplar Ave,
Memphis TN 38138-
3939. 901/753-7886.

Welcome Home
1110 Market St, Suite
Fc3, Chattanooga TN
37402-2866.
423/265-2039.

Kay Uniforms
1307 Chilhowee Ave,
Knoxville TN 37917-
7709. 423/522-3361.

Kay Uniforms
3216 E Stone Dr,
Kingsport TN 37660-
6710. 423/288-5682.

**Aus-Tex
Manufacturing Co.**
400 W Church St,
Greeneville TN 37745-
3277. 423/638-2881.

**Tennessee River Mill
Outlet**
Ft Crockett Village,
Lawrenceburg TN
38464. 615/762-
6260.

**Tennessee River Mill
Store**
2500 Pillow Dr,
Columbia TN 38401-
4375. 615/381-0748.

**Wilson's The Leather
Experts**
5252 Hickory Hollow
Pkwy, Antioch TN
37013. 615/731-
5883.

SHOE STORES

Shoe Show
6520 Chapman Hwy,
Knoxville TN 37920-
6570. 423/579-5614.

Shoe Show
2021 N Highland Ave,
Jackson TN 38305-
4949. 901/668-5458.

FURNITURE STORES

Potters Furniture Warehouse
Hwy 52 W,
Jamestown TN
38556. 615/879-5846.

DT McCall & Sons
601 Water St,
Carthage TN 37030.
615/735-0165.

Fleming Fine Furniture
4791 Burbank Rd,
Memphis TN 38118-6302. 901/365-9216.

Forsythe Oak Outlet
206 E Reelfoot Ave,
Suite 4, Union City TN
38261-5700.
901/885-5777.

Furniture Liquidation Center Antioch
1805 Antioch Pike,
Antioch TN 37013-3311. 615/832-4905.

Grand Piano & Furniture Co.
300 Broad St,
Kingsport TN 37660-4206. 423/246-1333.

Heilig-Meyers Furniture
1030 US Highway 45
Byp, Jackson TN
38301-3256.
901/668-0496.

Heilig-Meyers Furniture
783 W Poplar Ave,
Collierville TN 38017-2543. 901/854-0112.

Royal Discount Furniture
122 S Main St,
Memphis TN 38103-3621. 901/527-6407.

Rhodes Furniture Co.
15115 Old Hickory
Blvd, Nashville TN
37211-6301.
615/833-0207.

Welcome Home
307 River Rock Blvd,
Murfreesboro TN
37129-4819.
615/895-3206.

Yellow Gables Home Furnishings
Hampton Plaza,
Clarksville TN 37040.
615/645-9894.

Baby Superstore
1580 Gallatin Rd N,
Madison TN 37115-2124. 615/860-2229.

MISC. HOME FURNISHINGS STORES

Color Tile Supermart
5072 Summer Ave,
Memphis TN 38122-4408. 901/682-8401.

Wallpaper For Less
Campbell Plaza
Shopping Center,
Columbia TN 38401.
615/380-9255.

Binswanger Glass Co.
7215 Winchester Rd,
Memphis TN 38125-2149. 901/757-8336.

HOUSEHOLD APPLIANCE STORES

Flamegas
1430 Old Belfast Rd,
Lewisburg TN 37091-3571. 615/359-1987.

Sears Outlet Store
640 Thompson Ln,
Nashville TN 37204-3608. 615/742-1237.

CONSUMER ELECTRONICS STORES

Super Dish Satellite Systems
316 S Anderson St,
Tullahoma TN 37388-3839. 615/454-1534.

COMPUTER AND SOFTWARE STORES

Radio Shack
Fort Henry Mall,
Kingsport TN 37664.
423/246-3022.

Tennessee Com Inc.
6213 Charlotte Pike,
Nashville TN 37209-3033. 615/352-1006.

Wesco Distribution Inc.
2606 Summer Ave,
Memphis TN 38112-2610. 901/458-7591.

RECORD AND PRERECORDED TAPE STORES

Pop Tunes Record Shops
797 W Poplar Ave,
Collierville TN 38017-2543. 901/854-5418.

Sam Goody
7620 Highway 70 S,
Nashville TN 37221-1700. 615/662-2438.

Waves Music
The Mall At Green
Hills, Nashville TN
37215. 615/269-9288.

DRUG STORES

Eckerd Drugs
Donelson Plaza Shpg
Ctr, Nashville TN
37214. 615/883-8511.

Wal-Mart Discount Cities
Jacksboro, La Follette
TN 37766. 423/566-5323.

Big B Drugs
1109 Huntsville Hwy,
Fayetteville TN
37334-3615.
615/433-7112.

Fred's Pharmacy
16280 US Highway
64, Somerville TN
38068-6152.
901/465-3657.

Baptist Pharmacy
Mid-State Medical
Center, Nashville TN
37203. 615/329-
5940.

USED MERCHANDISE STORES

Todd Factory Outlet
1280 US Highway 51
S, Ripley TN 38063-
5540. 901/635-4501.

SPORTING GOODS STORES

Champ's Sports
Bellevue Mall,
Nashville TN 37221.
615/662-7419.

Champ's Sports
Oak Ridge Mall, Oak
Ridge TN 37830.
423/481-8312.

Hibbett Sports
Three Star Mall,
McMinnville TN
37110. 615/473-
2795.

Hibbett Sports
Dyersburg Mall,
Dyersburg TN 38024.
901/286-2918.

Score
3437 Raleigh Springs
Mall, Memphis TN
38128-3806.
901/385-0770.

Sports Fantasy
5252 Hickory Hollow
Pkwy, Antioch TN
37013. 615/731-
3102.

Toys R Us
1755 Galleria Blvd,
Franklin TN 37067-
1602. 615/771-7744.

BOOKSTORES

Books a Million Inc.
1789 Gallatin Rd N,
Madison TN 37115-
2122. 615/860-3133.

Davis-Kidd Booksellers
113 N Peters Rd,
Knoxville TN 37923-
4908. 423/690-0136.

Family Bookstores
2162 Gallatin Rd N,
Madison TN 37115-
2004. 615/851-0145.

Waldenbooks
Paddock Place,
Nashville TN 37205.
615/352-6879.

Wallace's Book Store
1100 Liberty St,
Knoxville TN 37919-
2327. 423/637-7073.

STATIONERY AND OFFICE SUPPLY STORES

Officemax
2020 Gunbarrel Rd,
Chattanooga TN
37421-2663.
423/894-0458.

Officemax
1460 Union Ave,
Memphis TN 38104-
6729. 901/725-8180.

JEWELRY STORES

Gold Silver & Diamond Exchange
201 S Water Ave,
Nashville TN 37203.
615/320-6204.

Kay Jewelers
Oak Ridge Mall, Oak
Ridge TN 37830.
423/482-2321.

Sam's Fine Jewelry
125 John R. Rice
Blvd, Murfreesboro TN
37129-4165.
615/849-8414.

HOBBY, TOY, AND GAME SHOPS

Michaels-Arts & Crafts
6015 Stage Rd,
Bartlett TN 38134-
8311. 901/373-6151.

Michaels-Arts & Crafts
2174 Gallatin Rd N,
Madison TN 37115-
2004. 615/859-0196.

Old America Store
5027 Hixson Pike,
Hixson TN 37343-
3924. 423/875-4707.

Kay-Bee Toys
1800 Galleria Blvd,
Franklin TN 37067-
1605. 615/771-7675.

Toy Liquidators
3536 Canada Rd,
Arlington TN 38002-
9722. 901/386-4926.

GIFT, NOVELTY, AND SOUVENIR SHOPS

The Paper Factory
Carolina Pottery Outlet
Ctr, Blountville TN
37617. 423/323-
0522.

Kirkland's
4544 Poplar Ave,
Memphis TN 38117-
7510. 901/767-3897.

Paradies Shop
1 Terminal Dr,
Nashville TN 37214-
4110. 615/275-1155.

Stop Inc.
9888 Roberts Rd,
Baxter TN 38544.
615/858-3160.

Kirkland's
5252 Hickory Hollow
Pkwy, Antioch TN
37013. 615/731-
1003.

Visitors Center Gift Shop
2 Broad St,
Chattanooga TN

37402-1022.
423/266-7070.

Welcome Home
2850 Parkway, Pigeon
Forge TN 37863-
3347. 423/429-3287.

**LUGGAGE AND
LEATHER GOODS
STORES**

The Wallet Works
Genesis Rd, Crossville
TN 38555. 615/456-
0901.

Alan Bruce Bags Etc.
Belz Factory Outlet
Mall Annex, Sevierville
TN 37862. 423/428-
6111.

**SEWING SUPPLIES
STORES**

Laura Ashley
2129 Abbott Martin
Rd, Nashville TN
37215-2615.
615/383-0131.

Piece Goods Shop
107 Broyles St,
Johnson City TN
37601-2517.
423/282-9933.

**CATALOG AND MAIL-
ORDER HOUSES**

Express Fulfillment
2515 E 43rd St,
Chattanooga TN
37407-2619.
423/867-9081.

Shop at Home Inc.
5210 Schubert Rd
#12600, Knoxville TN
37912-3857.
423/688-0300.

FUEL DEALERS

Edwards Oil Company
105 Helton Dr,
Lawrenceburg TN
38464-2253.
615/762-5531.

S. TN Oil Co. Inc.
Industrial Park,
Lawrenceburg TN
38464. 615/762-
9600.

Amerigas
5201 Lamar Ave,
Memphis TN 38118-
7807. 901/363-4600.

Garland Coal Company
300 Forest Park Blvd,
Knoxville TN 37919-
5127. 423/588-9711.

**OPTICAL GOODS
STORES**

Royal Optical
7600 Kingston Pike,
Knoxville TN 37919-
5603. 423/691-8500.

Eye Clinic PC
138 Houston Ave,
Selmer TN 38375-
2127. 901/645-7255.

**Wells & Spivey Eye
Clinic**
2381 E Cedar Ave,
McKenzie TN 38201-
2222. 901/352-2473.

Eyear Optical
475 Highway 70 S,
Crossville TN 38555-
5105. 615/456-2420.

**Cole National Optical
Shop**
Governors Square
Mall, Clarksville TN

37040. 615/552-
7446.

Megamarket Optical
719 Thompson Ln,
Nashville TN 37204-
3624. 615/385-1515.

**MISC. RETAIL
STORES**

Iron Age Safety Shoe
331 Wilhagan Rd,
Nashville TN 37217-
1145. 615/367-1630.

**American Feed & Farm
Supplies**
309 Driftwood St,
Nashville TN 37210-
2103. 615/259-2033.

Pass Pets
Cool Springs Galleria,
Franklin TN 37064.
615/771-7616.

Pet Specialties Inc.
3 Maryland Farms,
Suite 328, Brentwood
TN 37027-5005.
615/377-3790.

Brooks Brothers
7615 W Farmington
Ave, Suite 26,
Germantown TN
38138-2820.
901/759-0479.

The Sunglass Shop
4419 Mall of
Memphis, Memphis
TN 38118-8408.
901/363-2414.

**The Sunglass Co.
Outlet Store**
2655 Teaster Ln,
Pigeon Forge TN
37863-3278.
423/429-8799.

For more information on career opportunities in retail:

Associations

**INTERNATIONAL ASSOCIATION
OF CHAIN STORES**
3800 Moor Place, Alexandria VA
22305. 703/549-4525.

**INTERNATIONAL COUNCIL OF
SHOPPING CENTERS**
665 Fifth Avenue, New York NY
10022. 212/421-8181. Offers
conventions, research, education,
a variety of publications, and
awards programs.

NATIONAL AUTOMOTIVE DEALERS ASSOCIATION
8400 Westpark Drive, McLean VA 22102. 703/821-7000.

NATIONAL INDEPENDENT AUTOMOTIVE DEALERS ASSOCIATION
2521 Brown Boulevard, Suite 100, Arlington TX 76006. 817/640-3838.

NATIONAL RETAIL FEDERATION
325 7th Street NW, Suite 1000, Washington DC 20004. 202/783-7971. Provides information services, industry outlooks, and a variety of educational opportunities and publications.

Directories

AUTOMOTIVE NEWS MARKET DATA BOOK
Automotive News, Crain Communication, 1400 Woodbridge Avenue, Detroit MI 48207-3187. 313/446-6000.

STONE, CLAY, GLASS, AND CONCRETE PRODUCTS

Growth in stone, clay, glass, concrete, and related materials is closely tied to the success of the construction industry. On the one hand, analysts believe that the fortunes of the construction industry should remain solid in the short term, despite the added pressure of an economy that has cooled from its torrid pace of growth in 1994 and early 1995. On the other hand, the longer-term forecast is for much slower growth, since infrastructure construction is dependent on declining local government budgets. In general, the stone, clay, glass, and concrete industry should see revenue growth of about 1 to 2 percent annually over the next few years.

AFG INDUSTRIES, INC.
P.O. Box 929, Kingsport TN 37662. 423/229-7200. **Contact:** Rick Stapleton, Director of Human Resources. **Description:** AFG Industries, Inc. is a nationwide flat glass manufacturer. **Subsidiaries include:** American Flat Glass Distributors, Inc. (AFGD).

AMERICAN FLAT GLASS DISTRIBUTORS, INC. (AFGD)
2341 Beaver Creek Drive, Powell TN 37849. 423/938-2020. **Fax:** 423/947-2018. **Contact:** Tommy McNeil, Branch Manager. **Description:** Founded in the early 1960s, AFGD specializes in architectural insulated glass units and custom tempering. The company was originally founded as Southern Wholesale Glass, Inc. In 1983, AFG Industries, Inc. purchased Southern Wholesale Glass, Inc. and changed its name to American Flat Glass Distributors. Today, AFGD manufactures a complete line of insulated glass units for commercial and residential applications. Products include clear, tint, and reflective glass; wire glass; and equipment for the handling, storage, and transportation of glass. A customized order entry system allows orders to be processed upon receipt and shipped the following day. There are 19 AFGD locations throughout the United States in metropolitan areas, with the largest facilities at Marietta, GA and Opelousas, LA. **Common positions include:** Blue-Collar Worker Supervisor; Branch Manager; Clerical Supervisor; Credit Manager; Customer Service Representative; Industrial Engineer; Industrial Production Manager; Management Trainee; Manufacturer's/Wholesaler's Sales Rep.; Mechanical Engineer; Metallurgical Engineer; Operations/Production Manager. **Educational backgrounds include:** Business Administration; Engineering; Finance; Marketing; Sales. **Benefits:** 401K; Disability Coverage; Life Insurance; Medical Insurance; Profit Sharing; Savings Plan; Tuition Assistance. **Corporate headquarters location:** Atlanta GA. **Other U.S. locations:** Nationwide. **Subsidiaries include:** AFGD Canada. **Parent company:** AFG Industries, Inc. **Operations at this facility include:** Manufacturing; Sales. **Listed on:** Privately held. **Number of employees at this location:** 75. **Number of employees nationwide:** 1,000.

ARCH ALUMINUM & GLASS COMPANY
3142 Connahbrook Drive, Memphis TN 38116. 901/332-6883. **Contact:** Debbie Wilson, Office Manager. **Description:** A glass manufacturer. Glass is not made on-site, but the company's services include cutting, tempering, insulating, fabricating, polishing edges, and cutting holes. If given a pattern or sketch, the company will create a piece of glass to meet those specifications. **Corporate headquarters location:** Pompano Beach FL.

CHASE INSTRUMENTS CORPORATION
P.O. Box 68, Rockwood TN 37854. 423/354-4206. **Contact:** Paula Tarver, Manager of Human Resources. **Description:** A manufacturer of laboratory, hospital, and scientific glassware for a worldwide market. Products include test tubes and slides.

GALLATIN ALUMINUM PRODUCTS
P.O. Box 1987, Gallatin TN 37066. 615/452-4550. **Contact:** Human Resources Director. **Description:** Manufactures glass products such as windows.

GEMTRON CORPORATION
615 Highway 68, Sweetwater TN 37874. 423/337-3522. **Contact:** John Canada, Director of Human Resources. **Description:** Manufactures decorative and flat glass.

GENERAL SHALE PRODUCTS CORPORATION
P.O. Box 3547, Johnson City TN 37602. 423/282-4661. **Contact:** Joanne Gilmer, Human Resources. **Description:** A producer of blocks, bricks, ready-mix concrete, sand, and other products. The company ships its products across the United States and Canada, primarily focusing on territory east of the Mississippi River. General Shale produces over 1 billion bricks each year. The company was founded in 1928 with the merger of two Tennessee brick plants. Since then, General Shale has become one of the nation's largest brick manufacturers, operating 17 plants in 12 cities. In addition to manufacturing, the company is involved in solving engineering, architectural, and construction problems. **Other U.S. locations:** Huntsville AL; Atlanta GA; IN; Corbin KY; Louisville KY; Elizabethton TN; Kingsport TN; Knoxville TN.

ROGERS GROUP, INC.
421 Great Circle Road, Nashville TN 37228. 615/780-5668. **Fax:** 615/780-5813. **Contact:** Roger Denton, Director of Employee Relations and Development. **Description:** Engaged in the crushed stone, building materials, asphalt construction, and limestone products mining business. **Common positions include:** Accountant/Auditor; Civil Engineer; Computer Systems Analyst; Cost Estimator; Human Resources Specialist; Mechanical Engineer; Mining Engineer; Structural Engineer. **Educational backgrounds include:** Business Administration; Engineering. **Benefits:** 401K; Dental Insurance; Disability Coverage; Life Insurance; Medical Insurance; Pension Plan; Tuition Assistance. **Special Programs:** Internships. **Corporate headquarters location:** This Location. **Other U.S. locations:** Indiana; Kentucky; Ohio; Tennessee. **Operations at this facility include:** Administration; Divisional Headquarters; Manufacturing; Regional Headquarters; Sales. **Listed on:** Privately held. **Number of**

employees at this location: 100. **Number of employees nationwide:** 1,500.

TILECERA
300 Arcadia Boulevard, Clarksville TN 37040. 615/645-5100. **Contact:** Ron Irlinger, Human Resources Manager. **Description:** Manufactures ceramic wall and floor tile.

VULCAN MATERIALS COMPANY
P.O. Box 7, Knoxville TN 37901. 423/577-2511. **Fax:** 423/579-2948. **Contact:** James Barontini, Director, Human Resources and Administration. **Description:** Produces crushed limestone. **Common positions include:** Accountant/Auditor; Administrative Services Manager; Attorney; Blue-Collar Worker Supervisor; Buyer; Civil Engineer; Clerical Supervisor; Computer Programmer; Computer Systems Analyst; Credit Manager; Electrical/Electronics Engineer; Geologist/Geophysicist; Human Resources Specialist; Industrial Engineer; Manufacturer's/Wholesaler's Sales Rep.; Mechanical Engineer; Metallurgical Engineer; Mining Engineer; Operations/Production Manager; Property and Real Estate Manager; Purchasing Agent and Manager; Quality Control Supervisor. **Educational backgrounds include:** Accounting; Business Administration; Computer Science; Engineering; Liberal Arts. **Benefits:** Dental Insurance; Disability Coverage; Employee Discounts; Life Insurance; Medical Insurance; Pension Plan; Savings Plan; Tuition Assistance. **Corporate headquarters location:** Birmingham AL. **Other U.S. locations:** Nationwide. **Operations at this facility include:** Administration; Divisional Headquarters; Sales. **Number of employees at this location:** 65. **Number of employees nationwide:** 6,600.

Note: Because addresses and telephone numbers of smaller companies change rapidly, we recommend you call each company to verify the information below before inquiring about job opportunities. Mass mailings are not recommended.

Additional employers with under 250 employees:

GLASS AND GLASS PRODUCTS

Binswanger Glasscraft Products
P.O. Box 17242, Memphis TN 38187-0242. 901/388-1334.

Contour Industries Inc.
P.O. Box 69, Surgoinsville TN 37873-0069. 423/345-2000.

Energy Saving Products Inc.
537 N Blythe St, Gallatin TN 37066-2223. 615/452-1240.

Harman Automotive Industries Inc.
P.O. Box 4628, Sevierville TN 37864-4628. 423/428-0168.

CRUSHED AND BROKEN STONE

Perstorp Components
2409 Industrial Dr, Springfield TN 37172-5014. 615/384-6265.

SAND AND GRAVEL

Dixie Cement Co.
P.O. Box 14009, Knoxville TN 37914-1009. 423/522-1171.

Premier Refractory & Chemicals Inc.
101 Jonesboro Rd, Erwin TN 37650-1094. 423/743-4125.

Quazite
291 Industrial Park Dr, Lenoir City TN 37771-3216. 423/986-5533.

Schuller International Division Manville
P.O. Box 309, Etowah TN 37331-0309. 423/263-1229.

Kingsport Foundry & Manufacturing
P.O. Box 880, Kingsport TN 37662-0880. 423/224-1100.

KAOLIN, CLAY, CERAMIC, AND/OR REFRACTORY MINERALS

HC Spinks Clay Co. Inc.
P.O. Box 820, Paris
TN 38242-0820.
901/642-5414.

ASPHALT

Ford Construction Co. Asphalt Plant
P.O. Box 527,
Dyersburg TN 38025-0527. 901/285-1938.

Standard Construction Co.
7434 Raleigh
Lagrange Rd, Cordova
TN 38018-6224.
901/754-5181.

CEMENT

Signal Mountain Cement Co.
1201 Suck Creek Rd,
Chattanooga TN
37405-9700.
423/886-0800.

TILE

General Shale Products Corp.
P.O. Box 446,
Knoxville TN 37901-0446. 423/522-0051.

CONCRETE, GYPSUM, AND PLASTER PRODUCTS

Tennessee-Luttrell Co.
P.O. Box 75, Luttrell
TN 37779-0075.
423/992-3841.

EARTH AND MINERALS

Crossville Ceramics
P.O. Box 1168,
Crossville TN 38557-1168. 615/484-2110.

JM Huber Corp.
P.O. Box P, Etowah
TN 37331-6016.
423/263-2241.

Perfect Equipment Corp.
P.O. Box 1154,
Murfreesboro TN
37133-1154.
615/893-0643.

MINERAL WOOL

Celotex Corporation
1760 Aaronwood Dr,
Old Hickory TN
37138-4251.
615/847-0955.

For more information on career opportunities in stone, clay, glass, and concrete products:

Associations

THE AMERICAN CERAMIC SOCIETY
735 Ceramic Place, Westerville
OH 43081. 614/890-4700.
Offers a variety of publications,
meetings, information, and
educational services. Also
operates Ceramic Futures, an
employment service with a
resume database.

NATIONAL GLASS ASSOCIATION
8200 Greensboro Drive, Suite
802, McLean VA 22102.
703/442-4890.

Magazines

GLASS MAGAZINE
National Glass Association, 8200
Greensboro Drive, McLean VA
22102. 703/442-4890.

ROCK PRODUCTS
MacLean Hunter Publishing
Company, 29 North Wacker
Drive, Chicago IL 60606.
312/726-2805.

TRANSPORTATION

According to Labor Department estimates the number of jobs in the air transportation industry will increase faster than average. Passenger and cargo traffic should increase in response to a rise in population, incomes and business activity. Employment in other air transport activities will also increase as more aircraft are purchased for business, agriculture, and recreation. Despite this expected growth, jobseekers should expect strong competition as the number of applicants for airline jobs exceeds the number of jobs available. Not only are airline jobs highly sought after, but the industry has been going through a period of consolidation, and today more and more of the business is concentrated with a handful of the major carriers, such as American, Delta, and USAir.

In the trucking and warehousing industry, the number of jobs created is very closely related to the health of the national economy. Competition in the industry is intense, both among truckers and with the railroads. Trucking companies compete by slashing rates or offering more customized service. Motor carriers must quote rates high enough to cover costs but low enough to remain competitive. Still, job opportunities for truckers are expected to be good. In some areas, companies have had trouble recruiting well-trained drivers. Although some routes have switched to intermodal transportation and recent downturns in the economy have eased some driver shortages, turnover is relatively high. That should ensure a steady supply of jobs.

On the railroads, the use of both freight and passenger rail will climb. And according to the U.S. Commerce Department, increased trade and stronger freight rates should help the performance of U.S. flag liner companies operating in the Asian markets. Domestic use of water transportation should also increase, especially between Alaska and the lower 48 states.

APEX EXPRESS CORPORATION
P.O. Box 100906, Nashville TN 37224. 615/242-5552. **Contact:** Tim Moore, Controller. **Description:** A trucking and general commodities firm. **Common positions include:** Claim Representative; Computer Programmer; Customer Service Representative; Department Manager; General Manager; Management Trainee; Services Sales Representative. **Educational backgrounds include:** Marketing. **Benefits:** Dental Insurance; Life Insurance; Medical Insurance; Pension Plan; Profit Sharing. **Corporate headquarters location:** This Location.

CENTRAL PARKING CORPORATION
2401 21st Avenue South, Suite 200, Nashville TN 37212. 615/297-4255. **Contact:** Human Resources. **Description:** Central Parking Corporation is a leading provider of parking services in the United States. The company operates over 1,200 parking facilities containing approximately 475,000 spaces including 95 international facilities with approximately 26,610 spaces located in 31 states, the

District of Columbia, Puerto Rico, the United Kingdom, and Mexico. Since 1991, the company has added an average of approximately 120 properties to its operations each year. The company believes that its leadership position in the parking industry is the result of applying professional management strategies to a consolidating industry historically managed by small local operators, understanding the needs of the parking public, applying technology to parking services, retaining employees through proprietary training programs, and using an incentive compensation system that rewards performance. The company provides parking management services at multi-level parking facilities and surface lots. It also provides parking consulting services, shuttle services, valet services, parking meter enforcement services, and billing and collection services. The company's clients include some of the nation's largest building owners and developers of mixed-use projects, major office building complexes, sports stadiums, hotels, and municipalities. Parking facilities operated by the company include, among others, certain terminals operated by BAA Heathrow International Airport (London), the Prudential Center (Boston), Busch Stadium (St. Louis), Reunion Arena (Dallas), Coors Field (Denver), Oriole Park at Camden Yards (Baltimore), and various parking facilities owned by the Hyatt and Westin Hotel chains, the Rouse Company, Faison Associates, May Department Stores, Equity Office Properties, and Crescent Real Estate. **Corporate headquarters location:** This Location.

FEDERAL COMPRESS AND WAREHOUSE INC.
165 Madison Avenue, Memphis TN 38103. 901/524-4000. **Contact:** Human Resources. **Description:** Stores and warehouses cotton.

FEDERAL EXPRESS CORPORATION
P.O. Box 727, Memphis TN 38194. 901/369-3600. **Contact:** Steven Priddy, Vice President of Personnel. **Description:** Corporate headquarters offices for the air freight corporation which offers delivery services in the United States and 187 other countries. The company's fleet consists of 462 aircraft and over 30,000 delivery vehicles. The company also operates a business logistics service. Hubs and major sorting centers are in Alaska, Illinois, Indiana, California, New Jersey, and Tennessee. **Common positions include:** Cargo Handler; Computer Programmer; Customer Service Representative; General Manager; Human Resources Specialist; Marketing Specialist; Public Relations Specialist; Services Sales Representative. **Educational backgrounds include:** Computer Science. **Benefits:** Dental Insurance; Disability Coverage; Employee Discounts; Life Insurance; Medical Insurance; Pension Plan; Profit Sharing; Savings Plan; Tuition Assistance. **Corporate headquarters location:** This Location. **Operations at this facility include:** Administration; Divisional Headquarters; Manufacturing; Regional Headquarters; Sales; Service. **Number of employees at this location:** 8,000. **Number of employees worldwide:** 100,000.

M.S. CARRIERS
P.O. Box 30788, Memphis TN 38130-0788. 901/344-4708. **Fax:** 901/344-4798. **Recorded Jobline:** 901/344-4333. **Contact:** Employment Manager. **Description:** M.S. Carriers is an irregular route, truckload carrier transporting a wide range of commodities in the eastern two-thirds of the United States, and the provinces of Ontario and Quebec, Canada, with interline service to Mexico. The

company can transport any type of freight (except certain types of explosives, household goods, and commodities in bulk) from any point in the continental United States to any other point in another state over any route selected by the company. The company's primary traffic flows are between the middle South and the Southwest, Midwest, central states, Southeast, and Northeast. The principal types of freight transported are packages, retail goods, nonperishable foodstuffs, paper and paper products, household appliances, furniture, and packaged petroleum products. **NOTE:** All job openings are listed on the company jobline. Please apply only for those specific job listings. **Common positions include:** Accountant/Auditor; Automotive Mechanic/Body Repairer; Buyer; Clerical Supervisor; Computer Programmer; Computer Systems Analyst; Customer Service Representative; Financial Analyst; Human Resources Specialist; Purchasing Agent and Manager; Sales Representative; Transportation/Traffic Specialist. **Educational backgrounds include:** Accounting; Business Administration; Computer Science; Finance; Marketing. **Benefits:** 401K; Dental Insurance; Disability Coverage; Life Insurance; Medical Insurance; Profit Sharing; Tuition Assistance. **Corporate headquarters location:** This Location. **Other U.S. locations:** Atlanta GA; Chicago IL; Columbus OH; Port Clinton OH; Drums PA; Nashville TN; Dallas TX; Martinsburg WV. **Operations at this facility include:** Administration; Customer Service; Marketing; Purchasing; Sales; Service. **Listed on:** NASDAQ. **Number of employees at this location:** 450. **Number of employees nationwide:** 3,200.

MARK VII, INC.
965 Ridge Lake Boulevard, Suite 103, Memphis TN 38120. 901/767-4455. **Contact:** Ms. Kelly Shaw. **Description:** Mark VII, formerly MNX, Inc., is one of the country's leading providers of single-source transportation services to some of the largest shippers in the world. Through its customer-driven approach, Mark VII provides shippers multi-modal transportation solutions in an ever-changing marketplace. The transportation market is evolving into three segments -- equipment providers, equipment users, and logistics managers. Mark VII facilitates the link between equipment providers and equipment users. The company provides a full complement of logistics management services such as dedicated fleet, warehousing, and risk management, as well as the component services involved in these activities. With over 90 offices across North America, Mark VII is one of the largest transportation services companies in the United States. The company's areas of operation include: Intermodal, Trucking Services; Carload, International, Dimensional Traffic; Consolidation & Distribution Services, and Air Freight. Services include double stack, trailers, and containers on rail cars; trucks; and ocean-going transportation. Commodities transported include paper, food, empty containers, retail products, and household goods throughout the U.S. and internationally. **Subsidiaries include:** TemStar, which operates 500 refrigerated trailers; and truck operations such as Driver Training Academy, Career Credit, Fuel Management, and Missouri-Nebraska Express.

NORFOLK SOUTHERN CORPORATION
West Carters Valley Road, Church Hill TN 37642. 423/521-1431. **Contact:** Personnel Department. **Description:** This location is a railroad.

OMC FISHING BOAT GROUP, INC.
STRATOS BOATS
931 Industrial Road, Old Hickory TN 37138-3692. 615/847-4034. **Toll free fax:** 800/934-1592. **Contact:** Mr. Lanny Simpson, Human Resources. **Description:** A manufacturer of fiberglass fishing boats. **Parent company:** Outboard Marine Corporation produces marine products including outboard motors and engines under brand names including Johnson, Evinrude, and Cobra; and boats under brand names including Donzi, Four Winns, Grumman, Seaswirl, Javelin, Sunbird, Suncruiser, Ryds, Quest, Stacer, Roughneck, and Chris-Craft. The company also produces replacement parts and accessories, offers boat rentals, and provides related financial services.

SEA RAY BOATS, INC.
2600 Sea Ray Boulevard, Knoxville TN 37914. 423/522-4181. **Contact:** Luanne Jarnagin, Director of Human Resources. **Description:** One of the nation's leading manufacturers of recreational pleasure boats. Sea Ray offers a line of nearly 60 models in seven product families, including Sport Boats, Sport Cruisers, Sport Yachts, Yachts, Laguna fishing boats, tournament-quality Ski Rays, and Sea Rayder jet boats. Sea Ray builds pleasure boats from 65 to 130 feet, Sea Ray family ski boats from 18 to 21 feet, Laguna fishing boats from 16 to 31 feet, and the Sea Rayder water jet-powered boat. Distribution is through approximately 180 dealers worldwide, with international sales accounting for 15 to 25 percent of sales. Sea Ray is part of the Brunswick Corporation, one of America's oldest companies (founded in 1845) and one of the largest corporations in the United States. Sea Ray, together with other divisions, makes Brunswick the world's largest producer of marine engines and boats. **Other U.S. locations:** Phoenix AZ; Merritt Island FL; Palm Coast FL; Sykes Creek FL; Vonore TN. **Parent company:** Brunswick Corporation.

VOLVO PINTO MARINE PRODUCTS
200 Robert Wallace Drive, Lexington TN 38351. 901/968-0151. **Contact:** Carol Wallsmith, Manager of Human Resources. **Description:** Produces marine products including outboard motors and engines. The company also produces replacement parts and accessories, offers boat rentals, and provides related financial services.

Note: Because addresses and telephone numbers of smaller companies change rapidly, we recommend you call each company to verify the information below before inquiring about job opportunities. Mass mailings are not recommended.

Additional employers with under 250 employees:

RAILROAD EQUIPMENT

Norfolk Southern Corp.
3125 N Central St, Knoxville TN 37917-5139. 423/521-1431.

Rail Bearing Service Inc.
5336 Counsellor Ln, Knoxville TN 37914-6627. 423/524-8353.

SHIP/BOAT BUILDING AND REPAIRING

OMC Fishing Boat Grp
880 Butler Dr, Murfreesboro TN 37130-6101. 615/895-5190.

Supra Sports Inc.
P.O. Box 144,
Greenback TN 37742-
0144. 423/856-3035.

T&S Boats
1658 Taylor Town Rd,
White Bluff TN
37187-4008.
615/797-5001.

**LOCAL AND
INTERURBAN
PASSENGER TRANSIT**

K-Trans
1135 E Magnolia Ave,
Knoxville TN 37917-
7786. 423/522-5000.

Service Transport
400 Industrial Dr,
Jackson TN 38301-
9613. 901/424-0567.

Averitt Express
2580 Bells Hwy,
Jackson TN 38305-
8848. 901/668-6768.

Tennessee Rural Metro
160 Campbell Station
Rd Public, Knoxville
TN 37922. 423/675-
3434.

TRUCKING

**AAA Cooper
Transportation**
1100 Visco Dr,
Nashville TN 37210-
2210. 615/242-2376.

**Ace Transportation
Inc.**
606 Fesslers Ln,
Nashville TN 37210-
2817. 615/244-6803.

ADT Automotive Inc.
435 Metroplex Dr,
Nashville TN 37211-
3109. 615/333-1400.

**Advance
Transportation Co.**
210 Cole Ave,
Nashville TN 37210-
4706. 615/244-4023.

**American Freightways
Inc.**
877 Mitchell Rd,
Kingsport TN 37663-
3245. 423/349-6334.

Averitt Express
140 Terminal Rd,
Clarksville TN 37040-
5824. 615/648-0910.

Averitt Express Inc.
2640 Stephenson Rd,
Murfreesboro TN
37130. 615/893-
7794.

Averitt Express
101 Pressler Rd,
Dyersburg TN 38024-
6609. 901/286-5720.

**Carolina Freight
Carriers**
890 Visco Dr,
Nashville TN 37210-
2150. 615/726-2950.

**Carolina Freight
Carriers**
3665 E Raines Rd,
Memphis TN 38118-
6823. 901/363-5588.

**Celebrity Freight
Systems**
326 Wilson Pike Cir,
Brentwood TN 37027-
5240. 615/377-9206.

**Challenger Motor
Freight**
319 Fesslers Ln,
Nashville TN 37210-
2920. 615/256-6474.

**Consolidated
Freightways**
444 Calvert Dr,
Gallatin TN 37066-
5401. 615/452-6665.

CF Motorfreight
3365 E Stone Dr,
Kingsport TN 37660-
6779. 423/288-6112.

**Eagle Distributing
Company**
P.O. Box 27190,
Knoxville TN 37927-
7190. 423/637-3311.

**Expedited Transport
Associates**
RR 12 Box 225,
Cookeville TN 38501-
9812. 615/432-4767.

First Fleet Inc.
334 Industrial Dr SW,
Cleveland TN 37311-
8261. 423/479-7585.

**Glen McClendon
Trucking**
128 Market St NE,
Charleston TN 37310.
423/336-2876.

Milan Express Inc.
1091 Kefauver Dr,
Milan TN 38358-
3412. 901/686-7428.

Poole Truck Lines Inc.
1408 Lebanon Rd,
Nashville TN 37210-
3102. 615/255-4082.

Humboldt Express Inc.
450 Woodycrest Ave,
Nashville TN 37210-
4321. 615/255-8403.

Humboldt Express Inc.
345 Hill Ave, Nashville
TN 37210-4736.
615/242-5552.

KS & Co.
3891 Homewood Rd,
Memphis TN 38118-
6194. 901/794-2922.

Kenneth O'Lester Co.
142 Hartman Dr,
Lebanon TN 37087-
2516. 615/444-2963.

**Metro Transportation
Services**
2921 Ketchum Rd,
Memphis TN 38114-
6350. 901/743-4891.

Milan Express Inc.
825 Visco Dr,
Nashville TN 37210-
2149. 615/254-1752.

**Strickland
Transportation Inc.**
1007 4th Ave N,
Nashville TN 37219.

Nashville Auto Auction Inc.
1450 Lebanon Rd,
Nashville TN 37210-
3164. 615/244-2140.

National Horticulture Express
116 White St,
McMinnville TN
37110-2252.
615/473-5731.

Newberry's
15707 Highway 70 E,
Lenoir City TN 37772-
5433. 423/988-4330.

Optimara Distribution Inc.
1501 Lischey Ave,
Nashville TN 37207-
5106. 615/228-2683.

Ozburn Hessey Distribution
7355 Cockrill Bend
Blvd, Nashville TN
37209-1025.
615/350-9400.

Pemberton Transportation Service Inc.
2530 Mitchell St,
Knoxville TN 37917-
6138. 423/524-5592.

Pony Express Courier Corp.
381 Air Freight Blvd,
Nashville TN 37217-
2513. 615/399-7040.

Ryder Dedicated Logistics
1135 Riverside Blvd,
Memphis TN 38106-
2504. 901/775-0648.

Tenn Ohio Transportation Co.
155 N Conalco Dr,
Jackson TN 38301-
3665. 901/422-5548.

Priority Transportation Inc.
P.O. Box 751780,
Memphis TN 38175-
1780. 6018959400.

Roy Widener Motor Lines Inc.
707 N Liberty Hill Rd
#310, Morristown TN
37814-4915.
423/586-0561.

Wagner Electric Corporation
P.O. Box 1508,
Tullahoma TN 37388-
1508. 615/454-1800.

Sadler Bros. Trucking & Lease
436 Enos Reed Dr,
Nashville TN 37210-
4302. 615/256-4911.

Sharp Transport Inc.
P.O. Box 155,
Ethridge TN 38456-
0155. 615/829-2194.

South Eastern American
8596 US Highway 51
N, Millington TN
38053-1521.
901/873-4882.

TNT Holland Motor Express
615 Nestor St,
Nashville TN 37210-
2108. 615/244-2720.

Wallace Hardware Co. Inc.
P.O. Box 687,
Morristown TN
37815-0687.
423/586-5650.

Wilson Trucking Corporation
7125 Strawberry
Plains Pike, Knoxville
TN 37914-9637.
423/525-4081.

United States Xpress Inc.
2711 Knott Rd,
Knoxville TN 37921-
5320. 423/584-4600.

Hillis Inc.
126 Gulf Plant Dr,
McMinnville TN
37110-1736.
615/473-7700.

Pony Express Courier Corp.
140 Collins St,
Memphis TN 38112-
3810. 901/458-1988.

Ferodo America Inc.
1375 Heil Quaker
Blvd, La Vergne TN
37086-3518.
615/793-5177.

Old Dominion Freight Line
1250 Bridgestone
Pkwy, La Vergne TN
37086-3509.
615/793-2828.

Southland Truck Center Inc.
673 E Brooks Rd,
Memphis TN 38116-
3011. 901/332-8990.

A. Arpin of Memphis
1716 N Shelby Oaks
Dr, Suite 3, Memphis
TN 38134-7406.
901/388-5919.

Graebel/Nashville Movers Inc.
1418 Antioch Pke,
Nashville TN 37211.
615/781-2970.

WAREHOUSING AND STORAGE

Storage Trust
671 Myatt Dr,
Madison TN 37115-
2169. 615/865-3292.

United Refrigerated Services
1100 N Parkway,
Memphis TN 38105-
2415. 901/452-1611.

Kenco Warehouse
2100 Amnicola Hwy,
Chattanooga TN
37406-2305.
423/698-4011.

WATER TRANSPORTATION OF FREIGHT

K-Line America Inc.
5050 Poplar Ave,

Suite 535, Memphis
TN 38157-0501.
901/761-2001.

**Lykes Bros. Steamship
Co.**
235 Germantown
Bend Cv, Suite 2,
Cordova TN 38018-
7285. 901/757-1091.

**MARINE CARGO
HANDLING**

Hailey's Harbor Inc.
3730 Amy Lynn Dr,
Nashville TN 37218-
3813. 615/242-8435.

**AIR TRANSPORT AND
SERVICES**

Hassett Air Express
3079 Fleetbrook Dr,
Memphis TN 38116-
1609. 901/332-4614.

USAIR-USAIR Express
1001 Airport Rd,
Chattanooga TN
37421-2270.
423/490-5606.

**Memphis Shelby
County Airport**
P.O. Box 30168,
Memphis TN 38130-
0168. 901/922-8000.

**PASSENGER
TRANSPORT
ARRANGEMENT
SVCS.**

Worldclass Travel
315 Deaderick St,
Nashville TN 37201-
1114. 615/256-5900.

Wright Travel
6750 Poplar Ave,
Suite 118, Memphis
TN 38138-7407.
901/755-7000.

Norton Lilly Inc.
301 Washington Ave,
Suite 202, Memphis
TN 38103-1911.

For more information on career opportunities in transportation:

Associations

**AIR TRANSPORT ASSOCIATION
OF AMERICA**
1301 Pennsylvania Avenue NW,
Suite 1100, Washington DC
20004. 202/626-4000.

**AMERICAN BUREAU OF
SHIPPING**
2 World Trade Center, 106th
Floor, New York NY 10048.
212/839-5000.

**AMERICAN MARITIME
ASSOCIATION**
380 Madison Avenue, 17th Floor,
New York NY 10017. 212/557-
9520. A trade association which
offers collection and bargaining
services.

**AMERICAN SOCIETY OF TRAVEL
AGENTS**
1101 King Street, Suite 200,
Alexandria VA 22314. 703/739-
2782. For information, send a
SASE with $.75 postage to the
attention of the Fulfillment
Department.

**AMERICAN TRUCKING
ASSOCIATION**
2200 Mill Road, Alexandria VA
22314-4677. 703/838-1700.

**ASSOCIATION OF AMERICAN
RAILROADS**
50 F Street NW, Washington DC
20001. 202/639-2100.

**FUTURE AVIATION
PROFESSIONALS OF AMERICA**
4959 Massachusetts Boulevard,
Atlanta GA 30337. 404/997-
8097. Publishes monthly
newsletter which monitors the job
market for flying jobs; a pilot
employment guide, outlining what
is required to become a pilot; and
a directory of aviation employers.

**INSTITUTE OF
TRANSPORTATION ENGINEERS**
525 School Street SW, Suite
410, Washington DC 20024-
2797. 202/554-8050. Scientific
and educational association,
providing for professional
development of members and
others.

MARINE TECHNOLOGY SOCIETY
1828 L Street NW, Suite 906,
Washington DC 20036. 202/775-
5966.

**NATIONAL MARINE
MANUFACTURERS
ASSOCIATION**
401 North Michigan Avenue,
Suite 1150, Chicago IL 60611.
312/836-4747. A partnership of
three manufacturer groups: The
National Association of Boat
Manufacturers; The Association
of Marine Engine Manufacturers;
and The National Association of
Marine Products & Services.
Subscription to job listing
publication is available for a fee.

**NATIONAL MOTOR FREIGHT
TRAFFIC ASSOCIATION**
2200 Mill Road, Alexandria VA
22314-4654. 703/838-1810.
Works towards the improvement
and advancement of the interests
and welfare of motor common
carriers.

**NATIONAL TANK TRUCK
CARRIERS**
2200 Mill Road, Alexandria VA
22314. 703/838-1700. A trade
association representing and
promoting the interests of the
highway bulk transportation
community.

Directories

**MOODY'S TRANSPORTATION
MANUAL**
Moody's Investors Service, Inc.,
99 Church Street, New York NY
10007. 212/553-0300. $12.95
per year with weekly updates.

**NATIONAL TANK TRUCK
CARRIER DIRECTORY**
2200 Mill Road, Alexandria VA
22314. 703/838-1700.

**OFFICIAL MOTOR FREIGHT
GUIDE**
1700 West Courtland Street,
Chicago IL 60622. 312/278-
2454.

Magazines

AMERICAN SHIPPER
P.O. Box 4728, Jacksonville FL
32201. 904/355-2601. Monthly.

FLEET OWNER
707 Westchester Avenue, White
Plains NY 10604-3102. 914/949-
8500.

HEAVY DUTY TRUCKING
Newport Communications, P.O.
Box W, Newport Beach CA
92658. 714/261-1636.

ITE JOURNAL
Institute of Transportation
Engineers, 525 School Street SW,
Suite 410, Washington DC
20024-2797. 202/554-8050.
One year subscription (12 issues):
$50.

**MARINE DIGEST AND
TRANSPORTATION NEWS**
P.O. Box 3905, Seattle WA
98124. 206/682-3607.

SHIPPING DIGEST
51 Madison Avenue, New York
NY 10010. 212/689-4411.

TRAFFIC WORLD MAGAZINE
741 National Press Building,
Washington DC 20045. 202/383-
6140.

TRANSPORT TOPICS
2200 Mill Road, Alexandria VA
22314. 703/838-1772.

UTILITIES: ELECTRIC/GAS/WATER

With deregulation looming closer and closer, utilities are adjusting by cutting costs and providing better service. This is a good sign for the industry but a bad sign for jobseekers, as employment should remain just about flat. Job prospects in the utilities industry are probably best with large electric utilities, water supply facilities, and sanitary services right now. The most common positions with public utilities are precision production workers and operators, fabricators, and laborers.

THE ELECTRIC POWER BOARD OF CHATTANOOGA

P.O. Box 182254, Chattanooga TN 37422. 423/756-2706. **Contact:** Travis Boles, Supervisor of Human Resources. **Description:** The Electric Power Board is a nonprofit agency of the city of Chattanooga created in 1935, which provides electrical service to residents and businesses in the area surrounding Chattanooga. All electricity is purchased from the Tennessee Valley Authority under terms of a wholesale power contract. The service's retail rates are set to cover only costs of furnishing electric service to Power Board customers. In addition to the delivery of power, the company also provides related services to customers. These services include providing automatic dusk-til-dawn outdoor lighting to increase security, and tree trimming on request to reduce the loss of power during high winds or ice storms.

KNOXVILLE UTILITIES BOARD

P.O. Box 59017, Knoxville TN 37950-9017. 423/524-2911. **Contact:** Dennis Upton, Manager of Human Resources. **Description:** A utility company.

TENNESSEE VALLEY AUTHORITY

400 West Summit Hill Drive, Knoxville TN 37902. 423/632-3822. **Fax:** 423/632-7152. **Contact:** Jenna Robinson. **Description:** A federal government agency and one of the largest electric utilities in the nation. The Tennessee Valley Authority serves the Southeast region of the United States. **Common positions include:** Accountant/Auditor; Attorney; Biological Scientist/Biochemist; Chemist; Civil Engineer; Computer Programmer; Electrical/Electronics Engineer; Environmental Scientist; Librarian; Marketing Specialist; Technical Writer/Editor. **Educational backgrounds include:** Accounting; Biology; Business Administration; Chemistry; Communications; Computer Science; Engineering; Finance; Journalism; Library Science; Marketing; Mathematics. **Benefits:** Dental Insurance; Disability Coverage; Life Insurance; Medical Insurance; Tuition Assistance. **Special Programs:** Internships; Training Programs. **Corporate headquarters location:** This Location.

UNITED CITIES GAS COMPANY

5300 Maryland Way, Brentwood TN 37027. 615/373-0104. **Contact:** Human Resources. **Description:** United Cities Gas Company is primarily a distributor of natural and propane gas, operating in 10 states and serving more than 300,000 customers. The company's natural gas business generates 65 percent of its profits, and operates in eight states, including Georgia, Illinois, Iowa, Kansas, Missouri, South Carolina, Tennessee, and Virginia. United Cities' propane is distributed through the company's wholly-owned subsidiary, UCG Energy Corporation, which serves customers in North Carolina, Tennessee, and Virginia. United Cities Gas Storage Company provides United Cities and others with supplemental natural gas supplies through company-owned natural gas storage fields in Kentucky and Kansas. **Corporate headquarters location:** This Location. **Number of employees nationwide:** 1,300.

Note: Because addresses and telephone numbers of smaller companies change rapidly, we recommend you call each company to verify the information below before inquiring about job opportunities. Mass mailings are not recommended.

Additional employers with under 250 employees:

ELECTRIC SERVICES

Johnson City Power Board
100 N Roan St,
Johnson City TN
37601-4733.
423/434-4000.

Upper Cumberland Electric Membership
138 Gordonsville
Hwy, Gordonsville TN
38563-4608.
615/683-6162.

Duck River Electric Membership
1411 Madison St,
Shelbyville TN 37160-
3629. 615/684-4621.

Elizabethton Electric System
State Line Rd,
Johnson City TN
37601. 423/929-
8888.

Middle TN Electric Membership
810 Commercial Ct,
Murfreesboro TN
37129-4951.
615/890-9762.

Kingsport Power Co.
422 Broad St,
Kingsport TN 37660-
4208. 423/378-5000.

Mountain Electric Co. Inc.
2736 Whittle Springs
Rd, Knoxville TN
37917-3332.
423/521-4171.

Boone Hydroelectric Plant
301 Boone Dam Rd,
Kingsport TN 37663-
4135. 423/323-3629.

The Allen Fossil Plant
2574 Plant Rd,
Memphis TN 38109-
3014. 901/789-8400.

Bull Run Fossil Plant
1265 Edgemoor Rd,
Clinton TN 37716-
6270. 423/945-3430.

GAS UTILITY SERVICES

Columbia Gulf Transmission
4077 Booker Farm Rd,
Hampshire TN 38461-
4600. 615/285-2367.

Suburban Propane
1838 US Highway 51
S, Covington TN
38019-3622.
901/476-5211.

GAS AND/OR WATER SUPPLY

Tennessee-American Water
1101 Broad St,
Chattanooga TN
37402-2800.
423/756-5811.

For more information on career opportunities in the utilities industry:

Associations

AMERICAN PUBLIC GAS ASSOCIATION
Lee Highway, Suite 102, Fairfax
VA 22030. 703/352-3890.
Publishes a weekly newsletter.

AMERICAN PUBLIC POWER ASSOCIATION (APPA)
2301 M Street NW, Washington
DC 20037. 202/467-2970.
Represents publicly-owned
utilities. Provides many services
including: government relations,
educational programs, and

industry-related information
publications.

**AMERICAN WATER WORKS
ASSOCIATION**
6666 West Quincy Drive, Denver
CO 80235. 303/794-7711.

**NATIONAL RURAL ELECTRIC
COOPERATIVE ASSOCIATION**
1800 Massachusetts Avenue NW,
Washington DC 20036. 202/857-
9500.

<u>Directories</u>

**MOODY'S PUBLIC UTILITY
MANUAL**
Moody's Investors Service, Inc.,
99 Church Street, New York NY
10007. 212/553-0300. Annually
available at libraries.

<u>Magazines</u>

PUBLIC POWER
2301 M Street NW, Washington
DC 20037. 202/467-2900.

EMPLOYMENT SERVICES

NOTE: *While every effort is made to keep the addresses and phone numbers of these companies up-to-date, employment services often move or change hands and are therefore more difficult to track. Please notify the publisher if you find any discrepancies.*

TEMPORARY EMPLOYMENT AGENCIES OF TENNESSEE

ARVIE PERSONNEL SERVICES
1719 West End Avenue, Suite 116W, Nashville TN 37203. 615/321-9577. **Fax:** 615/321-4949. **Contact:** Janice Threalkill-Sawyers, President. Temporary Agency. **Specializes in the areas of:** Personnel/Labor Relations; Secretarial. **Positions commonly filled include:** Accountant/Auditor; Landscape Architect. Company pays fee. **Number of placements per year:** 200 - 499.

OLSTEN STAFFING SERVICES
162 Marketplace Boulevard, Building D, Knoxville TN 37922. 423/539-0200. **Contact:** Lisa Matthews, Branch Manager. Temporary Agency. **Specializes in the areas of:** Non-Specialized. **Positions commonly filled include:** Administrative Assistant; Bookkeeper; Clerk; Draftsperson; Factory Worker; Legal Secretary; Light Industrial Worker; Medical Secretary; Receptionist; Secretary; Stenographer; Typist/Word Processor. **Number of placements per year:** 1000+.

SOUTHERN TEMP, INC.
701 Cherokee Boulevard, Suite A, Chattanooga TN 37405. 423/266-8367. **Contact:** Mary North, President. Temporary Agency. **Specializes in the areas of:** Non-Specialized. **Positions commonly filled include:** Administrative Assistant; Bookkeeper; Clerk; Construction Trade Worker; Customer Service Representative; Data Entry Clerk; Draftsperson; Factory Worker; Legal Secretary; Light Industrial Worker; Medical Secretary; Receptionist; Secretary; Typist/Word Processor. **Number of placements per year:** 1000+.

STAFF BUILDERS, INC. OF TENNESSEE
6060 Primacy Parkway, Suite 441, Memphis TN 38119. 901/767-8233. **Contact:** Elizabeth Cude, Branch Manager. Temporary Agency. **Specializes in the areas of:** Non-Specialized. **Positions commonly filled include:** Accountant/Auditor; Administrative Assistant; Bookkeeper; Clerk; Computer Operator; Computer Programmer; Customer Service Representative; Data Entry Clerk; Draftsperson; Driver; EDP Specialist; Factory Worker; Health Services Worker; Legal Secretary; Light Industrial Worker; Medical Secretary; Nurse; Public Relations Specialist; Receptionist; Sales Representative; Secretary; Stenographer; Technician; Typist/Word Processor. Company pays fee.

PERMANENT EMPLOYMENT AGENCIES
OF TENNESSEE

ANDERSON McINTYRE PERSONNEL
6148 Park Place, Suite 100, Chattanooga TN 37421. 423/894-9571. **Fax:** 423/892-7413. **Contact:** Ms. M. McIntyre, President. Employment Agency. **Specializes in the areas of:** Administration/MIS/EDP; Advertising; Architecture/Construction/Real Estate; Banking; Computer Science/Software; Finance; Food Industry; General Management; Health/Medical; Industrial; Insurance; Legal; Manufacturing; Non-Profit; Retail; Sales and Marketing; Secretarial. **Positions commonly filled include:** Accountant/Auditor; Administrative Services Manager; Advertising Clerk; Branch Manager; Claim Representative; Clerical Supervisor; Computer Programmer; Computer Systems Analyst; Credit Manager; Draftsperson; Management Trainee; Paralegal; Physical Therapist; Physician; Travel Agent. **Number of placements per year:** 200 - 499.

AUSTIN-ALLEN COMPANY
8127 Walnut Grove Road, Cordova TN 38018. 901/756-0900. **Fax:** 901/756-0933. **Contact:** Mr. C.A. Cupp, General Manager. Employment Agency. **Specializes in the areas of:** Accounting/Auditing; Engineering; Personnel/Labor Relations. **Positions commonly filled include:** Accountant/Auditor; Ceramics Engineer; Chemical Engineer; Electrical/Electronics Engineer; Human Resources Specialist; Industrial Engineer; Industrial Production Manager; Materials Engineer; Mechanical Engineer; Metallurgical Engineer; Purchasing Agent and Manager. Company pays fee. **Number of placements per year:** 100 - 199.

CAREER PROFESSIONALS, INC. (CPI)
P.O. Box 1223, Morristown TN 37816-1223. 423/587-4363. **Contact:** Jim Beelaert, President. Employment Agency. **Specializes in the areas of:** Engineering; Food Industry; Printing/Publishing. **Positions commonly filled include:** Accountant/Auditor; Electrical/Electronics Engineer; Financial Analyst; Human Resources Specialist; Industrial Engineer; Mechanical Engineer; Metallurgical Engineer; Statistician. **Number of placements per year:** 1 - 49.

DUNHILL OF MEMPHIS, INC.
5120 Stage Road, Suite 2, Memphis TN 38134. 901/386-2500. **Contact:** Mike Rhodes, President. Employment Agency. **Specializes in the areas of:** Distribution; Engineering; Manufacturing.

ENGINEER ONE, INC.
P.O. Box 23037, Knoxville TN 37933. 423/690-2611. **Contact:** George Chaney, President. Employment Agency. **Specializes in the areas of:** Computer Science/Software; Construction; Engineering; Food Industry; Industrial; Manufacturing; MIS/EDP; Technical and Scientific. **Positions commonly filled include:** Aerospace Engineer; Agricultural Engineer; Ceramics Engineer; Civil Engineer; Computer Programmer; Electrical/Electronics Engineer; General Manager; Industrial Engineer; Mechanical Engineer; Petroleum Engineer; Systems Engineer. Company pays fee. **Number of placements per year:** 50 - 99.

EXPRESS PERSONNEL SERVICES, INC.
8807 Kingston Pike, Knoxville TN 37923. 423/531-1720. **Fax:** 423/531-3267. **Contact:** Celia Spinner, Owner. Employment Agency. **Specializes in the areas of:** Computer Science/Software; Engineering; General Management; Industrial; Manufacturing; Personnel/Labor Relations; Sales and Marketing; Technical and Scientific; Transportation. **Positions commonly filled include:** Administrative Services Manager; Biomedical Engineer; Branch Manager; Chemical Engineer; Clerical Supervisor; Computer Programmer; Computer Systems Analyst; Construction Contractor and Manager; Customer Service Representative; Electrical/Electronics Engineer; Emergency Medical Technician; General Manager; Human Resources Specialist; Industrial Engineer; Industrial Production Manager; Management Analyst/ Consultant; Mechanical Engineer; Metallurgical Engineer; Operations/ Production Manager; Purchasing Agent and Manager; Quality Control Supervisor; Sociologist; Software Engineer; Technical Writer/Editor; Transportation/ Traffic Specialist. Company pays fee. **Number of placements per year:** 1 - 49.

F-O-R-T-U-N-E PERSONNEL CONSULTANTS OF NASHVILLE
125 Belle Forest Circle, Suite 205, Nashville TN 37221. 615/662-9110. **Contact:** Tom Oglisby, President. Employment Agency. **Specializes in the areas of:** Food Industry; Manufacturing. **Positions commonly filled include:** Electrical/Electronics Engineer; General Manager; Human Resources Specialist; Industrial Engineer; Mechanical Engineer; Purchasing Agent and Manager. Company pays fee.

HESTER & ASSOCIATES
P.O. Box 4517, Chattanooga TN 37405. 423/265-0148. **Fax:** 423/265-6418. **Contact:** Mike Schoonover, Co-Owner. Employment Agency. **Specializes in the areas of:** Engineering; General Management; Industrial; Manufacturing; Personnel/Labor Relations; Technical and Scientific. **Positions commonly filled include:** Engineer; General Manager; Human Resources Specialist; Industrial Production Manager; Operations/Production Manager; Purchasing Agent and Manager; Quality Control Supervisor. Company pays fee. **Number of placements per year:** 1 - 49.

RANDALL HOWARD & ASSOCIATES, INC.
P.O. Box 382397, Memphis TN 38183-2397. 901/754-3333. **Contact:** Randall C. Howard, President. Employment Agency. **Number of placements per year:** 1 - 49.

J & D RESOURCES
6555 Quince Road, # 425, Memphis TN 38119. 901/753-0500. **Fax:** 901/753-0550. **Contact:** Jill T. Herrin, President. Employment Agency. **Specializes in the areas of:** Computer Science/Software. **Positions commonly filled include:** Computer Programmer; Computer Systems Analyst. Company pays fee. **Number of placements per year:** 50 - 99.

MADISON PERSONNEL
1864 Poplar Crest Cove, Memphis TN 31119. 901/761-2660. **Contact:** David White, Owner/Manager. Employment Agency. **Specializes in the areas of:** Accounting/Auditing; Clerical; Engineering; Food Industry; Legal; Manufacturing; Sales and Marketing; Secretarial. **Positions commonly filled include:** Accountant/Auditor; Administrative Assistant; Bookkeeper; Credit Manager; Financial Analyst; Legal Secretary; Marketing Specialist; Medical Secretary; Receptionist; Sales Representative; Secretary; Stenographer. Company pays fee. **Number of placements per year:** 50 - 99.

NORRELL SERVICES
1770 Kirby Parkway, Suite 330, Memphis TN 38138. 901/332-1110. **Contact:** Edna Crommett, Branch Manager. Employment Agency. **Specializes in the areas of:** Banking; Clerical; Finance; Insurance; Secretarial. **Positions commonly filled include:** Accountant/Auditor; Administrative Assistant; Biological Scientist/Biochemist; Chemist; Computer Programmer; Customer Service Representative; Data Entry Clerk; Factory Worker; Human Resources Specialist; Legal Secretary; Marketing Specialist; Medical Secretary; Receptionist; Sales Representative; Secretary; Stenographer. Company pays fee. **Number of placements per year:** 1000 + .

PIERCY EMPLOYMENT SERVICES
386D Carriage House Drive, Jackson TN 38305. 901/664-4400. **Contact:** Bea Long, Placement Consultant. Employment Agency. **Specializes in the areas of:** Administration/MIS/EDP; Clerical; Data Processing; Industrial; Secretarial; Technical and Scientific. **Number of placements per year:** 1 - 49.

RASMUSSEN & ASSOCIATES, INC.
P.O. Box 5037, Kingsport TN 37663. 423/239-6664. **Fax:** 423/239-4832. **Contact:** W.L. (Bill) Rasmussen, President. Employment Agency. **Specializes in the areas of:** Accounting/Auditing; Engineering; Finance; General Management; Manufacturing; Personnel/Labor Relations; Printing/Publishing. **Positions commonly filled include:** Accountant/Auditor; Budget Analyst; Buyer; Chemical Engineer; Chemist; Designer; Electrical/Electronics Engineer; Financial Analyst; General Manager; Human Resources Specialist; Industrial Engineer; Mechanical Engineer; Metallurgical Engineer; Nuclear Engineer; Purchasing Agent and Manager; Quality Control Supervisor; Software Engineer. **Number of placements per year:** 1 - 49.

SALES CONSULTANTS
P.O. Box 172286, Memphis TN 38187-2286. 901/761-2086. **Fax:** 901/761-9373. **Contact:** Wayne Williams, Principal. Employment Agency. **Specializes in the areas of:** Sales and Marketing. **Positions commonly filled include:** Manufacturer's/Wholesaler's Sales Rep. Company pays fee. **Number of placements per year:** 1 - 49.

SHILOH CAREERS INTERNATIONAL, INC.
P.O. Box 831, Brentwood TN 37024-0831. 615/373-3090. **Fax:** 615/373-3480. **Contact:** Mary Ann Webber, President. Employment

Agency. **Specializes in the areas of:** Insurance. **Number of placements per year:** 1 - 49.

STAFFING SOLUTIONS BY COBBLE
1801 Downtown West Boulevard, Knoxville TN 37919. 423/690-2311. **Contact:** Bill and Donna Cobble, Presidents. Employment Agency. **Specializes in the areas of:** Accounting/Auditing; Banking; Computer Science/Software; Finance; Office Support; Technical and Scientific. **Positions commonly filled include:** Accountant/Auditor; Administrative Assistant; Computer Operator; Computer Programmer; Data Entry Clerk; Engineer; Industrial Designer.

TENNESSEE JOB SERVICE
909 8th Avenue North, Nashville TN 37245-3700. **Fax:** 615/741-6106. **Contact:** Dan Lindsey, Personnel Director. Employment Agency. **Specializes in the areas of:** Non-Specialized. **Positions commonly filled include:** Accountant/Auditor; Administrative Services Manager; Architect; Attorney; Biological Scientist/Biochemist; Branch Manager; Budget Analyst; Buyer; Chemist; Computer Programmer; Computer Systems Analyst; Construction Contractor and Manager; Counselor; Dentist; Designer; Dietician/Nutritionist; Draftsperson; Economist/Market Research Analyst; Editor; Education Administrator; Engineer; Financial Analyst; Forester/Conservation Scientist; General Manager; Geographer; Geologist/Geophysicist; Health Services Manager; Hotel Manager/Assistant Manager; Human Resources Specialist; Librarian; Management Analyst/Consultant; Manufacturer's/Wholesaler's Sales Rep.; Mathematician; Meteorologist; Nuclear Medicine Technologist; Paralegal; Pharmacist; Physical Therapist; Physician; Physicist/Astronomer; Public Relations Specialist; Purchasing Agent and Manager; Radiologic Technologist; Recreational Therapist; Registered Nurse; Reporter; Respiratory Therapist; Restaurant/Food Service Manager; Science Technologist; Social Worker; Sociologist; Statistician; Teacher; Technical Writer/Editor; Underwriter/Assistant Underwriter; Veterinarian.

EXECUTIVE SEARCH FIRMS OF TENNESSEE

B.K. BARNES & ASSOCIATES
475 Metroplex Drive, Building 400, Suite 405, Nashville TN 37211. 615/832-9935. **Contact:** Mr. B.K. Barnes, President. Executive Search Firm. **Specializes in the areas of:** Accounting/Auditing; Administration/MIS/EDP; Banking; Engineering; Finance; General Management; Health/Medical; Manufacturing; Secretarial. **Positions commonly filled include:** Accountant/Auditor; Actuary; Bank Officer/Manager; Ceramics Engineer; Computer Programmer; Computer Systems Analyst; Credit Manager; Electrical/ Electronics Engineer; Financial Analyst; General Manager; Human Resources Specialist; Industrial Engineer; Materials Engineer; Mechanical Engineer; Metallurgical Engineer; Pharmacist; Physician; Restaurant/Food Service Manager. Company pays fee. **Number of placements per year:** 100 - 199.

INFORMATION SYSTEMS GROUP, INC.
6363 Poplar Avenue, Suite 336, Memphis TN 38119. 901/684-1030. **Fax:** 901/684-1068. **Contact:** Harold Lepman, President. Executive Search Firm. **Specializes in the areas of:** Computer Science/Software. **Positions commonly filled include:** Computer Programmer; Computer Systems Analyst. Company pays fee. **Number of placements per year:** 1 - 49.

MANAGEMENT RECRUITERS OF FRANKLIN, INC.
236 Public Square, Suite 201, Franklin TN 37064-2520. 615/791-4391. **Fax:** 615/791-4769. **Contact:** Roger H. Marriott, President. Executive Search Firm. **Specializes in the areas of:** Accounting/Auditing; Printing/Publishing. **Positions commonly filled include:** Accountant/Auditor; Budget Analyst; Cost Estimator; Customer Service Representative; Financial Analyst; General Manager; Manufacturer's/ Wholesaler's Sales Rep. Company pays fee.

MANAGEMENT RECRUITERS OF KNOXVILLE
9050 Executive Park Drive, Suite 16, Knoxville TN 37923. 423/694-1628. **Contact:** Jim Kline, Manager. Executive Search Firm. **Specializes in the areas of:** Accounting/Auditing; Administration/MIS/EDP; Advertising; Architecture/ Construction/ Real Estate; Banking; Communications; Computer Hardware/Software; Finance; Food Industry; General Management; Health/Medical; Insurance; Legal; Manufacturing; Personnel/Labor Relations; Printing/Publishing; Retail; Technical and Scientific; Textiles; Transportation.

MANAGEMENT RECRUITERS OF LENOIR CITY
530 Highway 321 North, Suite 303, Lenoir City TN 37771. 423/986-3000. **Contact:** Mr. R.S. Strobo, Manager. Executive Search Firm. **Specializes in the areas of:** Accounting/Auditing; Administration/MIS/EDP; Advertising; Architecture/ Construction/ Real Estate; Banking; Communications; Computer Hardware/Software; Finance; Food Industry; General Management; Health/Medical; Insurance; Legal; Manufacturing; Personnel/Labor Relations; Printing/Publishing; Retail; Sales and Marketing; Technical and Scientific; Textiles; Transportation.

MANAGEMENT RECRUITERS OF MEMPHIS
5495 Winchester Road, Suite 5, Memphis TN 38115. 901/794-3130. **Fax:** 901/794-5671. **Contact:** Wally Watson, General Manager. Executive Search Firm. **Specializes in the areas of:** Accounting/Auditing; Engineering; Finance; General Management; Industrial; Manufacturing; Personnel/Labor Relations; Sales and Marketing. **Positions commonly filled include:** Accountant/Auditor; Chemical Engineer; Electrical/Electronics Engineer; Financial Analyst; General Manager; Human Resources Specialist; Industrial Engineer; Mechanical Engineer; Operations/Production Manager; Quality Control Supervisor; Transportation/Traffic Specialist. Company pays fee. **Number of placements per year:** 1 - 49.

MODERN WOODMEN OF AMERICA
319 West McKnight Drive, # 201, Murfreesboro TN 37129. 615/896-7778. **Contact:** Mark A. Pody, Manager. Executive Search Firm. **Specializes in the areas of:** Finance; Industrial; Sales and

Marketing. **Positions commonly filled include:** Customer Service Representative; Financial Services Sales Rep.; Insurance Agent/Broker; Management Trainee; Securities Sales Rep.; Services Sales Representative. Company pays fee. **Number of placements per year:** 1 - 49.

MOORE & ASSOCIATES
531 Metroplex Drive, Suite 115A, Nashville TN 37211. 615/781-8060. **Contact:** Ernie Moore, President. Executive Search Firm. **Specializes in the areas of:** Accounting/Auditing; Administration/MIS/EDP; Finance; Food Industry; Health/Medical; Manufacturing; Personnel/Labor Relations; Real Estate; Sales and Marketing. **Number of placements per year:** 500 - 999.

THE MORGAN GROUP
P.O. Box 121153, Nashville TN 37212. 615/297-5272. **Contact:** E. Allen Morgan, Managing Partner. Executive Search Firm. **Specializes in the areas of:** Accounting/ Auditing; Administration/MIS/EDP; Finance; General Management; Manufacturing; Sales and Marketing. **Positions commonly filled include:** Accountant/Auditor; Bank Officer/Manager; Branch Manager; Budget Analyst; Computer Programmer; Computer Systems Analyst; Cost Estimator; Financial Analyst; Financial Services Sales Rep.; General Manager; Hotel Manager/Assistant Manager; Management Analyst/Consultant. Company pays fee. **Number of placements per year:** 1 - 49.

PERSONNEL LINK
3935 Summer Avenue, Suite #2, Memphis TN 38122. 901/327-9182. **Fax:** 901/324-7603. **Contact:** Mr. Leomell Klank, Recruiter. Executive Search Firm. **Specializes in the areas of:** Non-Specialized. **Positions commonly filled include:** Accountant/Auditor; Adjuster; Administrative Services Manager; Advertising Clerk; Biological Scientist/Biochemist; Blue-Collar Worker Supervisor; Branch Manager; Broadcast Technician; Brokerage Clerk; Budget Analyst; Buyer; Chemist; Chiropractor; Claim Representative; Clerical Supervisor; Clinical Lab Technician; Computer Programmer; Computer Systems Analyst; Counselor; Credit Manager; Customer Service Representative; Dental Assistant/Dental Hygienist; Dental Lab Technician; Draftsperson; EEG Technologist; EKG Technician; Electrician; Engineer; Financial Analyst; Food Scientist/Technologist; General Manager; Health Services Manager; Hotel Manager/Assistant Manager; Human Resources Specialist; Human Service Worker; Industrial Production Manager; Insurance Agent/Broker; Landscape Architect; Librarian; Licensed Practical Nurse; Management Trainee; Manufacturer's/Wholesaler's Sales Rep.; Medical Records Technician; Operations/Production Manager; Paralegal; Physical Therapist; Property and Real Estate Manager; Public Relations Specialist; Purchasing Agent and Manager; Quality Control Supervisor; Radiologic Technologist; Recreational Therapist; Reporter; Respiratory Therapist; Restaurant/Food Service Manager; Securities Sales Rep.; Services Sales Representative; Social Worker; Statistician; Surgical Technician; Surveyor; Transportation/Traffic Specialist; Travel Agent; Underwriter/Assistant Underwriter; Water Transportation Specialist; Wholesale and Retail Buyer. Company pays fee. **Number of placements per year:** 50 - 99.

QUEST INTERNATIONAL
123 Lake Haven Lane, Hendersonville TN 37075. 615/824-8900.
Fax: 615/264-3333. **Contact:** Bill Griffin, President. Executive
Search Firm. **Specializes in the areas of:** Food Industry;
Hotel/Restaurant. **Positions commonly filled include:** Hotel
Manager/Assistant Manager; Restaurant/Food Service Manager.
Number of placements per year: 1 - 49.

SALES CONSULTANTS OF NASHVILLE
7003 Chadwick Drive, Suite 331, Brentwood TN 37027. 615/373-
1111. **Contact:** Drew Foster, Branch Manager. Executive Search
Firm. **Specializes in the areas of:** Accounting/Auditing;
Administration/MIS/EDP; Advertising; Architecture/ Construction/
Real Estate; Banking; Communications; Computer
Hardware/Software; Electrical; Engineering; Finance; Food Industry;
General Management; Health/Medical; Insurance; Legal;
Manufacturing; Operations Management; Personnel/Labor Relations;
Printing/ Publishing; Retail; Sales and Marketing; Technical and
Scientific; Textiles; Transportation.

CAREER SERVICES

CAMBRIDGE CAREER SERVICES
300 Montvue Road, Suite B, Knoxville TN 37919. 615/539-9538.
Contact: Marta L. Driesslein, CPRW, Founder/President. Career
marketing firm. Scheduled and confirmed appointments required.
Description: Primarily focuses on maximizing job search efforts by
improving the presentation skills of jobseekers. Cambridge Career
Services develops a targeted job search plan geared toward current
employment trends. The firm teaches jobseekers to: identify and
describe the job skills required to match a company's specific need;
confidently respond to problems or interview questions; and generate
more job-seeking activity by locating and using non-traditional
sources. Cambridge Career Services is professionally certified to
create a personalized resume showcasing transferable skills and
problem solving abilities, using industry-specific language. The firm's
Career Success Package includes a free referral service, linking
qualified candidates to known job opportunities available from area
employers and employment agencies. Services are provided to entry-
through executive-level clients: Individual Career Counseling
/Outplacement and Transition; Transferable Skills Assessment;
Interview Preparation and Coaching; Personalized Resume
Development; Job Opportunity Referrals; and Ongoing
Encouragement.

INDEX OF PRIMARY EMPLOYERS

NOTE: *Below is an alphabetical index of primary employer listings included in this book. Those employers in each industry that fall under the headings "Additional employers" are not indexed here.*

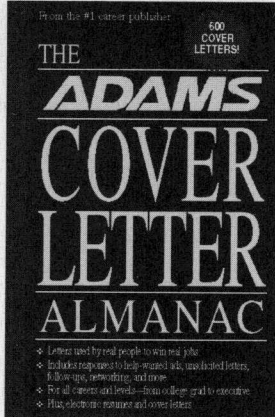